COLLEGE OUTLINE SERIES

HISTORY OF THE FAR EAST

MILTON W. MEYER

Professor of History
California State College at Los Angeles

the text of this book is printed
on 100% recycled paper

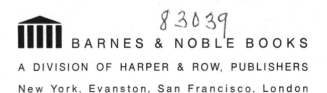

BARNES & NOBLE BOOKS

A DIVISION OF HARPER & ROW, PUBLISHERS

New York, Evanston, San Francisco, London

 For information address Harper & Row, Publishers, Inc., 49 East 33rd Street, New York, N.Y. 10016. Published simultaneously in Canada by Fitzhenry & Whiteside Limited, Toronto.

First BARNES & NOBLE BOOKS edition published 1972.

LIBRARY OF CONGRESS CATALOG CARD NUMBER: 77-16280

STANDARD BOOK NUMBER: 06-460135-8

To Susan, Mark, and Ruth

ABOUT THE AUTHOR

Milton W. Meyer is Professor of History at California State College, Los Angeles. He received his B.A. degree from Yale, his M.A. from Columbia University, and his Ph.D. from Stanford University. During the Second World War he served with the United States Army in England and in the Far East. From 1951 to 1955 he was with the United States Foreign Service in Djakarta and Hong Kong. He is the author also of *A Diplomatic History of the Philippine Republic; Asia: An Introductory Bibliography; Southeast Asia: A Brief History; Japan: A Concise History; India-Pakistan and the Border Lands;* and *China: An Introductory History.*

CONTENTS

MAPS

PREFACE

The purpose of this book is to provide for both the student and the general reader an introduction to Asia. The volume covers the history and present conditions of some two dozen political entities on the vast Asian continent, that sprawling geographical triangle from Afghanistan to Indonesia to Japan. It develops primarily the civilizations of India and China and secondarily those of the rim lands. The work is divided into five parts. The introductory chapters deal with the general scope and geographic setting of the continent and its individual countries. The second part relates to the ancient states of South, Southeast, East, and Northeast Asia. The third recounts the histories of traditional Asian kingdoms and empires. The fourth tells of Asia in its modern century, through the Second World War. The fifth narrates post-war developments of the individual nation states.

The author has had longtime interest in Asia. He was born and raised in the Philippines. In the course of the Second World War, he served in the United States Army in the China-Burma-India theater of operations. In the first half of the 1950's he was with the Foreign Service of the Department of State in Indonesia and Hongkong. His academic career has also been concerned with Asian studies. At Yale he was privileged to study with Professor Kenneth Scott Latourette, at Columbia with Professors L. Carrington Goodrich and Sir George Sansom, and at Stanford with Professors Thomas Smith and Arthur Wright. At Stanford Professor Claude Buss directed his doctoral dissertation, *A Diplomatic History of the Philippine Republic.* The appreciation of an Asian heritage has been enhanced through the experience of teaching Asian history for more than a decade to stimulating students at California State College, Los Angeles; of traveling in most of the countries he writes about; and of publishing books relating to Asian bibliographies and country or regional history texts.

ROMANIZATION OF ASIAN NAMES

The Romanization systems used in this Outline are flexible. Since names relating to traditional India and its sphere of cultural influence are phoneticized in a variety of ways, the simplest variations are adopted. The same holds true for Korean and Japanese terms, but the Wade-Giles system is followed for Chinese names. Diacritical marks have been omitted except for the aspirated consonants in Chinese (*ch'*, *k'*, *p'*, *t'*, and *ts'*). As is the practice in East Asia, wherever Chinese cultural patterns are present the family name precedes the personal.

PART ONE
INTRODUCING ASIA

Asia is the largest continent in the world. It is almost five times the size of the United States. Yet the name is no more than a geographic expression. The continent has no racial, political, cultural, religious, or historical unity. Its countries and its peoples are of seemingly infinite variety. The word "Asia" is derived from *Asu,* an early Greek word for sunrise. In the course of the Christian millennia, the Europeans used the term to include all the countries to their east. They also coined other designations for Asian subregions, such as the Near East, the Middle East, and the Far East, depending on their location vis-à-vis Europe. The Americans, facing Asia across the Pacific, quite logically in reverse order could have advanced the notions of the Near, Middle, and Far West. Asians of course had indigenous names for their own and neighboring lands.

The boundaries of Asia embrace some 17 million square miles of continental land masses, rim lands, and outlying archipelagoes. Over-all, they range 5,000 miles north to south and 6,000 miles east to west. Asia is separated from Europe within Russia by the Ural Mountains and the Caspian and Black Seas, and from Africa by the Suez Isthmus. These divisions are arbitrary features imposed by early geographers, for they are not physically imposing. The historical boundaries that this book follows are those of the Far East defined in its widest geographical extent. The term is broken down into component subregions of South and Southeast Asia, China and Inner Asia, and Northeast Asia.

South Asia centers on India, the largest country. To its east and west is a geographically split Pakistan. Other neighboring states include Afghanistan, Nepal, Bhutan, and Sikkim. Ceylon lies in the Indian Ocean, which also has island groups related historically to the continent. The second important region, Southeast Asia, covers ten administrative entities. It includes continental Burma, Thailand, Laos, Cambodia, and North and South Vietnam. Malaysia straddles between the mainland and the island of Borneo, while insular archipelagoes embrace Singapore, Indonesia, and the Philippines. East Asia centers on mainland China with its peripheral land and insular dependencies. Northeast Asia includes Korea and Japan.

1
THE STUDY OF ASIA

There are several reasons for the study of Asia as defined in this book. The first is geographic magnitude. These lands, 7.5 million square miles, constitute an area twice that of Europe. Communist China, known as the People's Republic of China, itself is slightly larger than the United States; India is a third the size. A second reason is that more than half the world's population live in Asia. With some two billion people, the continent has a population density three times that of the world as a whole. The two chief countries, mainland China with over 750 million and India with 550 million, total 40 percent of the global population. Pakistan, Japan, and Indonesia each have above 100 million, or half the population of the United States. Such extended and populous countries signify important economic, political, and demographic considerations.

Another factor important in the study of Asia is its racial, linguistic, and social complexity. Indo-European types exist mainly in South Asia; Mongoloid strains are predominant in East Asia; and Austro-Asian groups live in Southeast Asia. Linguistic groupings also roughly follow the traditional racial and geographical subareas. Aryan- and Dravidian-derived languages are spoken on the Indian subcontinent. In East and Northeast Asia, Sinitic peoples essentially relate to China, though Altaic roots are also present in Mongolia, Manchuria, Korea, and Japan. In Southeast Asia, Tibeto-Burmese forms a great part of mainland languages, while Malaysian tongues are found in southern islands strung out between Madagascar and Polynesia.

Asia is also of interest to students because of the depth and variety of its cultural history. Underlying racial and linguistic patterns are two main Asian traditions that spread across country borders. These are the Indic and Sinic cultures. India gave birth to the first and exported it to Southeast Asia. China fashioned the

U. S. S. R.
AFGHANISTAN
Kabul
Islambad
WEST PAKISTAN
C H
New Delhi
NEPAL
Kathmandu
INDIA
E PAK
BURM
Rangoon
CEYLON
Colombo
INDIAN OCEAN

Ulan Bator
MONGOLIA
Peking
KOREA
Seoul
Tokyo
JAPAN
I N A
PACIFIC
OCEAN
Vientane
Hong Kong
Hanoi
LAOS
VIETNAM
SIAM
Bangkok
CAMBODIA
Saigon
Phnom Penh
MALAYSIA
ASIA

second, which was adopted in parts of Southeast Asia, Korea, and Japan. There were also major nonindigenous cultural influences. Islam came in from the Middle East, beginning in the eighth century, and gave rise to Muslim-oriented societies on the Indian subcontinent and in insular Southeast Asia. Commencing in the 1500's, a final dimension was added to the Asian historical scene with the arrival of Western powers. Over the ensuing centuries these grew and expanded, directly to impose colonial empires, or indirectly to affect political destinies of those few countries remaining independent.

But the weight of tradition is strong: Asian philosophies, cultures, and religions are old. Much goes back very far, and past events condition contemporary actions. In India Hinduism, emerging some two millennia before Christ, embraced a congeries of philosophic schools, caste strictures, and sacred works. Around 500 B.C., Buddhism issued from its fold, the first of several complementary faiths that helped fashion the Indic way of life. With embellishments from these other schools, Hinduism crystallized by A.D. 1000. Islam then entered the subcontinent to leave its indelible heritage. In China, early traditions (collectively termed Sinicism, from the Greek *sinai* for "foreign") emphasized such concepts as the importance of the family, ancestor worship, and social hierarchy. Drawing from these beliefs and adding others, the Confucian cult was formally fashioned between the fifth and second centuries before Christ. It became and until the twentieth century remained the pre-eminent philosophic basis of the Chinese state, and it also influenced the political structure of neighboring states.

PROBLEMS IN ASIAN STUDIES

There are basic problems in understanding such a complex continent as Asia. In past eras, its countries were remote from Europe and the Americas. Vast sea and land areas separated the continent from the Occident. Only the most intrepid traveler from the West could surmount them. First it took years, then months, and eventually weeks to reach Asian ports and capitals. Moreover, Asians themselves were semi-isolated from each other by the same topographical barriers. It is surprising that as many indigenous traders and missionaries, especially Buddhists, traveled as widely as they did. But now the time and distance problems have been reversed. With the jetlike speed of communications and transportation, matters of Asia relating to continental and to world affairs complicate the international scene.

Overcoming cultural gaps between East and West was another problem. Easterners generally characterized Westerners as materialistic, imperialistic, expansionist, and not generous enough in extending aid for their pressing economic needs. Asians regarded themselves as spiritual in nature and inheritors of ancient traditions, which Westerners on the other hand interpreted, as confining and restrictive. The student of Asia faced linguistic and psychological barriers. Oral languages and written scripts were complicated and took years to master. Traditional philosophies were baffling to foreigners. Art, music, and literature were grounded in cannons and aesthetics unlike those in the West. Climates were hard for Westerners to endure, requiring not only physical but also mental reorientation.

Another basic problem in assessing the Asian scene is that of the coexistence of the old and the new. To what extent has modernization during the past century affected traditional values? In the cities its role is most apparent. High-rise buildings, imported goods, paved streets, and luxurious homes are in evidence in capitals and other urban centers. But village life continues in routines inherited over the centuries. Peasants plant rice, catch fish, obey headmen, and follow time-honored social customs. The widely proclaimed "revolution of rising expectations" does not seem to be universally accepted. Most of the people remain poor and illiterate.

Except for Japan, the problem of economic development remains critical, as Asian states strive to transform themselves into modern nations. The gap between the economically developed countries of the West and the underdeveloped ones of Asia is also reflected in issues of race and colonialism. The "colored" versus the white, the colonials against the "imperialists" are familiar themes in modern Asian history. Yet the confrontations cannot be seen strictly in East-West perspective, because racial tensions and territorial aggressions have been common among Asians themselves.

Contemporary Asian politics are more complex than a division of states into ideological categories of Communist, anti-Communist, and neutralist suggests. To the average Asian, concerned only with the difficult task of marginal subsistence, international cold or hot wars have little meaning. All he asks for is enough rice for the next meal and to be left in peace. To Asians who concern themselves with international affairs, there might be any number of conflicts between ideologies, neighbors, and power groupings. Each state has its own framework of international action and policy.

ASIAN STUDIES IN THE UNITED STATES

American involvement in Asia is of relatively recent origin, but three wars in the mid-twentieth century spurred interest. Prior to the Second World War, only a few Americans thought and wrote about Asian history and problems, and most of these individuals lived abroad.

China drew the greatest number of Americans, because United States interests in Asia were chiefly directed toward this large, populous, independent country. The first American ship to reach China arrived in 1784 in the southern port of Canton. Over the subsequent decades, American commercial, and then missionary, interests grew. The treaties between China and the West slowly forced doors wider to foreign rights and privileges. Beginning in 1844, Americans joined with Europeans in extending their enterprises the length and breadth of the land. With the growth of American commerce and missionary efforts, came concurrent political and diplomatic involvement. Until the period of the Second World War, China remained the chief consideration in American-Asian affairs; yet few could appreciate even at first hand the complexities of the changing Chinese political scene.

American presence also registered in Japan, geographically the closest Asian country to the United States. Following a pattern of continental expansion, Americans in fulfilling their "Manifest Destiny" did not stop at the shores of the Pacific but pushed on across the vast ocean to the Asian periphery. After Commodore Matthew Perry helped to open Japan in 1854, American interests, together with European, increased through treaty rights similar to those obtained in China. These included special commercial privileges and juridical rights. An independent modernizing Japan managed to terminate them at the turn of the twentieth century. Freeing itself of external political pressures, as no other Asian state could then do, Japan skyrocketed into the Asian scene and came into conflict with American interests. The political collision helped generate the spread of the Second World War to that part of the world.

When in 1898 the Philippines were acquired by the United States as a result of the Spanish-American War, Americans arrived for good in Southeast Asia. All the other countries there (as well as in South Asia except Afghanistan and Thailand) were in colonial hands, and the United States did not concern itself in the affairs of other colonial peoples. Nor was it invited to do so. Then followed three wars in three decades in Asia that involved the United States. With regional developments, due in great part to the rise first of Japanese militarists and then of Chinese Communists in the East Asian scene, Americans perforce discovered the existence and importance of the continent, in the cause and aftermath of the Second World War. The Korean and the Indochinese wars subsequently added materially to American involvement in Asian affairs.

SOURCES IN THE ASIAN HISTORY

Despite the selectivity and recency of American interests in Asia, there is no reason for lack of information on the continent. From prehistoric eras, archeology has revealed much. From historic periods, written material abounds. The Chinese have a literate tradition extending over three and a half millennia. The written characters that they use today can be traced back to similar forms in use around 1500 B.C. Over the centuries, private and official Chinese historians wrote voluminously. While little remains of their original books, the basic works of history, literature, and philosophy were copied and recopied, to be transmitted down through the ages. A sense of history preoccupied the Chinese intellectuals, who took pride in their long continuous heritage.

Around the third and fourth centuries A.D., Korea and Japan, borrowing from the Chinese script, began to develop their own literate traditions.

India, despite generalizations characterizing the country as nonhistorical in outlook, had works of history. Dating from approximately 2000 B.C., a native literary tradition eventually crystallized in Sanskrit. It reconstructed some aspects of ancient life through the media of old hymns, epics, genealogies of royal families, poetry, and prose works. In Southeast Asia, indigenous written sources came much later, with the arrival of Indic traditions. Between the ninth and nineteenth centuries, local chroniclers intermingled fact and fiction in their accounts of Burmese, Thai, and Malaysian life. Almost all the Asian states had precolonial annals, which included folklore, legends, and historical accounts.

There were also early foreign records of Asia. Asians wrote about each other long before the Westerners depicted their societies. Dating from approximately the third century B.C., these accounts included Chinese dynastic historians as well as diaries kept by traders, state officials, Buddhist pilgrims, and other travelers. Japanese went to China, Chinese to India, and Indians to Southeast Asia. In terms of over-all numbers they were only a handful, but they left behind fascinating accounts, mixing fact and fiction, of the regions which they visited or heard about.

With the advent of Alexander the Great and his troops into North India, in the last quarter of the fourth century B.C., Westerners began to write with firsthand knowledge, at least about India. Their accounts were supplemented by those of Chinese Buddhist pilgrims, who traveled to the historic home of Buddhism. Later Islamic historians who accompanied the conquering Turks and Mongols added their versions. With the coming to Asia of individual medieval Europeans as missionaries and traders (such as the Polos of the thirteenth century), accounts filtered back to or were published in Europe of the richness and vastness of Asian lands. During the Middle Ages, the Crusades and the Church inspired Europeans to traverse Asia for riches and converts.

These travelers were followed by representatives of Western European chartered trading companies, who, on behalf of their sovereigns, initiated the colonial empires. They kept extended records of their activities. When in the nineteenth century,

European crowns succeeded the companies as colonial rulers, state representatives continued voluminous accounts. In politically independent China and Japan, foreign traders and church representatives also chronicled events. But wherever they were compiled, the colonial works tended to stress Western activities and achievements. Not much was recorded on what the inhabitants thought or how they felt about the alien presence.

During the twentieth century, there emerged a growing corps of native nationalistic writers. Asian historians of the new nations stressed indigenous backgrounds and accomplishments and downgraded achievements of colonial regimes. Polemics of the colonialism issue clouded much of historical output. Asian countries published in their own language or in English newspapers and periodicals which included a wide variety of news and range of political interpretation. There was available in the West a good deal of source material on Asia, and centers for Asian study were established in academic and nonacademic institutions.

2

GEOGRAPHIC SETTING

Asia has a variety of topographical features, including deserts, jungles, mountains, plains, rivers, and extended coastlines. The overwhelming majority of the population live along coasts, near rivers, and in delta lands. But much of the continent is unattractive. Extensive areas are too cold, too dry, too mountainous, too infertile, or too remote for habitation. Mountains and plateaus cover two-fifths of the continent, and they support only a limited number of pastoral people. The Pamirs in Central Asia constitute the modal mountain system. From the four-to-five-mile-high Pamir knot, the "Roof of the World," mountain ranges fan out in all directions, including the famous Himalayas to the east. The main Asian rivers rise in Tibet, but there is no single riverine system. From Tibetan-centered ranges the Yellow, Yangtze, and West rivers flow east to the China plains and coastal regions. Into Southeast Asia meander the Mekong and Irrawaddy. Into India traverse the three main rivers of the subcontinent: the Brahmaputra, the Ganges, and the Indus.

Asian climate is continental and extremely varied. In summer the heated interior warms the air, causing it to expand and rise. The resultant low pressure sucks in air from the relatively cooler surrounding seas. Moist winds blow into the continent from the Indian and Pacific oceans, drenching the coastal areas but losing precipitation and force as they proceed west and north. In winter the reverse climate pattern occurs. Chilled air develops a high-pressure land area from which the winds blow outward to regions of low pressure, hovering over peripheral oceans still warm from the summer sun. These winter and summer winds, or monsoons, were important to the economy of the continent. The early sailing ships that carried trade were literally blown to and from destinations by seasonal winds. In addition to the basic monsoon pattern, sporadic cyclonic storms and hurricanes or typhoons (a term derived from the Western transliteration for the Chinese "big wind") brought additional rains.

With respect to natural resources, while over-all reserves are not known for certain, Asian countries do not seem to be well-endowed with energy or fuel sources. Supplies of iron, coal, and oil are limited, though rubber and tin are plentiful in Southeast Asia. The use of atomic power as a fuel source, now introduced into Asian lands, will probably change the basic energy potentials. Except in Japan, industry has scarcely began to develop. Agricultural pursuits absorb the energy of approximately four-fifths of the people. All societies had intensive agricultural economies, based essentially on rice culture with its great use of manpower. Because of intensive population pressures generated on food-producing areas and relatively inefficient methods of production, this agrarian output barely sustains life. Some Southeast Asian countries grow enough food for consumption and for export, but most Asian states must import food to sustain their millions.

The effects of geography on Asian historical development have been several. The Indic and Sinic centers of civilizations, located in fertile riverine and irrigated areas, were separated from the Mediterranean centers by high mountains, vast steppes, and great deserts. Such early contacts with the West as were established were tenuous and of sporadic nature. Some commerce and diplomatic relations were conducted among Asian states themselves. China and India, the principal countries, were semi-isolated from each other, east from south, chiefly by the Himalayas, though their cultures met in Southeast Asia. The traditional Asian countries and kingdoms, large and small, were usually self-sufficient in basic commodities. Few incentives existed in the agrarian self-contained monarchies to explore for the purpose of expanding trade. This situation changed when the West arrived with mercantilistic doctrines and patterns of international trade.

SOUTH ASIA

The entity of greatest geographical extent in South Asia is India. It occupies most of the subcontinent, while border states, land and insular, of large and small dimensions, surround it.

India. India is the heartland of South Asia, a great triangle bounded on the north by mountains and on two sides by oceans. An enormous land, India is the size of Europe without Russia. The central east-west Vindhya range, up to a mile in height, forms a dividing line between north and south. North India consists of a mountainous arc, extending from the Persian Gulf east to the Bay of Bengal. Paralleling the mountains to the south are deserts, as well as the Indo-Gangetic river system. Here are three main rivers: the Indus, with its five tributaries in the Punjab ("Five Rivers"); the Ganges, with many branches; and the Brahmaputra, snaking from Tibet into East Pakistan. For empires in North India, the rivers provided convenient transportation systems and sources of water for irrigated crops. South of the Vindhya range lies the rocky Deccan ("South") plateau, 1,000 to 2,500 feet high. Demarcating this plateau are the steep Western Ghats ("Stairs") and the less forbidding Eastern Ghats. These ranges are bordered on the west by the Malabar coast, on the east by the Coromandel or Carnatic coast. Few good harbors exist on the little-indented Indian coastlines. New Delhi is India's capital; the largest cities include Bombay in the west, Madras in the south, and Calcutta in the east.

Though India experiences all types of climate, it is essentially tropical. Monsoons, arising in the Arabian Sea and the Bay of Bengal, bring rains between June and September, with the amount of rainfall varying greatly according to land features. Indian resources include a variety of mineral deposits, but reserves are not outstanding. Oil and coal deposits are not extensive, though there is a large northeastern iron belt. There is a good deal of potential hydroelectric power, and dam projects are high in official priorities. Like the rest of Asia, India is primarily agricultural. Only half the land is arable, but in the cultivated areas are produced oil seeds, cattle, sugar, flax, and cotton. Rice, as in most other Asian countries, is the main crop.

The course of Indian history has to a great extent been determined by geographical features. The deserts, hills, and plateaus tended to divide people internally, particularly between north and south. The vast riverine plains of the north were most conducive to fostering empires, which only occasionally spilled south into the Deccan, an effective land barrier. The great mountain chain that fenced off India from the rest of the world favored

AFGHANISTAN
WEST PUNJAB
Peshawar
Cease-fire line
Srinagar
TIBET
Indus
Lahore
HIMACHAL PRADESH
Chandigarh
Simla
Brahmaputra
BAHAWALPUR
PUNJAB
BALUCHISTAN
UTTAR PRADESH
SIKKIM
N.E. FRONTIER
New Delhi
NEPAL
Punakha
Lucknow
Katmandu
BHUTAN
KHAIRPUR
Jaipur
ASSAM
RAJASTHAN
Ganges
Shillong
SIND
Patna
Karachi
MANIPUR
BIHAR
MADHYA PRADESH
Dacca
GUJARAT
BENGAL
TRIPURA
Bhopal
Narbada
Ahmedabad
Calcutta
Junagadh
I N D I A
BURMA
ORISSA
MAHARASHTRA
Bhubaneswara
Bombay
ARABIAN SEA
Hyderabad
BAY OF BENGAL
Panjim
GOA
ANDHRA PRADESH
MYSORE
Bangalore
Madras
ANDAMAN IS.
MADRAS
KERALA
Trivandrum
CEYLON
NICOBAR IS.
Colombo
SOUTH ASIA
Jammu and Kashmir (Disputed area)
Pakistan
Miles
0
200
400
600

the creation of a distinctive civilization, one which was moulded, however, by two major invasions from the northwest. The ancient Aryans gave India its first historic culture, and the medieval Muslims brought their own culture and introduced communalism. From the sea came the modern West, which brought political stability and modernization to the land. In 1947 India received independence.

Border Lands. Created by the partition of British India in 1947, Pakistan consists of eastern and western areas, a thousand miles apart, inhabited by Muslim majorities. East Pakistan has a smaller area but a larger population. It lies mainly in the Ganges-Brahmaputra delta area, centering on Dacca, the provincial capital. The land is subject to floods, grows rice and jute, imports food, and is overpopulated. West Pakistan, on the Indus river system, is drier, produces wheat and cotton, and exports food. It comprises 85 percent of the land area but has less than half the population. It has more natural resources than East Pakistan, but they are not sufficient for industrialization. The national capital, originally coastal Karachi, was relocated in the 1960's to Islamabad, a new planned city in the northwest.

Mountainous Afghanistan, northwest of Pakistan, is a landlocked country whose strategic location has subjected it to frequent invasions, particularly by tribes and armies on their way to India. In the nineteenth century it was involved in the European struggle for power in Asia. Kabul is the capital.

Nepal, a landlocked country lying between India and China, extends from the Ganges plain to the Himalayas. Kathmandu is the capital.

Bhutan, an Indian protectorate, is closely related to Tibet, to which it is joined by a number of Himalayan mountain passes. Sikkim, another Indian protectorate, is also in the Himalayas. Both countries have been involved in border disputes between India and China.

Ceylon is a large island in the Indian Ocean, connected with the mainland by the Adam's Bridge sandbars. The land has varied geographical features. In the northern lowlands the economy is based chiefly on manufacturing, commerce, and food-processing. The coastal plains are wet and fertile, producing tea, rubber, and coconuts. The capital, Colombo, is a seaport on the Indian Ocean.

Trincomalee, a fine and strategically important harbor, is on the Bay of Bengal. The central highlands are also used for plantation crops. From ancient times Indians, first the Sinhalese and then the Tamils, migrated into the island. The former were Buddhists, the latter Hindus. Practicing variant religions and speaking different languages, the two groups have had communal problems since the British granted independence in 1948. In the Indian Ocean also are scattered archipelagoes, some of which were exposed to early Indian and later European political and cultural influences.

SOUTHEAST ASIA

Southeast Asia is a mountainous region with thick covering forests. Several main rivers serve as travel routes: the Red River through North Vietnam; the Mekong through Laos, Thailand, Cambodia, and South Vietnam; the Chao Phraya through Thailand; and the Irrawaddy through Burma. The over-all regional climate is hot and equable. A rainy season lasts from June through September in the countries north of the equator.

Rice is the staple of the Southeast Asian economy. Other food crops, including soybeans, peanuts, and corn, are grown by peasants in small plots. Plantations produce rubber, sugar, coconut products, hemp, cocoa, quinine, tea, coffee, and spices. Though relatively well-off in food products, Southeast Asia is poor in raw materials. Minerals in the various countries include some tin, aluminum, chromium, manganese, tungsten, nickel, zinc, iron ore, and gold.

Mainland Southeast Asia. The westernmost country in mainland Southeast Asia is Burma, bordering on India and Pakistan. With a long history of independent kingdoms, in the course of the nineteenth century Burma came under British rule. Regaining independence in 1947, it re-entered international life. The Irrawaddy Valley is the agricultural center. Mountains or upland areas surround it. The capital, largest city, and trade center is Rangoon. Mandalay, up the Irrawaddy River, is the second city. Rice, forest products, oil, and precious stones are main products of the Burmese economy. The Burmans are the main ethnic group, but sizable minorities, including the Shans, Kachins, and Karens, in the peripheral areas pose political problems.

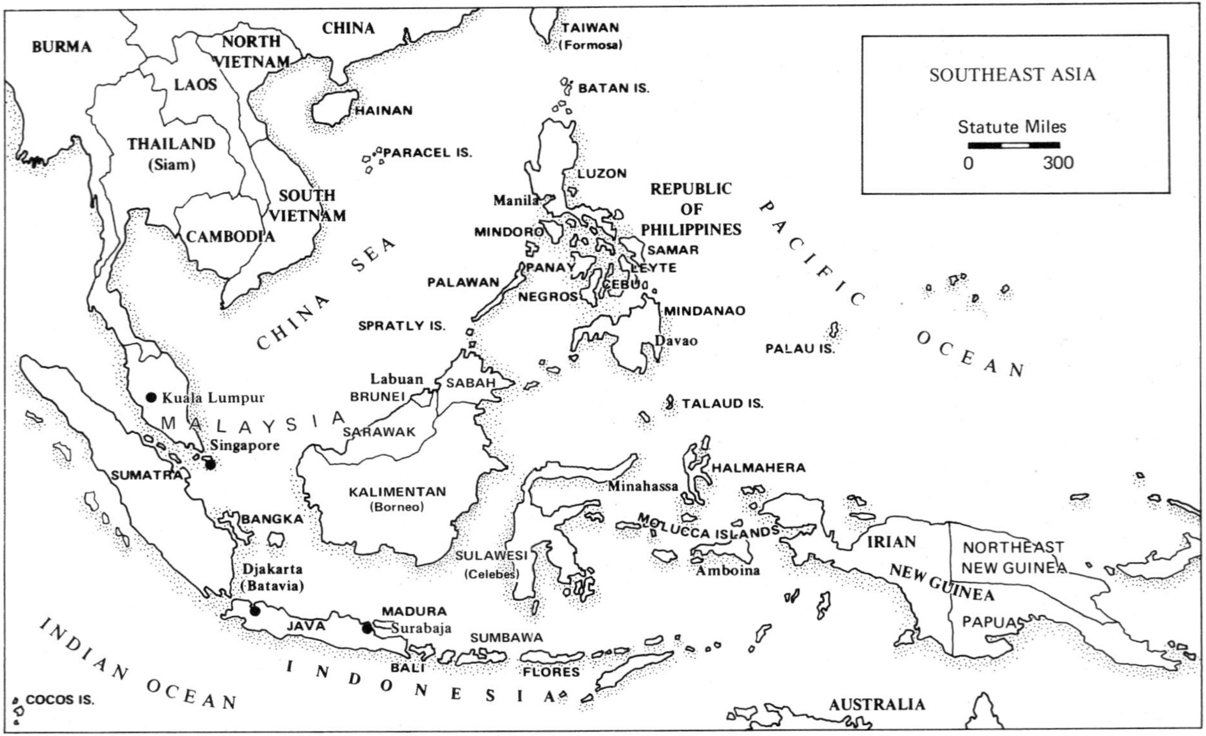
SOUTHEAST ASIA
Statute Miles
0
300
BURMA
CHINA
NORTH VIETNAM
LAOS
THAILAND (Siam)
CAMBODIA
SOUTH VIETNAM
HAINAN
PARACEL IS.
TAIWAN (Formosa)
BATAN IS.
LUZON
Manila
REPUBLIC OF PHILIPPINES
MINDORO
SAMAR
PANAY
LEYTE
CEBU
NEGROS
PALAWAN
MINDANAO
Davao
PACIFIC OCEAN
PALAU IS.
CHINA SEA
SPRATLY IS.
Labuan
BRUNEI
SABAH
SARAWAK
Kuala Lumpur
MALAYSIA
Singapore
SUMATRA
KALIMENTAN (Borneo)
TALAUD IS.
HALMAHERA
Minahassa
BANGKA
SULAWESI (Celebes)
MOLUCCA ISLANDS
Amboina
IRIAN
NORTHEAST NEW GUINEA
NEW GUINEA
PAPUA
Djakarta (Batavia)
JAVA
MADURA
Surabaja
SUMBAWA
BALI
FLORES
INDONESIA
INDIAN OCEAN
COCOS IS.
AUSTRALIA

Thailand ("Land of the Free") lies to the east of Burma. Earlier known as Siam, the country kept its independence in the course of colonial rule in Southeast Asia, thanks to the political astuteness of its kings and to Anglo-French rivalry in the area. The north and west are mountainous. In the east is the infertile Korat plateau. The south leads into the Malay Peninsula, which in early times supported small kingdoms that capitalized on trade routes from the Bay of Bengal to the Gulf of Siam. Other empires flourished in the central and northern reaches of the fertile Chao Phraya Valley. Bangkok, the capital, was founded in the late eighteenth century by the last Thai dynasty. Now it is an important regional entrepôt and focal transportation point.

East of Thailand are the states of Indochina: North and South Vietnam, Cambodia, and Laos. Communist North Vietnam (the Democratic Republic of Vietnam) comprises the Red River and coastal plains. Mountain ranges parallel the coast. The chief cities are Hanoi, the capital, and Haiphong, the main port. South Vietnam (the Republic of Vietnam) centers on extensive Mekong delta lands. With rice and rubber plantations it is more fertile than North Vietnam. Saigon is the capital and chief port. Vietnam has been traditionally divided into warring kingdoms; the French imposed only an arbitrary unity on the land. The division into North and South Vietnam was made by the 1954 Geneva Conference as a temporary expedient to end colonial and guerrilla warfare. Cambodia, with Phnom Penh as the capital, is watered by the large Mekong River. The country had a succession of early empires. Laos, the least-developed Indo-Chinese country is hilly and landlocked. Vientiane is its administrative capital, while Luang Prabang is the royal capital, a dual structure reflecting past indigenous imperial rivalries.

Insular Southeast Asia. The Malay Peninsula, a thousand miles long, extends from the Asian mainland toward the Indonesian islands. Its long mountain range is covered by forests. On the west coast are large rubber plantations, the mainstay of the economy. Early kingdoms, continually fighting among themselves, occupied the isthmus. In an imperial process that culminated in the early twentieth century, Malaya and Singapore, as well as North Borneo, Brunei, and Sarawak, came under some form of

British rule. In 1957 Malaya achieved independence, with Kuala Lumpur as its capital. In 1963 the Federation of Malaysia was formed; it included Singapore, Sabah (North Borneo), and Sarawak. Brunei, a small British protectorate in Borneo, chose to remain outside the federation. In 1965 Singapore left the federation and became an independent state. Communalism is the main problem in Malaysia, with its sizable numbers of Malays, Chinese, and Indians.

Indonesia, the most important Southeast Asian country, lies to the south and west of the Malayan Peninsula. With some 115 million people (half the population of Southeast Asia), it consists of a long (over 3,000 miles) island chain straddling the equator. The simplest geographical pattern is to distinguish between Java and the Outer Islands. Java, the main island, is overpopulated but rich in agricultural resources. It contains the capital, Djakarta, and three-fifths of the country's population. Among the largest of the Outer Islands, Sumatra, 1,000 miles long, is underpopulated and possesses oil deposits and rubber plantations. Mountainous Borneo (Kalimantan) is comparatively underdeveloped. Celebes (Sulawesi) produces copra, coffee, and spices. Many lesser islands string out eastward from Java and Celebes toward Australia. Indonesia produces quinine, pepper, kapok, rubber, hemp, copra, palm oil, and tea. Java and South Sumatra were the sites of important empires until Westerners arrived in the sixteenth century. The Dutch then extended their sway over the region. On August 17, 1945, the Indonesians proclaimed their independence, though the Dutch did not recognize the act until four years later.

The Philippine archipelago, comprising over 7,000 islands, lies between Formosa and Borneo. The majority of the islands are small, uninhabited, and unnamed. The eleven largest contain 95 percent of the population. There are three main island groups. Luzon, in the north, is the most important island. Its capital, Manila, was founded in 1571 by the Spanish. Then come the central Visayan islands. In the south is the large and underpopulated island of Mindanao. The Philippines never had important kingdoms, and even under three centuries of Spanish rule, remained outside the mainstream of Southeast Asian history.

Effects of Geography. One effect of geography on Southeast

Asia has been the development of distinctive architecture, which utilizes thatch, wood, and bamboo products. Another is that the scarcity of raw materials has hampered the growth of industry. A third and most important effect is historical. Because of its extended size, differing groups of peoples, races, and ideas funneled into the area. Local empires waxed and waned, generally in coastal, river, or delta regions. People in native city states and kingdoms, though semi-isolated from each other, engaged in continual warfare and in turn were dominated territorially or culturally by India, China, and Islam. Then Westerners arrived, to establish colonial regimes, which collapsed in the aftermath of the Second World War. Into contemporary times, Southeast Asia, a relative power vacuum, has attracted outside interests to complicate regional problems and issues.

CHINA AND RIM LANDS

Sprawled above South and Southeast Asia is China. This huge country consists of China Proper and its border regions, which have veered in and out of the Chinese political orbit.

China Proper. China Proper constitutes only one-third of the total area of China but contains 95 percent of the people. It may be divided into northern, central, southern, and western regions. The first three are centered on the country's three main river systems.

North China. The Yellow River waters the North China plain, which supports one-fourth of China's population. The river's name derives from the great amount of silt that it carries. Some 2,700 miles long, it rises in Tibet, drops precipitously in its upper course, and then gradually unfolds in great bends through western and northern China. Relatively shallow and wide, it is not easily navigable. The North China plain produced the earliest historic centers of Chinese civilizations and was the site for most of the dynastic capitals. Peking and Tientsin, the two biggest cities, are on the northern fringe of the plain. The growing season in North China is short, and a year's rainfall averages only twenty-five inches. The main crops include such dry land grains as legumes, wheat, millet, and kaoliang (a type of millet). The region has some oil resources and 85 percent of China Proper's

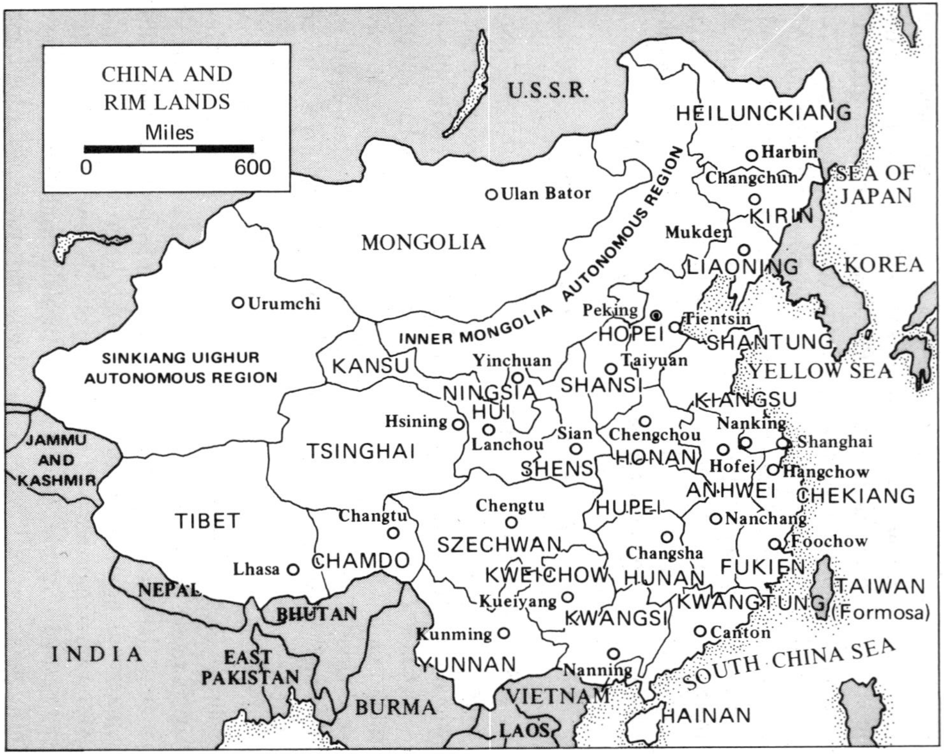
CHINA AND
RIM LANDS
Miles
0
600
U.S.S.R.
HEILUNCKIANG
Harbin
Changchun
SEA OF
JAPAN
KIRIN
Mukden
LIAONING
KOREA
MONGOLIA
Ulan Bator
INNER MONGOLIA AUTONOMOUS REGION
Urumchi
Peking
Tientsin
HOPEI
SHANTUNG
SINKIANG UIGHUR
AUTONOMOUS REGION
KANSU
Yinchuan
Taiyuan
YELLOW SEA
NINGSIA
HUI
SHANSI
KIANGSU
Hsining
Lanchou
Sian
Chengchou
Nanking
Shanghai
JAMMU
AND
KASHMIR
TSINGHAI
HONAN
SHENSI
Hofei
Hangchow
ANHWEI
CHEKIANG
Chengtu
HUPEI
Nanchang
TIBET
Changtu
Changsha
Foochow
SZECHWAN
CHAMDO
Lhasa
KWEICHOW
HUNAN
FUKIEN
TAIWAN
(Formosa)
NEPAL
BHUTAN
Kueiyang
KWANGTUNG
KWANGSI
Kunming
Canton
INDIA
EAST
PAKISTAN
YUNNAN
Nanning
SOUTH CHINA SEA
BURMA
VIETNAM
LAOS
HAINAN

coal reserves. About half a dozen of Communist China's two dozen provinces lie in North China.

Central China. The Yangtze River is the artery of Central China, a transition zone between north and south in geography, culture, and crops. In its upper reaches, it also rises in Tibet and breaks through the mountains into the central plain. Some 3,200 miles long (the fourth longest river in the world), it is navigable in its lower course. Central China is the country's economic rather than political heartland. At least three of its subregions have 70 million or more people. Though the region was less important historically than the north, some national capitals have been located in the lower Yangtze Valley, and big cities exist on or near the river. In the central area is the industrialized tri-city complex of Wuhan: Hankow, Wuchang, and Hanyang. Farther downstream is Nanking, one-time capital of China. Hangchow, which Marco Polo in the thirteenth century characterized as the most beautiful city in the world, is in the delta region. Shanghai, with over ten million people on a tributary near the Yangtze mouth, is the biggest city on the Eurasian mainland. Hills and mountains are more noticeable here than in North China and the climate is wetter. Some wheat is grown, but rice is the paramount crop, tea is an important secondary one. Scattered mineral deposits are found in the mountains, and iron ore is located around Wuhan.

South China. The West River flows through South China, a region crisscrossed by numerous mountain ranges. Some 900 miles long, the river flows into the South China Sea near Canton, the largest and oldest urban center in South China. Tributaries flow into it or into the sea. The climate is rainy and humid. Rice and tea are the major crops. Some mineral resources exist. To eke out a sufficient livelihood is difficult in the marginal south coastal provinces. It is from two such provinces that most of the Chinese have emigrated overseas. South China was never important as a national political center. Far from central and northern capitals, it was a center for rebellion.

West China. Like South China, West China is mountainous. The chief agricultural center, taking its name from the color of the shales and sandstone, is the Red Basin of Szechwan ("Four Streams") province, which feeds over a hundred million people. The Yangtze flows through gorges, as do the Mekong and other rivers that traverse south to Southeast Asian delta lands. The western region of China Proper was the latest to be incorporated into the political empires, and over the millennia semi-autonomous states and tribes existed there. Though the region from time to time received refugees, West (like South) China was never the political center of a unified country. Some natural resources exist, but life in most of West China is difficult. Chengtu, in the Red Basin, is the chief city.

Effects of Geography. The effects of the geographical environment upon China Proper were several. Though a diversity of topographical features exist, the land was conducive to the development of a fairly unified culture. Except for the peripheral ring of mountains, the internal barriers of hills did not hinder the southward spread of peoples and ideas. From early centuries, the concept of *Chung Kuo* (Middle Kingdom) was in part fostered by the geographic unity of China, first in the historic North China plain, and then, by extension through succeeding empires, into all China Proper. The Chinese vary in temperment and physical appearance, but not to the same extent as do, say, the Indians. Despite geographical barriers, over the centuries, through the intermingling of races and assimilation by the Chinese of alien ideas and blood into their own life, from ancient times they emerged as a relatively homogeneous people.

China's Borders. Beyond China Proper are insular and land border areas that from time to time have been incorporated into Chinese empires. These include Tibet, Sinkiang, Mongolia, Manchuria, Formosa, and the Ryukyus.

Tibet. One million square miles in area, Tibet is a mountainous country, half of it a plateau over 15,000 feet high. Only some two million people live in this widespread region. Agricultural and mineral resources are minimal. Tibet has experienced independent kingdoms off and on, but Chinese interest dated from A.D. 650, when an expedition entered the capital, Lhasa. In the thirteenth century, the Mongols incorporated Tibet into their empire, and Kublai Khan, the greatest of the line in China, set up the rule of priest-kings. A dyarchy arose, with the Panchen Lama as spiritual leader and the Dalai Lama as temporal ruler. In the eighteenth century the Manchu sent several expeditions into Tibet. After 1912, the Nationalist Chinese held the border land, and in the 1950's the Chinese Communists established control over it.

Sinkiang. The last of the major outlying border lands to be brought into the Manchu empire, Sinkiang ("New Territory") was created in 1884. Twice the size of Texas, it has a population of about four million, of whom the majority are Turkish-speaking Islamic peoples, mainly Uighurs, related to tribes of central Russian Asia. The main settlements, in the oases fringing the northern and southern borders of the Tarim Basin, constituted the links in the historic trade and travel routes between China, India, and the West. The region's dry desert air has preserved many artifacts of Chinese history. In Tunhuang was found the world's oldest extant printed book, dating from A.D. 868. After the downfall of the Manchu in the early 1900's, local warlords arose. They alternated their allegiances between the Russians and the Chinese. When the Chinese Communists took over the province, Russian influence was eliminated, though border problems continued to plague the two neighbors. In the great desert areas of Sinkiang, the Chinese Communists have conducted nuclear tests.

Mongolia. The Mongolias formed a transition zone between Chinese and nomadic culture. Inner Mongolia, periodically incorporated into Chinese territory, was Sinicized. Most of the seven to eight million inhabitants are Chinese. Across the forbidding Gobi Desert is Outer Mongolia, an independent state, with over one million inhabitants. Though it was rarely part of their empires, the Chinese perennially claimed suzerainty, or control, over the land. It was the source of marauding tribes, who periodically made inroads, in all or part of China. From it came the Mongols, who established the largest land empire in world history. With the rise of Soviet Russia in the 1920's, a time when China was torn by strife, Outer Mongolia went into the Russian political and ideological orbit.

Manchuria. To the east of Mongolia lies Manchuria, known to Chinese as the "Three Eastern Provinces." Over fifty million people live within the half-million-square-mile area. Manchuria is rich in coal, iron, and timber, as well as in agricultural resources. Dating from the second century B.C., Chinese colonies existed in South Manchuria. Expansionist Chinese emperors in later times periodically reasserted control. On the other hand, Manchuria, was also the source of invasions into China, the last of which was that of the Manchu in the mid-seventeenth century. After the downfall of the Manchu, Chinese warlords ruled Manchuria. They tried to stem the Japanese, who from 1905 gradually expanded control over all of Manchuria, and in 1932 established the puppet state of Manchukuo. In the final days of the Second World War, the Russians by international agreement, for one year occupied all Manchuria. Upon their withdrawal, Chinese Nationalists and Communists competed to fill the political vacuum; the Communists eventually won control.

Formosa. Formosa, which the Chinese call Taiwan ("Terraced Bay"), lies across the Formosa Strait from mainland China. It has been in and out of historic Chinese empires. It has a checkered historical background, and its international title was open to varying legal and political interpretations. As early as A.D. 605, the Chinese claimed it but colonization proceeded unevenly. In 1206 the island officially became a Chinese protectorate under only tenuous control. In the sixteenth century, the Dutch and the Portuguese tried to establish commercial depots. During the Manchu conquest of the mainland, many Chinese refugees fled to Taiwan. Eventually incorporated into the Manchu empire, the island attracted more Chinese immigrants. It was at first administered as part of Fukien Province (which is located directly opposite on the mainland), then in 1886 as a separate province. In 1895, as a result of Chinese defeat in the Sino-Japanese War, title went to the Japanese, who colonized it for half a century. In 1945, after the Japanese surrender ended the Second World War, Chiang Kai-shek's Nationalists troops occupied Taiwan. Four years later, it became the home of his refugee government. A fertile island, Taiwan grows a variety of crops, including rice, sugarcane, and forest products. Taipei is the chief city and the capital of the Nationalist regime.

The Ryukyu Islands. Stretching out northeast from Taiwan are the Ryukyus. The archipelago consists of three principal island groups, of which Okinawa, with its capital of Naha, is the most important. In the seventh century A.D., the Chinese invaded the islands and began to extract tribute. In the 1600's, the Japanese also received tribute. In 1854 Commodore Matthew Perry concluded a treaty with the ruling house. The anomalous international status was forced to a solution by the Japanese, who incorporated the islands into their empire, over Chinese protests, in 1879. After the Second World War, for strategic considerations, the islands were placed under the administration of the United States, while the Japanese retained sovereignty. This arrangement, confirmed by the 1951 Japanese peace treaty, was in effect for several decades.

EFFECTS OF GEOGRAPHY. The border lands ringing China have had effects on the Chinese. They influence climatic patterns and, in Tibet, give rise to the chief rivers of the country. The western and northern peripheries were the sources of repeated invasions. From what is now Manchuria, Mongolia, and Sinkiang came people who conquered China Proper in part or in whole. For their part, strong Chinese emperors from time to time expanded in these self-same areas, especially through Sinkiang into Central Asia. But the vast expanses of deserts and mountains tended to inhibit sustained contact by land between China and the rest of the world. And for the generally non-seagoing Chinese, the oceans to the east helped to isolate the country until the Westerners arrived from that quarter with their gunboats.

China in North Vietnam and Korea. Chinese territorial and cultural influences also spread into peripheral countries where geographical obstacles could be surmounted. Over the centuries, strong Chinese emperors and dynasties periodically dispatched missions to neighboring lands and claimed suzerainty over them. Most of these diplomatic and military missions were "hit-and-run" operations, with no lasting historical significance. But North Vietnam and Korea came under strong and long-lasting Chinese territorial and cultural domination.

NORTH VIETNAM. Chinese political interest in Southeast Asia was especially directed toward a geographically contiguous North Vietnam. As early as the third century B.C., the Chinese temporarily subdued Vietnam to a distance some 250 miles north of present-day Saigon. As a result of subsequent campaigns, by 111 B.C. North Vietnam was physically annexed into the Chinese empire. This territorial and administrative incorporation, extending to approximately the 17th parallel, continued until A.D. 939. To North Vietnam in this millennium, the Chinese exported their writing, Confucian ethics, law codes, and bureaucratic structures.

In later eras, though Chinese expeditions only unsuccessfully penetrated North Vietnam, their ideologies remained. North Vietnamese leaders into contemporary regimes considered well the risks involved in living next to an expansive China.

Korea. Korea was subjected even more persistently than North Vietnam to Chinese political and territorial pressures. A peninsular country, Korea (somewhat larger than Minnesota) is 600 miles long and 135 miles wide, with mountain ranges cross-hatching the land. Located near powerful states, Korea experienced foreign political pressures from ancient into modern eras. Prior to the second century B.C., Chinese colonies had been founded in the north. In the third century A.D., as Chinese influence declined, Korea divided itself into the three main states of Koguryo, Paekche, and Silla. In the south a Japanese-sponsored state persisted into the mid-sixth century A.D. Among the Korean states, warfare was continuous. In the seventh century, Silla sought Chinese aid against its two rivals. Silla won but in the process became Sinicized. About this time from China came Buddhism, which Koreans not only adopted but re-exported to Japan.

In the ninth century, as Chinese dynastic protection declined, Silla fell. The royal house of Koguryo emerged in newfound prominence and established the Wang dynasty (850–1392). But the country, now known as Korai, stayed in a tributary position to China. The successor Yi dynasty (1392–1910) also continued to acknowledge Chinese suzerainty. After the mid-nineteenth century, the modernizing and expanding Japanese reaserted traditional political interests in Korea. Expelling first Chinese and then Russian presence, they assimilated the country as a colony, called Chosen (1910–1945). After the Second World War, international power struggles continued in Korea but with some new parties and differing ideologies involved. In 1945 the country was divided (like later Vietnam) into what were meant to be temporary military zones of Russian and American occupation, but the line crystallized at the 38th parallel. North of it is Communist-dominated Democratic Republic of Korea with a capital at Pyongyang, and south of it is the anti-Communist government of the Republic of Korea with its capital at Seoul.

JAPAN

Japan was exposed to Chinese cultural and political influence over the centuries, but the water barrier provided an effective deterrent to any Chinese conquest. Japan, divided into some four dozen prefectures or provinces, is a thousand-mile-long archipelago consisting of over four thousand islands, of which four are the most important. The southermost main island is Kyushu ("Nine Provinces"). Closest to the Asian mainland, it was traditionally the first to receive new immigrant waves and cultural impulses from China and Korea. To its east lies Shikoku ("Four Provinces"), never in the mainstream of Japanese history. Across the beautiful Inland Sea from Shikoku and Kyushu is Honshu ("Main Island"), the largest, most populated, and most historic home island. To its north is Yezo or Hokkaido ("Northern Sea Circuit"), a cold and underpopulated island, inhabited by the aboriginal Ainus.

Japanese topography is mountainous. Hundreds of volcanoes exist, some of which, including Mount Fuji, have been active in historic times. In addition to sporadic volcanic eruptions, earthquakes are a frequent calamity. Heavy stresses on the earth's crust result from great differences in elevation within short latitudes. The plains of Japan, only one-fifth of the total land mass, produce most of the food for the hundred million people. The chief plains are in Honshu. Tokyo, the capital, is on the large Kanto plain; the city of Nagoya is in the west on the Nobi plain; the ancient cities of Nara and Kyoto and the commercial centers of Osaka and Kobe are on the Kansai plain in the west. Japan is limited in resources as well as fertile land. While the country has sufficient copper, it possesses few coal, iron, and oil deposits. Hence as Japan modernized and its industrial base expanded, it had to turn abroad for guaranteed sources of and access to natural resources.

Japan has a temperate climate conditioned by continental wind and climate patterns. Winter winds from the continent usually carry cold dry air, though sometimes they pick up precipitation over the Japan Sea. From the opposite direction, warm southwest summer winds bring plentiful rains. Two gulf streams

CHINA
U.S.S.R.
KOREA
SEA OF JAPAN
KOREA STRAIT
SHIKOTAN
HABOMAI IS.
REBUN
RISHIRI
KITAMI
Nemuro
Asahigawa
Kushiro
HOKKAIDO
HIDAKA
Otaru
Sapporo
Muroran
OKUSHIRI
Hakodate
Aomori
Hachinohe
KITAKAMI
Morioka
Akita
Sendai
Yamagata
SADO
Niigata
Nagaoka
MIKUNI
MTS.
HONSHU
Utsunomiya
Nagano
Takaoka
Toyama
Tokyo
Yokohama
Kamakura
Kanazawa
KISO
Fukui
Gifu
Nagoya
Shimizu
Shizuoka
Ichinomiya
Okazaki
Hamamatsu
Toyohashi
CHUGOKU
MTS.
Kyoto
Otsu
Nara
Ise
Kobe
Osaka
Okayama
Wakayama
Pusan
Hiroshima
Takamatsu
Tokushima
Kure
Shimonoseki
Moji
Nogata
Kochi
TSUSHIMA
Yawata
SHIKOKU
Fukuoka
Sasebo
Kumamoto
GOTO IS.
Nagasaki
KYUSHU
Kagoshima
TANEGA
YAKU
JAPAN
Miles
0
150

also affect the climate. The warm Japan Current flows north along the Pacific coast, while the cold Okhotsk Stream surges southward through the Japan Sea. Though rivers are few, water is in abundance. Thanks to an abundant rainfall supply, vegetation abounds, the country is lush, and forest products are available. Wood is the chief structural ingredient of traditional homes and public buildings.

As in other Asian lands, geographic factors have helped to fashion Japanese life and culture. The surrounding waters produced a variety of fish, the chief source of protein and an economic mainstay for the people. Land conditions were most suitable for rice production, which remained the traditional source of wealth. Geographic factors also had social and cultural influences. The length of the country resulted in a racially mixed people, arriving from northern and southern points of origin on the continent. Because of a favored geographical location, those Honshu plains bordering the Inland Sea and the Pacific coast became the political centers of early Japan. Geographic semi-isolation helped the Japanese to retain many of their traditions and fostered cultural conservatism. While absorbing many ideas from abroad, the Japanese kept much that was indigenous.

PART TWO
EARLY ASIA
(To the Thirteenth Century)

The earliest centuries of Asian peoples were formative ones. Prehistoric people lived in sites scattered throughout a great continental triangle that ranged from North China to Java to West India. The first Stone Age cultures may have evolved independently, but in their later phases migrations occurred—from the Middle East into India, from China into Southeast Asia, from the continent into Japan. The oldest settled communities generally located along riverine or coastal areas and drew their livelihood from fertile, rice-producing basins or from maritime activity. These in time gave rise to early kingdoms and later empires.

Between 2000 and 1500 B.C., came the first outlines of the two chief historic cultures of the continent—the Indic and the Sinic. Their respective core doctrines embodied Hinduism and Confucianism. Much later, in the first centuries of the Christian era, the first historic states arose in the rim lands of Northeast and Southeast Asia. Out of India came Buddhism, the world's first universal religion. Though the faith eventually died out in the land of its birth, it peacefully spread in one form or another throughout Asia, particularly between the fourth and eighth centuries A.D. Islam then came into the continent in two streams, one via India to the Malayan world, and another via Inner Asia into China. By the thirteenth century, all basic Asian philosophies and religions had been established.

Over the centuries, the Asian states organized their governmental structures. Yet the political pattern that emerged in most countries was one of internal division, of warring kingdoms, of competing principalities. From time to time, India and Southeast Asia built empires of note. These came and went usually in short periods, though some in Korea and Japan were more continuous.

THE FAR EAST
c. 200 B.C.

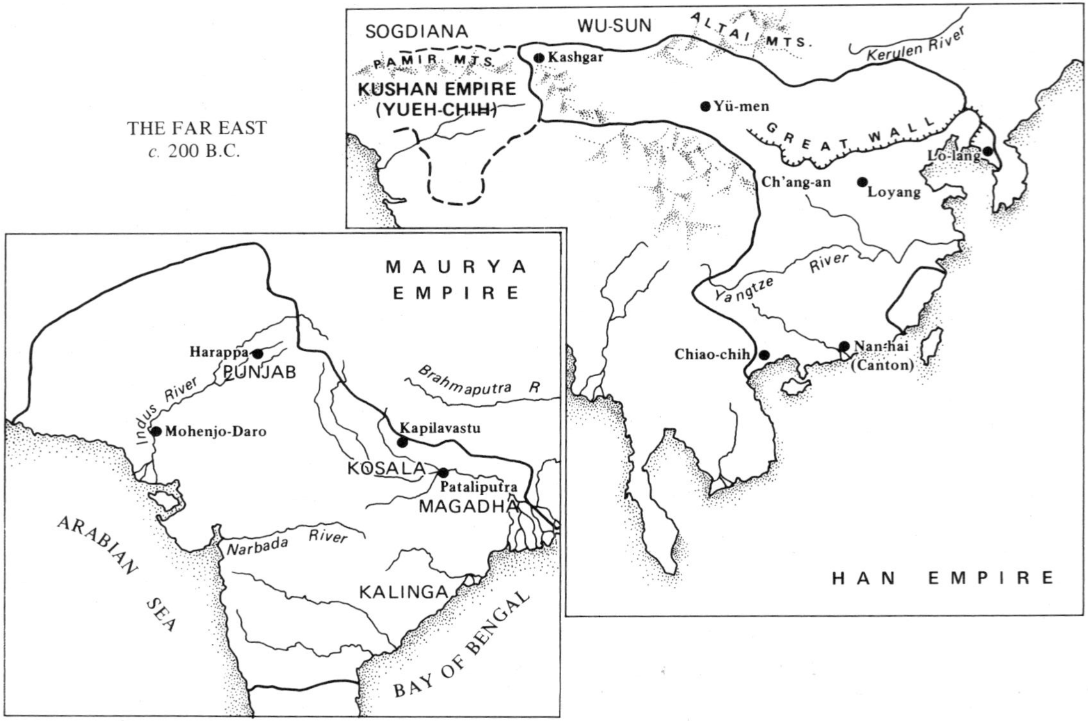

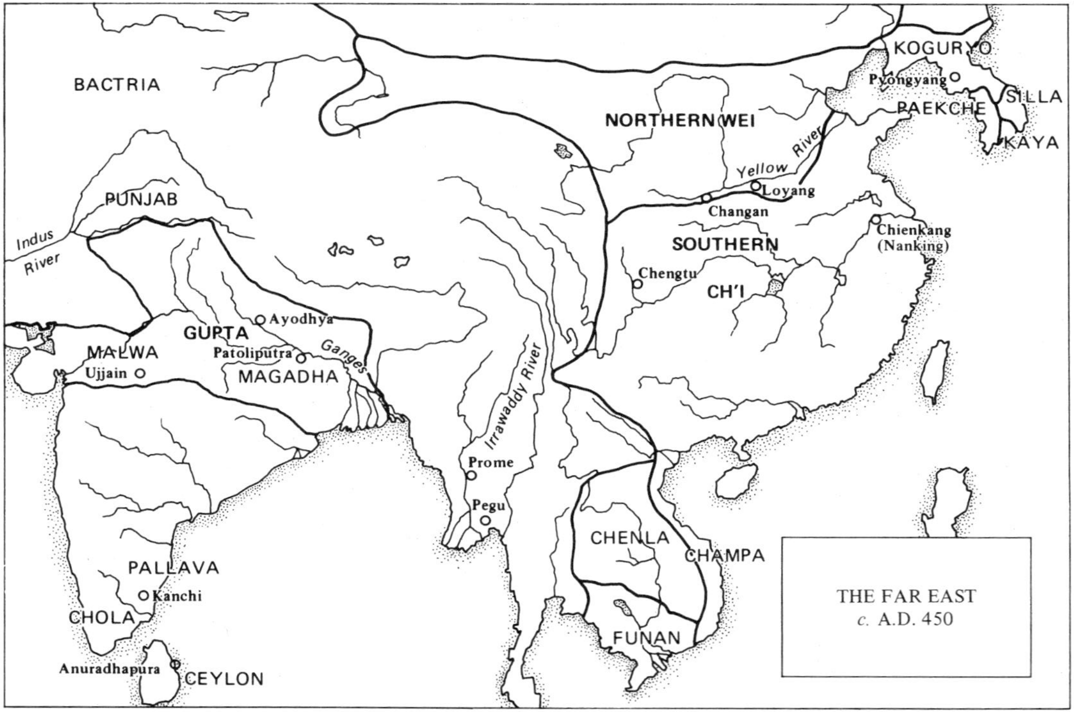
BACTRIA
NORTHERN WEI
KOGURYO
Pyongyang
SILLA
PAEKCHE
KAYA
Yellow River
Loyang
Changan
Chienkang
(Nanking)
SOUTHERN
CH'I
Chengtu
PUNJAB
Indus River
GUPTA
Ayodhya
MALWA
Patoliputra
Ganges
Ujjain
MAGADHA
Irrawaddy River
Prome
Pegu
CHENLA
CHAMPA
FUNAN
PALLAVA
Kanchi
CHOLA
Anuradhapura
CEYLON
THE FAR EAST
c. A.D. 450

But it was China, despite extended periods of disunity, that appeared over the millennia to have achieved the greatest degree of political and cultural continuity. Dynasties came and went as in other lands, but Chinese political inertia kept its momentum through ongoing bureaucratic, philosophic, and ideological bases of state.

By the thirteenth century, it was only China that had achieved stability and was to keep it. Korea was stagnating. Japan was disintegrating into a feudal pattern. Southeast Asian kingdoms, small and divided, were warring. In India, the Muslims had imposed their rule in the north, but Islam compounded rather than cemented Indian political divisiveness.

3

SOUTH ASIA
To 1206

The word *India* is derived from the Greek name for the Indus River, which ancient Indians called the Sindhu. On that river centered the earliest recorded civilization of the subcontinent. Then from the West, around 1500 B.C., came the Aryans, whose culture eventually spread into the Gangetic plain. With the invaders came the refinement of Hinduism, antecedents of which traced back to the Dravidians, the earlier inhabitants. Around 500 B.C., arose other faiths, chief of which was Buddhism. By that time early historic kingdoms had commenced. In the millennium between 500 B.C. and A.D. 500 they flourished. Those in the north, including the first empire, the Mauryan, were affected by foreign incursions; those in the south, collectively known as the Tamil lands, remained more aloof. Toward the end of the period in the Gangetic plain flourished the Gupta empire, a dynasty characterized by political and cultural activity, including the spread of Buddhism. After its fall, for another five centuries political fragmentation returned to the subcontinent with warring northern, central, and southern kingdoms. Around A.D. 1000, into this political disarray Islam came from the west in the guise of the marauding Turks. Within two centuries, they had conquered large areas of the north. Islam was in India to stay.

ANCIENT INDIA
(To 500 B.C.)

The Dravidians in the Indus River valley left the first record of Indic civilization, though evidence of prehistoric man exists. In time the Dravidians were conquered by nomadic Aryans who settled first in that area and subsequently fanned out into the

Gangetic plain. The first Hindu literary, political, and social structures resulted from interaction between the newcomers and the earlier inhabitants. By 500 B.C., the basic concepts of the orthodox faith were established, but coming into being were two chief heterodox religions, Jainism and Buddhism, which also left their mark in Indian thought.

Indus Civilization. Traces of man on the Indian subcontinent date back to around 400,000 B.C. From sites in the Soan River valley in northwest India, as well as from others in Gujarat and Madras, have come various primitive tools, dating to the Paleolithic (Old Stone) Age. Like their counterparts elsewhere, the prehistoric people of India were nomads who hunted and gathered food. They banded together as small groups in isolated settlements, whose shelters were carved-out rocks or simple huts. Of the ensuing Mesolithic (Middle Stone) Age, nothing definite can be gleaned. In the Neolithic (New Stone) Age, which entered the subcontinent between 10,000 and 6000 B.C., man settled down in fixed communities and practiced agriculture. He performed simple rites of animism and buried his dead in cemeteries with megaliths (stone blocks) serving as tombs. He used the potter's wheel and produced painted pottery and clay figures.

Remains of village life dating from the third millennium B.C. have been found in the lower Sind and Baluchistan. These villages resembled those in nearby Middle Eastern countries. The people built mud brick homes and used copper implements. They worshiped bull figurines, associated with a fertility goddess. Their ethnic origins are unclear, and their culture patterns, as indicated by pottery forms and burial customs, were varied.

During the period from 2500 to 1500 B.C., archeological discoveries to the east in the Indus River valley indicate a highly advanced urban civilization developed by the Dravidians. The cities, though widely scattered, were remarkably similar in cultural patterns. There were two chief centers, Harappa in North Punjab and Mohenjodaro ("Mound of the Dead") to the south, each several miles in circumference. Built of brick, they had walls, straight streets, multistoried houses, and well-laid out blocks, with citadels in the western quarter. Bathrooms with brick pipes as drainage systems conducted water out into street sewers.

The Indus people produced fruits, vegetables, wheat, and

barley. They used cotton, domesticated animals, and traveled in wheeled vehicles. They had written symbols, but these have not yet been deciphered. From some sixty sites have come pottery remains of varying colors, including clay toys similar to those in use today. Figurines of different types are dressed in the Hindu girdled apparel, with an elaborate headpiece. Many distinctive carved seals have also been uncovered. On these were inscribed symbols and figures, some of which later became symbols of Hinduism: the bull, serpent, swastika (signifying well-being), and a man surrounded by animals, sitting yoga-style with hands pointing to earth. (The cow, sacred to later Hindus, is not depicted.) What is known of early Indus religion is derived from the seals, which reveal an emphasis on fertility symbols, certain animals, and a prototype of a god of destruction.

Aryan Culture. After a millennium duration for causes unknown, the Indus civilization collapsed. Perhaps already decaying internally, the cities were conquered by the next invaders, the militant Aryans ("Kinsmen" or "Nobles"), who arrived about 1500 B.C. in migrant waves from the west. They brought with them their tribal system, which became established in India, and settled down into autonomous villages and towns, which eventually spread out into the Gangetic plain. They imposed their way of life on the local inhabitants or pushed them south.

The usual Aryan town was centered on some building or natural feature which served as an assembly place. The town walls had four gateways, each with a bamboo or wood observation tower. No art is extant from the Aryan period, but some aspects of life were developed that helped to shape classical Hinduism. The Aryans practiced cremation and believed that the dead were judged in the next world. They worshiped nature gods and also propitiated demons and ghosts. The chief deities included Indra, the prototype of the aristocratic Aryan warrior; Agni, the fire god; Rudra, the rain god; and Dyaus (Zeus), the sky god.

As sacrificial rites become more complex, Brahmans, who performed them, evolved into a priestly class. The Brahminical rites and formulas were outlined in the earliest Indian literature called *Vedas* ("Knowledge"). There were four Vedas, of which the oldest and most important is the *Rig* ("Rich") Veda. They consisted of hymns, incantations, and chants in both verse and prose form, which were handed down orally for centuries before being written. The Aryan period between 1500 and 1000 B.C. is sometimes designated as Vedic India because of the importance of these works. (Doctrines of transmigration, caste system, and cow veneration do not appear in the earliest Vedas; they were later additions to Hinduism.)

The next Aryan period, between 1000 and 500 B.C., is termed the Epic Age. Most of the source material for life during this era is drawn from two great epics whose main outlines were shaped at this time. The longest poem in the world, the *Mahabharata* ("Descendants of Bharata") is an anthology describing succession disputes and civil wars that raged in a Ganetic kingdom. It includes the *Bhagavad Gita* ("The Lord's Song"), a poetic dialogue of religion and ethics. The other epic, the *Ramayana,* narrates the personal and political vicissitudes of Prince Rama and his noble wife Sita.

Hinduism. By 500 B.C., with the development of an Indic civilization centered on the Gangetic plain, Hinduism emerged, as an unstructured and nonevangelizing religion. At the priestly level, Brahmans performed their intricate, esoteric rites. A number of gods were worshiped; the main ones were Brahma the creator, Vishnu the preserver, and Siva the destroyer. The mass of the people embraced a wide variety of animistic and simple folk beliefs and deified animals. Though it appeared fairly elastic in theology, Hindu orthodoxy possessed a core of commonly accepted beliefs and concepts. One was *varna* (class or caste), derived probably from race and occupation. At the top of the class structure were the Brahmans (priests). Next came the Kshatriyas (warriors and nobility), then the Vaisyas (traders and artisans), and finally the sudras (serfs). Each caste was divided further into thousands of subcastes, or *jati.* Outside the traditional castes were the millions of untouchables, whom Gandhi was to call *Harijan* ("Children of God").

The moral code that incorporated the principles of Hinduism was called *dharma.* Associated with it was *karma,* the doctrine that consequences of one's deeds carry over from one life to the next. Related to reincarnation, karma, because of one's good or evil actions, conditioned the course of future transmigrations. But through them one aspired finally toward release, or *moksha,* into the world soul, or ultimate reality. Other important Hindu doctrines included *maya* (the idea that the material world is illusory), and *ahimsa* (the principle of nonviolence toward life). Idealistic and otherworldly in nature, Hinduism tended to resign its believers to their contemporary fates, though it offered hope of betterment in a future life. Because of its disinterest in the here-and-now, orthodox Hinduism presented problems in the modernization of India.

Other Hindu literary works achieved canonical status, though they were of less exalted nature than the Vedas. *Brahmanas,* were prose texts explaining Vedic hymns. Appended to them were the *Forest Texts,* used by mystics and ascetics as further guides. Around 600 B.C., appeared the *Upanishads,* which expounded more metaphysical doctrines. The Upanishads and their later elaborations into the twentieth century were collectively termed *Vedanta* ("End of the Veda"). Associated with literature but not considered divinely inspired are the *sutras,* traditional learning summarizing laws and ritual.

Other Faiths. Alongside Hinduism, other faiths developed, of which the most important were Jainism and Buddism. Their founders reflected the changes in North India during the late Epic Age. The founders of the new religions lived for the most part in the lower Gangetic region, and were comparatively unaffected by the caste system. With the rise of new cities, urban classes, and a welter of small kingdoms, came unrest and new ideas. Both Jainism and Buddhism accepted such Hindu beliefs as rebirth, maya, and ahimsa, but both protested against some of the restrictions in the growingly rigid class structure.

JAINISM. Vardhamana Mahavira ("Great Hero") was the founder of Jainism. The traditional account of his life (*c.* 540–468 B.C.) relates that he was the twenty-fourth in a line of prophets of Kshatriya background, who appeared periodically over billions of years. Mahavira was born to a noble family in what is now Bihar state. At the age of thirty, he left home in search of salvation. After twelve years of wandering, he found enlightenment, and he propounded his doctrines until his death thirty years later. Subsequent doctrinal schisms arose, but Jains generally shared some common beliefs. They held that all matter possessed living souls and was graded into five categories, with the highest having all five senses. Like Hindus, Jains sought release from the ceaseless rounds of birth and rebirth by building up merit. Ascetic in nature, Jainism never spread in India, but its monks made great contributions to science.

Buddhism. Though Buddhism eventually died out in India, it spread to other lands and had a profound effect in Asia. Its founder was Siddhartha Gautama (*c.* 567–487 B.C.), also called Sakyamuni ("Sage of the Sakyas," a tribe into which he was born in what is now Nepal). Gautama, son of a ruler in Kapilavastu, was brought up in luxury as heir to the throne. However, becoming aware of human suffering, at the age of twenty-nine, he renounced his position and family to become a wandering monk. After six years of trying various paths to knowledge, including mortification of the body, he reached enlightenment while meditating under a bo (fig) tree. Accepting the Hindu doctrine of karma and transmigration, the Buddha ("Enlightened One") taught that one could escape this cycle through an ethical life. In its simplest doctrinal form, the Buddha enunciated "four truths." Life consists of suffering; suffering is caused by desire; to stop suffering one has to rid himself of desire; he can banish desire by the eightfold path: right belief, right purpose, right speech, right conduct, right occupation, right effort, right mindfulness, and right concentration. This path would lead one to *nirvana,* the extinction of desire and annihilation of self. Until his death at the age of eighty, the Buddha expounded his faith through oral teaching to the disciples who gathered around him.

EARLY KINGDOMS AND EMPIRES (500 B.C.–A.D. 500)

With the establishment of Hinduism as the chief religion and philosophy of the state, and others in minor but growing competition, by 500 B.C. the first historic kingdoms of India came into being. The settled Aryan life over the centuries began to spawn larger political entities, of which the first notable one, Magadha and the Maurya dynasty, centered on the mid-Ganges plain. This dynasty produced India's first emperors, including Asoka, one of the greatest of them all. After this dynasty, India broke up into small warring kingdoms not only in the north but also in the central Deccan and south. Some kingdoms were Hindu-oriented; others were Buddhist. The Gupta, also from the central Ganges area, reunited much of India, and this age was one of cultural brilliance and political expansion. By A.D. 500, India not only had recorded several impressive empires, but the Indic way of life, in a combination of Hinduism and Buddhism, had spread into Ceylon and parts of Southeast Asia.

The Mauryan Empire. After 500 B.C., sources of information on Indian history included Western writings as well as indigenous Hindu, Buddhist, and Jain texts. These accounts tell of the rise of kingdoms in North India. The most important was Magadha, located in what is now southern Bihar. Established by the Saisunagas of the Kshatriya class about 650 B.C., the state had ten dynastic rulers of this line, which in 362 B.C. was replaced by the Nandas. After forty years of rule, the latter in turn were overthrown by Chandragupta Maurya, who established the great Mauryan dynasty.

By the time Magadha state had come on the scene in the east, Westerners had entered the Indus Valley in the west. In the mid-sixth century B.C., Cyrus the Great, who founded the Achaemenian dynasty in Persia, expanded his empire into the western Sind. His successor, Darius I, during the Buddha's lifetime pushed into the Rajputan Desert and West Punjab, which he called Gandhara. In 480 B.C. Darius' son Xerxes employed Indian troops in his invasions of Greece. For over a century and a half, the conquered portions of Punjab and Sind constituted a province of the Achaemenian empire, and there was a great deal of contact between India and Persia.

In 330 B.C. Alexander the Great conquered Persia and began his expansion into the east. Pushing into Central Asia three years later, his army crossed the Hindu Kush Mountains. After wintering in the vicinity of Kabul, it crossed the Indus over a bridge of boats in early 326 B.C. (the earliest authenticated date in Indian history) and conquered a number of localities and tribes. The ruler of the Hindu city of Taxila in Gandhara welcomed Alexander, and according to Greek sources, killed cattle to feed his guests. (The foreigners noted the practice of *suttee*, the self-cremation of widows.) Alexander then advanced to the Beas River, where his troops, after years of campaigning, mutinied.

Forced to turn back, the conqueror returned to the Indus, sailed to its mouth, and proceeded homeward by land along the Persian Gulf.

Alexander's Indian conquests were insignificant from a military point of view. There are no references to him in ancient Indian literature, though the Greek colonies that he established in Central Asia eventually influenced Indian art. However, his expedition shook up the balance of power among the native Gangetic states and Magadha benefited from the political reshuffling. Its young king, Chandragupta Maurya, became the first historical Indian emperor. Initiating the dynasty (322–184 B.C.), he located on the Ganges his capital of Pataliputra (Patna), which was a large and imposing city. Chandragupta was an able and conscientious ruler. He expanded his empire east and west and defeated the Alexandrian ruler Seleucus Nicator. The treaty settlement gave the Indian emperor Greek cities in Afghanistan and northwest India as well as Seleucus' daughter in marriage. According to accounts of the Seleucid ambassador, Megasthenes, the Mauryan kingdom was idyllic and peaceful. The emperor maintained a large standing army, comprising infantry, cavalry, elephants, and chariots. The realm was divided into three provinces, and a civil bureaucracy with six presiding boards, was organized. A secret service system operated throughout the empire. Agriculture provided the mainstay of Mauryan economic life, but there was also a good deal of commerce, which was highly regulated. Irrigation systems existed, and good post roads linked key areas.

According to tradition, Chandragupta Maurya abdicated after some years to become a monk. His son Bindusara was also an able ruler, but Asoka his grandson (r. 273–232 B.C.) was the most renowned of all Indian emperors. Asoka expanded the Mauryan empire and in a bloody southern campaign won Kalinga (now Orissa) on the east coast. The war was militarily successful; but Asoka, remorseful for the terrible loss of life involved, turned to Buddhism. He devoted his later years to promoting the faith, which he made the official religion of India. Perhaps, like Constantine's, his motivation for conversion was in part political, to transcend religious and ideological differences in the land. Asoka supported a large number of Buddhist priests and founded religious houses. A royal relative reputedly converted Ceylon. On rocks and pillars (fourteen of the latter stand today) Asoka had engraved Buddhist edicts which exhorted his people to follow the faith and eschew Hinduism. He also promoted economic reforms throughout the temporarily unified land.

North India. After Asoka's death, his empire went into decline. Taxila and Kalinga broke away. In 185 B.C. what was left of the kingdom in the Gangetic plain went over to the Sungas (185–73 B.C.), whose realm was not a centralized empire but a confederacy with overlords and vassals.

A large part of North India fell to foreign conquerors. The first invaders were Greeks expanding from Bactria, an Asian country which had revolted against the Seleucids and became an independent kingdom. The Bactrian general Menander established a dynasty over Gandhara and Mathura. He and his successors were called Yavanas in local histories. Menander became a Buddhist, and his conversion is recounted in a catechismal Buddhist work, *The Questions of Milinda.* A bilingual culture arose, fusing indigenous and Greek ideas. The Greek legacy also included art and sculpture, but its political impact was not significant.

Other invaders eventually succeeded the Greeks. In 135 B.C. the Scythians (or Sakas), who had been pushed out of Bactria by other nomads from China, entered the Indus Valley from the north. They spread to the south, to Punjab, and east to the Deccan. From the west, the Parthians (or Pahlavas) also invaded the Indus Valley, and by the end of the first century B.C. had gained ascendancy in the northwest. Gondophernes, one of their line, was said to have been converted to Christianity by the apostle Thomas. Subsequently, the Kushans (or Yüeh-chih, as the Chinese termed them), who had earlier forced the Sakas from Bactria, fanned into North India from the Oxus Valley, where they had displaced their traditional enemy and established several principalities.

Kanishka was the greatest ruler of the Kushans. (The date of his accession varies between A.D. 78 and 144 because of conflicting chronologies.) His realm extended over Kashmir and much of the Indus and Ganges valleys, with its capital first at Peshawar and later at Mathura. He adopted and propagated Buddhism. The Gandhara style of Buddhist sculpture, derived from Greek art, developed in his kingdom, which because of its border location was culturally influenced by the Hellenistic West; and the kingdom was an entrepôt for trade between the Orient and Rome. In A.D. 99 Kushan ambassadors were received and entertained by the Roman emperor Trajan. Thus, wedged between Hellenistic and Sinic cultures, the Kushans extended Indian contacts with other nations.

Central and South India. Displacing the Sungas briefly on the eastern Gangetic plain were the Kanvas (73–23 B.C.). They were soon replaced by the Andhra line (28 B.C.–A.D. 225), of the Deccan, which had now become an Indian power. The Andhras were Hindus but tolerated Buddhism, and during their rule great Buddhist monuments were built. Among them were the Karli cave monastery in the Western Ghats; the great marble stupas (temples) in the central Deccan; and other stupas at Amaravati on the Kistna River. The Andhras in turn were ousted by the Pallavas (no relation to the Pahlavas), who established another independent state in the central Deccan. Also religiously tolerant, the Pallavas accepted Buddhists and Jains. They engaged in trade with countries of Southeast Asia, to which they also sent missionaries. Farther to their south three other Hindu states flourished. Chola sprawled along the eastern Coromandel coast; Chera (Kerala) arose on the western Malabar coast; and Pandya was located in the far south. In these centuries, the earliest historic Indian immigrants moved into Ceylon, where by the fourth century B.C., they had established their capital at Anuradhapura in the north of the island. These Sinhalese, as they were termed in Ceylon, were converts to Buddhism and developed their chief city into a large political and religious center, with some Buddhist stupas larger than the Egyptian pyramids.

While the Kushans developed land trade routes, the Tamil states turned to the sea. Westward they traded with the Roman empire via the Persian Gulf and the Red Sea, and they sent an embassy to the Roman emperor Augustus in the first century B.C. In a trade pattern that persisted into the modern era, India exported more to the West than it imported. Romans paid in bullion for luxury goods, cotton, precious woods, and rare animals. The Romans also established permanent trading agencies in South India and Ceylon, where Roman coins have been found. Eastward the Tamils sailed along the Bay of Bengal or across it to Southeast Asia, bringing religious and political ideologies as well as trade to that region.

The Gupta Empire. After the Kushan collapse, the Guptas (A.D. 320–480) founded the next great empire in North India. They brought peace and prosperity to most of the country, stimulated foreign contacts, and patronized the arts. Chandragupta I founded the line. On the throne only a decade, he extended his rule in the Ganges Valley by marriage and military campaigns, and he rebuilt Pataliputra as the capital of the state. Under his son Samudragupta, the empire became the dominant power in India. Ruling almost half a century (330–375), Samudragupta expanded control over all the Ganges Valley, south into the Deccan, and over a number of frontier tribes and kingdoms. The monarch was a devout Hindu and an extremely able and cultured man, skilled as a writer, musician, and poet.

The son whom Samudragupta chose to succeed him ruled as Chandragupta II (375–413). Establishing a new capital in north-central India, he conquered the western Saka states and Bengal. An account of his reign by Fa-Hsien, a Chinese Buddhist pilgrim, noted that the higher castes abstained from liquor and meat, which were consumed only by the lower castes and the untouchables (to whom he made the first specific reference). Kumaragupta, next in line on the throne, continued centralized Gupta rule for another four and a half decades.

The Gupta was a creative age. During this period the *Mahabharata* and the *Puranas* were completed. In the first half of the fifth century, Kalidasa, the greatest Indian poet and dramatist, composed the lyrical poem *Cloud Messenger* and the epic play *Shakuntala*. Buddhist and Hindu images proliferated. The Gupta Buddha became stereotyped in a sitting position with a smooth, rounded body. Great Hindus and Buddhist shrines, monasteries, and temples were built in the open or hewn out of rock. The famous Ajanta caves, excavated in the Deccan over five centuries, depict religious and secular themes through wall paintings and sculpture. Medical science progressed. Mathematicians formulated equations and fixed the value of *pi*. The decimal system, including a symbol for zero, was outlined. Astronomers posited the law of gravity, observed the earth's daily rotation, and noted solar eclipses. Metallurgy was advanced. Kumaragupta erected a solid iron monument, commemorating his father Chandragupta II, that has never rusted.

Spread of Buddhism. Under Gupta patronage, Buddhism spread. The Buddha had bequeathed oral precepts to his followers, foremost of whom was Ananda. In time Buddhist canonical literature crystallized into the *Tripitaka* ("Three Baskets"), consisting of monastic rules, the Buddha's sayings, and metaphysical works. In an attempt to preserve doctrinal unity, ecumenical councils were called from time to time over the ensuing centuries, but by A.D. 100 two basic Buddhist forms had emerged, both lasting to this day. Hinayaha ("Lesser Vehicle"), the conservative form, attempted to maintain the original doctrine of the Buddha, emphasizing salvation by the eightfold path. But it also came to glorify the historical Buddha, who had not considered himself a savior of men. Hinayana is followed today in Ceylon, Burma, Thailand, Cambodia, and Laos. (The religion is equivalent to that of a state church.) Mahayana ("Greater Vehicle") was the changed branch of Buddhism. Originating in North India, it spread into China, Korea, Japan, and Vietnam. Over the centuries, Mahayana evolved fundamental differences from Hinayana. Its adherents looked to salvation by faith in a number of buddhas, in addition to the historic one. They also revered *bodhisattvas*, who though ready for individual salvation, compassionately postponed it until they could save others along with themselves. Instead of nirvana, Mahayana believed in afterlife concepts of heavens and hells.

Buddhism in both its forms entered Indian pictorial art and literature. Hundreds of *jatakas* (birth stories) recounted traditional episodes from the Buddha's previous lives. Because of his holiness, the Buddha himself was not portrayed until Greek cultural influences arrived in India around the beginning of the Christian era. Symbols of his life and teaching were used instead. The lion represented the Buddha himself; the elephant his majesty; the horse his role as a world ruler; and the bull the sign of the zodiac under which he was born. Buddhist universities were founded, among which Nalanda, in present-day Bihar, was the greatest, attracting many foreign students. Buddhist concepts were exported by Indians to Southeast Asia, where by A.D. 500 these ideas, coexisting with Hinduism, helped fashion ideologies for early kingdoms in Burma, Thailand, Cambodia, South Vietnam, Malaya, and Indonesia. Other Indians, as well as Chinese pilgrims, carried the faith to East Asia. Buddhism was on its way to becoming the world's first universal religion.

POLITICAL FRAGMENTATION (A.D. 500–1206)

After the Gupta empire met its inevitable decline, India once again broke up into principalities, a pattern by now familiar in Indian history. Northern, central, and southern powers competed for political supremacy over the subcontinent, but none was able to approximate the boundaries of the earlier Maurya or Gupta. It was into this fragmented India that Islam was introduced. It took hold first in the north but later spread into peripheral regions.

North and West India. After a century and half, the Gupta empire broke up. Again through northwest passes came aggressors, this time the Huns, from Central Asia, who also overran much of Europe. The White Huns, a Bactrian branch, first conquered Afghanistan and then in the mid-fifth century entered India. Though at first contained by the Gupta, they whittled away at the North Indian empire, which eventually paid tribute to them. India once more became balkanized. In Central Asia the Turks managed to break up the Hun empire, but in India the invaders were assimilated and some of their descendants, notably the Rajputs ("King's Sons"), were influential in later Indian history.

In North India one major dynasty appeared briefly. In 606, at the age of sixteen, Harsha Siladetya came to the throne in East Punjab. Within six years he had established an empire in North India, which he ruled from Kanauj, near present-day Lucknow. The city had gardens and parks, as well as Buddhist monasteries and Hindu temples. Harsha established diplomatic relations with Tibet, to whose monarch he married off a daughter, and also with the Chinese capital in North China. A Chinese Buddhist pilgrim, Hsüan-tsang, described the monarch as a wise, compassionate ruler who listened to complaints of his subjects. A patron of the arts, he composed three dramas. Every fifth year he gave away his treasury's surplus wealth to the poor. A religious eclectic, he revered Siva, the Buddha, and a solar god. Hsüan-tsang noted that Buddhism appeared to have declined in vigor and that Indians practiced suttee and worshiped various goddesses.

In 647 Harsha died, leaving no heir. A usurper claimed the throne. He had the misfortune to attack a visiting Chinese diplomatic mission, whose leader fled to Tibet. There the emissary gathered troops and returned to defeat the Indian, who was then carried off to China. In North India there followed a five-hundred-year period of warring Hindu kingdoms. Yet learning progressed, with Sanskrit becoming the established classical language, while vernaculars such as Hindi, Gujarat, and Bengali, were also recognized. In the eighth century, the Pala kings came to power in the lower Ganges. They accepted Buddhism, but combined it with Tantrism, which stressed magical spells and portents. In 1125 the Palas were replaced by the Brahman Senas, who remained in power until the advent of the Muslims. By then, Buddhism, in both its Hinayana and Mahayana versions, had disappeared from the North Indian scene, having been absorbed back into Hinduism.

Central and South India. Other states developed in Central and South India. In Rajputana the princes restored Hindu culture. In Maharashtra, around present-day Bombay, the Chalukya reigned (550–853). They were temporarily conquered by the Rashtrakuta from the Deccan, who carved out the famous cave temples at Ellora in the Deccan and at Elephanta, an island in the Bay of Bombay. The Chaluyka dynasty ruled again from 973 to 1318, when the Muslims arrived.

Between the sixth and the eighth centuries the Pallavas ruled the Madras area, with Kanchi as their capital. Pallava merchants and missionaries established trade and religious ties with Southeast Asia. The Pallavas, like the Tamil states of Pandya and Chera, eventually became vassals of the Cholas, who emerged as the most powerful South Indian state in the tenth and eleventh centuries. In the course of the thirteenth century, their rule broke up, and their empire was divided between the Muslims and another Hindu state.

Over these centuries, Hindu Tamils continued to migrate into Ceylon, where they drove the earlier Buddhist Sinhalese from their capital of Anuradhapura, in the mid-eighth century A.D. The Sinhalese relocated in the south at Polonnaruwa, where they built another grand royal and religious capital. After reaching its height in the twelfth century the city was sacked, again by Tamils, who forced the inhabitants to withdraw into the central Ceylonese mountain fastness.

Tamil culture in South India enhanced popular Hinduism and proved resistant to Buddhism. In one religious development, Vishnu and Siva emerged as the chief gods, with their avatars, or incarnations, in several manifestations. In another development ascetics propounded *bhakti,* devotion to a world soul as the way of salvation. Though bhakti was an ancient element of Indian religion, it was the holy men from the south who popularized the doctrine in their travels throughout the land.

Advent of Islam. Islam arrived in force in India several hundred years after its origin. Muhammad, or Mohammed (570–632), the founder of Islam, was an Arabian merchant. In visions he received revelations, which he recorded in the Koran, Islam's holy book. The name *Islam* means "resignation" to the will of Allah, or God. Muhammad's followers were Muslims (those who "surrender" to Allah's will). His creed was simple but dogmatic: "There is no God but God, and Muhammad is his prophet." Islam's "five pillars" included ritual purification, prayer, almsgiving, fasting, and pilgrimage, if possible, to Muhammad's birthplace, Mecca. Puritanical in nature, with an absence of ritual, the faith forbade idolatry and music in mosques. Islam believed that all Muslims formed one congregation, that true believers belonged to one world, which could be enlarged by holy war, or *jehad.* But Jews and Christians as People of the Book (Old Testament), were tolerated if they paid a poll tax, or *jizya.* A caliph was considered the prophet's temporal successor, but the position came to fall most often on the monarch who could command the greatest allegiance.

Islam's development was influenced by historical and cultural factors. Two main streams of thought emerged: the orthodox Sunni, and the heterodox Shia, which through the Sufi movement stressed mysticism. In spite of theological schisms and counterclaims to the caliphate, Islam expanded rapidly in the Middle East, Central Asia, and Europe during the first century and a half of its existence. Arabs brought the faith to India. As early as 712, converted Arabs settled in the lower Sind area and around present-day Bombay, where they developed Muslim communities but did not expand their religious activities. Instead, the main Islamic thrust into India came three centuries later from Persia via converted nomad Turks in Central Asia. By 998, a Turkish Islamic state was established in Afghanistan, eighty miles south of Kabul. From this state, called Ghazni, the first sizable Muslim forces entered India.

In 1018 Mahmud of Ghazni invaded North India in two major campaigns. Sacking temples and laying waste cities, he left as his legacy the stereotype of a rampaging Muslim. From his campaigns there is reference to *jauhar*, a practice associated with proud Rajput warriors who, faced with overwhelming odds, killed their families and went forth to certain death. The invader eventually returned to Afghanistan, where he died in 1030.

In the twelfth century, Mahmud's successors gave way to another Turkish dynasty. In 1175 Muhammad of Ghur, like his predecessor, sallied into India from Afghanistan. Remaining in North India, he located his capital at Delhi, a strategic site commanding access to both the upper Indus and Gangetic plains. Local rajahs, rent by internecine rivalries, were swiftly conquered. During his three decades of rule, Muhammad presided over an area that extended from Ghur to Bengal. In 1206 he was assassinated. Aibak, a former slave, who had become Muhammad's viceroy and general, then assumed command. He initiated a new dynasty, and India entered another historical era.

4
SOUTHEAST ASIA
To 1300

As in South Asia, sites in Southeast Asia date back to prehistoric time. Man is old to the region. Over the centuries, waves of people, probably originating in South China, emigrated to Southeast Asian mainland and insular regions, to form the racial and linguistic bases of people now living there. Following the primitive indigenous cultures, by the last centuries B.C. Sinic and Indic cultures had been introduced. The former, commencing in the late second century B.C., confined itself mainly to North Vietnam. The latter, in both Hindu and Buddhist forms, began to manifest itself strikingly in the second century A.D. The Indian cultural legacy was perhaps the most significant feature of this period in Southeast Asian history. With the more sophisticated imported ideologies, came records of the first kingdoms. Arising by A.D. 600, these kingdoms took hold in North and South Vietnam, Cambodia, Thailand, Burma, and Indonesia. They drew strength, mainly in coastal or delta regions, from favored agricultural resources or, lacking these, from maritime pursuits. Between 600 and 900, some of these kingdoms grew in power; some faded out; still others began life. Between 900 and 1300, an imperial high point was reached with the Angkor dynasty in Cambodia, the Pagan empire in Burma, and the Srivijaya kingdom in South Sumatra. But warfare was endemic among the states, and the Mongol invasions from China in the latter half of the thirteenth century helped change the political patterns of mainland Southeast Asia.

PREHISTORY

Southeast Asian peoples are among the most ancient in the world. Skeletal remains that date back a million years have been discovered. The first great historic wave of immigrants came from the north, beginning around 2500 B.C. (approximately contemporaneous with the Indus Valley civilizations). These were sedentary Malay types who brought rice culture with them. Originating in Chinese territory, the people trekked southward into Southeast Asia; later groups followed their paths. Successive migrant waves pushed back earlier settlers into the hills and jungles or intermarried with them. By the Christian era, four main racial and linguistic families had developed. Originating in West China, Tibeto-Burman was spoken in northern and central Burmese river valleys. Mon-Khmer was used in the lower reaches of the same river valleys and delta areas as well as in the Chao Pharya and Mekong River plains. Malaysian was utilized in central Vietnam and the archipelagoes, and Annamese elsewhere in Vietnam. After the arrival of Chinese, Indian, and Arabic cultural influences, written variations of these oral tongues arose.

The Stone Age. Evidence of the Stone Age has been discovered in Southeast Asia by physical and cultural anthropologists. From Paleolithic sites in Java have come human remains and artifacts that reveal the transition from apeman to civilized man. Called *pithecanthropus* (from the Greek "apeman"), the earliest human types were tool-makers, utilizing coarse chopping and scraping utensils of stone, petrified wood, or bone. They were nomads, who did not settle down to grow crops. Later discoveries, also in Java, reveal more advanced beings, like the Australian aborigines today.

When the human form emerged toward the end of the period, there followed a succession of more culturally advanced tribes that moved down into the region from the north. These people of the later Mesolithic Age appeared in Southeast Asia in three great waves. First came the Australoid or Veddoid people, a dark-skinned race with curly but not woolly hair. Their descendants survive in some of the hill tribes of Indonesian islands. Then came the Negritos, small woolly-haired people, whose descendants survive today in Malayan and Philippine jungles and mountains. The third group were the Melanesoids, whose descendants are found in the South Pacific islands and Australia. A transition stage, Mesolithic culture utilized increasingly advanced bone and stone implements and made pottery.

About 2500 B.C., the Neolithic Age dawned with the arrival from the north of the Malays and Indonesians, whose descendants populated much of insular Southeast Asia. From the Proto (Older) Malays descended some interior tribes of Indonesia, including the Bataks and Minangkabaus of Sumatra and the Dyaks of Borneo. From the succeeding groups called Deutero (Second) Malays come coastal people: Malays, Javanese, and Balinese. All used tools of polished stone and simply decorated pottery. They were animists, believing that spirits, good and evil, pervaded the natural world. They revered a rice goddess. They grew food crops, particularly rice, which was cultivated in dry lands or in irrigated fields. They domesticated water buffaloes and pigs. They lived in small communities headed by priests and priestesses, who were associated with fertility cults, and they followed social law called *adat*. They constructed megaliths and dolmens, large stone monuments, perhaps used for worship or rituals. They developed puppet plays and practiced cremation involving either actual remains or puppets representing the deceased.

The Metal Ages. Around 300 B.C., other immigrants from the north inaugurated the Metal Ages. Termed Dongson (after the Vietnamese village where its artifacts were first discovered), the bronze and iron culture spread in Southeast Asia. The people of this time irrigated fields, domesticated animals, and practiced navigation. In social life women held an esteemed position; inheritance, descent, and family were traced through the maternal line. Their animistic religious pantheon included a variety of local gods, but paid special attention to those of the mountains and the seas. They venerated ancestors. Their art forms, similar to the Chinese of the time, portrayed men and animals in stylized representation. Their early communities grew and eventually formed the bases of kingdoms that received cultural impulses from China or India.

ANCIENT KINGDOMS (To A.D. 600)

Sources on ancient kingdoms of Southeast Asia derive from archeological evidence and from Chinese and Indian annals, compiled from on-the-spot observations or hearsay evidence. Direct

Sinic rule was restricted to geographically contiguous North Vietnam, but the Chinese enjoyed commercial and diplomatic relations with Southeast Asia at large. They utilized land routes into North Burma, though elsewhere sea lanes provided the chief source of international contact. From India, farther distant, came decisive and persisting cultural influences, radiating out chiefly through maritime routes. Diffusion of Indian culture proceeded variously—through cultural colonies established by Indian priests or traders, through conversions experienced by local rulers and elite groups, or through travel of individual Southeast Asians to India. In the early Indianized states Hindu and Buddhist ideas, voluntarily accepted and appropriated, coexisted in local kingdoms of Cambodia, South Vietnam, Thailand, Burma, and the Malayan world.

Funan. Funan (*c.* 150-550) was the first empire in Southeast Asia. The name derives from a Chinese transliteration of the ruler's title in Khmer, "King of the Mountain." According to a Pallavan legend, a Brahman founded Funan by marrying a Naga tribal princess, and he introduced Indian ritual to the country. The first capital, Vyadhapura ("City of Hunters"), was located in Cambodia probably during the first century A.D. The Khmer monarchs claimed semidivinity as evidence by their title, a royal appellation derived from Hindu political thought and one that was adopted by rulers of later neighboring kingdoms. Associated with Naga origins was the royal nine-headed cobra, an art motif carried down into modern eras. The heartland of the kingdom was the rice-rich, low-lying Mekong Delta. Because of the country's many interlacing canals, Chinese travelers wrote about "sailing through Funan." Through energetic campaigns, Funan extended its borders to include all Cambodia, some of Annam, the Chao Phraya Valley, and portions of the Malay Peninsula.

From the third century A.D., Funan maintained formal ties with China. A Chinese account, written at that time describes the king and nobles of Funan shaded by umbrellas and riding majestic elephants. The main buildings of the capital were of brick covered with lime plaster. The ruler, probably a Buddhist, kept Sanskrit court records. Gold and silver statuary existed; taxes of pearls and perfumed woods were imposed on subjects. The people, whom the chronicler described as black, frizzy-haired, and half-naked, lived in bamboo houses and worked in fields growing cotton, rice, and sugarcane.

In the late fourth and fifth centuries, Indianization advanced more rapidly, in part through renewed impulses from the Pallava and Gupta empires. But Funan rulers continued diplomatic ties with China, and Chinese accounts provide information on later Funan. Though Buddhism was tolerated, Siva was the patron deity of the realm. Sanskrit was used, and the suffix *varman* ("protected by"), a term used by Kshatriyas in India, was added to royal names. No architectural monuments remain from the period, but Gupta style images were fashioned. Following Hindu practice, widows and widowers did not remarry. Ashes of the deceased were placed in containers and thrown into the rivers or seas. Royal processions continued in sumptuous style, with musicians, guards, elephants, and white umbrellas. In the first half of the sixth century, relations with China were particularly close. One Funan king traded with South China ports and sought aid against an eastern enemy, Champa. But by the mid-sixth century, Funan had succumbed to pressures from the north; other Khmers, rising in South Laos, invaded the kingdom and replaced the Kaundinya line with a new dynasty.

Champa. Funan's eastern neighbor, Champa, was similarly influenced by India. Settling chiefly on southern Vietnam coastal plains, the early Chams had a primitive culture. With meager agricultural resources, they lived chiefly by fishing and hunting. In the course of the first century A.D., Indian merchants settled on the Champa coast. With the advent of the Indians came Hinduism and a more advanced culture. According to one rock inscription, around the beginning of the third century a Hindu ruler named Sri Mara founded the kingdom of Champa and conquered the surrounding tribes. About this same time, Champa appears in Chinese records as Lin-yi, with its capital at Indrapura on the Bay of Tourane (Danang).

As in Funan, Indianization spurted during the Gupta period in the late 300's and the 400's. Hindu strains were more apparent than Buddhist. A Siva cult existed. The people practiced suttee, eschewed beef, and followed Hindu chronology. In what was essentially a unitary form of government, Champa's three main provinces were divided into some three dozen districts, presided over by officials with incomes assigned from estates or taxes. An assembly of nobles decided matters of succession, which proceeded along a matriarchal pattern. Buildings were erected first of wood, then of brick; but few ruins remain today. Devoted to the seas, the Chams developed commercial relations with China and India. Sustaining livelihood mainly from commerce, Champa lasted quite long—into the fifteenth century—despite continual wars with neighboring lands.

Thailand and Burma. Into lower Thailand and coastal Burma came the Mons, who were related to the Khmers. Some settled in the Chao Phraya Valley; others moved on to the Irrawaddy Delta. Acquiring Indian culture from the country of Telugus in the Deccan, the Mons became known as Talaing. By the third century A.D., early Hinduized kingdoms, more Buddhist than Brahman, were in evidence. Chief among them were Dvaravati and Thaton. The former, on the right bank of the Chao Phraya, north of present-day Bangkok, was important by A.D. 500. The latter flourished across the mountains on the Tenasserim coast in Burma. Very receptive to Indian cultural forms, the Mons filled a historic role of transmitters of this culture. Though no pre-A.D. 500 inscriptions are extant, some brick structures have been uncovered. Coexisting with the Mons in Central Burma were the Pyus, the earliest historic inhabitants, who located on the Irrawaddy at Srikshetra ("City of Splendor") near present-day Prome. The city gates, protected by guardian spirits, were thirty-two in number (as were the provinces), a figure relevant to the legend of the Mount Meru, the Hindu center of the world.

The Malay World. In the Malay world, a handful of states became Indianized. Dating from the fourth century A.D., the earliest Malayan inscriptions in Kedah are Buddhist. The state of P'an P'an existed on the upper isthmus. In 515 a Chinese visitor described there a Brahman court and at least ten Buddhist monasteries. Another state, Lankasuka, was established at the eastern end of an important portage crossing to the Bay of Bengal. According to Malay tradition, the settlement was founded, probably at the beginning of the second century A.D., by a prince called Mahawangsa, who bestowed the place name. There fragments of Chinese pottery dating between the third and sixth centuries have been discovered. According to a fifth-century

Chinese annal, the state possessed harbor facilities, as well as agricultural and natural resources that included perfumed woods. The Malay ruler, wearing a sleeveless cotton garment and accompanied by a bodyguard, rode the ubiquitous elephant.

In Borneo, there were a few Indianized ports. In West Java, Purnavarman arose in the mid-fifth century. In Central Java, Ho Ling was noted in Chinese annals, which recorded missions in the fifth and sixth centuries. More agricultural than commercial, Ho Ling drew upon a plentiful source of Javanese labor and produced a surplus of food. Its people enjoyed shadow plays, danced to gongs and drums and depicting war exploits.

Chinese in Southeast Asia. Less pervasive than the Indian, the Chinese sphere of influence more particularly embraced North Vietnam, whose political and racial origins trace back to China. Around 1000 B.C., the Yüeh state existed in the fertile valley of the Yangtze River. Over the ensuing centuries, stronger tribes forced the Yüehs to migrate south, and eventually some ended up in North Vietnam. The Yüehs practiced irrigation, fished, and used poisoned arrows in hunting and warfare. In 214 B.C. their land was incorporated into the Chinese empire. Six years later, after the emperor's demise, a Chinese general proclaimed an independent kingdom, Nam Yüeh, or Nam Viet (a variant term), with a capital at Canton. Shortly afterward, the state became the vassal of a reinvigorated Chinese empire and remained so until 111 B.C., when it was annexed. The Chinese emperor divided Nam Viet, which included North Vietnam, into seven counties.

Sinic culture spread into the region. Chinese loanwords appeared in Vietnamese business, education, and philosophies. At first it was difficult for the Vietnamese to comprehend sophisticated Confucian precepts; not until A.D. 189 were Vietnamese accepted into government service. Around A.D. 200, with the disintegration of the Han dynasty in China, North Vietnam became a refuge for Chinese scholars. Eventually the Vietnamese elite appropriated the Chinese classics and ideologies, while the masses turned to Mahayana Buddhism. In village life, peasants identified themselves with local spirits as well.

The Chinese early developed trade and diplomatic relations with Burma, which it bordered on the east. By 128 B.C., a land route from India through Burma to China was in use. In A.D. 97

Roman envoys traveled this road to Yung-ch'ang, a Chinese prefecture on the upper Mekong River. T'an, a state in Burma, sent envoys and gifts to the Chinese capital in A.D. 94, 97, and 120. In 342 Yung-ch'ang was abolished during a period of Chinese political strife, and the land route was closed for three hundred years.

Chinese merchants and diplomats traveled in other areas of Southeast Asia, but they left no lasting effect. Some Buddhist pilgrims also recorded impressions. Fa-hsien, returning from Ceylon to China after a stay of a decade in India, in 414–415 passed through Borneo or West Java. Beached for some months at a port called Yeh-po-ti, he noted the predominance of Hinduism and the absence of Buddhism. After him other pilgrims and monks traveled the sea route. In 424 a Buddhist priest called Gunavarman on his way home from Ceylon stopped at Cho-po (Borneo?) and converted the ruler to Buddhism. Chinese records note other embassies that arrived during the first half of the fifth century from that principality.

EARLY EMPIRES (A.D. 600–900)

Between the seventh and tenth centuries, empires subject to Indic and Sinic culture flourished in Southeast Asia. In Cambodia, the state of Chenla, replacing Funan, persisted for two and a half centuries, to be in turn annexed by the Kambuja dynasty of Angkor. From North Vietnam, the Annamese under Chinese domination engaged in perennial warfare with the Chams to the south. In Thailand Mon kingdoms continued, but in Burma the political situation became more complex with the Mons, Pyus, and Burmans competing for power. There appeared in southwest China a new state, Nan-chao, which was to influence the course of mainland Southeast Asian history. Perhaps the most important empires of the period appeared in Indonesia: the Srivijaya in South Sumatra, and the Sailendra in Central Java. Around A.D. 850, these two united, with a capital in Sumatra. Though dying out in India, Mahayana Buddhism grew in Southeast Asia. China continued to assert imperial prestige, more through commercial and diplomatic ventures than by direct conquest.

Cambodia. Former vassals of Funan, the Chenlas moved south from Laos into the lower Mekong Valley. It took them many decades to consolidate their conquest. The founding of the state was a co-operative venture of two brothers, Bhava-varman (r. 550–600) and Mahendravarman (r. 600–611), who worshiped Siva and Indra. The third in line, son of the latter, Isanavarman (r. 611–635), completed the task of conquest. The new rulers retained the hereditary ministers of Funan but moved the capital to Isanapura. Around 700, the kingdom divided into two parts: Upper (Land) Chenla, and Lower (Water) Chenla. The more vigorous Upper Chenla embraced some thirty provinces and dispatched missions to China. Its leaders followed the Harihara cult, worshiping both Siva and Vishnu. Lower Chenla fragmented into five dynastic units, warring constantly with neighboring and overseas states. For a time they became tributary to the Sailendra of Central Java.

In 802 Lower Chenla was reunited as the Khmer Kingdom of Kambuja under Jayavarman II. A prince from a minor Khmer state who had spent some time in Java, he cast off Sailendra authority, though he was related to that family. His successors expanded the domain. Information on the early Khmer empire derives mainly from buildings. Dating back to Funan, a devaraja cult existed that emphasized the divine essence of kingship, a concept supported by both Hinduism and Mahayana Buddhism. The naga-serpent tradition was assimilated, and Saivite temples were erected. During their lifetimes, rulers lived in wooden palaces; after death they were transferred to stone temples and mausoleums. Based on Indian concepts, royal capitals, surrounded by walls and moats, symbolized the universe. In the center of the "World City" was the Meru mountain-temple. Within it was the image of Vishnu, Siva, or a buddha with whom the god-king had identified himself.

Vietnam. In these centuries, North Vietnam continued within the Chinese empire. Though the Vietnamese sporadically revolted, they remained secure not only in Chinese territorial limits but also in the Sinic culture sphere. Chinese officials supervised affairs and collected taxes. Chinese schools, political institutions, customs, and script became dominant in the ruling classes. In the late seventh century, the Chinese T'ang dynasty established there the protectorate of Annam (*an*, country of peace, i.e., China, and *nam*, south), from which period the term came into use for North and Central Vietnam. To the south Champa continued to exist, though warfare was endemic between the two states. When not fighting, Champa sent trade missions to China. In a favored location, Champa was an intermediate point for ships from India and Persia on the way to China as well as for the spice trade from the Indies.

Thailand and Burma. The Mons in Thailand persisted in the Dvaravati kingdom. In the course of the eighth century, some of them migrated northwest and founded Haripunjaya, near modern Chiengmai. Their counterparts in Lower Burma increased control in Thaton. The Pyus, however, found themselves in more constricted areas in the central Irrawaddy Valley at Srikshetra. Their power was circumscribed not only by the Mons but also by hill tribes to the east. And in the north the state of Nan-chao, founded in southwest China, around A.D. 750, also pressed down on them. In the 790's, a Chinese historian described Pyu society. Buddhism prevailed; young monks (seven to twenty years old) had shaved heads and lived in monasteries. Women wore ornaments and topknotted hair adorned with flowers and precious stones. In 822 Nan-chao invaded the kingdom. In the same century Burmans, also from China, entered Burma, began to absorb the Pyus, and founded several small states in Central Burma. However, little is known of Burman history before the eleventh century.

The Malay World. In the Malay Peninsula, small kingdoms continued but greater powers now rose in Indonesia. By the seventh century, Srivijaya, located near modern Palembang in South Sumatra, had emerged as the chief one. Chinese records referred to the kingdom first as Kan-to-li, then San-fo-ts'i. In A.D. 670 Srivijava sent an embassy to China. Straddling the strategic Malacca Strait as well as the Sunda Strait between Sumatra and Java, Srivijaya based its strength on maritime activity and founded various coastal colonies to further its commerce. It conquered most of Sumatra, the Malay Peninsula, and West and Central Java. Its rulers helped put Jayavarman II on the Khmer throne. The Chinese

Buddhist pilgrim I-ching described seventh-century Srivijaya as a center of Hindu and Buddhist learning as well as trade.

Simultaneously in East Java the Sailendra arose in the state of Mataram to displace Ho Ling. Ninth in line but the first important ruler was Sanjaya, who ascended the throne in 732. Initially Saivite by faith, the Sailendra, like Funan, derived authority from the title of "King of the Mountain." About A.D. 750, Mahayana Buddhism spread to Central Java where for a time it prevailed over Hinduism. The later Sailendra were great temple builders. They erected Buddhist monuments of which the most famous was Borobudur, dating to 772 and erected by King Pancapana, known also as King Vishnu. It is one of the architectural wonders of Southeast Asia. Representing Mount Meru, the cosmic mountain, Borobudur is Indian in idea but Javanese in application. A square pyramid built on a natural rock hill, it consists of eight terraces, five of which are square-cornered and three circular, the latter having seventy bell-shaped stupas. The top is mounted by a domed stupa a hundred feet high. There are three miles of terraces with wall niches for Buddha images and friezes depicting the life of the Buddha but in Javanese context.

The Sailendra periodically fought the neighboring states of Kambuja, Annam, and Malayu on Sumatra. In 832 the dynasty lost out when the only adult successor in the line, a woman, married the ruler of a rival state. Balaputra, the queen's younger brother, tried unsuccessfully to gain the throne. He fled to Srivijaya, around A.D. 850, and he married into that state's dynasty. With his departure, Buddhism died out in Central Java, and Hinduism regained prominence.

THE GOLDEN AGE (A.D. 900–1300)

The Golden Age in Southeast Asia witnessed the apex of the Khmer empire of Kambuja in Angkor. In the twelfth century, its architecture reached a climax, with the construction first of Angkor Wat, probably the most extended religious edifice in the world, and then of Angkor Thom, a grand royal city. Neighboring Annam, at long last in the mid-tenth century, threw off the Chinese yoke. It initiated native dynasties, which continued warfare with

Champa. From Nan-chao the Thai moved southward to establish their first kingdoms in the Chao Phraya Valley. Under the Burmans, the Pagan empire reached its apogee. Srivijaya continued its commercial empire from a South Sumatra base, while in Central and East Java three states—Mataram, Kediri, and Singosari—succeeded each other. From India, in the early eleventh century came Chola invasions of the Malayan world. From China, marauding Mongols not only sealed off land routes to the West but pushed campaigns into mainland Southeast Asia. From the Middle East and India, Muslim traders established small commercial communities in Indonesia. At the time these had little effect on existing Indic culture patterns, but after 1300 Islam became important in the insular world of Southeast Asia.

Cambodia. Between A.D. 900 and 1100, the rulers of Kambuja consolidated rule over all Funan and expanded into neighboring areas. Locating in the Angkor region and imposing indirect rule over outlying areas, they received tribute from dependencies. The monarchs had Hindu pretensions, while the mass of people remained in the Mahayana Buddhist fold. But rulers were tolerant and erected temples to Siva, Vishnu, Brahma, and the Buddha. Rajendravarman (r. 944–968), who united Upper Chenla and Kambuja proper, built Phnom Bakeng and Bantaey Srei, a beautiful jewel-like temple. His son completed other monuments and began new ones.

In the twelfth century the empire reached its height. Suryavarman II (r. 1113–1150) engaged in northern campaigns and warred against the Chams but paid tribute to China. In his kingdom he instituted a road system, built reservoirs, and expanded irrigation works. He is most noted for constructing Angkor Wat, a temple to Vishnu, with whom he identified himself. Intended as his mausoleum, it was not completed until after his death. Covering almost a square mile, the buildings were erected of stone from nearby hills; a specially built canal transported the stone to the construction area. The temple is surrounded by moats and walls, and the vast courtyard is approached by stone causeways. The main structure itself is several-tiered. At four corners are symmetrical towers shaped like lotus buds (sacred in Asian art), and at the center is a crowning tower over two hundred feet high. Extended pillared galleries, ornamented by bas-relief, depicting scenes from Indian epics but with indigenous spirit, line the temple proper.

Following Suryavarman's death, Kambuja was for a time thrown into turmoil. Peasants revolted and a usurper gained the throne. In 1177 Chams invaded the land and captured Angkor. In the confusion the usurper was killed and members of the former dynasty recovered the throne. Jayavarman VII (r. 1181–1219) drove out the Chams and pursued them into home territory. Near Angkor Wat he erected Angkor Thom, a royal city with defensive walls and moats. A Mahayana Buddhist, this king erected temples, the most notable of which was the Bayon. A pyramidal mass, it is crowned by a tower with four huge identical faces portraying the bodhisattva Avalokitesvara with whom the king identified himself.

Whether of Hindu or Buddhist persuasion, Cambodian monarchs followed Indian rituals at court. A hereditary group of Brahmans led by a chief priest perpetuated the devaraja cult. They provided the advisers to the king as well as court instructors, teachers, and physicians. They recited Hindu poetry, read Indian classics, and composed in Sanskrit grammar. Other chief ministers of state supervised administration, armies, arsenals, courts, and police. Because of succession problems resulting from a king's many sons (by numerous wives) all claiming the throne, a Grand Council, convened by the chief minister after the monarch's death, resolved claims. Since royal descendants for five generations back were eligible claimants, intense rivalry usually resulted. Among the lower echelons of society were three separate classes: commoners, slaves, and hill peoples. The Khmer calendar utilized a seven-day week and thirteen-month year. The land was extremely fertile; fruits and vegetables were plentiful; and up to three annual crops of rice could be produced.

Imperial decline came as continuous local wars drained treasuries and royal energies. Conflicts with neighboring states and kingdoms resulted in a loss of land, labor, and revenue. The religious surges ceased and the building splurge ended. In the course of time, the mass of people were converted by simple-living Buddhist monks from hierarchical Hinduism and elaborate Mahayana Buddhist forms to the less involved Hinayana faith, which stressed simplicity of ritual, lay participation, and abolition of classes. The kings' claims to divinity were thus cut away.

Vietnam. In the last decades of the Chinese T'ang dynasty, the Sinic hold over North Vietnam weakened. In the 860's the Chinese could not protect the capital Hanoi from incursions of Nan-chao. In 906 the T'ang gave the Vietnamese the right to select one of their own as governor to replace the Chinese viceroy. With gradual Vietnamization came indigenous strength. In 939 a local leader called Ngo Quyen declared independence. The Chinese still claimed suzerainty over the land, though their forces lost control. As a result of continual turmoil in forcing out the Chinese, North Vietnam lay impoverished and ravaged for decades. But the indigenous first Le dynasty (1009–1225) brought some semblance of economic recovery. It also renewed wars with Champa. The perennial warfare in part was due to population pressures in the north that pushed Annamese southward toward the rich and less populous Mekong delta lands. The Le monarchs nibbled away at Cham domains, which over the century constricted in size. In turn, North Vietnam suffered Mongol depredations emanating from China. In 1257 Hanoi was sacked, and repeated threats in the 1280's brought temporary alliance between Nam Viet and Champa against the northern marauders. But when the threat disappeared, Vietnamese again turned their attention toward the south.

Thailand. While the Mon kingdoms of Dvaravati and Haripunjaya persisted, new alignments shaped up in the north. Over these centuries, at least three migrant groups pressed down from the Nan-chao area into north mainland Southeast Asian river valleys and plains. Known collectively in China as Tai (Great), those who migrated into the Chao Phraya area adopted the aspirated form, Thai (Free); into Laos came the Lao; into Burma moved the Shans (the probable origin of the name Siam). In these new areas the Tai settled among the earlier inhabitants and contributed to racial admixtures. By the end of the eleventh century, the Thai were recorded in North Thailand in a small state called Payao. In the course of the next century, they moved farther south. After 1200, they appeared in the central plains, where they began to establish the first Thai kingdoms of note.

In 1238 the Thai overran Sukhotai, in Central Thailand, which was part of the Khmer empire. By 1300, another Thai state was established at Chiengmai, also a Khmer dependency. The second son of the conqueror of Sukhotai, Rama Khamheng ("Rama the Brave," r. 1283–1317), was the most distinguished of the line. At his capital he erected a great fortress with triple walls and four gates enclosing palaces and lakes. He pushed control into North Malaya and ended Mon rule in Dvaravati, whence he adopted Hinayana Buddhism. During his reign, not only was the new faith assimilated but so also were Khmer linguistic attributes and culture. Thai language was reduced to Mon letters, and temples were erected to Buddhist deities. Though the Mongols did not invade Thailand, their absorption of Nan-chao pushed more immigrants south. The Thai monarch nonetheless retained ties with China; twice he visited the Mongol emperors in Peking and also dispatched five tribute missions.

Burma. In these centuries, the first notable Burman empire emerged, the Pagan (1044–1287), founded by Anawrata. Uniting the various small kingdoms, Anawrata (d. 1084) located his capital in a semi-arid spot on the central Irrawaddy. The king was renowned for both his military and his administrative accomplishments. He developed and extended irrigation systems which assured and increased food supplies, thereby providing a base for military expansion. He rounded out his boundaries to include Pyu, Mon, and Shan territory and annexed parts of South China. A convert to Hinayana Buddhism, he made the court a focus of religious activity. He borrowed heavily from Mon culture and adopted its script. He and his successors made Pagan into a city patterned on Indian styles of architecture. In 1090 the great Buddhist Ananda temple was dedicated. Meanwhile, Pagan maintained formal diplomatic relations with China. In 1287, in the course of Mongol invasions, Pagan was destroyed. Burma once again fell into a pattern of political disarray.

Indonesia. Minor states carried on in the Malay Peninsula, but more important ones grew in Indonesia. In Central and East Java several states, more Hindu than Buddhist, arose in succession.

Mataram (900–1050) first appeared in Central Java, where the Brahman rulers constructed beautiful Prambanan temples. After 929 the state's center of political power moved east as it became a maritime kingdom dependent on overseas trade. Its most notable ruler, Airlangga (r. 1019–1049), who was of Balinese background but took an East Javan bride, presided over a kingdom centered near Surabaya. Under his leadership East Java grew in importance. A worshiper of Vishnu, he tolerated Buddhism and Saivism. No architectural monuments date from his time, but there is a large body of Indo-Javanese literature concerning his rule. On his death, the realm, subjected to Srivijaya attacks from Sumatra, split apart.

That part of the Mataram state known as Kediri recouped losses. Airlangga's son-in-law took advantage of momentary Srivijaya troubles not only to rebuild his kingdom but also to conquer Java and outlying areas. Like its predecessor, Kediri developed into a commercial power. Its rulers subscribed to the Vishnu cult. In 1222 a palace revolution ended the dynasty, which was succeeded by a new East Javanese regime at Singosari. This dynasty's most famous ruler was Kertanagara (r. 1268–1292), who asserted sovereignty over most of Java, and whose forces for some seventeen years threatened the Sumatran kingdom. In turn, Singosari felt pressures from Mongol China. Kertanagara refused to pay tribute to an ambassadorial mission and treated it summarily. In 1292 Peking dispatched an expedition to chastise the Indonesian monarch. But by then the political conditions had changed; Kertanagara had been killed by a usurper related to the Kediri line. Kertanagara's son Vijaya formed an alliance with the Mongols to oust his rival. Once this was accomplished, he in turn expelled his temporary allies and began a new empire, the Majapahit, in East Java.

In Sumatra, after 850 the reinvigorated Sailendra line ruled over Srivijaya. In 1025 the state was invaded from Chola, a kingdom on the Coromandel coast of India. The Indians won some military victories but left no political realignments abroad. After the crisis passed, Srivijaya expanded again, reaching Formosa by the end of the twelfth century. In a favored location, it controlled trade channels both to China and to India. In the early thirteenth century, according to a Chinese account, it had some fifteen vassal states. But then its decline set in. Political and economic competition came from Javanese states and neighboring Malayu, a former vassal. By 1300, Srivijaya had lost its grip on the strategic

Malacca Strait. Moreover, Islam had arrived with the first Muslim communities having been founded in North Sumatra. From there, in the thirteenth century, Islam spread to other settlements in the Malacca region on the Malay Peninsula, where it caught permanent hold.

5
CHINA AND INNER ASIA
To A.D. 220

The Chinese traditionally have intrepreted their history as a succession of some two-dozen dynasties over the past four thousand years. Because of this fact, their historical record appears more orderly and continuous than that of India or Southeast Asian political entities. The traditional Chinese dynasties, according to the chronicles, were founded by good moral rulers and ended by debauched evil monarchs. History thus became a repetition of personalities in such a pattern with dynasties quite like one another, though their duration varied greatly—between four years and nine centuries. Modern interpretations of Chinese history complement the personal dynastic factor by developing economic, political, and cultural aspects. New rule usually commenced with a period of peace, prosperity, and demographic growth, during which power was consolidated and territory expanded. But as time went on and as government expenses grew, adverse trends became noticeable. Loss of revenue, decline of imperial prestige, and constriction of territory followed. The already hard-pressed peasants became worse off; crop failures were widespread; public works fell into disrepair. Rebellions ensued, and in the military free-for-all, one leader would finally emerge victorious and begin a new rule.

As in South and Southeast Asia, man is ancient to China. The earliest traditional dynasty, that of the Hsia, arose when the Indus River civilization was flourishing in India. By the time of the second, that of the Shang, the people had fashioned a distinctive way of life on the North China plain. Following the Shang, came the Chou, whose rule was the longest in Chinese history. It was in this period, politically chaotic but intellectually creative, that the basic philosophies with their classics were created. The Chou fell to the Ch'in, who began the Chinese empire. The Western-designated term *China* derives from this first imperial dynasty. The Chinese themselves, reflecting an ethnocentric outlook, traditionally referred to their land as *Chung Kuo* (Middle Kingdom). After the Ch'in came the long-lived Han, in the course of which the Chinese imprint was stamped in East Asian civilization.

ANCIENT CHINA (To 1122 B.C.)

The racial origins of the Chinese are dimmed in time. Artifacts of Stone Age cultures have been discovered in scattered sites. But the China of history arose along the banks of the Yellow River on the North China plain. The Hsia is the first traditional dynasty, though as yet it is unsupported by archeological evidence. The ensuing Shang was a period when some of the earliest Chinese traditions were fashioned. As the earliest historic Chinese, the Shang bequeathed a distinct culture. Their kings exercised control over arts and crafts. They promoted writing, used chariots, and practiced rituals. Their society consisted essentially of the few rulers and the many who were governed. Through rites of ancestor worship that projected their origins back into antiquity, the Shang perpetuated the close-knit family system. They reached high artistic standards, and their script was remarkable. From their cultural center in the Yellow River plain, they radiated Chinese civilization out into peripheral areas.

Prehistory. Differing theories exist to account for the racial origins of the Chinese people. According to one theory, they migrated to China from Central Asia or the Middle East. According to another, they began in Southwest China or India. A third argument posits their evolution independently in North China. However they arrived or evolved, the Chinese founded their civilization on the Yellow River plain, probably because of its fertility and its climate, then more temperate than it is today.

Archeology confirms the tradition that the ancient Chinese evolved in the northern plain, where they developed primitive cultures on or near rivers. These date back to the Paleolithic Age, which in China lasted from around 500,000 B.C. to 20,000 B.C. In

1927, at Chou-k'uo-tien, thirty miles southwest of Peking, an archeological expedition discovered remains of the pre-human Peking man from this era. Paleolithic man used fire, hunted a variety of animals, wore beads, and painted his teeth red. In the later part of the Paleolithic Age, glaciers moved into China. The climate changes resulted in turbulent winds that blew soil, some of which settled as fertile friable loess in the Yellow River area.

There is as yet no definitive archeological record to support extensive life in the Mesolithic Age in China. But the Neolithic Age, which began at an unknown time and ended around 2000 B.C., evolved through three subperiods based principally on types of pottery fashioned. Characterizing the first stage was grey pottery, discovered in North China sites. It was of poor quality but varying types, including tripods and colanders. The second period was noted for painted pottery, made on the potter's wheel with geometric designs. The third period was that of fine black wheel-made pottery. These early Chinese cultivated by stone-bladed hoes, raising vegetables and growing millet. They domesticated pigs and dogs and produced tools of polished or ground stone. They hunted with bows and arrows, wore clothes of skin or hemp, and lived in sunken pit dwellings. By the end of the period, life was relatively well advanced. The political center of one area in the western Shantung Peninsula was a big city surrounded by a mile of walls built of pounded earth. The Neolithic culture, which spread down to the Yangtze coastal area, ended when bronze artifacts came into use during the supposed Hsia dynasty.

Chinese myths and legends also center on the North China plain as the cultural homeland. These stories reveal ancient Chinese values and beliefs. They stressed the importance of family ties, noted the dominance of agriculture, portrayed the rule by priest-kings, and depicted a man-centered society. According to the chronicles, which vary somewhat, the Creator P'an Ku shaped the universe over a period of eighteen thousand years, a multiple of the sixty-year Chinese lunar cycle. There then followed long periods of rule by celestial, terrestrial, and human emperors, all in variation of the sixty-year cycle. Subsequently came several outstanding monarchs, who were the inventors of many arts and crafts. Among them was Huang Ti ("Yellow Emperor"), considered the grand ancestor of the Chinese race. Several more kings followed in succession not by eldest son but by ablest man. The last of these founded the first traditional dynasty, that of the Hsia.

The Hsia. As described in early Chinese histories, the Hsia dynasty is dated from 2205 to 1766 B.C. (or 1994 to 1523 B.C. according to another early source). Much relating to the period is legendary. If it did exist, the Hsia (like most other Chinese Paleolithic and Neolithic cultures) was located near the banks on the middle reaches of the Yellow River. During the course of the five-century dynasty, seventeen sovereigns reportedly ruled over groups of city-states. According to later Chinese histories, the basic outlines of the personal factors in the dynastic cycle were already established in the evolution of the Hsia. Yu, a model emperor, founded the Hsia. Chieh, the depraved last monarch, was overthrown in revolt by the people led by the good T'ang, a descendant of the Yellow Emperor. As noted previously, everything is as yet conjectural about the Hsia, but all Chinese traditional accounts accepted its existence.

The Shang. The first authenticated dynasty in China is that of the Shang (1765–1123 B.C., or *c.* 1500–1027 B.C. according to another chronology). Its people developed on the North China plain a remarkable civilization. Archeological finds that document the period include inscribed divinations on oracle bones and shells. As the earliest specimens of Chinese characters, about 2,500 signs are recognizable to this day. In this type of scapulimancy, a sharp instrument incised the characters on tortoise shells or flat animal bones. In time, questions and detailed answers were recorded. These more involved inscriptions generally consisted of one-to-five dozen characters. Typical subjects of divination related to advice on matters of sacrifices, war, hunting, fishing, journeys, weather, crops, and illness. The Shang also composed on wooden or bamboo slabs, but these media have long since disappeared through the toll of time.

Another important source of information on Shang life derives from pottery and highly developed inscribed bronzes. When patterns appear, they tend to be geometrical ones or conventionalized designs (like those of American Indians). One such popular stylized representation is the animal mask, a front head-on view of an animal head, like a ram's, with the ears spread out and the design centered on a nose-eye axis. Bronze was not only utilized but it was cast and smelted in some form of blast furnace. Metal artifacts include weapons and ceremonial vessels in many shapes and forms. Shang bronzeware is represented by tripods, round or square pots mounted on four legs, covered pots with movable handles, and varieties of drinking cups. Most bronzes have turned green because of chemical action resulting from burial of over three millennia.

Other information on the Shang dynasty derives from literature composed in later eras. Most of this relates to the nobility. In its early years, the ruling house, which derived its name from the god *Shang Ti* ("Ruler Above"), probably occupied several capitals. Around 1400 B.C., it settled down in the marshes of Yin on the banks of a tributary of the Yellow River near modern An-yang. The royal domain encompassed the area from what is now Peking in the north to the Yangtze in the south, from the sea in the east to present-day Kansu Province in the west. Nine monarchs, with an average reign of thirty years, ruled at An-yang. Succession was either brother to brother or father to son. Kings performed the most important rites. They led armies of infantry and chariots into battles, and conducted hunts. They had a centralized bureaucracy of councillors, historians, diviners, and priests. Hereditary nobility presided over substates. In a city-state pattern of rule, the nobles followed, supported, or fought the kings, who in turn protected or fought them. The Shang regulated their activities of war and peace according to the lunar calendar, which reckoned a ten-day week, a three-week month, and a two-month cycle. The 360-day year covered six two-month cycles, which were periodically reconciled with solar time by adding an intercalary week or two.

The advanced development of arts and crafts presupposed a skilled artisan class who executed the bronze works, shaped jewels, especially those of jade, and manufactured white and glazed pottery. Silk, a commodity ancient to China, was woven. Shang people played musical instruments, such as okarinas and musical stones. They produced sculpture up to a yard in length, but no examples of this art form are extant. A merchant class traded in various commodities, including salt, shells, and metals brought from a distance to the capital. The mass of people practiced agriculture, the mainstay of the economy. The peasants used hoes, spades, and foot plows in the fields. The chief crop was millet; possibly wheat and irrigated rice were raised. Farmers utilized animals, including pigs, sheep, goats, cattle, and horses. They lived in simple one-roomed thatched huts or in crude Neolithic-type pit dwellings and loess caves carved into the hills. There is no proof that Shang society materially depended on slave labor.

The dynastic decline of the Shang repeated the pattern of the Hsia. Chou Hsin, the last Shang ruler, was supposedly tyrannical. His long-suffering subjects rose in revolt under Wu Wang (King Wu) and his brother Chou Kung (Duke of Chou). The remnants of the Shang royal family and their loyal adherents went into exile. Korea traces its traditional beginnings to one such group of royal refugees. Others retreated to Central China. In new environs they diffused Chinese culture.

THE CHOU (1122–221 B.C. or 1027–221 B.C.)

The origins of the Chou are unknown. By the time Chinese annals record the state, it was centered on the Wei River, a tributary of the Yellow River. Its capital was Hao, near present-day Sian in Shensi Province. (This well-watered and fertile area near the Yellow River's last bend was also to provide capital sites for several future Chinese dynasties.) Unlike the Shang brother-to-brother pattern, Chou succession was from father to son. After the king of Wu and his brother overthrew the Shang, they established the new dynasty. On the fringe of Sinic culture, the Chou location permitted the coexistence of a border martial outlook and a sophisticated settled civilization. Population figures are not available for the Chou dynasty, but it is possible that by the end of the period China was the most populous country in the world.

In the first four and a half centuries of rule, the Earlier or Western Chou maintained the political center of power in the Wei Valley. Like the Shang, they ruled over a triangular area extending from South Manchuria to the Yangtze to Kansu Province. Then they moved their capital farther west. Through continued wars and strife, feudalism—in the sense of a politically divided and decentralized country—arose. The troubled Later or Eastern Chou epoch is sometimes further subdivided. Such subperiods include the "Spring and Autumn Epoch" (722–481 B.C.) and the "Warring States" (403–221 B.C.), both eras named after historical books. However, despite the political turmoil, the Chou was an era of intellectual creativity, cultural development, and literary and philosophic activity.

The State. The political head of the Chou realm was the king (*wang*), who lived at the central capital. Assisting him were a chief minister and six subordinate ministries: imperial household, agriculture, army, religion or rites, punishments, and public works. An elaborate appointive bureaucracy, based on wealth and family, serviced the state. The land was divided into circuits, each with an official in charge. Because of the country's large area, poor transport, and weak rule, the kings delegated authority to their lords or vassals, who kept courts in their own political and religious centers. Fighting among leaders became endemic and grew harsher over the decades. By the end of the period a dozen states were contending for political mastery. One—the Ch'in—finally triumphed, to establish China's first empire.

In their continual wars, the Chou leaders utilized three-man chariots and infantry units with long bows and crossbows. In later times cavalry was introduced, probably from Central Asia. Because of their mobility and speed, horses changed the nature of warfare. In their religious life, the Chou worshiped *T'ien* (Heaven), a Supreme Being sometimes taken for Shang Ti, the ancestral deity. As mediator between heaven and earth and between nature and man, the king performed at ceremonies the rite of *kowtow*, the three kneelings and nine prostrations. Chou gods, like earlier ones, were portrayed more as superhuman beings than divinities. In their social affairs, the Chou, like the earlier Shang, divided into two main groups, the rulers and ruled. Aristocratic clans worshiped through a hereditary head a common ancestor. The lords enjoyed unrestricted power in their domains. They owned the land, but their stewards supervised its cultivation. Nobles ate meat and were fond of drink. By the third century B.C., chopsticks were in use. The governed class consisted mainly of peasants, who continued a primitive Neolithic existence and observed fertility and animistic rites. Artisans executed bronzes, which now became massive, bulky, uninspiring, and formal. Merchants conducted trade and commerce, chiefly by barter. By 500 B.C., metallic currency was developed. Chinese scholars noted lunar and solar eclipses and were aware of the movements of the planets Jupiter and Saturn. They developed geometric equations, used *pi*, and practiced trigonometry.

The Economy. Agriculture was the keystone of economic life. The main crops now included millet, wheat, barley, and rice. The ox-drawn plow was used. The most prominent agrarian feature (which might have been a post-Chou projection) was the well-field system, derived from the character for well (*ching*),井. In this system the land was given to eight peasant families. Each tilled its own field as well as the central one in common for the lord. As land became impoverished, it was periodically reassigned. Not until the third century B.C. did peasant proprietorship arise. Farmers were not bound contractually to the land in a feudalistic manner, but they had little chance to improve their lot. With the fashioning of some iron agricultural and military implements in the Chou, China entered the Iron Age.

Culture. The Chou was a time of intellectual activity. Amidst the warfare of the day and times of political flux, men sought to re-examine or to confirm traditional values. They proposed alternative philosophies to resolve political chaos and restore normal relations. Feudal lords gathered around them philosophers, advisers, and writers to discuss issues as well as to enhance their own prestige. Most of the thinkers to a great extent borrowed upon or appropriated from earlier religious beliefs of the Chinese people. Chou philosophers asked the time-honored questions that their counterparts in other lands posed with regard to the nature of man, the appropriate bases for human society, and its salvation in anarchic times. But Chinese philosophers, unlike Indian, in particular stressed political thought, accented a concern to improve society, and sought realizable political utopias.

CONFUCIANISM. Confucianism, which stresses the value of the "middle way," was only one of several important schools of the day but emerged as the paramount one after the Chou. Confucianism as a word does not exist in China or in East Asia. Its equivalent is *ju chiao* ("learning of the literati"). Its founder was

Confucius (a Latinized name), known in Chinese as K'ung Fu-tzu or Master K'ung, who was a contemporary of the Buddha. His traditional dates are 551–479 B.C. Born of wealthy background in the Chou state of Lu on the Shantung Peninsula, he held various local government posts and traveled about North China, hoping to convert some lord to his philosophy. Though at the time, he gained no followers, Confucius became the model teacher and moralist for later generations.

The most important Confucian ideas are outlined in the *Analects,* a work in terse and cryptic dialogue form between the master and his disciples. The philosopher was interested not in metaphysics or the afterlife but in contemporary affairs. His models were past heroes, including the ancient emperors and the founders of the Chou dynasty. The doctrine stressed five basic relationships: those between ruler and subject, husband and wife, father and son, elder and younger brother, and friend and friend. All individuals filled assigned roles in a hierarchical society. The Confucian program called for a government by ethics, the training of character, and the social ideal of the educated gentleman-ruler. It held that good government resulted from educated men executing proper rituals. The training for this type of man included the cultivation of five inner virtues: integrity, righteousness, loyalty, reciprocity, and human-heartedness.

Later disciples added their own tenets to Confucian thought. Mencius, or Meng Tzu (372–289 B.C.), was the most important. His philosophy is contained in a book that bears his name and is written also in dialogue style. He concluded that man was essentially good, but that this innate moral worth was adversely altered through environmental factors. To overcome this moral drag, one had to practice self-cultivation through proper ritual and behavior. In political affairs Mencius confirmed the necessity of rule by good example and the right of subjects to revolt against evil kings, who because of wrongdoing had lost the Mandate of Heaven. Another disciple of Confucius was Hsün Tzu, or Hsün K'uang (*c.* 300–237 B.C.). As a teacher and politician, he also outlined his views in a book called by his name. Contradicting Mencius, Hsün Tzu claimed that, because of conflicting personal drives as well as politically inchoate times, man was essentially imperfect though education could improve his nature.

In its original Chou form, Confucianism embraced differing and apparently contradictory outlooks. Yet all had common ideological denominators (some derived from earlier Sinicism): agnosticism, involvement in contemporary affairs, concern for man's duty to man, the importance of education, the propriety of ethical conduct, the improvability of human beings, and emphasis on ritual. These ideas were not only elaborated in works attributed to Confucius and his colleagues but were also developed in the so-called "Five Classics" compiled in the Han dynasty. These later became the standard works for educated men to study and to emulate. Though tradition attributed to Confucius their authorship or editorship, it is doubtful that he wrote any of them; in fact most of their sources predated him. Much in the books is spurious. They are all old, and the ancient phraseology and esoteric interpretations render their sense the more difficult. The Five Classics are compilations of poetry, divination, ritual, and two histories: a general one of China and a specific one of Confucius' home state.

The *Classic of Poetry* (*Shih Ching*), an anthology of several hundred songs or poems probably composed between the tenth and seventh centuries B.C., deals with various subjects relating to life, love, politics, and rites of Chou (and Shang) times. The *Classic of Divination* (*I Ching*) is a diviner's handbook. The extended work elaborates the meaning of trigrams (☰, ☱, ☲, ☴, ☳, ☵, ☶, ☷,) and hexagrams which replaced scapulimancy. The *Classic of Ritual* (*Li Chi*) is a second-century B.C. compilation of earlier material relating to etiquette. The *Classic of History* (*Shu Ching*) is a work of general Chinese history of fifty-six chapters (probably only half are genuine). The work includes a number of statements attributed to various rulers and ministers from ancient times through the Early Chou. Lastly, the *Spring and Autumn Annals* (*Ch'un Ch'iu*) is a chronology of events dated between 722 and 481 B.C. in Lu, Confucius' home state. The title denotes an agricultural year, with its planting and harvesting seasons. The work is similar in nature to the histories of other Chou states.

Other Philosophies. Second in importance to Confucianism as a school of philosophy was Taoism. This rose in the peripheral states of the Yangtze Valley, but it incorporated such ancient Sinic beliefs as mysticism, spirit worship, and yoga-type breathing exercises. As a doctrine of protest, it de-emphasized ritual and authority, holding that man should related to nature rather than to society. Classical Taoism, much of which is vague, derives essentially from two figures. The founder, Li Erh, better known as Lao Tzu ("Old Master"), is said to have lived in the sixth century B.C. His authenticity has been questioned because the earliest reference to him is in a brief passage in a work of history written four centuries after his death. Attributed to him is a book, bearing his name, which is a repository of a variety of beliefs. A second main Taoist figure was the historical Chuang Tzu (369–286 B.C.), a contemporary of Mencius. In a book derived from his name, he expressed Taoist ideas through poems, parables, and metaphors. He sought to free the individual from his own inner intellectual restrictions as well as from impinging external circumstances.

Taoism advocated the principle that man should blend into the Tao ("The Way"), the nameless, the non-being. Tao is the underlying principle in which everything has its being. Harmony with Tao is attained through the mystical approach, intuition, and illumination rather than through rational processes. Merging consists of inaction, of yielding passivity (*wu wei*). As an analogy, the Taoist often used the simile of soft dripping water wearing down hard rock. Taoists also advanced the idea of unity of opposites. There had to be rules because anarchy existed; reverence for ancestors was necessary because impiety was prevalent. Like Confucians, but on differing bases, Taoists advanced the ideal of political primitivity, in which they preferred to see no good or evil action and no suffocating ritual. Their ideal was a small state, where one could hear dogs bark and cocks crow in a neighboring state yet remain unconcerned about its affairs. Later popular Taoism inverted some of the early intellectual and political doctrine by stressing through protoscientific experiments the use of magic, the quest for immortality, and the search for elixirs to prolong life.

Other schools of thought existed in the Chou period but they tended to lose ground during later dynasties. The Dialecticians through sophistic arguments posed linguistic, semantic, and philosophic propositions. The Naturalists were interested in the question of origins. They made much of yang-yin concepts, or complementary opposites, with the former connoting positive and strong ideas, the latter negative and weaker ones. Mo Ti, or Mo Tzu (470–391 B.C.), in a book bearing his name, propounded a doctrine of universal love, defined not in the Confucian sense of graded love but as loving others as one's self. He also believed in a moral heaven and, somewhat unusual in Chinese thought, looked on Shang Ti as a personal Being. The individualistic and pessimistic Yang Chu, of the fourth century B.C., was a solitary figure who founded no school and gathered no followers. His negative thought left little imprint in Chinese philosophy.

The legalist school had the most immediate impact on political life. The rulers of Ch'in, who overthrew the Chou and established the Chinese empire, adopted its ideas. Among its adherents were various prime ministers, including Li Ssu, the adviser to China's first emperor. Holding that the prince could and should follow any tactic in order to obtain and to maintain power, the Legalists emphasized authoritarianism in politics. They believed that the prince was all-wise; the people knew nothing. The Legalists enacted stringent laws that brought wide-ranging rewards and punishments. The idea of an authoritarian ruler had always been present in Chinese political thought, but the Legalists elaborated the concept and gave it political orthodoxy.

EARLY EMPIRES
(221 B.C.–A.D. 220)

In 221 B.C. a political revolution in China occurred when the Ch'in initiated the imperial structure. Kings now escalated into emperors, and centralized bureaucracies grew powerful. Succeeding the short-lived Ch'in, the Han consolidated gains and expanded Chinese rule into East and Central Asia. The long dynasty, in both the earlier and later phases, was creative. Where the Ch'in laid the imperial foundations, the Han rounded out the political superstructure. Confucian bureaucrats served the imperial government, and official scholarship abounded. The first great individual works of history were compiled. In science inventive genius manifested itself. A variety of arts were practiced. North Korea, South Manchuria, Central Asia, and North Vietnam adopted Chinese cultural patterns through voluntary or imposed means. Taking justifiable pride in the dynasty that first left a definite imprint in the East Asian historical scene, later generations of Chinese, including the Communists, have designated themselves as Han Chinese.

The Ch'in **(*221–206* B.C.)** The Ch'in dynasty was essentially a one-man rule. But despite its brief imperial duration, it had a long background. As early as the eighth century B.C., the state arose in the Wei Valley, where the Chou had earlier commenced political life. In a region peripheral to both nomadic and Sinic influences, the Ch'in simultaneously absorbed two ways of life. Over five centuries, its kings slowly expanded their domains. By 221 B.C., they had conquered all China as it then existed. Strong men and Legalist ideas contributed to Ch'in success. In the pre-imperial phase, ministers who subscribed to the views of the Legalists advanced authoritarian bases for a strong state and ruler. What the kings had earlier practiced over their limited but growing domains was later put into effect throughout the Chinese empire.

Li Ssu, an advocate of forceful measures, became the minister to the young king, who founded the empire as Ch'in Shih Huang Ti. The new imperial name was noteworthy. *Shih* meant "First," and *Huang Ti* derived from the word for the celestial Being. A complex and fearless man, the emperor meant to brush away old kingdoms and establish precedent through the creation of a new imperial structure. Foreshadowed by earlier policies, his domestic programs emphasized conformity and centralization. At Hsien-yang, his capital near the site of the Early Chou capital and of modern Sian, he erected a huge palace. Maintaining a great bureaucracy, he divided China into many counties grouped into several dozen provinces, each with a military governor, civil administrator, and lesser supervisory officials. As in the earlier pre-imperial phase of Ch'in rule, peasants were given ownership of private lands, subject to tax. The emperor placed stringent controls over nobility. Through measures of forced labor, he shifted populations about China according to work projects and military necessity. The state maintained public works, built canals, and operated an efficient network of roads. The ancient Chinese written language was formalized into one basic style, which has persisted to this day. Fearing opposition or subversion, the emperor effected, upon Li Ssu's advice, a program of thought control. Intellectuals who opposed him were killed off and books with ideas antagonistic to the Legalistic tradition were burned.

In his external programs, Ch'in Shih Huang Ti expanded China's frontiers. In the north he consolidated links of the Great Wall, whose chief purpose was temporary containment of nomadic invaders until Chinese troops arrived on the scene. But the wall was continually breached and never stopped any strong invading forces from entering North China. It was primarily a type of symbolic cultural demarcation with the area south of it designated as Chinese and that north of it as "barbarian." In western campaigns, the emperor contained the Huns (whom the Chinese called Hsiung-nu), long-time active on China's borders. He expanded his borders south, where no strong tribes blocked Chinese emigration and military campaigns. By 214 B.C., Ch'in troops had penetrated down northern and central Vietnamese coastal and valley areas to modern Hué. Their action foreshadowed almost twenty-two centuries of Chinese interest or involvement in the southern neighbor.

***The Early Han* (*206* B.C.–A.D. *9*)** Though Ch'in Shih Huang Ti had believed that his empire would last for ten thousand generations, it died with him. In the succession struggles that ensued, his heir and minister were killed, and a new dynasty assumed the Mandate of Heaven. Liu Pang (or Chi), a village official of peasant background from East China in the Han Valley, fought his way to the top. Winning out over military rivals, he established the dynasty with a capital at Ch'ang-an, which, like the Ch'in capital, was near modern Sian. Accepting the previously fashioned imperial structure, he continued Ch'in centralization but gradually replaced Legalists with Confucianists to act as bureaucrats and tutors to the heir. In an apparent political retreat, he temporarily authorized local lords to collect taxes. Militarily, he faced the continued menace of the Hsiung-nu in the north and west, and in one campaign he was actually surrounded by them. He bought himself off through the marriage of a Chinese princess to a Hun chieftain. After Liu Pang's death, one of his consorts, Empress Lü, who had borne him a son, temporarily took charge of imperial affairs. The empress presided with a firm hand and appointed her own relatives to top positions. After her death, her family was massacred by those loyal to the throne.

Half a century later, the Early Han reached its height in the reign of Han Wu Ti ("Martial Emperor"), who ruled from 141 to 87 B.C. One of the greatest Chinese emperors, he brought prestige to his dynasty through domestic and foreign accomplishments. He reinstituted the imperial rituals of sacrifices to Heaven and to Earth. He fashioned a firm and centralized government. A bureaucracy in eighteen grades flourished at the capital, with officials appointed from the ranks of the wealthy and educated. An examination system was inaugurated to recruit additional men. The traditional Chinese distinction was kept between the rulers and the ruled, but the former were now appointed officials rather than hereditary aristocrats. Strong economic steps supported the domestic programs and foreign campaigns. Those measures were directed more toward filling state coffers than improving public welfare. State monopolies and licensing systems were reinvigorated from earlier times. The emperor established the "leveling" system, which provided for granaries to store surplus crops bought in times and areas of plenty to sell in times and places of scarcity.

Han Expansion. Han Wu Ti embarked upon campaigns to defend China against border tribes, including the Hsiung-nu. The emperor continued the Ch'in expeditions to the south, where by 111 B.C. North Vietnam was absorbed into Chinese territory. He also dispatched troops into Korea and South Manchuria. In 108 B.C., these areas were assimilated into China as Ch'ao-hsien. Transformed into a center of Sinic culture, Korea in later centuries exported Chinese ideas to Japan. The emperor also initiated measures to extend the Great Wall westward. In great campaigns numbering up to 100,000 men, he fought the Huns. He also used diplomatic strategy against border tribes. In 139 B.C. he sent the soldier-statesman, Chang Ch'ien, to Central Asia with instructions to make an alliance with the Yüeh-chih, who had been driven out of Mongolia by the Hsiung-nu. The Chinese emissary was not successful in his mission, because the Yüeh-chih in their new surroundings were not concerned about fighting their former enemies. But after spending twelve years in the area, Chang Ch'ien returned home with many notes and observations on Central Asia. In 115 B.C. his second mission to the Ili Valley was also unsuccessful. Chinese continued to probe westward. By 42 B.C., they were in Russian Central Asia, where they might have met Roman forces. By then, the Chinese were some two thousand miles away from their capital of Ch'ang-an, much farther than the contemporary Romans were from theirs in the opposite direction.

CULTURE. One of the most noticeable features of Early Han times was the emergence of a modified Confucianism. The core doctrine appealed to rulers because of its emphasis on ritual, form, order, and imperial prestige. But borrowing from Legalism, Han Confucianism advocated an efficient authoritarian bureaucracy. Appropriating from Taoism and the Naturalist school, it assimilated popular ideas such as yang-yin, the five elements, concern with divination, the search for long life, and belief in physical immortality. Scholars defined the Classics, added commentaries, and transmitted ancient texts. In 124 B.C. Han Wu Ti founded an imperial university patterned on Confucian thought. It was also during his reign that China's first great historian lived. Ssu-ma Ch'ien, a scholar and bureaucrat, composed the *Historical Records* (*Shih chi*), a general history of China from ancient times to his day.

Wang Mang's Regime **(A.D. 9–23).** After Han Wu Ti there were no more emperors of note until a century later when the line was replaced briefly by a usurper, Wang Mang, who assumed the throne after having served as regent for two young emperors. His brief dynasty was considered neither a separate one nor as part of the Han, but was simply glossed over by Confucian historians. On the throne Wang Mang revived the Legalist tradition of strong authoritarian rule. He augmented the bureaucracy, initiated more monopolies, and cornered the gold market. He revived the "leveling" system and extended agricultural loans to peasants. He decreed the nationalization of the land and the abolition of slavery, but these edicts proved ineffectual and were shortly dropped. Wang Mang's wide-ranging reforms cost him the support of the bureaucracy. Toward the end of his one-man dynasty, signs of decline grew. Adverse harvests plagued the land; frontier defenses eroded; and officials reported numerous natural disasters and rebellions, including a peasant uprising in Shantung led by the "Red Eyebrows." But since the rebels lacked administrative experience and any alternate program for efficient government, the rebellion withered away. Amidst political confusion and insurmountable problems, Wang Mang died.

The Later Han (A.D. *23–220*) Under the Later Han, the empire was reconsolidated. In the civil war that followed the death of Wang Mang, Liu Hsiu, a relative of the former ruling house, emerged victorious. He relocated the capital at Lo-yang. On the throne, the new emperor, called Kuang Wu Ti ("Shining Martial Emperor"), re-emphasized the role of Confucian scholars. He restored the territorial limits of the Early Han, maintained a Chinese grip over North Vietnam, and established relations with Japan. The first mention of Japan in Chinese annals was made in A.D. 57 when a Japanese mission received at Lo-yang a gold seal (discovered in 1789 on Kyushu Island in Japan) which read "King of Nu of Wa (Vassal of) Han." At that time, Japan was politically organized into "a hundred tribes"; Nu was probably one of them. The Chinese, displaying a culturally superior attitude toward both the Japanese states and people, designated them as *wa* ("dwarf").

The second ruler of the Later Han was Ming Ti ("Enlightened Emperor"). On the throne from A.D. 57 to 75, he reconquered Central Asia and subdued the northern border tribes. This feat was essentially accomplished by the statesman-explorer Pan Ch'ao, aided by local intrigues and local levies. The Chinese conquered lands as far west as the Caspian Sea. Only the Persian province of Parthia lay between China and the Roman Empire. (The Romans knew China as Serica, the "Silk Country.") Pan Ch'ao sent an emissary to Ta Ch'in, the Chinese designation for the Roman or Hellenistic world, but the mission turned back after reaching the head of the Persian Gulf. After Pan Ch'ao's death in A.D. 102, Chinese influence in Central Asia waned.

Culture. Pan Ch'ao came from a distinguished family. His sister Pan Chao was China's first woman essayist, and his brother Pan Ku was China's second great individual historian. Carrying on where Ssu-ma Ch'ien left off, Pan Ku blocked out a dynastic history, the *History of the Earlier Han* (*Ch'ien Han Shu*). In delineating only one dynasty, and only a part at that, this history became the prototype for all later dynastic annals of China.

Augmenting scholarship was progress in scientific matters in which the Han also showed inventiveness and ingenuity. They wrote about sunspots, recorded earthquakes, utilized sundials and the water-powered mill, experimented with drought-resistant rice strains, cast iron, and compiled works of medicine. In a major cultural development the Chinese manufactured paper to replace bulky wooden and bamboo slips. Paper dating from around A.D. 100 has been discovered in Han outposts in dry Central Asia. It was fabricated from fibers, bark, or rags. An early type of printing arose when the Classics, engraved on stone, were reproduced on paper by ink-rubbing techniques. Han art was varied. The Chinese played mandolins and zithers. They glazed pottery. They fashioned clay figurines of people, houses, and household items, which have been recovered from tombs. Some pictorial remnants exist in bas reliefs, on tomb walls, lacquer, shells, and tiles. Animal designs in silhouette, a Central Asian importation, are now outlined. But little remains of Han architecture except fragmentary military outposts and tombs.

Decline of the Han. For a century and a half after Ming Ti, there were no noteworthy emperors, but the Han dynasty persisted. Economic and political crises built up in the final decades. Bureaucratic offices were sold. Large landholders evaded taxes, the burden of which weighed on peasants. A growing population (some sixty million in the early A.D. centuries) competed for available land. Rebellions and military uprisings helped hasten the end of Han rule. In Shantung the Taoist-derived "Yellow Turbans" laid waste the countryside. In the southwest there operated another Taoist group, the "Five Pecks of Rice" band, whose members paid that amount of grain in dues to their cult masters. These and other rebellious groups were eventually put down by Han generals, three of whom emerged to contend for the imperial title. But none had the military capability to unite China. Instead of the political reunification of the country that usually came with the establishment of a new dynasty, a divided China followed.

6

CHINA AND INNER ASIA A.D. 220–1279

After the Han, political division lasting three and a half centuries fell upon China. Feudalism reappeared and fighting became endemic. But Chinese culture did not die out. In the north it merged with fresh infusions from non-Chinese rulers. Chinese continued to migrate south. For the first time the Chinese population center of gravity shifted to the Yangtze Valley, where purely Chinese monarchs ruled over constricted kingdoms. The over-all term for the Chinese period of political division is the Six Dynasties because out of the welter of petty principalities, Chinese historians sifted what they considered the legitimate succession of six imperial dynasties. The Sui, a short-lived dynasty like that of the Ch'in, reunified the land. Then followed the long and glorious T'ang. This was an era, resembling the Han, of territorial expansion and cultural activity. The Sui and T'ang rulers utilized, modified, and strengthened the political, economic, and social institutions bequeathed to them. But originality and creativity were less striking than in previous dynasties. After the T'ang, a period of political division (designated as the epoch of the Five Dynasties) once again ensued. This time the division was of shorter duration than that which followed the Han, lasting only some five decades. China was reunited by the Sung but on a more constricted territorial basis because of nomadic inroads in the north.

POLITICAL DIVISION (A.D. 220–589)

Traditional Chinese historians term this time of political division the Six Dynasties and subdivide it into several eras of varying duration. Between A.D. 220 and 265, three kingdoms arose to dispute succession to the late Han dynasty: the Wei, considered legitimate, at Lo-yang, the old capital; the Shu Han, at Chengtu; and the Wu at Nanking.

The subperiod of the Three Kingdoms was considered a romantic era by later Chinese writers. In fact it was a time of turbulence and military campaigns. The rulers of Wei, a warlike and highly centralized state, continually fought neighboring tribes and states. They maintained relations with Central Asian countries as well as with Japan. The Shu Han, in the fertile Red Basin, were in a favored geographical location with natural mountain barriers. The Wu, in the lower Yangtze Valley, developed maritime and land connections with South and Southeast Asia, including Funan and Champa. In the mid-third century, a Chinese mission from Wu reached India, and their narrative is the first one-the-spot Chinese record of India. Succeeding the Wei, the Chin (265–420) managed to reunify more of China Proper, first in its western branch at Lo-yang (265–316) and then in the eastern branch at Nanking (317–420). Upon its breakup after a century of rule, there followed greater fragmentation in the land. This subperiod is that of the Northern and Southern Kingdoms (420–589), with fourteen of them coming and going in the north, while another four, considered orthodox, succeeded each other in the south at Nanking.

The Northern Wei. In the north, the most notable dynasty to emerge was that of the Northern Wei (386–534), founded by the Toba people. Subjected to peripheral Chinese influence even before they captured Lo-yang, the Toba absorbed rather than rejected Chinese culture. They adopted and patronized Chinese institutions, assumed Chinese surnames, and defended Chinese civilization against new incursions from the north, mainly from the Turks. They effected strong military measures to insure political viability. For taxation purposes they instituted the equal-field system, in which all able-bodied peasants were assigned specific tracts. They refined the concept of mutual responsibility through the "three chiefs" system in which a line of command ran through village, neighborhood, and association chiefs. They adhered to Buddhism and created beautiful statuary.

Culture. Not only in the Northern Wei but generally

throughout China culture spread and flourished despite political turmoil. Chinese inventiveness continued. The science of cartography grew. Tea and other food crops came into use. In this era lived Ku K'ai-chih (*c.* 344–406), China's first great individual painter. Hsieh Ho, who lived around 500, outlined the canons of painting which came to be regarded as definitive by later generations. China's greatest calligrapher, Wang Hsi-chih (321–379) also flourished. The Chinese compiled works on philosophy and phonology. The origin of tones in spoken Chinese is unknown, but by the fifth century the four tones in mandarin were in evidence. The literati composed poems and wrote works of criticism and scholarship. Around 500, the *Thousand Character Classic* appeared. A unique work that was later used for instruction in the primary grades, it capsulated Chinese history and the Confucian doctrine into 250 four-character lines, with no character repeated. Confucianism persisted in religious and philosophic life, though the Classics were subjected to a growing critical spirit. Taoism experienced growth. In the southwest the Chang family papacy, instituted in the Later Han, with its hierarchy of priests to pope advanced the popular aims of happiness, longevity, and wealth.

Buddhism. In religious life, Buddhism recorded the greatest strides. Its introduction, development, and growth in China was a remarkable story. It was perhaps the only fundamental ideology imported into China prior to the coming of the modern West. Buddhism is not a proselytizing religion, and its adherents did not use force in preaching the word. No holy wars marked its spread. It was not imposed on the Chinese, who adopted it, however, only after they had modified it to a great extent. Arising in India, Buddhism provided the major cultural link between South and East Asia. Just when and how Buddhism arrived in China is uncertain. Tradition relates that Emperor Ming Ti of the Later Han dreamt of a golden statue, identified later as the Buddha. By the era of the Three Kingdoms, Buddhism had gained scattered pockets throughout China. Pilgrims helped to spread the faith to China. Indians came to China, and Chinese went to India. Initially the faith was embraced by wealthy and powerful families and rulers in north and south. Later it spread to the masses.

The adoption of Buddhism by the Chinese was in some ways paradoxical. Evolving out of Hinduism and traditional Indian philosophers, Buddhism in this context was alien to some Chinese outlooks. It was mystical and otherworldly; tended toward pessimism; and advocated celibacy, asceticism, and mendicancy. However, the amended form, Mahayana Buddhism, with its doctrine of salvation by faith in buddhas and bodhisattvas, could appeal to Chinese. It seemed to fulfill some basic demands of the human spirit which existing native religions and ethical systems could not meet. It provided a relief from Confucian ritual and determinism. It was an escape outlet from the numerous wars and political confusion of the times. In art it exerted a powerful aesthetic and intellectual attraction. Its ideas contributed to literature, astronomy, letters, and philosophy. It introduced elaborate religious ceremonies. It influenced Taoism, whose adherents built temples and adopted heavens and hells. Because of the religious affinity, travel increased between China and the rest of East and South Asia.

Considered along with Confucianism and Taoism as one of the three main Chinese philosophical systems, Mahayana Buddhism waxed during the Six Dynasties. It developed a number of sects in China, of which four eventually emerged as the most important. T'ien-t'ai, named after a holy mountain, held that salvation did not result only from enlightenment but from a variety of factors, including good works, study, discipline, morality, and insight. Ching-t'u ("Pure Land") preached that salvation lay in the Lotus Sutra, which emphasized the role of Amida, a buddha who dwelt in the pure land or western paradise. Chen-yen("True Word") stated that truth and existence derived from the Eternal Buddha, whose ultimate reality was suggested by magic symbols. Ch'an emphasized inner enlightenment leading to a conversion experience. Deriving from Dhyana in India and passed to Japan as Zen, this sect played a particularly important part in East Asian thought. Adherents of any of all sects worshiped various divinities, in addition to the historical Buddha and Amida; especially important were Maitreya, the buddha of the future, and Kuan-yin, the goddess of mercy. The wide-ranging appeals of Buddhist philosophies, personalities, and sects won many converts.

POLITICAL UNITY
(A.D. 589–906)

With the Sui came political unity once again. As their successor, the T'ang achieved another high mark in Chinese politics and society. Boundaries were extended; border states came under vassalage; and foreign contacts increased. The dynasty, embracing a population of some 130 million, spanned a culturally brilliant period that resembled the Han but was on a grander scale. Chinese of later days, particularly those in the south, called themselves Men of T'ang, in addition to the commonly used term of Han Chinese.

The Sui (589–618). The Sui reunified China under the rule of one emperor and one imperial family. The founder of the line was Yang Chien, also called the Wen Ti emperor (r. 589–604). Of Chinese stock but married to a Hsiung-nu, he was an official of the last of the small northern kingdoms that flourished during the period of political division. As emperor he again centralized the monarchy and bureaucracy. He located his capital at Ch'ang-an, the site of the Early Han capital of the same name. An able administrator, he brought Confucianism back to the forefront after Buddhism had held sway so strongly. Recruiting bureaucrats largely from fellow Northerners, he reinstituted and broadened the examination system. He kept the distinction between military and civilian officials, and he appointed the local bureaucrats. He replaced provincial units with prefectures and counties, and he extended to all China the equal-field system of the Northern Wei.

As frequently happened in the course of the dynastic cycle, the Sui reached its height in the rule of a successor, Wen Ti's son Yang Ti. Fond of power, pomp, and circumstance, Yang Ti erected vast palaces and not only maintained the royal capital at Ch'ang-an but also built subsidiary ones at Lo-yang and Yang-chou, in the lower Yangtze Valley. In projects that consumed great energies and many lives, he added to the Great Wall and extended the Grand Canal system, with the aims of improving internal transport, facilitating shipment of grain tribute to the capital, and supporting armies engaged in northern campaigns.

Yang Ti embarked on military campaigns and diplomatic adventures in borderlands. He encountered the usual troubles in the north and west with the nomadic peoples, in whose ranks were the unruly Turks, called T'u-chüeh. The emperor interfered in internal Korean affairs, but his campaigns there proved inconclusive. The Sui did not send missions to Japan, but the Japanese on their own initiative dispatched at least four embassies to Ch'ang-an. The Sui evidenced more direct interest in Formosa, where they sent exploring parties and armed expeditions. The emperor temporarily reasserted the prestige of the Chinese empire abroad, but his domestic and foreign policies cost the dynasty dearly. Yang Ti was killed by rebels, and the Mandate of Heaven passed to the T'ang.

The T'ang (618–907). The T'ang dynasty was founded by Li Yüan, who emerged victorious in the struggle for power after the collapse of the Sui dynasty. With the aid of Turkish allies, Li Yüan and his son Li Shih-min captured the capital, and the new emperor, known as Kao Tsu ("High Progenitor," a common imperial designation), was enthroned. Of aristocratic background, the family intermarried with non-Chinese families. The emperors kept their capital at Ch'ang-an, a traditional and logical center of power in the productive Wei Valley. By the end of Li Yüan's rule, the country was pacified, and he abdicated in favor of his son.

Li Shih-min ruled as T'ang T'ai Tsung ("Great Ancestor") between 626 and 649. In the course of his reign he faced and resolved perennial problems of Chinese monarchs. He reinvigorated the central organs of government, rebuilt palaces, erected public works, and constructed canals. He dispatched armies abroad and subdued the desert tribes. Turning his back on Buddhism, he established Confucianism as the state cult and had temples erected to the philosopher's memory. He surrounded himself with an elaborate hierarchy of court aristocracy in nine grades, as well as bureaucratic officials of nine ranks in junior and senior grades. He kept the distinction between military and civil officials. He conscripted peasants as mass militia to serve in domestic and frontier military posts. He reinvigorated the examination system but did not hesitate to appoint able men from outside it. He divided the country into ten provinces, some 350 prefectures, and many subprefectures. Border princes, with

Chinese designations, ruled over non-Chinese areas. Pursuing active foreign policies, T'ang T'ai Tsung expanded west. With the help of newfound friends, the Uighurs, he wrested the Tarim Basin in Sinkiang from the Turks. Tibet, unified for the first time in 607, came into the Chinese sphere of influence. T'ang contacts extended into North India. In the northeast, the emperor did not actively intervene in Korean affairs, but his successor temporarily brought the whole of the peninsula under Chinese sway.

T'ang T'ai Tsung's son Kao Tsung, who succeeded him in this imperial title, ruled longer than his father. But toward the end of his reign, he came under the influence of an ambitious woman, Wu Hou, who had been the concubine of both father and son. The Empress Wu, one of the strong women in Chinese political annals, openly assumed control of the reigns of government after Kao Tsung's death. In 690 she appropriated the title of empress and became in fact China's only actual ruling empress. Strong-minded, able, and energetic, she showed Buddhism great favor. Finally forced out of office in 705 by disaffected court circles, she died shortly after the coup. Within a few years, one of her grandsons ascended the throne as Hsüan Tsung ("Mysterious Ancestor"), under whose reign (712–756) the T'ang reached its height and began its decline.

The new emperor was an ambitious, strong, and energetic administrator. He entrenched Confucian doctrine as the philosophy of state. In the expanding country, he raised the number of provinces from ten to fifteen. A patron of learning, he initiated the imperial gazette as the world's first newspaper and founded the Hanlin Yüan, an imperial academy of letters. In foreign affairs, he reasserted Chinese presence in Sinkiang and the Trans-Pamir areas. Large armies, some under non-Chinese leadership, campaigned in Central Asia. In 751 one Chinese army under a Korean general met Arab forces at Talas, in an epoch-making battle which resulted in containment of the Chinese. This event ended Chinese control in Central Asia. Over the ensuing five centuries the military prestige of the Chinese diminished markedly. Conversely, Talas also marked the beginning of Turkish expansion and consolidation of Central Asia, where Islam replaced Confucianism. In the southwest, Chinese forces met reverses when Nan-chao defeated invading T'ang armies. But North Vietnam remained in the imperial domain, and Korea maintained vassalage. Japan continued to dispatch missions to the capital until the mid-ninth century.

Various personal and state circumstances led to Hsuan Tsung's downfall. In later life, he appropriated the beautiful Yang Kuei-fei as a concubine. This romance linking emperor and commoner, age and youth, became a popular literary theme. The emperor and his consort placed under their patronage a young general of non-Chinese extraction, An Lu-shan. The ambitious general achieved control of large border armies and then turned against his sponsors. In 755 he captured Ch'ang-an, forcing the court to flee south, where Yang Kuei-fei was killed and the emperor abdicated. After two years, An Lu-shan was killed by his son, who in turn was murdered by a non-Chinese rebel. T'ang loyalists recaptured the capital, and the dynasty carried on for another century and a half.

A few T'ang ministers advocated reforms to shore up sagging economic fortunes. In 780 one of them initiated the Double Tax, which consolidated the multiple land, household, and personal assessments into two levies a year, collected in the sixth and eleventh months. Such reforms helped to keep the dynasty going, but personal and administrative decay was apparent. After An Lu-shan's revolt, court and factional struggles intensified. The equal-field tax system partially broke down. Extensive land areas reverted to tax-free estates and tax receipts fell off. Rebels and military men ransacked the land and captured the capital, where in 907 one of them set himself up in a new dynasty that presided over a limited area. Competing generals refused to acknowledge his supremacy in their own provinces. Once again in a politically divided China kingdoms came and went in north and south.

The State. As befitting T'ang prestige, their capital and bureaucratic structure were of grand proportions. Ch'ang-an, then probably the largest city of the world, had an estimated population of some two million. Thronging with Chinese and foreigners, the walled city was laid out in a rectangular fashion, measuring five by six miles. Main thoroughfares ran on north-south and east-west axes. Inside the walls lay the imperial city with the government quarters. Inside that was the separate complex of the imperial palace and grounds. Two public market places provided for the exchange of goods. The remaining areas of the city were divided into blocks, each with its own administration. In the capital the central organs of government operated. The Imperial Secretariat established policies; the Imperial Chancellery reviewed them; the Secretariat of State Affairs executed them. The traditional six boards, as well as other offices, continued to operate. The Board of Censors effected internal controls by reporting directly to the emperor cases of maladministration and misgovernment. In local government, the three-tiered structure embraced provinces and circuits among provinces, prefectures, and subprefectures. Through the examination system, based essentially on Confucian doctrine, the bureaucracy was recruited.

The Economy. In economic affairs, the equal-field system was the keystone of early T'ang finance. Each able-bodied male between the ages of twenty-one and fifty-nine received just over thirteen acres of land, of which he could permanently own a fifth. Other individuals received varying tracts. The aims of the system were to insure direct government collection of taxes from cultivators and to prevent land from falling into the hands of powerful large landholders. The T'ang developed various types of tax policies. Taxes in kind imposed the delivery of unhulled grain in fixed amounts. Taxes in produce other than grain were placed on other foodstuffs and on handicrafts, such as textiles. The labor tax demanded from able-bodied adults twenty days a year of service to the state, though the service could be commuted with money or commodities. To keep track of population and fiscal matters, elaborate land registers and censuses were formulated. Commercial imposts were also set on merchants and artisans, and city inhabitants were taxed. Copper cash circulated, and paper money was utilized. Merchants who deposited money in provincial offices for safety received receipts, which in time became known as "flying money" and gained usage as currency.

Culture. T'ang scholars showed interest in science. Gunpowder was developed for pyrotechnical purposes. Optical lenses were introduced, and medical knowledge increased. Many new plants and vegetables were developed. Tea became a widespread drink. The use of paper spread to Central Asia through Chinese captured by Arabs in the Battle of Talas. From there it went on to western Asia and eventually to Europe. Wood-block printing was a significant invention, for which the time was ripe because the materials involved in it—paper, ink, and brush—were present. There were widespread religious, bureaucratic, and examination requirements for multiple copies of similar texts. One source of printing was the black and white reproductions of rubbings on paper taken off stone engravings. Another source was imprints made by large seals used for official purposes. By the seventh century, wood-block illustrations or texts in full pages had evolved. The earliest complete Chinese book printed by the wood-block method is a Buddhist sutra dating from 868 which is now in the British Museum. (Later, in the eleventh century, the Chinese discovered movable print, but they did not take to it because the numerous small metal or wood plates with the characters were easily lost or cumbersome).

T'ang writers produced a large number of scholarly works, including compendiums and encyclopedias. Among the more noted Confucian scholars was Han Yü (768–824), a statesman, author, and essayist. The short-story form flourished, but drama remained in incipient form.

Poetry reached new heights and was composed by emperors and commoners alike. Three names emerged as the greatest Chinese poets. Li Po (701–762) was a Taoist. He was a carefree wanderer and lover of wine. A minor official, at different times he affiliated with various pleasure-seeking groups. Reflecting his personality and outlook, his poetry is spontaneous and lyrical. His close friend Tu Fu (712–770) was a poet of a different mould. Also a minor bureaucrat, he was an idealistic and conscientious man who depicted the suffering and adversity of his personal and official experiences. Po Chü-I (772–846), of a later generation, wrote in a simple vernacular style. With few allusions to abstruse Classics, he struck a popular chord in his verses. Though he pursued an erratic and uneventful official career, he achieved poetic fame that spread to Korea and Japan.

While little exists from T'ang architectural examples, much can be derived from Buddhist temples in Japan of the same period. Sculpture rose and declined with the fortunes of Buddhism. The T'ang sculpted Buddhas as well as small secular objects of art. Painting flourished. Wu Tao-hsüan (also called Wu Tao-tzu), who died in 792, was China's first great landscape artist. Two painting schools arose. A northern one was noted for realism, precision, and clear style; a southern one painted in more subdued, impressionistic style. The T'ang enjoyed music, examples of which died out in China but carried on in Japan.

In philosophic life, Confucianism continued to grow. The Classics were studied anew and were engraved on stone. Taoism, with its appeals of mysticism and elixirs of life, remained popular. Buddhism reached its greatest heights and began its decline. Chinese pilgrims went to India to search out latest texts and doctrines. Among the more famous, Hsüan-tsang (602–664) used Central Asian routes. A great scholar and author, he translated or composed works equivalent in scope to twenty-five times the size of the Bible. Meanwhile, Japanese pilgrims and students traveled to China. One of the more notable was the monk Ennin, who was in China between 838 and 847, and who left a detailed account of Chinese life in the later T'ang. There was some persecution of Buddhists; T'ang emperors did not officially subscribe to the faith, and Confucian nativists attacked Buddhist spiritual precepts and temporal grandeur. Over the ensuing centuries Buddhism tended to recede in importance. What was left of it after the T'ang became Sinicized. As in India, the older, more established faith absorbed the newer.

Foreign Contacts. In the earlier T'ang period, the Chinese pursued contacts with the outside world, displaying an unusual interest in overseas trade routes. Either through direct conquest or by ideological example, the T'ang exerted political influence in peripheral areas. Four protectorates were neatly defined with capital cities that surrounded the Middle Kingdom: An-hsi to the west, An-tung (which today is a city in Manchuria) to the east, An-pei to the north, and An-nan to the south. Chinese centralized institutions were copied by rulers in Tibet, Nan-chao, Korea, and southeastern Manchuria. In the seventh to ninth centuries, Japan succumbed to waves of Sinicization. Conversely, in the chief cities of the T'ang, there were many foreigners who practiced their own faiths, including Judaism, Manichaeism, Mazdaism (or Zoroastrianism), Nestorian Christianity (a heresy from Roman Catholicism), and Islam. In times of peace and prosperity as in the T'ang, the Chinese not only exported cultural values but proved themselves tolerant of alien ideas and presence.

DIVISION AND PARTIAL UNITY (A.D. 906–1268)

With the fall of the T'ang came another period of political division, but this time of only some five decades. Then the Sung, receiving the Mandate of Heaven, reunified a great portion of China Proper. But because of persistent pressures from northern nomads, their territorial limits gradually shrunk. First ruling from the north, they were later forced south by ever increasing non-Chinese military might to locate their capital south of the Yangtze. The enforced southward migration temporarily sustained their fortunes until Mongol might overtook them.

***Five Dynasties* (*906–960*).** Internal division and civil strife followed the collapse of the T'ang. The period was one of general administration breakdown and civil wars. The empire was split among small states, some of which in the north were dominated by alien rulers. However, five successive northern states considered legitimate carried on. The first two had capitals at Lo-yang and the last three at Kaifeng, farther to the east. To win orthodoxy and to seal links with antiquity, the constricted states appropriated high-sounding dynastic names from earlier periods. A concurrent succession of ten kingdoms, mainly in the south, competed for power in the continual struggles to reunify the country. Though extensive fighting and difficult times characterized the period, the most significant fact was that political reunification of much of China resulted after only half a century. Never again was mainland China split into competing regional political units even for so long as five decades. In times of division, whether under native or foreign rule, the vision of unity, Chung Kuo, the Middle Kingdom, persisted.

***The Sung* (*960–1279*).** Because of the continual and ever expanding pressures from nomadic tribes to the north, China progressively weakened and shrank in size during the Sung. This dynasty, like the previous Chou and Han, was split into two periods, but now into a northern and southern succession rather than western and eastern. The Northern Sung (960–1127) ruled from Kaifeng, the capital during the last three of the Five Dynasties. The Southern Sung (1127–1279) eventually located at Hangchow in the Yangtze delta area. Chao Kuang-yin (927–976), a general from the last of the Five Dynasties, founded the new regime. He regained Central and South China, and by the time he died, had crushed all but two states. His brother and successor carried on, but he was not able to retake all Chinese territory. After him, the Northern Sung line deteriorated. None of the later monarchs displayed any noticeable administrative or political acumen, though Hui Tsung, the eighth and last of the northern branch, was a patron of the arts.

Invasions from the North. The chief problem that the Northern Sung emperors had to face, and which they attempted unsuccessfully to resolve, was the recurring threat of non-Chinese pressures generated from the north and northwest. In Inner Mongolia and Manchuria were the Khitan. Founding a dynasty called Liao (907–1125), they pushed south of the Great Wall and located in present-day Peking. From their tribal name is derived *Khitai,* the Russian word for China, and *Cathay,* which during Marco Polo's time the Europeans called China. The Ju-chen were another border group impinging on the Chinese. Also from Manchuria, they were at first vassals of the Khitan, whom they defeated in alliance with the Chinese. But after the joint venture, the Ju-chen guests refused to leave North China and instead drove the Sung south. In Peking the new conquerors, adopting Chinese culture, supplanted the Liao dynasty with one of their own, the Chin (1125–1230). A third people, the Tangut, originating in Tibet, located in Ning-hsia in northwest China as the state of Hsi Hsia (1030–1230). In the latter year, like a whirlwind out of the north, came still another group, the Mongols. Under Genghis Khan they conquered both the Tangut and Ju-chen and started the Mongol rise to power in China Proper.

Reforms of Wang An-shih. Amidst adverse fortunes, the chief Northern Sung councillor, Wang An-shih (1021–1086), tried to implement administrative reforms. In a latter-day effort, much like the Double-Tax policy of the T'ang, he sought to strengthen the economic and military bases of the state. In some ways an innovator, he nonetheless remained within the Confucian fold and cited the Classics as sanctions for his proposals. Concerned for agriculture as the mainstay of the economy, he propounded, as Wang Mang and others had done before him, extensive state monopolies over commerce, ever-normal granaries, and an effective equal (or square) field system. He sought to impose taxes on all types of property and effected a state budget (an unusual move because Chinese political thought did not embrace the principle of imperial fiscal accountability). He attempted to bolster frontier defenses by assessing military and supply quotas on families in the border areas. Because his ideas were so broad and all-encompassing, they met with widespread opposition, and within his own lifetime none was effectively put into use.

The Move South. Five decades after Wang An-shih's death, the Sung had moved South. The Ju-chen, continuing unruly, raided the capital Kaifeng, capturing the emperor Hui Tsung and several thousand members of his court. Imperial remnants fled south to revive their fortunes from Hangchow. To forestall any more depredations, the Southern Sung paid an annual tribute, as had their predecessors, to the Ju-chen. Militarily weak but culturally creative, the Sung kept up in Central and South China the institutions that had previously existed for all China, but in contracted form. The examination system, based on Confucian ideas and dating to the Early Han, now became firmly based. As in the T'ang, examinations were held various in subjects, but only those that related to the Confucian classics led to the highest offices. Held every three years, the first round of examination at the prefectural level saw only 1 to 10 percent of candidates placing successfully. Those who passed went on to examinations administered at the capital, where only another 10 percent passed. These in turn qualified for the "palace examination," which weeded out others and ranked and rated the remaining ones. In this way, about half of the official positions were filled. The other half were filled through direct appointments, purchase of office, or other methods.

The Economy. The Sung tried to cope with basic financial and economic problems. They imposed the usual land taxes; but shrinking territory, growing population, and modest agricultural production led to declining tax yields. As one policy to keep solvent, the government matched rising financial obligations by minting more currency. In commerce, domestic trade grew beyond the government market places, though the Sung tried to exert the usual government controls over economic life. Trade guilds and merchant associations sprang up. They were grouped by trades in various localities or streets called *hang* (or *hong* in southern Chinese). Maritime commerce flourished, especially in South China, where Canton was the center of activities. In an arrangement convenient for Chinese, foreigners lived in designated quarters of port cities under their own laws. In the cities arts flourished, and those who could afford it enjoyed a luxurious life. Rich men took concubines and imposed on their women the practice of foot-binding, a custom with supposed erotic connotations of unknown origins but unique to China.

Culture. In science, the Sung displayed inventiveness. The Chinese now manufactured gunpowder for military ends and used explosive projectiles and hand grenades. Blocked by non-Chinese tribes from expanding on land, the Sung turned to the sea and developed navies. The compass was in use by 1119. Chairs at home and sedan chairs on the road came into general use. In computations the Chinese used the abacus and adopted the zero, introduced from India. With Buddhism ebbing, there was little Sung sculpture of note. But other aspects of artistic life were rich. Multistoried pagodas of brick or colored glazed tiles were erected. Artisans created beautiful porcelains, some monochrome and others multicolored. Impressionistic landscape painting reached an apogee. The dreamy landscapes were inspired by the migration southward to new scenery, Taoist quietude, the effects of the meditative Ch'an Buddhist sect, and a general tendency of the times to withdraw inwardly in spirit. Using a minimum of detail and subordinating man to nature, painters executed their lovely scrolls, which in their theory were microcosms of the natural world.

The art of wood-block printing became widespread. Classics, as well as dynastic histories, encyclopedias, and various scholarly works, were produced. Some editions survive today. The ranks of prominent scholars included the historians Ou-yang Hsiu (1007–1072) and Ssu-ma Kuang (1019–1086) and the versatile Su Tung-p'o (1036–1101). Neo-Confucianism emerged from the intellectual creativity of the time as the most important development. It was most closely associated with Chu Hsi (1130–1200), the last and greatest scholar of the school. Coming to full bloom in the Southern Sung, Neo-Confucianism derived from Taoism a belief in a universal world force or principle. Buddhism, especially the Ch'an sect, contributed the concepts of prolonged meditation and sudden enlightenment. Affected by other schools of thought, the Sung philosopher posited the validity of universal reason and the duty of the scholar to investigate mental and ethical phenomena. Neo-Confucianism advanced a dualistic *li* (the principle) and *ch'i* (the matter). Chu Hsi also resolved the longstanding Confucian ambiguity over the nature of man in favor of Mencius, who had considered it essentially good. Predisposed toward that philosopher, Chu Hsi included the work attributed to the master among the Four Books: *Book of Mencius;* the *Analects;* and two sections of the *Classic of Ritual,* those of the *Great Learning* (*Ta Hsüeh*) stressing individual self-cultivation, and the *Doctrine of the Mean* (*Chung Yung*). Through its Neo-Confucian form, the ancient philosophy received its last major imprint.

By the end of the Sung, China had achieved cultural stability. Established in defined context, the way of life associated with traditional China persisted into the modern-day world. Within the geographic boundaries of the country, the Chinese political, economic, and social facets of life operated in a fairly harmonious coexisting fashion. What has been termed early modern China began to emerge. Cities grew; commerce widened; the scholar-gentry, recruited principally from Confucian examinations, ran the state. A *Pax Sinica* descended. Cultural stability was both a boon and a bane. On the one hand, it bequeathed an extended era of relative peace and prosperity, a major accomplishment for any country at any time. But, in the long run, it turned out to be a liability, because an insulated China with outmoded institutions could not adequately resist the later ideological or military confrontation from the modernizing West.

7
NORTHEAST ASIA
To 1185

In Northeast Asia, as part of the Sinic cultural sphere, Korea and Japan evolved patterns both dissimilar and similar to the Chinese way of life. Though their ancient inhabitants differed from the Chinese linguistically and culturally, in early centuries of the Christian era, Korea and Japan became subject to Chinese influences. They adopted and adapted the Chinese script and literature, administrative procedures, political ideas, economic organs, artistic forms, and Buddhism as modified by the Chinese in the Mahayana version. But cultural absorption did not stifle individual creativity. In some respects Koreans and Japanese differed not only from the Chinese but also in a number of ways from each other. And while Korea was repeatedly invaded by the Chinese, the overseas Japanese were never politically absorbed into Chinese empires.

KOREA

Through cultural and political ties Korea more than Japan is closely identified with China. The peninsula had a mixed historical legacy. In its central geographic position, Korea received North Asian, Chinese, and Japanese influences. Its ancient peoples and languages derived from the north; its basic culture came from China; it experienced Japanese political presence. Early kingdoms centered in the more agriculturally productive areas of West and South Korea; and, because of proximity to China and Japan, they became subjected to pressures from those countries. The medial Korean geographic position bestowed not only historic diversity but perennial international problems for its leaders and kingdoms.

Early History. The Koreans are of mixed racial background. The northern strain resembles the Manchurian and Mongolian, while the southern one is similar to southern Japanese. Over the millennia Chinese presence in the peninsula added a Sinic strain. Not much is gleaned from the Paleolithic Age, but by the Neolithic, around 2000 B.C., tribes from North Asia appeared. Organized under hereditary aristocratic rule, the spoke Altaic or Turkic-Mongol. Koreans, more infused than were the Chinese by northern tribes, developed a toneless polysyllabic language rather than a tonal, monosyllabic Sinic type. As evidenced by remains of camp sites and shell mounds, the ancient Koreans were nomads who fished and hunted. Their pottery had comb markings, a design unusual to China. They were animistic in religious practice, considering some nature spirits as ancestors. Like Southeast Asians, they erected dolmens, a practice unknown to China. They worshiped natural deities, many of whom were malevolent (an outlook quite unlike that of the Japanese who did not develop a demonology). Women shamans and mediums were important in placating evil spirits.

According to a Korean myth, the first state to appear was one ruled by the the Kija family (Chi-tzu in Chinese). It was founded in the late twelfth century B.C. by a member of the Shang royal line, who fled with several thousand followers to escape the Chou. In South Manchuria and North Korea he established the state of Choson (*Ch'ao-hsien* in Chinese), a name, including the Japanese variant, Chosen, later applied at times to all Korea. In the fourth century B.C., new waves of people appeared from the north and east. Tungusic tribes from Manchuria, fleeing the Hsiung-nu, arrived in North Korea with iron and bronze. Other tribes from China brought agriculture. Around 190 B.C., a man called Winman (Wei Man in Chinese), who was either of Chinese background or a Korean in Chinese employ, usurped the throne of Choson. He created a new state, centered at modern Pyongyang.

With the rise of the Ch'in and Han dynasties in China, from that quarter came expansionist drives, especially under Han Wu Ti. In 109–108 B.C. Chinese armies conquered Choson for the purpose of outflanking the Hsiung-nu and preventing any possible alliance between them and the Koreans. In South Manchuria and North and Central Korea, the Chinese established four commanderies, which were subdivided into prefectures. By 75 B.C., the number had been reduced to one, Lo-lang, at Pyongyang. With a population of some 400,000, including many Chinese immigrants, Lo-lang was an early center of Sinic culture. Tomb excavations of wealthy Chinese in North Korea have revealed Han-type artifacts. In the third century A.D., a separate commandery, Tai-fang, was established on the west coast. By A.D. 313, after the demise of the Han and political turmoil in China, both colonies had fallen to Koreans.

Three Kingdoms. Three Korean kingdoms then competed for power. Initially, the most important was Koguryo, founded in 37 B.C. Of Tungusic background, it expanded rule from South Manchuria as Chinese contracted into Lo-lang. Its people hunted and ranged the plains. Originally numbering five tribes, Koguryo later consolidated into a single entity. Its three-tiered society was organized into aristocratic chieftains, warrior bands, and serfs and slaves. After their conquest of Lo-lang, the country began to receive Sinic culture, including some Confucianism, law codes, science, and a political structure. In A.D. 372 Buddhism officially arrived from China. In 427 the Koguryo capital was moved from South Manchuria to Pyongyang, where Sinification proceeded at a more rapid pace. A Chinese bureaucratic administration, drawing financial strength from agricultural and labor taxes, replaced the traditional aristocratic tribal organization.

To the south a second kingdom, that of Paekche, flourished in the Han Valley. Dating to 18 B.C., the state enjoyed a prosperous agricultural base. Sealed off by Koguryo from land routes to China, it developed maritime contacts instead. In 384 it adopted Buddhism. Though the country was economically viable, its leaders were not well-organized politically or militarily, and on this account they suffered from depredations of the northern neighbor.

In a more remote location to the southeast, lay Silla, founded in 57 B.C. Silla was never occupied by Chinese armies, nor in its early centuries did it receive Chinese ideology. Its society was organized along hereditary lines. The first two ranks (termed "Bone Ranks") governed the state, while young warrior bands, Hwarang, formed the military corps. Not until the sixth century did Sinic ideas make headway. In 528 Buddhism was adopted, and by then Chinese political ideology had also entered.

Political Unity. With the reunification of China under the Sui, its emperors renewed expansionist campaigns in the Korean peninsula. Koguryo fought back, and the Chinese found it hard going. The T'ang then allied themselves with Silla, with whose help in the 660's they destroyed first Paekche (despite Japanese intervention) and then Koguryo. The T'ang wanted to incorporate Korea into their empire, but Silla thought otherwise. Warfare erupted between the former allies, and the Chinese had to content themselves with the northern fourth of the land. Silla remained autonomous but sent tribute missions to Ch'ang-an. Meanwhile, Silla conquered Mimana, a Japanese colony that had existed for some centuries on the southern tip of the peninsula. This first political unification of Korea proved lasting. From the end of the seventh century, when Silla assumed control of most of Korea, into the twentieth, Korea existed as an independent country within traditionally recognizable boundaries. Next to China, it was the oldest state in East Asia.

Sinification. Politically independent but culturally receptive, Silla became a miniature T'ang. Both through direct contacts with China and by rule over the more Sinicized Paekche and Koguryo, it acquired Chinese ideas. From the capital at Kyongju and five subcapitals, a centralized government presided over provinces, prefectures, and districts. In 788 the Confucian examination system was introduced, but it was confined to the upper classes, where the Bone Ranks still held importance. Mahayana Buddhism was easier to absorb than Confucian precepts, and it gained in mass popularity. Monasteries waxed rich; monks traveled; temples and pagodas were built; and Buddhist sculpture was fashioned. Koreans journeyed to China on religious or secular missions, and the returned students became respected scholars. The T'ang utilized Korean commerce and military acumen; one Korean general commanded a Chinese army that penetrated into the northwest fringes of India. Despite basic differences between spoken Chinese and Korean, Silla adopted the Sinic characters. In the late seventh century, a Confucian scholar developed a system called *idu* that used characters for phonetics rather than for ideology, but the reform did not catch on.

Silla reached its height between the mid-seventh and mid-eighth centuries. But as the T'ang faded, so did Silla. Indices of dynastic weaknesses appeared in the Korean kingdom. Succession struggles ensued; peasants revolted; tax receipts fell·off; centralized government weakened. In 901 one Wang Kon, claiming descent from the earlier Koguryo rulers, raised the standard of rebellion which by 936 brought all of the land under his dynasty, the Koryo (a contracted version of the earlier name and one from which the modern Korea derives). In the course of repeated civil wars, the long-lingering aristocratic ranks and earlier tribal loyalties disappeared. The Chinese political and administrative structure filled the vacuum all the more.

With a capital at Kaesong, the Koryo presided over a united country until 1392. The centralized government had the traditional six ministries of the Chinese central apparatus, as well as the usual provincial, subprefectural, and district divisions. In 958 the Chinese examination system was instituted. However, as in earlier kingdoms, class lines were respected. Though the traditional aristocratic Bone Ranks had disappeared, descendants of associates of Wang Kon were favored. They formed the apex of society; commoners and other "low-born" provided its bulk. Wealth was concentrated at the capital, but with the negligible role of merchants in the new dynasty, the economy lagged. Art did not flourish, though beautiful celadons (porcelain of varying shades of green) were fashioned. Mahayana Buddhism, particularly the Ch'an and T'ien-t'ai sects, grew. The Tripitaka was printed by wood-block prints, but popular beliefs were incorporated into Buddhist theology. With the subsequent growth of nomadic military prowess along China's northern borders, came changes also in Korea's political life. The Koryu had to pay tribute first to the Khitans and then to the Ju-chen. But as was the fate of the Sung in China, so Koryu fell eventually under the onslaught of the Mongols.

EARLY JAPAN
(To A.D. 794)

The Japanese call their country Nippon or Nihon, transliterations of Chinese characters *Jih-pen* that mean "Land of the Rising Sun." The Western term similarly derives from the Chinese. Marco Polo, who traveled to China in the thirteenth century, heard there of the islands to the east. When his memoirs were transcribed in Europe, the term was written as *Chipango,* which in time became Latinized as Japan. Little definite can be said about the early Japanese, but they seem to have had prehistoric ties with both northern continental Asian peoples and southern insular ones. Though of diverse background, by A.D. 400 the Japanese had become a racially homogenous people, unified by common language and culture and centered along the Inland Sea, particularly in the Yamato plain near Kyoto.

Expanding from this centrally located and agriculturally rich base, the early Yamato rulers won control over neighboring tribes. They sent missions to Korea and China. Sinic culture that embraced Mahayana Buddhism, artistic forms, and political and economic systems, came into Japan after A.D. 400. Increasingly subject to Chinese ideas, the Yamato monarchs finally focused at Nara, where the court settled down for a period of seven and a half decades in what was Japan's first recognizable capital.

Prehistory. Physical and cultural anthropology reveals similarities between the Japanese and northeastern as well as southeastern Asian peoples. In prehistoric times waves of immigrants probably came into Japan from both directions. The aboriginal people, the Ainus, however, are proto-Caucasian. Archeological finds record successive cultures in ancient Japan. Paleolithic finds are few. The first important culture dates to the Mesolithic, which in Japan lasted from about 3000 to 300 B.C. This culture is called Jomon, which in Japanese means "cord pattern," because much of its pottery had such a pattern impressed on it. Other artifacts include shell mounds, stone weapons, and *haniwa* (clay figures representing men and animals). The Jomon people were nomads who hunted and fished. They lived in sunken-pit houses constructed of thatch and bark with a central hearth. They were animists who apparently worshiped natural objects more from reverence than fear.

With the Japanese Neolithic Age came the next culture phase, the Yayoi (from the name of a Tokyo site where a pottery type more advanced than the Jomon was discovered). Yayoi culture began in Kyushu and from there spread to the rest of Japan. A settled people, the Yayoi practiced rice cultivation. This period lasted from about 300 B.C. to A.D. 300. In its latter years iron and bronzeware were cast. Among the more significant artifacts are mirrors, swords, spears, and bells called *dotaku.*

The Tomb culture (*c.* A.D. 300–600), sometimes considered the last phase of the Yayoi, was introduced by immigrants from Korea. The name of the culture derives from its high earth tombs (*tumuli*) and stone burial chambers, in which have been found haniwa, jewels, mirrors, and swords.

The Yamato State. A Chinese account of A.D. 300, during the transition phase between the Yayoi and the Tomb cultures noted the presence in Japan of a hundred states, or tribes, whose people farmed, fished, and practiced weaving. Chinese histories written after the fifth century A.D. told of the political unification of Japan in the Yamato plain.

By about the mid-first century B.C., Yamato rulers of the Yayoi period had begun to dominate the others. Over the centuries they spread their rule through the Inland Sea area and South Japan. They conquered Izumo, another main center of early Japanese political life, on the Japan Sea in Southern Honshu. They also had connections with Korea, where for a time they had a foothold on the south coast. At first the Yamato kings exercised authority indirectly through various clans. But with the rise to power of other and stronger clans in the capital area, by the sixth century the Yamato monarchs had been relegated to a subordinate position. However, though they did not rule in fact, they kept the throne and claimed divine status. Great clans (*uji*) exercised semi-autonomy and tried to gain control over the ruling Yamato family. This type of indirect monarchy was an aspect of Japanese political life that persisted into the twentieth century. Families came and went as spokesmen for the emperor, but never in history was the imperial family overthrown, as so often happened in China.

Yamato society, like that of early Korea, was hierarchical and hereditary. The aristocratic uji headed subsidiary occupational groups (*be,* or *tomo*), who provided the necessary economic and agricultural support services. The imperial clan traced its ancestry to the Sun Goddess, while other clans claimed descent from lesser divinities. Within the groups, the immediate family was the basic unit. Generally the eldest male presided over family affairs. Monogamy was the usual practice, but those who could afford it had secondary wives. Yamato religion was called Shinto, a Chinese-derived term meaning "Way of the Gods" (to distinguish it from Buddhism and other beliefs). Early Shinto comprised various cults, whose beliefs and practices included animism, fertility rites, ancestor worship, and nature deification. In its pantheon were many heroes, gods, goddesses (chief of whom was the Sun Goddess), and *kami,* any superior being or spirit. Its simple rites emphasized ritual cleanliness.

Sinification. To this culture, the Japanese then added an element of Sinification. From about A.D. 400 to 550, the Japanese absorbed Chinese ideas slowly and without conscious effort. But with the establishment of the Sui and T'ang dynasties on the mainland, around A.D. 600 acceleration of the process occurred. By that time the course was dictated not only by Chinese prestige but also by practical politics as the Japanese rulers and their advisers realized the need to strengthen the authority of the central government over the uji. Sinification was a voluntary and selective process. The Chinese (unlike the later Mongols) had no interest in conquering Japanese territory or imposing their culture upon the Japanese.

Buddhism was a major importation. Tradition relates that in 552 the Korean kingdom of Paekche sent a Buddhist image and sutras to Yamato, with a proselytizing message and also an implied request for Japanese military support against rival Korean states. The uji divided over the desirability of shoring up Paekche's fortunes and of adopting Buddhism. The result was that Paehche received little aid, but the Soga uji, wishing to increase their prestige, adopted the new religion. Buddhism in Japan as sponsored by the Soga had its ups and downs. Eventually it achieved importance under the Soga statesman-prince, Shotoku Taishi.

Shotoku, who acted as regent (593–622) for his empress aunt, was a devout Buddhist, a Confucian scholar, and a practical politician. He advanced Buddhism as part of an over-all policy to centralize government under the imperial family. Some of his doctrines were formulated in the "Seventeen Article Constitution" of 604, traditionally attributed to him. The constitution urged the uji to adopt Buddhism, to recognize the supremacy of the emperor, and to stop factional politics. Shotoku also appropriated secular Sinic concepts, including the Chinese calendar and hierarchical bureaucratic system, and he sent several large official missions to China. The Soga line declined after Shotoku's death, and eventually was superseded by the Nakatomi clan.

Another massive attempt at Sinification was made by the Nakatomi, renamed the Fujiwara, through the Taika ("Great Transformation") reforms of 645–650. In these reforms, all land was nationalized and subject to redistribution on the basis of households, determined by periodic censuses. As in T'ang China, there were three main taxes: a grain tax in kind, a tax on other products, and a labor tax. Provinces grouped by circuits (*do*) were administered from the central government. The best-known was the Tokaido ("Eastern Sea Circuit") from Kyoto to Tokyo, stations of which were later portrayed in wood-block prints. (The Tokaido is now roughly the route of the fastest train in the world.) If these comprehensive policies had been carried out, the uji system would have been broken up. However, in practice, the reforms were of a nominal nature. Even where implemented in part, the new political forms were merely added to existing administrative patterns. As so often happened in the course of Japanese history, compromises were made between imported theory and established fact. Although absolute in theory, monarchs continued to fall under the dominance of the uji families, a tendency increased by frequent abdications.

The Nara Period. Yamato emperors frequently moved their capitals on estates scattered about the plain. Perhaps the chief reason for this continual movement was the concept of ritual impurity from the death of a ruler. But in 710, borrowing the idea of a permanent capital from the Chinese, the Japanese established Nara as their capital. The new city was built in the rectangular pattern of the Chinese capital of Ch'-ang-an but on a much smaller scale.

The court was characterized by elaborate rituals and ceremonies. Orchestral and dance forms imported from China included the *gagaku,* a musical tradition which lasted at the Japanese court until contemporary times. Administrative codes were drawn up for an elaborate bureaucracy which emphasized aristocratic connections. Duties of official organs were defined. Provincial governors, appointed by the emperor, were usually men of high rank who received income from land revenues as well as from their office. District magistrates were usually local clan leaders. At the bottom of the scale were free commoners and those in bondage as serfs or slaves. Land was allocated on the basis of rice production with adjustments for sex, age, and status of household members. All lands were subject to tax, but in time the nobility and the monasteries gained immunity through their influence at court, and the burden of taxation increasingly fell on peasants.

Culture. The Nara period was creative. The two main Japanese sources of ancient history date to the era: the *Kojiki* (*Record of Ancient Matters*), compiled in 712, and *Nihon Shoki* or *Nihongi* (*History of Japan*), compiled in 720. The two classics shaped Japanese mythology and history to enhance imperial claims to legitimacy. Their creation myths were concerned mainly with the procreation of many deities, including the Sun Goddess (Amaterasu), whose descendant Jimmu Tenno was said to have founded Yamato state. Collections of poetry, the *Kaifuso* (*Fond Recollections of Poetry*) and the *Manyoshu* (*Collection of Ten Thousand Leaves*), were compiled in 751 and 760 respectively. Most of the poems were *tanka,* consisting of five lines with thirty-one Japanese syllables in a 5-7-5-7-7 pattern. Chinese characters were the basis for written Nara literature, but problems of this borrowing resulted in Japan, as in Korea, because monosyllabic Chinese vocables and written characters had to be translated into polysyllabic oral and written Japanese. Some Chinese characters (*kana*) were adopted because they were like Japanese phonetics, while other Chinese characters (*kanji*) were utilized for ideas.

Growth of Buddhism. Buddhism spread in Japan during the Nara period. The imported doctrine filled a religious vacuum, since Shinto lacked moral teachings. By admitting Shinto gods as buddhas and bodhisattvas, Buddhism received added strength. Six Mahayana sects flourished, mainly at court and among the elite; Buddhism was not yet a popular religion in the land. The most important was the Hosso, which stressed enlightenment through the power of the mind. Its chief temple, the Horyuji, was founded by Shotoku Taishi in 607. The Golden Hall of the Horyuji, rebuilt several decades later, is probably the oldest wooden building in the world. The Kegon sect was introduced in 736 by a Chinese monk. It stressed a cosmological harmony under

Roshana, the universal Buddha. In Kegon art, the Buddha of the harmonious whole is equated with Dainichi, the Sun Goddess. Such a Nara Buddha image is in the Todaiji ("Great Eastern Temple"). A bronze statue, 53-feet high, it was built by the devout Emperor Shomu (r. 724–749), following a pestilence in the land. The emperor's widow bestowed to the monastery the Shosoin, a log warehouse containing many valuable imperial belongings which still exists. The emperor's daughter, the Empress Shotoku (no relation to the earlier Shotoku Taishi), was also a devout Buddhist. She had a million Buddhist charms printed, many of which remain today as the earliest examples of wood-block printing. After her death in 770, because she had mixed Buddhism with politics to the extent of falling in love with a monk, the influence of religion at court waned. Japan also shied away from women rulers thereafter.

HEIAN JAPAN (A.D. 794–1185)

After some years at Nara, the court moved again, eventually to settle at Heian, modern Kyoto. There it remained for over a millennium, though political power from time to time came to reside in families and areas in the provinces. The Heian era was a gold age of Japanese culture. Sinification eased off, and traditional Japanese aesthetics came to the fore in art and literature. Buddhism began to radiate out from the imperial and monastic centers into the countryside. The political divisiveness increased in the latter decades of the Heian. While the court carried on aesthetic pursuits at the capital, peripheral areas of Honshu grew in importance.

The State. The emperor Kammu, seconded by the Fujiwara clan, wanted to get away from the influence of the great Buddhist monasteries, whose growth in and around Nara, ironically, his predecessors had encouraged. In 784 he transferred his court and capital to nearby Nagaoka. But a decade later, because bad omens and epidemics plagued the new site, the emperor undertook another move, this time to Heian ("Peace and Tranquility"). Like Nara but on a larger scale, Heian was laid out in the Chinese capital pattern.

Despite Kammu's efforts to strengthen imperial rule, the

monarchy remained weak. The court emphasized ritual and etiquette, concerning itself with trivia which left little imperial time for political and economic problems. The Fujiwara family continued to exert indirect control over the monarch by cornering a monopoly of privileges and by providing empresses for the imperial family. During an emperor's minority, a Fujiwara was regent, and after the monarch attained majority, a Fujiwara became *Kampaku* (dictator), in essence the same position. Under Fujiwara tutelage, the practice of emperors retiring or withdrawing to a monastery became pronounced. Because of the early age of imperial retirement, sometimes there were two ex-emperors living at the same time as the titular ruler.

In the course of the Heian era, modifications took place in Japanese political and economic life. The Chinese-derived central bureaucracy declined in power, and the provincial aristocracy gained wealth and influence. New and simplified government agencies included an audit office, which handled taxation, and a bureau of archivists, which drafted imperial decrees and arranged imperial audiences. Police commissioners supplanted palace guards and army conscripts as enforcers of the law.

The Rise of Feudalism. The financial structure established by early Yamato rulers continued to weaken as tax exemptions increased. As in medieval Europe, peasants who were subject to tax commended their lands to a tax-free lord or monastery, thereby gaining exemption. In exchange for commendation, the peasant received certain rights and benefits. Mutual rights concerning to produce of the land were known as *shiki;* tax-exempt private estates were called *shoen.* In spite of imperial decrees issued from time to time in an attempt at regulation, the tax-free holdings of nobles and monasteries continued to increase.

These political and economic conditions resulted in the growth in Japan of a feudal system. Its economic base consisted of widely scattered autonomous tax-free estates and semi-independent provincial land holdings. Its military base came from a rising military class. As central authority declined in the provinces, so rose the authority of local chieftains and their followers. There were widespread disorders, including depredations of provincial *bushi* ("warrior-gentlemen"), piracy on the coastal and inland seas, fighting among militant Buddhist forces, and uprisings of the aboriginal Ainus. To suppress the Ainus, the Emperor Kammu levied troops under the command of a general called *Sei-i-tai-shogun* ("Great Barbarian-Subduing General"), abbreviated as *shogun*. This military commission became a permanent fixture and in later centuries was the power behind the Japanese throne. Meanwhile, rival clans emerged to challenge Fujiwara dominance. In the latter half of the twelfth century, the Taira and the Minamoto families began a thirty-years' war with each other, which was finally won by the Minamoto in 1185. There ensued a period in Japanese history known as the Kamakura, from the location of the Minamoto headquarters.

Culture. As provinces grew in power and Japan became increasingly decentralized, culture reached new heights at the Heian court. The traditional Japanese architectural style was developed. This so-called Fujiwara style was characterized by light, airy pavilions set in subdued and harmonious landscapes. Secular painting on scrolls portrayed *Yamato-e* ("pictures of Yamato"). A poetry anthology, the *Kokinshu* (*Ancient and Modern Collection*), compiled by imperial order, included 1,100 poems, almost all in tanka form. Prefacing this work was the Tosa diary, an early example of Japanese prose, describing the author's journey home to Heian from Tosa in Shikoku. Novels were composed relating court life. Sei Shonagon, an observant and witty woman writer, developed this theme in her *Pillow Book*. Most notable was Lady Murasaki Shikibu's *Genji Monogatari* (*The Tale of Genji*), probably written during the early eleventh century. This great historical novel, the masterpiece of Japanese literature, tells of the life and loves of the noble Prince Genji and portrays in detail the aristocratic court life.

Development of Buddhism. Buddhism continued to grow in influence and to win converts, expanding from the capital into the provinces. Buddhism influenced Japanese ways, but Japan also shaped Buddhism. Shintoism assimilated buddhas and bodhisattvas. Buddhist simplicity was changed to conform with Japanese hierarchical patterns in doctrine and monastic orders.

Additional Buddhist sects followed the Chinese model; the most important were the Tendai and the Shingon. The Tendai (T'ien-t'ai) was founded by the monk Saicho (767–822), who had gone to China on a mission. Upon his return in 803, he established his temple at Mount Hiei, northeast of Heian. His doctrine proclaimed the universal Buddha, but held that one could achieve salvation through meditation, virtue, good works, and scripture reading. The Shingon (Chen-yen, or "True Word") was founded by Kukai (774–835). Also a traveler to China, Kukai was a Japanese cultural hero known as Kobo Daishi ("Great Teacher"), to whom was attributed the invention of kana writing and the introduction of tea. Locating at Mount Koya monastery, near modern Osaka, he also preached the universal Buddha but stated that the path to salvation lay through the arcane True Word, which the master of the sect passed on just before his death to his foremost disciple. The doctrine gave rise to great works of art, including paintings of *mandalas,* depicting religious ideas in schematic form.

In time the number of chief popular gods, as in China, came down to some half dozen: the historical Buddha, the universal Buddha, Amida, Kannon (Kuan-yin in Chinese), Miroku (Maitreya in Chinese), and Fudo, a fierce indigenous god. Ennin, a monk of Mount Hiei who traveled in T'ang China, combined esoteric (secret) with exoteric (popular) teachings. He and other monks emphasized the doctrine of divine love and compassion, holding that the believer could achieve salvation merely by invoking holy names, an act called *nembutsu.* This promise of ready salvation by faith won many converts in following generations.

In the history not only of Japan but of Asia, the rise, spread, and geographic realignment of Buddhism was a remarkable feature. In both India and China, the faith had atrophied, while in Southeast Asia, Mahayana had been replaced by the Hinayan version, so strong in Ceylon. By the thirteenth century, on the other hand, Mahayana Buddhism was entrenched in Japan, as in Korea, countries geographically remote from the land of its birth, India. Though the religion eventually faded away in the two major continental Asian countries, in part losing its identity through assimilation into indigenous thought, Buddhism proved resilient in one form or another in Asian rim lands.

PART THREE
TRADITIONAL ASIA
(Thirteenth to Mid-Nineteenth Centuries)

Between the thirteenth and mid-nineteenth centuries, the indigenous religious and philosophic patterns of traditional Asia became set. In South Asia, Hinduism received few accretions. In China, Neo-Confucianism provided a fundamental base of Chinese stability. In peripheral lands of the continent Buddhism waxed—Hinayana in much of Southeast Asia, and Mahayana in Vietnam, Korea, and particularly in Japan, where a nativistic tinge was added. Islam did not materially progress in South or Inner Asia, but it took strong hold in insular Southeast Asia. And in the latter half of the period, with the advent of the West came Christianity, which left little religious imprint on Asia (except in Spanish Philippines), but bequeathed potent secular ideas associated with Westernization.

In this era, political patterns of traditional Asian countries and regions varied. All had organized social structures and were reasonably well governed, over longer or shorter periods, in extended or constricted areas. In India, the chief Islamic kingdoms flourished in the north, while others came into being in the south or border lands. The usual specter of divided warring kingdoms in Southeast Asia persisted. China's historical inertia, despite two periods of alien dynastic rule, generally prolonged political, cultural, and social stability. Korea continued to reflect the China pattern. But Japan fell into an extended period of feudalism with the country, at first politically divided and then reunited, frozen into distinctive social patterns as decreed by its leaders.

Then into traditional Asia came the West. For the Occident the timing was propitious, inasmuch as traditional states were

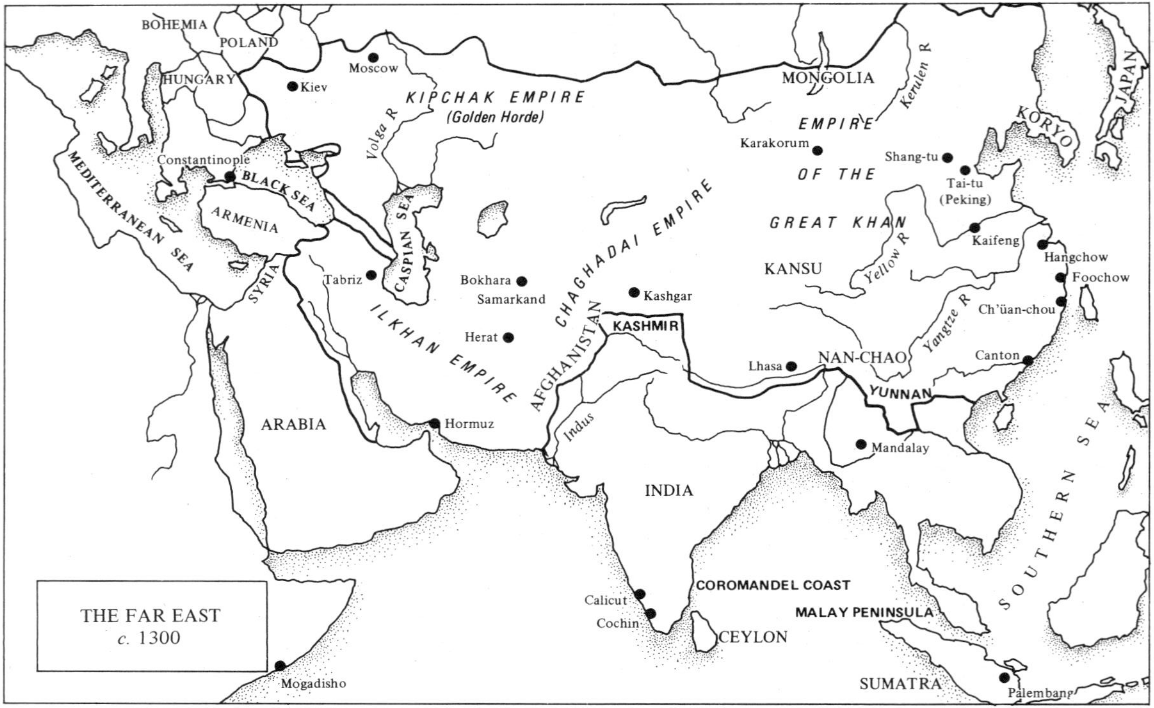
THE FAR EAST
c. 1300
BOHEMIA
POLAND
HUNGARY
Moscow
Kiev
KIPCHAK EMPIRE
(Golden Horde)
Volga R
MONGOLIA
Kerulen R
EMPIRE
OF THE
GREAT KHAN
Karakorum
Shang-tu
Tai-tu
(Peking)
KORYO
JAPAN
Constantinople
BLACK SEA
MEDITERRANEAN SEA
ARMENIA
CASPIAN SEA
SYRIA
Tabriz
Bokhara
Samarkand
CHAGHADAI EMPIRE
Kashgar
KASHMIR
AFGHANISTAN
ILKHAN EMPIRE
Herat
Hormuz
ARABIA
Indus
INDIA
Lhasa
NAN-CHAO
YUNNAN
KANSU
Yellow R
Yangtze R
Kaifeng
Hangchow
Foochow
Ch'üan-chou
Canton
Mandalay
SOUTHERN SEA
Calicut
Cochin
COROMANDEL COAST
MALAY PENINSULA
CEYLON
SUMATRA
Palembang
Mogadisho

either very stable or else disintegrating. The most conspicuous meeting ground of East and West was in war and diplomacy. But in their contacts, in peace or strife, both Westerners and Asians thought themselves superior to the other. The initial Occidental expansion, from the sixteenth through the eighteenth centuries, was essentially a mercantilistic search for economic gains and for colonies to consolidate them. But in the nineteenth century, an intensified Western expansion resulted from a diversity of motives, not only economic but also including strategic, political, industrial, and missionary considerations. As the Portuguese and Spanish faded in importance, French and Dutch interests grew. Russia and the United States made their presence felt, but it was Great Britain that took the lead.

Because of its long peninsular shape exposing it to maritime penetration, and because of its relative proximity to Europe, India came first under Western dominance. Southeast Asian countries (except Thailand) also began to experience Occidental presence, though empires, except for the Spanish Philippines, were not consolidated until after 1850. China kept aloof; only grudgingly and under force did it capitulate to initial Western demands of the mid-nineteenth century. Korea held the West at bay. It was Japan, after centuries of following most successfully an isolationist policy, that responded most ardently to Westernization.

8

SOUTH ASIA 1206–1858

With the inception of the Slave Dynasty, Islamic kingdoms became a conspicuous feature of Indian history. They were generally confined to the north, but occasionally spread into the Deccan. The Slave Dynasty and the four following dynasties are collectively designated the Delhi Sultanate. Then came the Mogul line, which in the course of the first several centuries produced some notable monarchs. During the period, while Hindu states waxed and waned, Islam grew. Conversions proceeded in various ways. The sword helped, but this method was more the exception than the rule. Theological persuasion, political motivation, and migration added converts. As individuals or as groups, Indians were won over. There were particularly many conversions in the Punjab and lower Bengal, a geographic polarization of the faith which later caused religious and political complications. Also compounding problems was the advent of Westerners, of whom the late-arriving English were to register the most lasting effect, first through the East India Company and then through the crown.

THE DELHI SULTANATE AND SUCCESSOR STATES (1206–1526)

From Delhi the five Islamic dynasties of Turkish background ruled varying areas of North India. As foreign rulers, they imported not only their religion but also their language, literature, and art forms. An uneasy religious and cultural coexistence resulted with Hinduism. Some aspects of Islam could be reconciled with the Hindu way of life; others could not. Meanwhile, in the Deccan other kingdoms, both Hindu and

Muslim, arose. Not strong enough to overthrow the Delhi Sultanate, they warred among themselves and left little lasting political or cultural legacy to the subcontinent.

Turkish Dynasties. The Slave Dynasty (1206–1290) initiated the Delhi Sultanate. Its founder Aibak, a former Turkish slave, ruled for only five years before his death in a polo accident. He was succeeded by another Turkish general, who chose his daughter Raziya as his successor. A commanding personality, Raziya as queen made many enemies at court, and she and her husband were assassinated. The dynasty lasted only another two and a half decades. It was succeeded by a short-lived dynasty, the Khalji sultans (1290–1320). The founder of this dynasty was murdered by his nephew Alauddin, who usurped the throne. Comparing himself to Alexander the Great, Alauddin (r. 1296–1315) repelled several Mongol invasions and warred in Rajputan and Tamil land. A strict Muslim, he laid a heavy hand on Hindus through poll taxes and other imposts.

The Tughluqs (1320–1413) came next. Muhammad Tughluq (r. 1325–1351), son of the founder, was an outstanding, though eccentric, ruler. He and his kingdom were described in a work by Ibn Batuta, an Arab traveler. Next in line was Firoz Shah (r. 1351–1388). His administration was typical of Turkish rule. The king was the commander-in-chief of the armed forces. Generals, usually princes, governed the provinces, maintaining detailed accounting systems, which were audited by the central government. Officials received compensation through revenues and assigned tracts of land, which, along with poll taxes on non-Muslims, was a chief source of state income. Firoz Shah was a complex man. On the one hand, he was a strict Muslim who enforced the Hindu imposts, forbade the construction of Hindu temples, and demolished some existing ones. On the other hand, he abolished heavy and cruel punishments, kept public works in good shape, and drew on the services of capable ministers, one of whom was a converted Brahman.

Then came the pillage of Delhi in 1398–1399 by the Mogul conqueror Timur (Tamerlane). In the political confusion resulting from the invasion, the Sayyid dynasty (1414–1451) came to the throne. They were followed by the Lodi, an Afghan tribe, during whose rule (1451–1526), sultanate territory was reduced to Delhi and its environs. Other Muslim and Hindu states contended for mastery in a fragmented North India. Finally, in 1526 the Moguls replaced the disintegrating Delhi Sultanate.

Effects of Turkish Rule. The heritage of Turkish rule was mixed. One legacy was the Urdu language (in use today in Pakistan), which included Hindu, Persian, and Turkish words. In philosophy Islam monotheism complemented a Hindu theistic strain apparent in the *bhakti*, or salvation by faith. The Delhi Sultanate continued the Hindu political pattern of confederated vassal states acknowledging, through tribute and taxes, the supremacy of the central government. Turkish rule left relatively undisturbed the life of the masses; its political, religious, and economic restrictions affected the Hindu leaders more than the populace. But though Muslims were in a minority, their predominant political power in the north lasted until the English replaced them.

Other States. Central and south autonomous states, both Hindu and Muslim, arose with the breakup of Turkish control. Among the latter were those established in Gujarat, Malwa, and Kashmir. The most important, however, was the Bahmani kingdom. In 1347 Muslims in the Deccan revolted against Tughluq domination. Their leader claimed descent from Bahman, an early Persian king. Under his successors, the kingdom grew until it straddled the Deccan from coast to coast. Its monarchs conducted almost incessant warfare with neighboring states in campaigns that involved the first use of artillery in Indian history. After a century and a half, the kingdom broke up in 1518 into five parts: Bidar, Golconda, Berar, Ahmadnagar, and Bijapur. The last was the chief successor state and had an architecturally imposing capital. These five kingdoms were later absorbed into the expanding Mogul empire.

The contemporary kingdom of Vijayanagar ("City of Victory") was more nativistic. It was founded by two Hindu brothers who converted to Islam but later went back to their original faith. Their dynasty (1336–1565) ruled most of India south of the Kistna River. The capital, with over half a million inhabitants, was grandiose, spreading seven miles north to south. The government included a council of ministers, provincial viceroys, and district magistrates. Vijayanagar provided a geographical, political, and religious barrier to the spread of Turkish-Islamic rule into Tamil land, where popular Hinduism continued. But though united in religion, South Indians spoke a variety of languages, and partly because of regional tensions, the state fell apart. In 1565 the capital was destroyed by Bahmani, and the kingdom, already weakened by international forces, came to an end.

THE MOGULS (1526–1858)

The Moguls (an Indian term applied to Central Asian Muslims, and also spelled *Mongol, Mughal,* or *Mughul*), like the Turks, invaded North Asia from Afghanistan. Their empire eventually included almost all the subcontinent. The early Mogul rulers were notable personalities; Akbar, the third in line, was the most outstanding. Where the Turks initiated, the Moguls consolidated. And when the British fell heir to the Indian empire, it was Mogul political precedent from which they heavily borrowed.

Mogul Rule. The founder of the dynasty was Babur ("Tiger"). Fifth in line from Timur, and also descended from Genghis Khan, he came to the throne at the age of eleven. After consolidating his kingdom in Afghanistan, he directed his efforts toward North India, then divided under the Lodis. Asked by the local governor to come into Punjab and help resolve royal conflicts, the conqueror did not stop there but marched into Delhi, which he took in 1526. Until his death four years later, he campaigned ceaselessly to pacify North India, winning a notable victory over the Rajputs. Babur combined the virility of nomadic Central Asian life with the aestheticism of North Indian culture. A remarkably versatile individual, he composed poetry and wrote his memoirs.

Babur's eldest son, Humayun, a less forceful figure, succeeded him. Political unrest soon developed, and an Afghan noble, Sher Khan, usurped the throne, assuming the title of Sher Shah. An able man, he quelled revolts, enforced law and order, and supervised a highly organized administration. The kingdom was divided into 47 provinces, which were subdivided into dis-

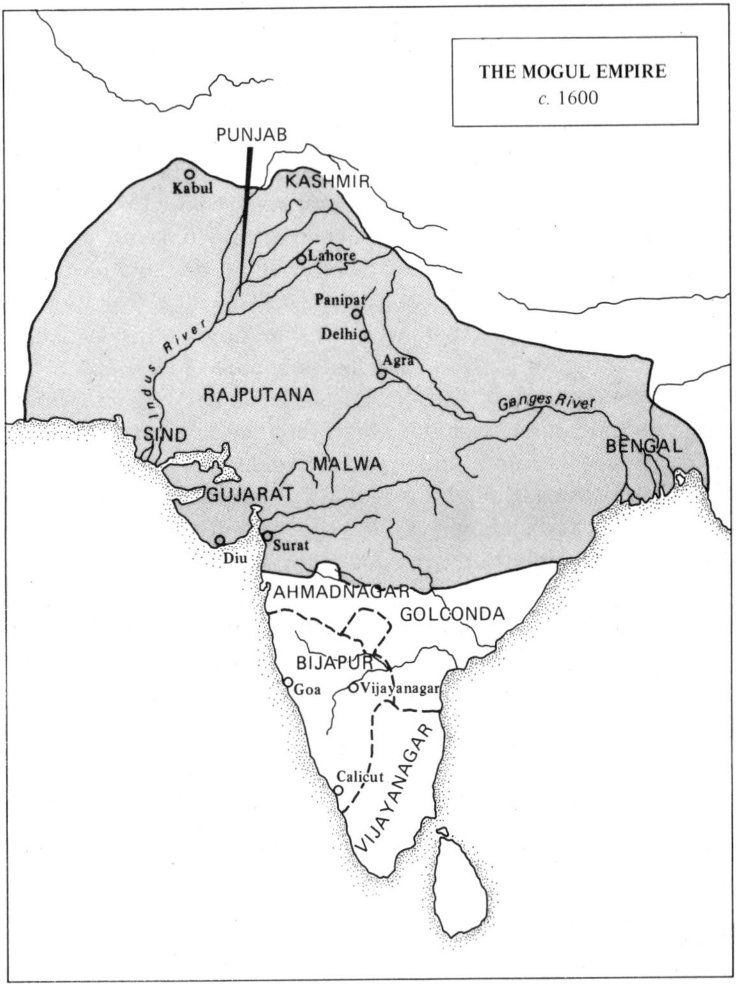
THE MOGUL EMPIRE
c. 1600
PUNJAB
KASHMIR
Kabul
Lahore
Panipat
Delhi
Agra
Indus River
Ganges River
RAJPUTANA
SIND
MALWA
BENGAL
GUJARAT
Surat
Diu
AHMADNAGAR
GOLCONDA
BIJAPUR
Goa
Vijayanagar
Calicut
VIJAYANAGAR

tricts with village clusters. Each district had a military governor, a judge, a treasurer, and two accountants, writing in Hindi and Persian. Land revenue collections, payable in kind or cash, were assessed at between one-fourth and one-third of the average crop yield. Tree-shaded post roads with resthouses at intervals were constructed. Sher Shah practiced religious toleration and permitted Hindus to hold office. He standardized the silver rupee at 180 grains, a ratio continued by later Moguls and also by the British. After ruling only five years, Sher Shah died in battle in 1545. His son took over command for nine years, but upon his death, succession disputes arose. Thereupon Humayun returned from exile in Kabul to retake Delhi, but he died within seven months.

Humayun's son Akbar, who became king at thirteen, ruled (at first through a regency) for half a century (1556–1605). He was a contemporary of Elizabeth I of England. An extraordinary man, the most famous of the Mogul line, he was an artist, politician, statesman, and military commander. He united North and Central India, though his realm was not so extensive as that of some other Indian emperors. His first capital was at Agra; then it moved for a time to nearby Fatephur Sikri. In fact, the nerve center of the empire accompanied him wherever he campaigned in India. Politically tolerant, Akbar presided over an empire of some hundred million people. He gained Hindu good will by venerating the cow, suspending the *jizya,* and employing Hindus in office. He won Rajput loyalty by extending privileges and concessions and marrying into their ranks.

Akbar was noted more for his administrative measures than for his conquests. His bureaucracy was essentially fourfold, consisting of court, military, civilian, and finance officials. Akbar was the supreme military commander. The regular army was not large, but its ranks could be swelled in time of need by militia and irregular contingents. The central government was headed by a prime minister and included a civil service. Serving the governors of the fifteen provinces were civilian and military *mansabdars,* graded according to the number of horsemen they could supply to the army upon imperial request.

Elaborating on Sher Shah's system, Akbar kept the financial administration, which was headed by a *diwan,* separate from political affairs. In the provinces, revenue officers were responsible for assessment and collection of the land taxes and for receiving customs duties and salt taxes. The assessment for land cultivation was based on factors such as soil fertility, kind of crop, and extent of acreage. The tax, paid in cash, averaged one-third of the produce.

Akbar also interested himself in religious matters. Growing increasingly discontented with orthodox Islam, in 1579 he issued an edict that gave him the sole right to adjudicate religious issues. The next year, he disavowed Islam as the state religion and proclaimed his own "Divine Faith." A syncretic religion, it appropriated elements from Islam, Persia, and Christianity (whose missionaries had begun to arrive at court). Though Akbar's religion did not outlive him, his political and financial structures persisted and formed the basis for British administration. The Urdu language also continued from his reign.

Akbar's son Jahangir reigned from 1605 to 1627. His administration was not so effective as was that of his father. Preoccupied with costly and ostentatious ceremonies, he lost western territory to the encroaching Persians and the throne was usurped by his son Shah Jahan. This emperor is remembered primarily for the construction in Agra of the surpassingly beautiful Taj Mahal, a mausoleum for his wife. The project employed twenty thousand workmen over a fifteen-year period (1632–1647). During Shah Jahan's reign, culture flourished and no major military campaigns threatened the country. In 1665, during the monarch's illness, his four sons contended for the throne, and Aurangzeb won out.

Aurangzeb (r. 1658–1707) at first attempted to gain the support of his subjects by prudent measures. He employed non-Muslims and lightened taxes. But in the latter part of his reign, he became increasingly intolerant and militant. With huge entourages he endeavored, with no success, to conquer the Deccan, the Achilles heel of so many northern rulers. In Auranzeb's reign the Mogul empire reached its greatest territorial extent, but its effective rule progressively weakened. After his death in 1707, the Mogul line, though still ruling in Delhi, produced no more outstanding monarchs. Other Indian states competed for power, but it was the advent of the West instead that sealed the dynasty's fate.

OTHER STATES

A growing indigenous power during the period of Mogul dominance was that of the Sikhs ("Disciples") in the Punjab. The faith was founded by Nanak (1469–1538), one of the Hindu Kshatriya class. His tolerant monotheistic creed, influenced by the bhakti and Sufi movements, emphasized doctrine less than a mystical devotion to God. Nanak was the first of a line of ten leaders, or gurus. The fourth established Amritsar as the sect's religious center. The last guru, murdered in 1708, completed the sect's scriptures called *Granth* (*Treatise*). He organized his followers into a militant, tightly knit group, who wore turbans and adopted Singh ("Lion") as surnames. Within a century, the Sikhs were predominant in the Punjab.

Later Mogul rulers also lost their grip over neighboring Afghanistan. In the eighteenth century, Persians invaded the land. One of them, Ahmed Shah, in 1747, established the Durani dynasty, a unified government extending over most of the present-day country. Several times he invaded India and twice sacked Delhi. After his death in 1773, his kingdom partially disintegrated; but his family retained power until 1826, when Dost Mohammed ended it. The new conqueror waged continuous war with the Sikhs and came into conflict with the British, who through the East India Company, in the mid-nineteenth century were poised on his borders.

Another state formed in the wake of the rearranging Indian political pattern was the Hindu kingdom of Maratha, or Maharashtra (the Sanskrit form), located in the Western Ghats and the Deccan, centered at Poona. It achieved power under an outstanding military leader, Sivaji (1627–1680). He managed to create a viable kingdom, but his successors could not perpetuate his administrative system. After Sivaji's death, the king's importance declined while that of the Brahman prime minister, or *peshwa*, increased. The office at Poona became hereditary and increasingly more powerful, while military leaders established what domains they could in a type of loose Maratha confederacy.

To its east and south in the Deccan arose Hyderabad. Originally under Mogul rule, around 1724 it began to exercise an increasing independence from Delhi. Lesser principalities existed farther to the south. Indians from Tamil land continued to migrate into Ceylon. For some centuries the Sinhalese, from their relocated capital of Polonnaruwa managed to contain them but were forced farther south in the central mountainous area, where they located at Kandy, their last capital. Meanwhile, other alien groups were arriving in the island. Attracted by Ceylon's spices, traders from Arab countries appeared in the twelfth and thirteenth centuries. Following on their heels were earliest representatives of European lands.

Decline of the Moguls. With the rise of new names and states, the South Asia political configuration altered. After the death of Aurangzeb, no strong Mogul leader emerged. The Rajputs were a powerful military group, but they remained a politically disunited state, as did the Marathas. The united Sikhs grew in power but lacked sufficient strength to overthrow the Mogul mastery. While states rose and fell, village India continued in its traditional life as councils (*panchayats*), headmen, priests, and farmers went about their daily rounds. Meanwhile India's scattered cities became more important as trade increased. India exported varied foodstuffs and commodities: silk, cotton, spices, rice, sugar, indigo, tobacco, and oil seeds; its chief imports were luxury goods. Though international trade was not a mainstay of Indian economy, it attracted Europeans to the country.

ADVENT OF WEST

Europeans arrived on the Indian subcontinent from the south and by sea, a departure from the usual invasion routes by land from the west and north. The Portuguese came first and settled at Goa, which they made their headquarters for a commercial empire. Their Indian presence was never influential, nor was that of lesser European powers. The French were more deeply involved, but the English won out over all European rivals. Through the East India Company they expanded interests until 1858, when the British crown assumed sovereignty. The English conquest of India was quite amazing. A small, distant, maritime country with a different history, England subjugated a large, populous subcontinent with ancient traditions and complex social structures. It started the process of modernization in India, the first country in Asia to be exposed in any appreciable manner to Westernization.

The Portuguese. In search of trade, slaves, and direct access to Asian wealth, the Portuguese began maritime explorations of the African west coast. Bartholomeu Diaz rounded the Cape of Good Hope in 1486. The next step was to reach Asia. In 1498 Vasco da Gama, with three vessels, reached the Malabar Coast just north of Calicut. He returned to Portugal after a two years' voyage with a valuable cargo of spices. In 1500 Pedro Cabral commanded an expedition of thirteen ships that, taking a western route to India, discovered Brazil. Two years later, da Gama returned to India and founded a trading post south of Calicut at Cochin.

The flag followed the vessel. In 1505 the Portuguese government appointed Francisco de Almeida as the first viceroy in India. He was succeeded several years later by Affonso de Albuquerque, who secured Portuguese control of strategically located islands and ports in the Indian Ocean area. In 1510 he seized the port of Goa, which became the headquarters of Portuguese political, commercial, and religious interests in the East. The Portuguese also established posts at Diu and Daman and in the lowlands of Ceylon.

After a century the Portuguese colonial cause atrophied, though the small country retained its three colonies in India into the mid-twentieth century. The Portuguese left in India an image tarnished by religious bigotry and commercial opportunism. But they introduced basic crops, including potatoes and corn; Renaissance art, which survives in their cathedrals; and their lingua franca, which was used in Indian ports for hundreds of years.

The Dutch. The Dutch replaced some of the Portuguese commercial interests in India and all of them in Ceylon. In 1602 the Dutch Parliament granted a charter to a joint-stock company, known as the Dutch East India Company, which developed commercial trade ventures in Indian ports and in coastal Ceylon. Unlike the Portuguese, the Dutch did not concern themselves with religious proselytizing. After some success in Indian ventures, they turned their attention to the East Indies. By 1759, they had relinquished their interests in India and little remained from their outposts there. But they stayed in Ceylon until the British, during the Napoleonic Wars, appropriated their commercial and political ventures on the island.

The Danes and the French. During the seventeenth century, other European states arrived in India. In 1616 the Danish East India Company was organized, but its operations were never extensive. The French arrived in 1664, when Colbert, the finance minister of Louis XIV, founded the French East India Company. In 1668 the first French factory, or trading center, was established at Surat, and in 1674 the French purchased the port of Pondicherry, which became their Indian center. However, the French did not secure a large portion of Indian commerce or territory.

The English. The English in India followed the traditional colonial sequence of voyages, organized commercial ventures, and then territorial acquisitions. In the seventeenth century, at least two chartered companies were formed in England; in 1707 they were amalgamated into what was known as the English East India Company. In 1612 the first permanent English factory was established at Surat. Others sprang up along the east coast. In 1639 the ruler of Madras ceded a desolate piece of land to the British, who built on it Fort St. George. Out of this settlement grew the modern Indo-British city of Madras.

During the subsequent English civil war, the country's commercial enterprises abroad were temporarily curtailed, but they were renewed following the restoration of the Stuarts. In 1668 the East India Company received Bombay from Charles II, who had acquired it from Portugal as part of his wife's dowry. Though the climate was unhealthy, the English built up their second post also into an important urban center. They established another center in Bengal but were forced to withdraw because of Mogul pressures. Returning in 1691, after a successful campaign against the Moguls, they established Fort William near the settlement of Calcutta. Thus by 1700, the British were strategically placed on the subcontinent—west in Bombay, south in Madras, and east in Calcutta. In these settlements a council of merchants chose their president, or governor. The three presidencies, as the settlements were called, were administered from London by Company directors.

Anglo-French Rivalry. The English and French fought

each other in India in the course of their European Wars, the War of the Austrian Succession (1740–1748) and the Seven Years' War (1756–1763).

In the course of the first war the shrewd French governor of Pondicherry, Joseph Dupleix, managed to make the Indian state of Hyderabad a French protectorate. He sought through taxes to impose the costs of French colonial rule on native rulers. He also utilized military contingents of native troops, called *sepoys,* under foreign commanders.

Robert Clive (1725–1774) was the English rival of Dupleix. At eighteen, he came to Madras as a clerk in the English East India Company. Later becoming a soldier, the ambitious Clive made a name for himself in military campaigns of the Company. In 1756 the governor (*nawab*) of Bengal with French support attacked the English and imprisoned them in their own fort (the "Black Hole of Calcutta," an incident later exaggerated by British historians). The following year British and Indian troops under Clive decisively defeated the French and their Indian allies at Plassey. Thereafter, the British assumed direct rule in Bengal.

Company Rule. In his two terms of office as governor of Bengal (1758–1760 and 1765–1767), Clive expanded the East India Company's trading privileges there. In 1765 the *diwani* transferred to the Company the right to the financial administration of Bengal, Bihar, and Orissa. In 1772 the Company directly appropriated revenue rights over these rich provinces.

Another outstanding British administrator was Warren Hastings, who like Clive went to India as a clerk and rose to governor-general (1772–1785). Hastings centralized and strengthened the administration of the Company's Indian holdings. During his tenure, Parliament passed the Regulating Act of 1773 which provided for government supervision of the Company's Indian affairs and established Calcutta as Company headquarters. The India Act of 1784 placed more restrictions on Company activities. After Hastings came Lord Cornwallis (1786–1793), the general defeated at Yorktown. During his efficient regime, the Indian Civil Service was placed on a merit basis.

Lord Wellesley, brother of the Duke of Wellington, was governor-general from 1798 to 1805. Wellesley sought to advance British power in India through direct or indirect Company rule over native states. During his regime, Company authority was extended to almost all India. Wellesley also encouraged Indian education and established a college to train Company officials. In 1798 Ceylon was made a crown colony.

The Napoleonic Wars ended with the British in control of all the French possessions in India except for a few colonies. The Charter Act of 1813 terminated the Company's commercial monopoly and opened Indian trade to all Englishmen. It also permitted missionaries to enter India and appropriated an annual sum for native education.

In the course of succeeding decades, further conquests expanded Company authority in India and its borders. Ceylon was brought under united British rule in 1815 when the central area under the indigenous Kandy monarchs was conquered. In a treaty the next year with Nepal, the British received certain Gangetic areas and replaced the Nepalis as protectors of neighboring Sikkim. Company jurisdiction encroached on Maratha borders. By the time of Lord Bentinck, governor-general from 1828 to 1835, European liberal ideas had repercussions in India. As governor-general (1828–1835), Bentinck undertook a program of reform. He permitted some qualified Indians to enter civil service ranks, abolished suttee, and suppressed Thugs, who practiced ritual assassination.

In 1838 the first Afghan War erupted, as a result of Anglo-Russian rivalry in Central Asia. Following this conflict, which ended badly for them, the British, in 1842, annexed the Indian kingdom of Sind to buttress their position in the northwest. Earl Dalhousie (1848–1856) was the last great governor-general. An experienced civil servant with reforming zeal, he sought to improve India's schools, penal system, public works, irrigation methods, and communications. In foreign policy, he pushed into Sikh territory, annexed the Punjab, and appropriated other areas through indirect political measures.

Effects of English Administration. Under a succession of forceful leaders, Company administration consolidated. In some princely states through British advisers it ruled indirectly; in so-called British India, Company rule was direct. Despite some reforms, all top civilian and military positions remained in English hands. In its judicial system the Company utilized Hindu or

Muslim law according to the defendant's religion, supplementing this with British legal procedure. Indians held lower judicial positions. The nature of colonial education was a subject of controversy in England. Those who advocated European over native learning won out, and in 1835 English supplanted Persian as India's official language. In the decades to come Indian intellectuals who had been indoctrinated with Western culture provided the impetus for the Indian nationalist movement.

Various types of financial assessments were made by the Company. Cornwallis decreed an annual charge of three million pounds on the province of Bengal. In order to expedite payment, the *zamindars* (tax collectors under the Moguls) were allocated the land if they did not already hold it. In Madras and much of Bombay, the *ryotwari* (from the word for "peasant") system imposed the land tax directly. In Central, North, and West India, the *mahalwari* (from the word for "estate") imposts were levied on villages, whose headmen collected it. In commerce British machine-made goods, especially textiles, flooded Indian markets, violating the country's traditional foreign trading patterns. Not only was there a greater volume of trade, but Indians were importing more than they exported. In other areas the Company recorded some progress. It introduced steamships on internal waterways, constructed some roads and railroads, and inaugurated a post office system.

Transfer of Control to the Crown. In 1857, a century after the Battle of Plassey, came the epochal Sepoy Mutiny. Its immediate cause was introduction of a British rifle cartridge, allegedly greased with either beef or pork fat, which had to be bitten before use—an act of impiety to both Hindus and Muslims. Refusing to use the cartridges, Sepoys at Meerut near Delhi mutinied and were thereupon imprisoned. The incident sparked sympathy from other Indian troops, who killed their British officers, freed the prisoners, and marched on Delhi. Widespread resistance followed, though most violence occurred in the Ganges Valley. Some native princes joined the rebellion; others remained loyal to the British. After a year and a half the rebellion was crushed. Rebels were executed, or they vanished. Some native princes were killed or dispossessed. The British used the occasion to terminate the last remnants of Mogul rule. Company jurisdiction itself had become increasingly anachronistic over the decades, and the mutiny sealed its fate. On November 1, 1858, a royal proclamation transferred sovereign authority over India from the Company to the crown. Two decades later, in 1877, Queen Victoria was proclaimed Empress of India. In line as yet another foreign dynasty, the British crown, in subsequent decades, reigned either directly or indirectly over a greater extent of the subcontinent than had any previous native or alien emperor. And it was the Company that had laid the basis for empire.

9
SOUTHEAST ASIA 1300–1850

In the over-all five-and-a-half centuries after 1300, Southeast Asia witnessed the rearrangement of indigenous states, the advent of Islam in the insular world, and, most important, the arrival of the West. In the earlier half of the period, between 1300 and 1600, while Kambuja atrophied, a new monarchy was established in Laos. The Vietnamese finally absorbed Champa. In Thailand, the successive kingdoms of Sukhotai and Ayuthia were the most important. In Burma, the political divisiveness resulting from Mongol invasions continued. Various Burman kingdoms competed for power not only among themselves but also with the Mon and Shan. In the archipelagoes, the long-lasting Srivijaya empire came to an end, while that of Majapahit waxed. Islam came to stay, and its most notable political center was the flourishing port of Malacca on the Malay Peninsula. Also by 1600, the Iberian powers of Portugal and Spain were in the island world for good.

Between 1600 and 1850, other Western powers—Dutch, French, and English—began gradually to consolidate their holdings in various Southeast Asian areas. Though Thailand kept political independence, Indochina gradually came under French rule, while Burma began to fall to the British, who were expanding from India. Parts of the Malayan world also went to the British; the major portions fell to the Dutch. In the Philippines the Spanish ruled supreme. The Portuguese contracted holdings to one spot, Timor, in Indonesia. Unlike India, where the British evolved as the main Western power, Southeast Asia experienced a handful of colonial masters. And modernization proceeded more slowly than in India, partly because of the fragmented colonial patterns and policies.

MEDIEVAL STATES (1300–1600)

The Mongol invasions of the thirteenth century helped to rearrange political patterns of mainland Southeast Asia. From China they sent more people streaming southward down the river valleys, as well as temporarily occupying some lands. After suffering depredations from the north, the Vietnamese, in their historic march south, absorbed Champa. In Laos the first main kingdom, Lan Xang, arose. The Khmer empire, ended in the Angkor area by Thai invasions, relocated at present-day Phnom Penh, where it survived in gradually constricted form, with eastern pressures from Vietnam and western pressures from Thailand. In the Chao Phraya Valley, Sukhotai reigned supreme until overtaken by another Thai kingdom, that of Ayuthia near modern Bangkok. The muddied Burmese situation clarified somewhat with the reimposition of Burman rule over most of the land under the Toungoo dynasty. In the insular world, Majapahit was the chief state and helped hasten the fall of Srivijaya. Into the political vacuum of the Malaccan Strait area came various states, including Malacca, which gradually fell to Islam. In the sixteenth century there arrived with the Portuguese and Spanish the Christian Bible and the Western gunboat.

Vietnam. In the course of the fourteenth century, more Cham land fell to the Vietnamese, but unrest developed in Hanoi. In 1400 the Tran monarch was deposed in a palace coup by a general, Ho Qui Li, who set up a short-lived dynasty. The Tran supporters requested and received Chinese aid; in 1407 a Chinese army helped to overthrow the Ho usurper. The Chinese remained in control of North Vietnam for a decade thereafter, trying to incorporate it again into their empire. In 1418 the Vietnamese rebelled, and under Le Loi in a ten years' war managed to oust the overstaying guests. Le Loi reimposed native rule but nonetheless sent a tributary mission to Peking, where the emperor recognized him as the king of Annam (a term now applied by the Chinese to all Vietnam).

The second Le dynasty (1428–1788) included Le Thanh Ton (r. 1460–1497), who finally in 1471 achieved mastery over the

Cham and began Vietmanese expansion across the Annamite chain into Laos. In their capital at Hanoi, the Le copied the Chinese central bureaucratic pattern with its six departments (finance, rites, justice, personnel, army, and public works). They conducted, as did China, the annual provincial and triennial regional and capital examinations for entrance to civil service posts. Further borrowed from the Chinese were the nine ranks, for both civilian and army officials, a hierarchy that lasted into modern times. The Chinese imperial dragon motif replaced the naga serpent of Hindu deities. But despite the Sinic overlay, indigenous Vietnamese religious practices persisted, and local native and ancestral spirits continued to be venerated.

Laos and Cambodia. To the west of Vietnam, the first historical kingdom was founded in Laos. In the upper Mekong Valley, a Tai chief named Fa Ngum, in 1353 united a number of small principalities into Lan Xang ("Kingdom of the Thousand Elephants"), with a capital at Luang Prabang. Fa Ngum annexed Vientiane and extensive territory on the west bank of the river. Buddhism was established by Hinayana monks brought in from Angkor. To the south, continued Thai encroachments on Angkor ended in 1431 with its capture and sack. Three years later, the Khmer regained Angkor and restored their prince to the throne but relocated their capital at Phnom Penh. The ancient Angkor monuments fell into jungle-covered ruins as Kambuja continued, in a weakened state, farther downstream the Mekong.

Thailand. In Thailand, the kingdom of Sukhotai declined after the reign of Rama Khamheng, and other states came to the fore. Most notable was Ayuthia in the lower Chao Phraya Valley, a rich agricultural region. Its founder King Ramatibodi (r. 1350–1369) reduced Sukhotai to vassalage status. He and his successors expanded Ayuthia's boundaries into Khmer territory, Chiengmai, Tenasserim, and the Malay Peninsula. Most notable of the later monarchs was King Trailok (r. 1448–1488). He reorganized and centralized the government apparatus with five departments (interior, agriculture, finance and foreign trade, royal household, and local government) and established a military arm. Classes held land proportionate to social status, from princes to commoners. Punishments were meted also according to social status. The aristocratic nature of state and society established by Ayuthia rulers persisted into the nineteenth century.

During the Ayuthia period (1350–1767), Hinayana Buddhism increased in popularity, partly as a result of contacts with the Khmers and partly because of direct relations with Buddhist centers in Ceylon. It became the official religion of the land, and so it remained. In the latter half of the sixteenth century, the political situation became more unstable with Burmese invasions. It was then that the temporarily united Burmese made two extended campaigns into the Chao Phraya Valley. As a result of the second invasion they sacked the capital and retained control of Ayuthia for fifteen years (1569–1584). Toward the end of the century, Phra Naret, a strong king, ended Burmese rule and in turn led two invasions of Burma. By 1600, Ayuthia had emerged once again as a leading Southeast Asian power.

Burma. In Burma, as a result of the late thirteenth-century Mongol invasions, the old Pagan kingdom disintegrated. A remnant of it was re-established at Ava, farther down the Irrawaddy near modern Mandalay. Other Burman kingdoms existed in Prome and Toungoo on the Sittang River. The Shan tribes remained strong in eastern hill retreats, while the Mons continued at Pegu. Among the various factions, continual but indecisive battles erupted, in the course of which Shans captured Ava. Central Burma broke up once again. Some Burmans fled to Toungoo, which, by the latter half of the sixteenth century, began to rise in prominence.

A reinvigorated Toungoo dynasty (1486–1752) retook Central Burma, defeated both the Shans and Mons, and carried expeditions into Thailand. The most famous of the line was Bayinnaung, ruling (1551–1581) first from Toungoo and later from Pegu, which he rebuilt. It was in his reign that Ayuthia was defeated and occupied for a decade and a half. He campaigned into Laos, temporarily subjugating Lan Xang, and also captured Chiengmai in Thailand. His son and successor Nandabayin lacked ability, and during his reign (1581–1599), Ayuthia, Lan Xang, and Chiengmai regained independence. By 1600, Burma had again broken up into petty kingdoms, among which were Ava, Prome, and Toungoo.

The Malay World. In East Java, the Majapahit empire, initiated by Vijaya, grew in power and lasted until the Portuguese arrived on the scene in the early sixteenth century. In its early existence, Majapahit was concerned with local controls. Then during the reign of Hayam Wuruk (1350–1389), the kingdom gained wider power. According to the epic *Magarakertagama,* composed by a Buddhist monk, the monarch's prime minister Gaja Mada extended Majapahit authority over a greater part of insular Southeast Asia. In 1377 Srivijaya, a long holdout, was conquered. Embassies were exchanged with China, from which centralized bureaucratic organs were adopted (revenue, justice, agriculture, and public works), headed by members of the royal house. A law code delineated lines of authority. Nobles of higher and lesser ranks, answerable to the king, governed local entities. Headmen presided over villages. After Hayam Wuruk's death, however, political disintegration set in.

In traditional Southeast Asia, there had been no great kingdoms on the Malay Peninsula. Though some city-states were established along Indian lines, they were not politically powerful. While Srivijaya lasted, South Sumatra, rather than the peninsula, controlled the straits. But concurrently with this kingdom's breakup Islam came into the political and religious vacuum. Initially brought by Arab traders from the Middle East, Islam was not accepted until Indians, mainly from the Gujarat area, were converted to the faith in the course of Turkish rule there. In the late thirteenth century, Marco Polo remarked on the presence of at least two Muslim communities in north Sumatra. In the course of the next century, Islam leapfrogged across the Malacca Strait to the peninsula, where Malacca, the most important trading community, was converted through the marriage of one of its rulers to a Muslim princess. Because of trading and ethnic connections with Java, Malacca re-exported the faith to that island, where it too began to take hold.

Meanwhile, Muslim traders and travelers brought the new faith from India. Prominent Indian Muslims intermarried with the elite and converted them. As was the case generally in India, conversions were made peacefully. The populace went along with rulers in subscribing to the new faith as they had to the earlier Hinduism and Buddhism. Some converted rulers were probably sincerely motivated by Islamic tenets. Others were attracted to commercial benefits, inasmuch as Gujarat Muslims brought welcomed and needed cotton goods to Southeast Asia. Other insular leaders, including those at Malacca, adopted Islam in part for political reasons, to counteract Buddhist Ayuthia and Hindu Majapahit. Beyond the Malay Peninsula, Islam did not take hold on mainland Southeast Asia, probably partly because of the absence of Indian Muslims in appreciable numbers and partly because of resistance from strongly oriented Hinayana Buddhist regimes.

Under its Muslim rulers, in the course of the fifteenth century Malacca flourished. Having little in the way of agricultural resources, it derived its strength mainly from commercial and maritime activity. It was in a strategic location at the narrowest width of the straits, and protected from the monsoons by both peninsular and Sumatran mountain ranges. Sultans or kings, advised by prime ministers, ruled the state. Other officials included the head of police and courts, a commander of the fleet, and four harbor masters, each dealing with assigned foreign traders and vessels. Income was derived from a basic 6 percent duty on foreign trade, plus 1 percent in "gifts." A domestic trade tax amounted to 3 percent, while additional levies were placed on food sales. The Malacca population was heterogenous; most were alien to the port. Javanese, Sumatrans, Persians, Chinese, Arabs, Parsees, Bengalis, and Gujarats rubbed shoulders. Goods of various countries—East Indian spices, Gujarati cotton, Chinese porcelains, and silks, Formosan foodstuffs—changed hands. The city developed rapidly, but it had to resist the approaches of Ayuthia and Majapahit. Its sultans admitted Chinese suzerainty and sent triennial tributary missions to China. Though it warred with neighboring small Malay states, none of them could conquer it. Its nemesis came in the guise of Portuguese.

Advent of West. The expansion of the Portuguese into Southeast Asia followed a logical pattern. After they obtained control of sea lanes to India, where their operations centered in Goa, their next step was to reach insular Southeast Asia, the source of spices themselves. In 1509 the ambitious viceroy Albuquerque dispatched Diogo Lopez de Sequeira to reconnoiter Malacca, where twenty of his men, including Ferdinand Magellan, were captured. Two years later, Albuquerque returned with a squadron of eighteen vessels, freed the men, and destroyed the town. The sultan fled but most of the foreign community were won over to Portuguese. The newcomers made Malacca a citadel and rebuilt it into the first European-type city in Southeast Asia. Costs of fortification were defrayed by duties on ships traversing the Malacca Strait. As in India, the Portuguese introduced Christianity with forced conversions, a theme new in Southeast Asian religious history. Missionaries, including the Jesuit Francis Xavier, came from Goa and used Malacca as a base for expeditions to China and Japan.

The Portuguese maintained trading posts in the Spice Islands themselves, notably at Tidore and Ternate. They signed commercial treaties with Burma, Siam, and Annam. Portuguese adventurers, called *feringhi,* entered the service of Southeast Asian kings. In South Burma Philip de Brito, "King of Syriam," ruled the port of Pegu (1599–1613); Diogo Veloso became a soldier of fortune in Cambodia and the Philippine Islands; others operated in the Bay of Bengal. But as in India, Portuguese colonial rule was undermined by internal weaknesses. The home country was never willing to reinvest in the colonies the wealth that it gained from them. Local Malay sultans fought the Portuguese but, unable to unite, they could not capture the city. It finally fell in 1641 to the Dutch. Thereafter the only remaining Portuguese possession in Southeast Asia was half of the Indonesian island of Timor.

Meanwhile, the Spanish, also in search of trade and converts, were pushing out to Asia. But whereas the Portuguese sailed eastward from Europe, the Spanish sailed westward. In 1519 Ferdinand Magellan reached the Philippines. With five ships he started out from Spain; rounded South America through the strait that bears his name; crossed the Pacific Ocean (which he named); and landed eventually at Cebu in the Visayan Islands. The Spaniards' high-handedness antagonized the at first friendly natives, and Magellan was killed in a conflict with them. What was left of his expedition continued to the Spice Islands, but only eighteen men on one ship, the *Victoria,* finally returned home, completing the first circumnavigation of the world in 1522.

Between 1525 and 1565, the Spanish sent five more expeditions to the Philippines, the first two from Spain and the others from Mexico. Heading the last was Lopez de Legaspi, who set out to colonize the islands. He first located at Cebu, but in 1571 moved the capital to Manila. Within five years, most of the Philippines fell to the Spanish. Hispanization of the culturally backward and politically fragmented archipelago was relatively easy. The people lived in scattered village settlements, called *barangays*. They were for the most part animistic in religion. There had been some earlier Chinese commercial and racial connections, as well as superficial Indian ties. Islam, on the other hand, had already begun to make inroads into southern islands until the Spanish arrested the trend.

By 1600, Spanish consolidation of the Philippines except for the Islamic south had been accomplished. But the Spanish came into conflict with the Portuguese in the Spice Islands. Though the Treaty of Tordesillas of 1494 and the Treaty of Saragossa of 1529 gave that area to the Portuguese, the Spaniards contested the claim. In the first half of the sixteenth century, rivalry continued until the Spanish withdrew, to concentrate on the Philippines. (This intrusion of European power politics became a recurring theme in Southeast Asian history and one over which indigenous people, though materially affected, had no say or control.)

SOUTHEAST ASIA AND THE WEST (1600–1850)

When the Europeans arrived, Southeast Asia was politically weak and divided. Dynastic problems and parochial jealousies consumed energies of petty despotic kings, while the ordinary man eked out his burdensome existence. He raised his family, planted rice, caught fish, and paid taxes. He obeyed his village headman and followed customary law. He continued to worship animistic gods through Hindu, Buddhist, or Islamic veneers. From outside Southeast Asia, no Asian power challenged Western expansion. India under Muslim leaders was fractionized; China and Japan were isolationist. In the absence of regional or continental resistance, European powers initiated their empires. Proceeding slowly at first, they gained footholds in varying mainland and insular areas. The two and a half centuries between 1600 and 1850 constituted the preparatory period for colonial rule in Southeast Asia. Except for the Philippines, it was not until after 1850 that empires were finally fashioned.

Thailand. In Thailand, by 1600 Ayuthia had evolved as the pre-eminent power on the mainland. In the course of the seventeenth century, it experienced short-lived foreign contacts. Its military service included Portuguese, Spanish, and Japanese adventurers, while the British, Dutch, and French sought commercial ties. The French became temporarily strong in 1685, when France and Ayuthia concluded a treaty of commerce and friendship. With the treaty came French-oriented advisers, including a prime minister, Constantine Phaulkon, who began his career as a cabin boy on a French ship. But three years after assuming office, while attempting to turn Thailand into a French protectorate, Phaulkon was killed in a coup. Thereafter the Thai shunned foreign contacts.

Ayuthia in its latter years disintegrated. Provincial governors established themselves as independent rulers. Once again the capital experienced destructive wars with, and occupation by, the Burmese. In 1767 P'ya Taksin, a Chinese general in Thai service, spearheaded resistance until he went insane. His successor, General Chakri, finally forced out the Burmese, and in 1782 established the dynasty bearing his name at Bangkok, a new capital farther downstream the Chao Phraya than Ayuthia. He took the regnal name of Rama I (from the Indian incarnation of Vishnu). The new monarch re-asserted rule not only in Central Thailand but also in peripheral areas. From his accession dates modern-day Thailand, with a history almost equal in time to that of the federal United States.

Rama's successors Rama II (r. 1809–1824) and Rama III (r. 1824–1851) concluded Siam's first modern treaties with the West. In 1822 the English East India Company sent John Crawfurd to initiate negotiations for commerce, but the Thai at the time disclaimed interest. Four years later, the British sent a second envoy, Captain Henry Burney. This time the Siamese, aware of recent British victories in Malaya and Burma, offered limited terms. Following on British heels came the Americans; in 1833 the first United States treaty with an Asian country was negotiated by Edmund Roberts. The Roberts treaty opened all Siam's ports to American ships, fixed port duties at 15 percent, provided for humane treatment of American sailors, and included a most-favored-nation clause (i.e., a stipulation that whatever concessions Siam granted another foreign state would be extended to the United States). The treaty, however, did not provide for consular representation. With the Western treaties came Western presence, but Chakri monarchs did not seriously set out to modernize the land until after 1850.

Vietnam. In Vietnam, after the death of Le Thanh Ton, the Le dynasty declined. Though the central government remained operative in Hanoi, its provincial powers were too extended. Local leaders asserted independence, and in 1527, a general, Mac Dang Dung, usurped the throne. He ruled in the north, while in the south at Hué, the rival Nguyen family, supported the cause of the deposed Le dynasty. But the Nguyen family in turn was divided. The Trinh, related to it by marriage, in 1592 overran the north, ended the Mac rule, and restored the Le line in Hanoi. The Nguyen remained in Hué. The Trinh tried without success to conquer Central and South Vietnam. During most of the seventeenth century, the two Vietnamese kingdoms coexisted, the boundary marked by a wall at Dong Hoi, north of Hué, running from the coast to the foothills. From their capital at Hué, the Nguyen princes extended Annamite power farther south, and by 1700 had acquired Saigon. Within another half-century they had opened up the whole Mekong delta area.

Political events in Vietnam then became more confusing. In the south three brothers, also called Nguyen but not related to the royal family, began their rise to power in 1771. First they took the Saigon area, then Hué, and finally Hanoi, in 1788. They divided the country into three subparts, one brother presiding over each; but this arrangement did not last long. By then the French were involved in Vietnamese politics.

As early as 1610, French Jesuits had labored in Indochina. The French East India Company was chartered in 1664. Over a century and a half, the French advanced their missionary and commercial interests. In 1787 Nguyen Anh (prince of the original Nguyen family), having been driven into exile at Bangkok, requested help from a French Catholic bishop in that city. The prelate went to France and obtained a treaty with the refugee monarch from Louis XVI. The subsequent outbreak of the French Revolution made Louis himself a refugee, but the bishop secured private volunteers with whose help Nguyen Anh recouped the throne at Hué in 1802. The king, now known as Gia Long, rewarded the French with territorial grants: the Bay of Tourane (Danang) and the islands of Touron and Pulo Condore. But Gia Long's successors instituted anti-French policies. The French were not in a position to intervene again until the Second Empire was established under Napoleon III.

Laos and Cambodia. In Laos, the Lan Xang kingdom was plagued with family quarrels and succession fights. By 1740, the country was divided into three parts: Luang Prabang, Vientiane, and Champassak, each a small, warring state. From time to time, Vietnamese and Thai incursions intruded into the Laotian domestic scene. After 1800 the two neighbors shared spheres of influence over northern and central areas: the Vietnamese at Vientiane and the Thai at Luang Prabang. A similar situation faced Cambodian kings. They lost the lower Mekong Delta to the Hué Nguyen, while the western and northern provinces fell to the Thai. By 1850 Cambodia was under joint suzerainty of its two historical enemy neighbors. Then the French stepped in and, in a fashion, saved Cambodian polity.

Burma. In Burma, also politically divided, the kings of Ava, Prome, and Toungoo competed for domination. It was the Ava line that eventually came out on top. Between the mid-seventeenth and late nineteenth century, the political gravity of Burma remained in so-called Upper Burma. The Toungoo dynasty relocated at Ava, far from the sea, and led a withdrawn, self-sufficient existence in the rich Irrawaddy basin. The kingdom was affected, however, by turmoil in China. When the Ming dynasty collapsed, and with the advance of the Manchu southward in 1658 the last of the Ming princes fled to Burma, where the enemy forces in pursuit besieged Ava itself. At this time the Thai temporarily recovered Chiengmai and Pegu, but Ava, after the Manchu retreat, took them back. The Burmans had less success in Lower Burma with the unruly Mons, who declared their independence and in 1752 took the capital city. With the fall of Ava came the end of the Toungoo dynasty.

The Mons remained in Ava less than a year. In Upper Burma at Swebo a Burman resistance movement began under Alaungpaya, who initiated Burma's last dynasty (1753–1885). When he prepared to attack Ava, the Mons suddenly evacuated the city and fled south to home territory. Alaungpaya pursued them and took their capital city of Pegu, as well as another settlement, Dagon, which he renamed Rangoon ("End of War"). Once again, most of Burma was reunited under one dynasty, and this time it remained so. In the course of Burman reconsolidation under the Alaungpaya line, the Mons ceased to exist as a separate people.

Alaungpaya, like his predecessors in earlier dynasties, turned his attention to Siam. He led an expedition against Ayuthia, but in 1760 he died in battle. Under his successor the war continued, and a second campaign directed at Ayuthia was successful. In 1767 the Thai capital was taken and plundered. The following year, as noted above, the Thai retook Ayuthia but moved to a new capital, Bangkok, nearer the sea. The Burmese also bore the brunt of more inroads from China. Under the strong Manchu leadership, Chinese forces in the late 1760's drove into North Burma; at one time they were only thirty miles from Ava. In 1770 peace terms were arranged, and the Burmese turned their attention once again to the Thai. Though Chiengmai seesawed in and out of Burmese hands, by 1800 the Burmans were out of Central Thailand.

The rest of the Alaungpaya dynasty was quite despotic. The principal agent for cultural unity was Hinayana Buddhism through the *sangha* monastic order. But sizable minority groups of differing persuasion were hard to absorb religiously or politically. The Mons were eliminated but not the Shans, Karens, Chin, Kachin, and Arakanese. Despite domestic problems, the Ava monarchs were bent on expansion. Contained in the east by growing Chakri might, they turned their attention westward. To that quarter they pushed into possessions of the English East India Company. Collision became inevitable.

In the southwest, the Burmans, after absorbing Arakan in the late eighteenth century, moved toward the Company's Indian center, Calcutta. In the northeast, they advanced into Assam, which the Company insisted was a British protectorate. In 1824 the first Anglo-Burmese War broke out over the latter encroachment. After a two-year war, a treaty was concluded. By its terms the Burmese paid the British an indemnity of one million pounds and allowed a British resident (ambassador) at Ava. Britain received the territories of Assam, coastal Arakan, and Tenasserim. The cessions hurt, and the Burmese developed strong ill feeling toward the British. As the Burman monarchs nursed their grudges at Ava, the East India Company began to develop economic projects in coastal, or Lower, Burma. But the British found it difficult to deal with the Burmese, and by 1850, another conflict was emerging.

The British in Malaysia. British political and commercial presence in the Malayan world predated those in Burma. In the late sixteenth century, English adventurers and freebooters, including Sir Francis Drake, operated in East Indies waters. The defeat of the Spanish Armada in 1588 was followed by a drive for English commercial expeditions. In 1591 James Lancaster headed a fleet sent by a London company to establish a trading post in the Spice Islands. The following year he landed at Penang, an island off the west Malayan coast, and took a cargo of spices back to London. Though this journey was not profitable, another London trading company secured a charter from Queen Elizabeth I in 1600. Two years later, Lancaster headed their expedition to Sumatra. The East India Company subsequently established trading posts at Bantam in Java, at Banda and Amboina in the Spice Islands, and at Benculen in Sumatra. But because of Dutch rivalry in Indonesia and the Company's preoccupation with India, British activity declined in Malaya. By 1700, Benculen was the only major British post in that area.

After the loss of the American colonies, and with growing commercial operations in China, the British reactivated interest in Southeast Asia. Quite fortuitously, they gained their first cessions. In 1782, the sultan of Kedah in North Malaya, in return for British aid in his war with the Chakri dynasty, offered to cede the island of Penang. The Company accepted the proposition and thereby acquired Penang though the sultan received no direct British support. In the course of the Napoleonic Wars, the European power alignments were transferred to the Southeast Asian scene. Because the Dutch were then allied with the

French, in 1811 British forces occupied Malacca and Java. Stamford Raffles, dispatched to Java as lieutenant-governor, set about to supplant Dutch political influence and economic interests with those of the British. He also introduced land and tax reforms in the islands.

In 1816 the Congress of Vienna returned the Indies and Malacca to the Dutch after only five years of British occupation. The indomitable Raffles then devoted himself to the acquisition of Singapore ("City of Lions"), then an island village south of the Malay Peninsula. In 1819 he induced the Company to buy the island from the sultan of Johore on the peninsula. The Dutch objected to this act; but after protracted negotiations, an Anglo-Dutch treaty in 1824 carved out spheres of influence. The Dutch quit Malacca and acknowledged pre-eminent British interests in Singapore and Malaya. In return, the British evacuated Benculen and some minor trading posts in Indonesia.

In the nineteenth century, Singapore grew into a major entrepôt. As a free port noted for efficient and just administration, it encouraged trade and attracted overseas Indians and Chinese. In 1826 the ports of Singapore, Penang, and Malacca were placed under an administration called the Straits Settlements. Four years later, this administration was placed under Company headquarters in Calcutta.

The Spanish in the Philippines. In the Philippines, over the centuries the Spanish imposed heavy-handed civilian and religious authority. The government was administered by a governor-general, assisted by a council and court in Manila. The provinces were placed under Spanish judges, tax collectors, land inspectors, and public works supervisors. In ecclesiastical structure, Manila was at first a bishopric and then in 1600 became an archbishopric. The Church founded schools on all levels, including the first university in Southeast Asia. International trade was minimal, though Chinese economic colonies in the archipelago traded with their homeland and participated as well in the galleon trade (1571–1811) with Acapulco.

Colonial domination also characterized the Philippine economic scene. Huge ecclesiastical and private estates presided over the destinies of hundreds of individuals. Spanish law, administration, religion, and language were propagated. Despite the fact that into the nineteenth century, there were relatively few Spaniards in the country, the Philippines became the first Westernized (though not modernized) country in Asia.

During the first half of the nineteenth century, there gradually arose a broadly based nationalistic movement as more Filipinos became educated at home or abroad, where in the more liberal atmosphere of mid-century Europe they picked up ideas if not of independence then of more autonomy. However, the Spanish granted few reforms.

The Dutch in Indonesia. In Indonesia, the Dutch built up their colonial interests. The first Dutch ships appeared in the area in 1596, and in 1598 several Dutch companies dispatched additional expeditions. In 1602 the first Dutch chartered company, called the Dutch East India Company, was formed. It was granted broad powers in the Southeast Asia area, similar to those of the British East India Company in India. In 1619 the Company occupied the town of Jacatra in West Java and renamed it Batavia (the ancient Roman name for Holland). Other foreign interests were forced out by the Dutch, who also brought local sultans under their rule.

In its first century of operation, the Dutch East India Company concentrated more on trade and commerce than on territorial expansion. But in the course of the 1700's, as it steadily increased its commercial interests it also acquired territory. In piecemeal fashion all Java came under its control, though in Central Java the sultanate of Mataram was made into two independent principalities, Surakarta and Jogjakarta. Meanwhile, the Company developed large plantations for growing export crops, including coffee and pepper. The labor force was comprised of natives recruited by local rulers who contracted with Dutch managers to deliver fixed quantities of crops.

The Company's administration in the archipelago was headed by a governor-general, assisted by a council and a civil service. Dutch residents, or governors, presided over the crazy-quilt native political patchwork of kings, sultans, and regents who ruled the people. Because of its prosperity, Java attracted Chinese immigrants, who became influential merchants and financiers despite sporadic persecutions directed against them. The presence of various races, gave rise to a plural legal system. *Adat* or native law, coming down from prehistoric times, honored Indonesian traditions; Chinese law obtained for that minority; and Dutch law prevailed for Europeans and Eurasians (persons of mixed Dutch and Indonesian blood).

For almost two centuries the Company acted as agent for the crown. But in the wake of the Napoleonic Wars its end came. After incurring financial losses over the years, in 1798 the Company was dissolved and the crown took over its operations. Java was temporarily (1811–1816) occupied by the British.

Upon their return, the Dutch imposed on Indonesia an authoritarian and strict rule, as a result of which unrest broke out in Java. A five-year revolt (1825–1830) ended with the defeat by the Dutch of Diponegoro, sultan of Jogjakarta. More Dutch political and economic controls were then imposed. These included the "culture system," whereby Indonesian peasants either devoted one-fifth of their cultivated field to the growth of export crops or spent one-fifth of their working hours on government plantations. Production increased in the most profitable crops of coffee, sugar, and indigo, and in the secondary crops of tobacco, cotton, pepper, and tea. Though winds of reform to liberalize colonial policies were now blowing in Europe, they were not felt in Indonesia until after 1850.

10

CHINA AND INNER ASIA 1279–1844

During the period between 1279 and 1844, for the first time alien dynasties ruled over all China. First came the Yüan (Mongol) dynasty, which defeated the Southern Sung. Under the great emperor Kublai Khan, it gave to the Middle Kingdom its most extended boundaries. Foreign domination in this instance was short-lived; it lasted less than a century. The Ming returned native rule to the land. But in the mid-seventeenth century, this dynasty went down under the onslaughts of another seminomadic group. The Ch'ing (Manchu), of alien origin, were the last of the some two dozen dynasties of China. Among their ranks in the first half of their rule were two notable personalities, the K'ang-hsi and Ch'ien-lung emperors. The latter, as the last of the great emperors of China, flourished at a time when the infant federal United States was just commencing national life. But it was during his reign and those of his successors that Westerners—Europeans and Americans—began to arrive in China to trade and to win converts to Christianity. Their way of life clashed with that of the Chinese, and it was the latter who gave in, with the forcible imposition on them by 1844 of the first treaty setlement.

THE YUAN (MONGOL) DYNASTY (1279–1368)

Climaxing the long historical process of border interaction between Chinese and non-Chinese tribes in favor now of the latter, the alien Mongols finally captured all China. In numbers only about one-twentieth of the Chinese at the time, they nevertheless imposed their rule over a great and populous country. But the conquest of China took decades to accomplish and the Southern Sung bitterly held out to the end. Some of the Mongol leaders, notably Kublai Khan, became Sinicized, but Chinese still resented the alien rule. It was during the Yüan period that the early modern European travelers—priests or traders—came into Mongolia and China. Among them Marco Polo was the most publicized, thanks to the memoirs he left of his lengthy sojourn in the land. But Westerners made little impact and the Chinese at the time merely tolerated their presence.

Dynastic Cycle. The Mongol rise to power began in Mongolia and in North China under Temuchin (1167?–1227), known to history as Genghis Khan ("Illustrious Ruler"). Little is recorded of his early life, but after a late start in military campaigns, he became famous in middle age, eventually emerging as overlord of all Mongolian tribes. From his capital at Karakorum (now only an archeological ruin), he sent out his hordes to conquer half the Eurasian heartland. In 1215 Peking fell to him, but only after Chinese traitors had admitted his troops. Enhancing the "Yellow Peril" stereotype associated with Mongol history, the barbarians plundered the capital and massacred the inhabitants.

Upon Genghis's death, his empire was divided into four khanates. His son Ogodai succeded to the one at Karakorum and reopened warfare against the North Chinese. As the Mongols under Ogodai penetrated farther south into China, they met more resistance. The Southern Sung in more hilly terrain put up a stiff fight. Not until 1279 did Kublai Khan, the grandson of Genghis, defeat the last of the Sung and absorb the rest of the country. But even before he mastered all China, the monarch had assumed, Chinese style, a dynastic name, that of Yüan ("Origin"). Ruling from 1264–1294, he moved to Peking and became a Chinese-type emperor. The Chinese, especially in the south which had not experienced alien incursions, as had the North, resented the new foreign rulers. But since the Mongols now governed all China, they could not be ignored. No Chinese government-in-exile operated, and there was no political alternative left; of necessity Chinese historians had to incorporate the Yüan as the next orthodox dynasty.

Mongol Expansion. Kublai not only subdued China but in ambitious foreign programs pushed into peripheral areas. In the south the Mongols conquered Nan-chao, many of whose Tai inhabitants fled, as noted previously, to Laos, Thailand, and

Burma. The Mongols launched expeditions against the Burmans in Pagan and the Vietnamese in Hanoi. They sent sea expeditions to Singosari and into the Malacca Strait. An unsuccessful attempt was made to subdue the Ryukyus. Kublai also launched two invasions of Japan. In 1274 he assembled in Korean waters a fleet that landed in November at Hakata Bay (now Fukuoka) in northwest Kyushu. In a one-day encounter the local Japanese put up a stubborn fight. A storm forced the fleet to withdraw, and the campaign suddenly ended. In 1281, after subduing South China, the Mongol emperor redirected his efforts toward the conquest of Japan. Two fleets, one from Korea and another from southeast China, rendezvoused again that summer in Hakata Bay. The Japanese, who had foreseen another invasion, put up another stiff fight. A hurricane came up, and, as in the previous campaign, helped to drive away the invaders. In Japan as elsewhere, Kublai's wide-ranging expeditions did not establish direct Mongol power, and resulting tributory relationships with South and Southeast Asian countries proved ephemeral.

Decline of the Mongols. After establishing an expansive empire in China under Kublai, the Mongols declined in power. The ruling line lost vigor. Unfavorable administrative factors displayed the usual syndrome related to dynastic decline. Famines, floods, heavy taxation, and revolts were noted. Rebellious groups headed by the White Lotus Society (dating from Sung times) erupted in South China and the lower Yangtze Valley and then spread north. As usual in Chinese history, the rebels infused agrarian distress with religious motivation, in this instance Buddhist heresies. Their cause came to naught. It remained for an organized military band, led by a former peasant, to overthrow alien rule.

Culture. The Mongols appropriated the Chinese bureaucratic structure to govern the country. A minority, they had to govern China as Chinese, yet keep power in their own hands to perpetuate political control. A dyarchy arose, with Mongol officials holding top civilian and most military offices, and Chinese in most other ranks. Kublai Khan appointed to office many foreigners, some of whom rose to be governors of provinces. He discontinued the civil service examinations and streamlined the central bureaucracy by consolidating ministries into four (finance, justice, war, and rites). In order to govern China more effectively, he moved from Karakorum to Peking, which he renamed Khanbalique (Cambaluc). Nearby Shang-tu (Xanadu) served as an alternate residence. The Mongols erected magnificent buildings in Peking, which was rebuilt by an Arab architect over a period of three decades. Kublai tolerated many religions and officially supported several creeds. His mother was a Nestorian. Despite foreign domination, Chinese culture progressed and literary activity broadened. Geographies and gazetteers were compiled. The suspension of the examinations for almost eight decades permitted scholars to experiment with non-Confucian literary forms. The novel became popular.

Under relative peace and prosperity, China, the Near East, and Europe entered into another era of cultural interchange. In an expansive age resembling the T'ang, safe land routes promoted trade, travel, and the exchange of ideas. Islamic influences and Persian art entered China. Sorghum, a major food crop, introduced from India, augmented the North Chinese diet. In turn, Europeans received from China paper money, playing cards, and works on medicine. Chinese influences crept into Persian miniature painting, architecture, music, and ceramics.

Early Westerners. A new dimension was added to Chinese international relations. Beginning with the mid-thirteenth century, Europeans arrived in China, initially as individuals and subsequently as representatives of the incipient Western European nation-states. Friars and traders came to Mongolia or China in search of converts or riches. Early emissaries of the Catholic Church to Mongolia included John of Plano Carpini (in Asia 1245–1247) and William of Rubruck (1252–1255). John of Monte Corvino in Peking (1307–1332) established the Catholic base in China. Among his colleagues was Odoric of Perdonne. Most notable of the traders was the Polo family. In the 1260's, Nicolo and Maffeo Polo traveled in Asia, including Peking, where Kublai received them. On a return trip they brought Nicolo's son, Marco. Between 1275 and 1292, the three entered the service of the Khan. Though the Venetian account of Marco Polo became famous in the West, Chinese histories do not mention the family.

With the collapse of the Mongols and return to nativistic rule in China came the end of Western church and trade. The friar

John of Marignolli (in China between 1340 and 1353) was the last medieval Catholic missionary to serve there. China once again turned inward, and for some centuries held off the West. Contacts with foreigners did not stimulate the Chinese to new ideas. Not only did early Westerners leave a negligible mark, but so did the Yüan themselves. As the first foreign dynasty to rule over all China, they added nothing fundamental to the Chinese way of life.

THE MING DYNASTY (1368–1644)

Considered typical of traditional Chinese dynasties, the Ming era was stable, peaceful, and prosperous. Scholar-gentry, once again recruited by examinations based on Neo-Confucian tenets, governed the state. Ming art grew stereotyped, but the novel proliferated. Cities flourished and were important centers of culture. China's territorial boundaries shrank drastically from Mongol limits, but population increased from around 60 million to over 100 million. Food production, including new crops introduced from the West, kept up with demographic growth.

Dynastic Cycle. In the wake of the Mongol breakup, many rivals contended for imperial power. Chu Yüan-chang (1328–1398) won out and founded the dynasty called Ming ("Bright"). The orphaned peasant lad, a Buddhist monk turned soldier, displayed military ability in his rise to the top. He first established a regional base of power in east-central China, then defeated local rivals, and finally marched on and took Peking in 1368. But he set up his capital at Nanking in the area he knew best. There he erected magnificent buildings and constructed high walls around the city. In consolidating his administration, he reverted to time-honored Chinese institutions. He filled government offices through civil service examinations. Of Buddhist background, he showed some favor to monks of that faith. Probing Central Asia, his troops encountered Tamerlane. The emperor's forces also fought against Japanese pirates who ravaged the China coast but were not able to cope successfully with them.

After Chu Yüan-chang's death, a civil war broke out between a grandson on the throne in Nanking and his uncle, a son

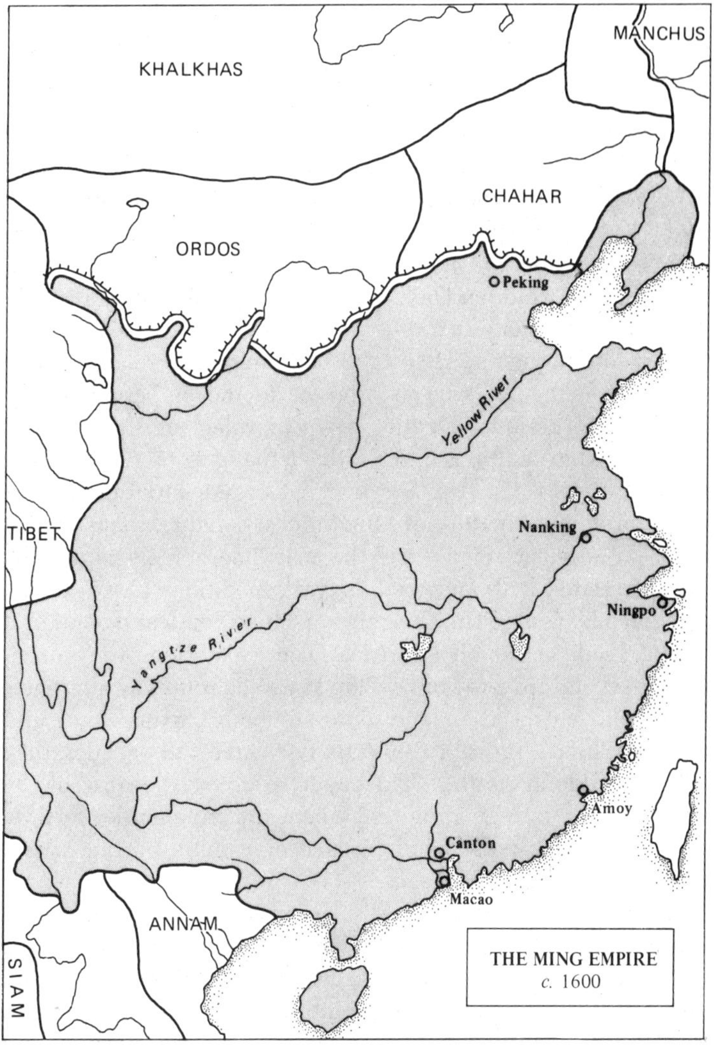
KHALKHAS
MANCHUS
CHAHAR
ORDOS
Peking
Yellow River
TIBET
Nanking
Ningpo
Yangtze River
Amoy
Canton
Macao
ANNAM
SIAM
THE MING EMPIRE
c. 1600

of Chu Yüan-chang, who centered his strength in Peking. The latter won out and assuming the throne as the Yung-lo emperor (r. 1403–1424), moved the seat of government back north. His reign marked the height of Ming power. In domestic affairs, Yung-lo effected the usual policies associated with a strong monarch: improving public works, conducting efficient tax policies, and pacifying border people. He extended Peking, which became a symbol of Ming monumentality and symmetrical architectural forms. Like the earlier T'ang capital of Ch'ang-an, the walled city contained a second walled area for bureaucratic residence, the Imperial City, within which a third walled complex contained the Forbidden City, where the imperial family resided.

Ming Expansion. In a program of imperial expansion, Yung-lo pushed into Mongolia. He established diplomatic relations with the Japanese shoguns, who as advisers to the emperors during Japan's feudal period were the *de facto* rulers of the country. He dispatched expeditions into North Vietnam, where the Chinese remained for two decades. His troops foraged into Burma. But the most prominent feature of Ming international relations during his and subsequent reigns was the maritime achievement. The emperor initiated long and costly naval expeditions (1405–1431), commanded by Cheng Ho, an Arab eunuch, to South and Southeast Asia and lands as far off as Africa. The expeditions were originated for several reasons: to develop sea trade routes as alternates to sealed-off Central Asian land routes, to import luxury items, and to reassert Chinese prestige. But after two and a half decades, they ceased as suddenly as they had begun, probably because of the high cost factor, bureaucratic resentment toward alien leadership, and the ever present Mongol menace of China's northern land borders, close to the capital.

In a return to traditional isolationist ways, the Ming emperors forbade Chinese ships to voyage beyond coastal waters and subjects were not allowed to leave the country. In foreign relations the Ming implemented the tribute system. A misnomer, the tribute system involved more than the exchange of gifts and the kowtow before the emperor. It embraced all aspects of interstate relations, such as the exchange of emissaries, the conduct of diplomatic relations, and the regulation of trade. The Chinese gave as well as took. The whole process probably proved more expensive to the Chinese, whose main aim was pacification rather than conquest of neighbors.

The State. First Nanking, then Peking, was a grand visible symbol of Ming rule. From the capital it continued and refined the three-part system of Chinese government, that of the civilian bureaucracy, military ranks, and censorate or auditors. The monarchs restored the six ministries (revenue, war, justice, rites, public works, and civil office). But with the growth of government and population, local administration became more complex. The Ming divided China into fifteen provinces with circuits, prefectures, subprefectures, and districts or counties. To insure effective tax collections, the Ming kept the usual detailed official land and population registers.

The Chinese educational and examination system became stereotyped. In government and private schools, the curriculum stressed Neo-Confucian philosophical interpretation of the Classics. A book widely used in primary instruction was the *Three Character Classic*, produced in the thirteenth century. The work was a concise summary of basic knowledge consisting of 356 alternately rhyming lines (the second and fourth), each with three characters. With variations, the examination system continued the three-tiered levels of tests at the prefectural, provincial, and central levels. The system recruited the best literary and scholarly minds, but it had drawbacks because the examinations dealt mainly with rote memory of the Classics and adhered to strict forms and styles. During the Ming, the bureaucratic ranks included probably half a million for all China.

After Yung-lo, though the dynasty persisted for over two centuries, there were no emperors of note. The bureaucratic machinery carried on until the mid-seventeenth century, when the dynasty ended. The collapse of the Ming came in the traditional manner. Inept monarchs, administrative abuses, agrarian revolts, growth of tax-free estates, and economic distress plagued the land. The Chinese were divided among themselves. Aspirants to the throne engaged in succession disputes. In the north, one Chinese general invited the leader of the growing Manchu forces in Manchuria to ally with him against a Chinese rival in Peking. The

Chinese general received the foreign aid and troops, who then refused to leave when Peking fell. Instead, the Manchu in time imposed their rule over all of China.

Culture. In intellectual thought, the Ming produced one famous philosopher, Wang Yang-ming (*c.* 1472–1528). His teaching adhered to many traditional Confucian ideas but was influenced by Ch'an Buddhism with its emphasis on intuition and meditation. Though his school became the vogue in Japan (where the founder was called Oyomei), in China it remained a minority one, for Neo-Confucianism had now been established as the state philosophy. Intellectual activity along other lines proceeded. Officials compiled local gazetteers, works of geography, and volumes of medicine, one of which classified 8,000 prescriptions and listed 900 vegetables and 1,000 animal and mineral drugs under 62 classifications. Illustrated encyclopedias were collated. Yung-lo himself ordered an encyclopedia to end all encyclopedias in a mammoth project that consumed the efforts of almost 2,200 scholars, who produced over 11,000 volumes. A 1615 dictionary listed over 33,000 characters according to 214 radicals, or roots, a lexicographic arrangement that persists to this day.

Reflecting the growth of city life with its non-Confucian literary public, the novel flourished. In the Ming at least four of the most popular works assumed final shape. The *Romance of Three Kingdoms,* attributed to a writer of the late fourteenth century, took as its setting the third-century period of political division and civil wars among the Three Kingdoms. *All Men Are Brothers* recounted legends about a minor bandit of Sung times who had been developed by professional storytellers into a Robin Hood character. The *Golden Lotus* was China's first important realistic novel. Strictly a non-Confucian book, the novel dealt with the pursuit of pleasure in city life, and it portrayed women characters realistically. *Monkey* narrated the story of an omnicompetent escort of the great seventh-century Buddhist pilgrim Hsüan-tsang.

Ming monumental sculpture included tombs of the early Ming emperors, with adorning figures, built near the capital. In other fields of art, artisans produced the blue and white porcelain patterns that have come to be associated with the Ming. Sung traditions persisted in landscape painting, but artistic inspiration was stifled by the codification of various theories of painting.

The Economy. New crops entered Ming China. Cotton was introduced and promoted by the government. From the New World came maize, or Indian corn, the sweet potato, and peanuts, which were planted especially in South China and helped to support population growth. Tobacco also entered and persisted in spite of the opposition of the governing classes to its use. From the Western Hemisphere also came a new coin, the Spanish silver peso. This gradually found favor and became so widespread in later centuries that the standard silver unit of Chinese currency, though indigenously minted, was sometimes designated as the Mexican dollar.

European Interests. During the Ming, Westerners representing national interests began to appear in China. Coming up into East Asia via Goa and Malacca, the Portuguese were the first to arrive. In 1517 the first official Portuguese mission, headed by Tomé Pires, anchored at Canton and proceeded to Peking. But because of their boorish manner, its members were returned south and imprisoned. The Portuguese made little dent in China, but in 1557 they received Macao, a small port near Canton, as a leasehold in return for their aid to the Ming against pirates ravaging the coast. An uninviting spot, Macao nonetheless became the anchor pin of European colonial exploits in China, the take-off point for Westerners. The Jesuits, associated mainly with the Portuguese national interest, soon followed; among them was Francis Xavier. Another Jesuit student, Matteo Ricci, sought permission to enter the Middle Kingdom. After a two-decade wait in Macao, he was finally allowed to proceed to Peking, where he revived the Catholic mission until his death in 1610. The Jesuits displayed all types of scientific devices at court in an attempt to gain access to those in top office, but their converts were few. However, they took back to Europe a favorable interpretation of Ming China, with its "philosopher-kings" and sophisticated society.

As the second national European interest in East Asia, the Spanish showed little desire to establish trading or mission posts. They concentrated instead on their Philippine acquisition, where the Chinese colonists developed trade ties with the homeland.

The Dutch were interested but unsuccessful in their attempts to establish Chinese toeholds. The French had no interests in Ming China. The Russians, extending across Siberia, unsuccessfully tried to reach the Ming court. The British came late to China, as they did to India, but they left the most definite imprint. In 1635 the first English vessel reached Canton. Two years later an expedition under Captain John Weddell blasted its way past river forts and Chinese opposition. The forceful British stance proved symptomatic as to the nature of future relations between China and the West. It also gave rise in Europe to a less laudatory interpretation of the Chinese than the Jesuit version.

With internal peace secured and little desire to experiment, the Ming reflected Chinese culturalism and unity. The realm was prosperous and inbred. The dynasty faced seaward and southward, but it still gave priority to Mongol and Central Asian problems. The maritime contacts, albeit temporary, forecast the nature of political events to come. Expansionist Western forces encroached on China, as they did in India, chiefly from the south and the sea, in contrast to traditional invasions from the north by land. At a time when the Western world had begun to expand, the Sinic counterpart had withdrawn. Only through force would it be coaxed out of its semi-isolation.

THE CH'ING (MANCHU) DYNASTY (To 1844)

Like the earlier Mongols, the Ch'ing, or Manchu, line consolidated its political hold over all China. It ruled the greatest extent of territory of any dynasty save for the Mongols. In some ways it resembled its alien predecessor. Both dynasties had strong leaders, who unified home territory before subjugating a weaker China. But the Manchus involved themselves more than the Mongols had with Chinese life and customs. In part because of this fact, they ruled the longer. Their emperors kept the Confucian bureaucracy and structure of state. But one problem with which they coped unsuccessfully was the persistent growth of Western power, which by 1844 had imposed the first treaty settlement.

Initial Rulers. The Manchus came from Ju-chen tribes, like those that had plagued the Northern Sung. Rising in Central and South Manchuria, the Manchus by the early seventeenth century had perfected an efficient military organization. They possessed a script derived from Mongolian. They had an effective leader in Nurhachi (1559–1626), the founder of the Manchu state. He followed in the tradition of Genghis Khan in a rise to power through consolidation of clans and tribes. In 1616 he proclaimed himself khan and appropriated the dynastic title of the Later Chin, to denote Ju-chen descent. Establishing his capital at Shen-yang (modern Mukden), he used Chinese captives and residents as advisers. Adopting Confucianism, he won the tacit support of Chinese in Manchuria, where three million of them went over to his side.

The Manchu line after Nurhachi fortunately had a succession of capable men to consolidate the kingdom. Abahai (1592–1643), the eighth son of the founder of the line, assumed the throne upon his father's death. He took the term *Manchu* (of obscure origin) to supersede the *Ju-chen* appellation. In 1636 at the capital he proclaimed the Ch'ing ("Pure") dynasty. Under his guidance, the Manchus conquered Inner Mongolia and subjugated Korea. They prepared for the conquest of North China, where troops broke through the Great Wall and knocked at the gates of Peking. Next on the Manchu throne was a young son of Abahai, a boy of nine who benefited from a strong regency under his uncle Dorgon. The regent ruled the Manchu kingdom until his death in 1651, by which time the Manchus were securely ensconced in Peking.

While Manchus encroached on Chinese territory, the Ming situation had become desperate. The Manchus' opportunity to replace Ming rule came in 1644, when Peking was overrun by a Chinese rebel army. Wu San-kuei, a fellow Chinese officer and rival, who guarded the Great Wall where it met the North China Sea coast, invited Manchu help to subdue his colleague. The Manchus obliged but then refused to leave Peking after it was captured. Ming remnants fled to the south and to Formosa, where they put up resistance for over a decade. It took the Manchus another fifteen years to complete the conquest of China, but revolts continued to plague the southern provinces.

But strong men continued in imperial position. K'ang-hsi, second of the dynasty in Peking (r. 1661–1722), was one of

China's greatest emperors. Also initially ruling through a regency, at fifteen he broke its power and appropriated political control. A man of great physical energy and intellectual ability, he loved the outdoor life and traveled extensively throughout his empire. Though originating nothing new in statecraft, he reinvigorated the political structure. He quelled the revolts in the south, including one by the former ally, Wu San-kuei. He promoted the well-being of his subjects. He initiated public works; encouraged literature and the arts; subsidized scholarship; financed new editions of the Classics; and composed sixteen short moral maxims. On his death his son, the Yung Cheng emperor, ascended the throne for twelve years (1723–1735).

More noteworthy was K'ang-hsi's grandson, the Ch'ien-lung emperor (r. 1736–1796). He achieved a long life and carried China to another height of political power at home and abroad. He rounded out the boundaries of China and extended military campaigns into Central Asia, Tibet, Nepal, and Burma. At home, through a policy of censorship, he tried to eliminate antidynastic literature. Yet he was interested in other types of learning, and he authorized the compilation of encyclopedias. Like his grandfather, he was a patron of the arts and letters. He achieved domestic order in China, which noted phenomenal increases in wealth and population, from around 110 million at the beginning of his rule to triple that number at its conclusion. In 1796 the emperor abdicated, not wishing to reign longer than his eminent grandfather. Three years later he died.

Manchu Expansion. It took a century for the initial Manchu emperors to consolidate China's borders. Taiwan came into the territorial fold and was eventually incorporated as part of coastal Fukien Province. Inner Mongolia, already under Manchu domination, was supervised by a Superintendency of Dependencies, first in Shen-yang and later in Peking. Sinkiang proved harder to assimilate. In the 1670's Galdan, one of many rebels there, with Tibetan support, conquered the Tarim Basin oases and pushed on to Peking but was defeated in the Gobi Desert. In Sinkiang itself, fighting continued sporadically for another century, but eventually it became the "New Dominion" in the Manchu empire. The Ch'ing also interfered in Tibetan affairs. They conducted three interventions there between 1720 and 1820, after which garrisons and advisers were permanently stationed at Lhasa, the capital. Under Chinese domination, the Dalai Lama and Panchen Lama, as spiritual and secular descendants of Buddhist deities, presided over the Tibetan Buddhist theocracy. From Tibet, Ch'ien-lung sent forces across the Himalayas into Nepal to pacify the Gurkhas, who were forced to recognize Chinese suzerainty.

Along the Burmese border wars also broke out. Despite the indecisive campaigns the Burmese king sent periodical tribute to Peking. Annamese rulers received investiture from the Chinese capital. Though Ch'ing rule did not effectively embrace other areas of Southeast Asia, Chinese cultural influence and physical presence manifested itself in peripheral countries. Into the newly established Southeast Asian colonies, emigrated Chinese, mainly from the marginal southeastern coastal areas. Abroad, Chinese quarters grew in the chief cities. Commercial relations were maintained with Western colonizers, who utilized them to promote trade interests in China. Chinese junks as well as Western ships carried products to South China ports, where other Chinese merchants, called *hong*, processed the merchandise.

Despite border successes, by 1800 the Manchu dynasty registered aspects of cyclical decline. Favorites amassed fortunes; bureaucrats became corrupt; and revolts broke out. The White Lotus group rampaged in the central Yangtze area, while other secret societies conducted anti-Manchu campaigns elsewhere. Following the abdication of Chien-lung, came weak successors, Chia-ch'ing (r. 1796–1820) and Tao-kuang (r. 1821–1850). It was during the reign of the latter that matters came to a head with the West.

Culture. In Manchu cultural life, little was new or striking. In Peking emperors erected more palaces, replacing those of the Mongol and the Ming, which remain to this day. Ceramic forms copied earlier models, though the K'ang-hsi and Ch'ien-lung periods were noteworthy in both monochrome and polychrome specimens. In painting there was imitation of previous masterpieces. Poetry and prose evidenced a commonplace inspiration. There was one outstanding novel, *Dream of the Red Chamber,* an autobiographical account in a riches-to-rags theme of a merchant family dealing in silk. In philosophy the school of *Han Hsüeh* ("Han Learning") sought to return to the original Classics of the Han rather than analyze the works as transmitted by the later Sung Neo-Confucianists. Another school termed "Statecraft," in anti-Manchu statements, sought reasons for Chinese weakness and political decline. These stemmed in part, they argued, from inbred attitudes and mistaken neo-Confucian concentration on human nature rather than on solving practical affairs of state.

During Ch'ing rule, China noted an increased use of land devoted to food crops, which helped sustain the population increase. The Chinese imported a variety of plants, some from the New World, including sorghum, corn, sweet potatoes, peanuts, potatoes, squash, and varieties of beans. The deleterious opium was also imported, chiefly from India. Imperial decreees forbade the sale or importation of opium, but despite the bans the drug was brought into the land by Western firms, which took over the trade. The importation of opium was the immediate cause of the first war between China and Western powers.

CHINA AND THE WEST (To 1844)

As Manchu rule progressed, Westerners came to China to stay. Initially they were restricted to Macao, but Peking later tolerated their part-time presence also in Canton, where trade developed between Western merchants and the South Chinese counterparts. But Westerners, chafing under commercial and individual restrictions, sought more rights in more ports. For their part, the rulers would not accede to such escalation of alien commercial ties. While the Chinese had long experience in dealing with "barbarians," the new Western breed would neither accommodate themselves to nor even tolerate adverse conditions. Matters came to a head in 1839 with the outbreak of the Sino-British conflict. When the undeclared war ended three years later, an unequal treaty was imposed on China, which did not gain reciprocal rights. Within another two years, other major Western countries, including the United States, received similar privileges. The first treaty settlement (1842–1844) marked the end of China's diplomatic isolation, but it left a permanent psychological scar in the Middle Kingdom.

Bases for Conflict. European and American interests in

China were chiefly commercial in nature, but religious groups were also present. The Jesuit Ricci's successors, especially Adam Schall and Ferdinand Verbiest, carried on in the capital from Ming times. During most of K'ang-hsi's reign, the emperor displayed a spirit of toleration toward them and other orders. But theological squabbles among the alien resident missionaries vitiated the cause. In the "Rites Controversy" (1628–1742), semantic debates ranged over appropriate Biblical translations. K'ang-hsi sided with the more tolerant Jesuits, and papal missions and others who formed a contrary verdict were expelled. Ch'ien-lung continued the strong policy of suppression. Catholic missions atrophied in China, not only because of hard-hitting Chinese policies but also because of conditions in Europe. The Jesuit order was proscribed by Pope Clement XIV in 1773, and the French Revolution and a secularist climate of opinion distracted from the evangelical spirit of missionary endeavor.

As missions declined in China, trade with the West increased. Economically self-sufficient, China, like India and Southeast Asian lands, did not need Western products. By the nineteenth century the Chinese desired from abroad only a few commodities (opium, furs, and certain foodstuffs). The Western merchants wanted tea and silk, the two traditional Chinese exports, on which they made great profits back home. Southern Chinese merchants co-operated with Western traders because they also profited from commerce. They often disregarded Peking's orders regulating international commerce. At Macao the Portuguese at first enjoyed a monopoly of trade. Other Western nationalities arrived, but in the ensuing centuries the English East India Company, expanding from India, overtook the Portuguese and all the others to become pre-eminent in the South China trade.

Because of official policy, trade was confined in the south to Macao and Canton. In the latter port, Peking sought to control foreign trade through the appointment of specific hongs, banded together into a *co-hong* (a type of guild) to handle commercial matters with aliens. The monopolistic system was regarded as an inequity by Westerners, who desired more flexible trade arrangements. In the so-called Canton trade, foreigners were confined in residence and business activity to a suburb (Shameen), though their ships discharged cargoes farther downstream at the Whampoa Island anchorage. They had to conduct operations through the merchant, or hong, assigned to them; each nationality was responsible to a certain hong who in turn was responsible to the *hoppo,* the customs superintendent for Kwangtung Province, of which Canton was the capital. Western merchants chafed under these limitations. But the Chinese made the rules, and if the aliens desired to trade, as they did for profit, they had to face inequities.

Russia was the only Western state to penetrate China by land from the north and into the capital, the place that counted the most. As early as 1656, a mission from the czar arrived in Peking for purposes of trade, but it met with no success. Subsequent missions were similarly unsuccessful, and occasional warfare erupted along the border. In 1689 a treaty at the border town of Nerchinsk settled Sino-Russian differences. It was the first treaty between China and a Western state, and an agreement concluded between equals rather one forced on China. The articles defined mutual boundaries, regulated commerce, and provided for extradition. Over the ensuing century, other agreements further refined the nature of bilateral relations.

In the south basic issues, besides trade matters, separated Westerner and Chinese. The former advanced the sovereign equality of nations; the latter kept up tributary notions and termed Westerners "barbarians," even in official correspondence. Western law guaranteed individual rights; Chinese jurisprudence posited group responsibility for individual wrongdoing. Westerners wanted fully publicized, low, and regularized tariffs; the Chinese imposed ad hoc, quixotic rates. Westerners objected to dealing only with the hong merchants; the Chinese refused to widen trade contacts. Western life and residence were restricted to Macao in the winter months and Shameen in the summer; the Chinese intended to keep it that way.

Western merchants became increasingly restive. Though spearheading the Western cause in the Canton trade, the British made little dent on Chinese rulers. In contrast to their contemporaneous successes in India, the English East India Company made little gain in expanding China operations. In 1787 it designated Lieutenant Colonel Charles Cathcart as special envoy to Peking to negotiate for improvements in trade conditions, but he died before reaching the capital. Five years later, Lord George Macartney was named chief of another mission, which reached Peking but was unsuccessful. In 1816 the British dispatched Lord Amherst, whose failure at the capital was more resounding than Macartney's. In 1834, the year after the monopolistic hold of the Company was abolished, Lord Napier was dispatched to Canton as the first Superintendent of British Trade to represent all British firms. He was similarly instructed to obtain concessions, but he never managed to depart Canton for Peking.

Like the British and other Europeans, the Americans desired additional rights in China, including rights equal to any which might be granted to third parties. This oft-enunciated plank of the Open-Door policy was as old as American presence in Asia. In 1784 the first American ship, the *Empress of China,* sailed for Canton from New York with a heterogeneous cargo, including furs. Other vessels soon followed. To regularize trade, resident American trading firms were soon established in Canton. In 1787 Samuel Shaw was appointed American consul, resident at Canton. As the first official United States representative in China, Shaw administered estates of Americans who died in Canton, disciplined mutinous sailors, and left an informative diary reporting some of his problems of office. Mission work augmented trade concern. In 1829 the first Protestants arrived in Canton, and other missionaries, including Catholics, soon followed. American naval vessels sailed upstream to Canton to remind the Chinese of an American iron fist within a velvet glove, a tactic the British were similarly pursuing.

The Opium War. The issue of opium triggered the first conflict. In 1839 Commissioner Lin Tse-hsü arrived in Canton from Peking to deal with the matter. He compelled Westerners to deliver their stocks, which were then mixed with salt, lime, and water, and dumped into the river. Protesting, the British retired to regroup forces in the nearby uninhabited island of Hong Kong. Conflict shortly erupted between the British and Chinese, but war was never declared. Chinese forces were defeated by the British in lopsided campaigns in South and Central China. In August, 1842, a peace treaty was signed on the deck of the *Cornwallis,* a British warship anchored off Nanking in the Yangtze River.

First Treaty Settlement. The terms of the Treaty of Nanking generally reflected immediate British and over-all Western objectives in China. Five ports—Canton, Amoy, Foochow, Ningpo, and Shanghai—all south of the Yangtze, were now opened to British trade. In these ports, the British could station a superintendent of trade or consular official and were granted rights in leased settlements or concessions (not necessarily cessions), where they might reside. In Canton the monopolistic co-hong was abolished and there, as well as in the other ports, the British could trade with whomever Chinese they wished. British-Chinese official intercourse was placed on a plane of diplomatic equality. Reflecting the mid-nineteenth century British free-trade philosophy, the treaty terms fixed the tariff at a low 5 percent ad valorem. As losers in the war, the Chinese paid an indemnity of $21 million. They also ceded Hong Kong in perpetuity to the British. The treaty stated nothing on opium, other than payment ($6 million of the over-all indemnity) for the confiscated lot.

In October, 1843, in the supplementary Treaty of the Bogue, the British elaborated commercial terms and received extraterritoriality in criminal cases. According to this principle of international law, foreigners in alien lands are tried according to their own law codes by their own judges. This second treaty also delineated the most-favored-nation clause.

Four months after the Treaty of Nanking was signed, President John Tyler of the United States requested Congress for authority to send an emissary to China to conclude a similar treaty. With Congressional approval, the post was conferred on Caleb Cushing of Massachusetts, a member of the House Committee of Foreign Affairs and a friend of the president's. In February, 1844, Cushing arrived in Macao, where the Chinese stalled him off. He then threatened to proceed directly to Peking to negotiate the treaty. The threat resulted in Chinese signature of a treaty, known after his name (or the Wang-hsia Treaty after a Macao suburb where it was concluded). Its terms followed in general those of the two British agreements (without any territorial cession), but the American version extended extraterritoriality to include civil as well as criminal cases.

Last of the major parties, the French concluded the Whampoa Treaty of 1844 along similar lines. With subsequent revisions, the treaties in the aggregate provided the legal basis for Western rights in China over the following century. Their all-encompassing terms included the opening of ports, regularizing of commercial representation, grants of leaseholds in concessions for residential purposes, territorial cessions, payment of indemnities, tariff controls, extraterritoriality in both civil and criminal cases, and freedom of worship. As a result of the treaties, Western presence came to the coastal provinces of China south of the Yangtze. But with it came increasing problems for the Chinese and Manchu. There was now no containing the alien thrust.

11
NORTHEAST ASIA
1185–1868

In Northeast Asia, the period from 1185 to 1868 constituted a time of relative isolation. While Korea continued to receive cultural impulses from China and remained a vassal of Chinese dynasties, Japan, thanks to its insular geographic position, continued to shape its historical destiny along policy lines set by its leaders. When in the mid-nineteenth century, the West arrived in both countries, the Koreans kept its emissaries at arm's length, but the Japanese, involved in a more forceful confrontation, opened their doors.

KOREA

Under the Koryo dynasty, Korea continued to be a vassal of China, but changing political events there were reflected in the peninsula. First invaded by the Khitan, it then allied with the Ju-chen, but was finally conquered by the Mongols. As the T'ang collapse earlier resulted in the end of the Silla in Korea, so the Mongol replacement by the Ming ended Koryo rule. In a succession fight, the commander of the Koryo forces, Yi Song-gye, deposed the monarch and initiated a new dynasty after his family name. The Yi dynasty (Li in Chinese) in Seoul endured over five centuries (1392–1910).

The State. In time-honored precedent, Yi Song-gye followed the Chinese political model in fashioning the central organs of government. Its main branches included the state council, secretariat, the six ministries, and censorate. Local government units included the usual provinces and their districts or counties. Of special importance were the "Merit Subjects" and "Minor Merit Subjects," Yi's close and less close associates, who filled top bureaucratic ranks. Entrance to office was filled mainly by the examination system on the Classics, but successful applicants were effectively limited to the upper class. The dynastic founder also embarked on a redistribution of the land, over which great confusion and tax-free estates had grown during the Mongol period. A wide range of civil servants benefited from new titles of land, and in time an officeholder-landlord (*yangban*) class rose. Below them, in the Korean social hierarchy were the "middle" people, the vast bulk of commoners, and the "lowborn" class. After the first century of rule, when the Yi was particularly creative and efficient, the dynastic decline commenced. It was manifested not by revolts and economic problems but rather in continued and disruptive bureaucratic factionalism and power struggles relating to court policies and personalities.

Culture. Under the Yi monarchs, Korea remained a vassal of the successive Ming and Ch'ing dynasties in China. Tribute was sent to Peking, which bestowed titles upon the peninsular kings. Cultural and commercial contacts remained close. Neo-Confucianism flourished as the state doctrine. The Chinese did not attempt to annex Korea physically; they were content to let their neighbor remain in tributary status. Many of Korean cultural traits derived from China. Mahayana Buddhism, the classical literature, civil service ranks, architectural forms, and the Chinese script were some of the more basic affiliations. Formal education stressed Confucian classics. There appeared scholarly works and histories, some of which were printed by movable type. The fifteenth century was a particularly creative one. In 1446 the fourth Yi ruler, Sejong, promulgated the *h'angul* (Korean letters) alphabet for the vernacular, but it was little used. Buddhist imagery continued. In ceramics, the beautiful Koryo ware was replaced by more commonplace pottery.

Foreign Relations. With Japan, Yi monarchs had problems. Japanese pirates infested coastal waters. In 1420 Korean and Japanese forces met in combat on Tsushima, an island in the strait that separates Korea from Kyushu Island. In the 1590's came serious Japanese invasions; Seoul was taken and Korean armies defeated. But guerrilla warfare plagued the occupiers and iron-clad Korean "Tortoise Boats" disrupted Japanese maritime connections with the home base. By the end of the century, the Japanese had evacuated but they left behind a desolate country and a heritage of bitterness. In 1609 a formal peace treaty between the Yi and the Japanese was negotiated on Tsushima Island.

A new threat then came from the north. As the Manchus were taking over North China, they spilled over into Korea, which accepted the Ch'ing suzerainty in accordance with the traditional Confucian pattern of elder-younger brother relationships as extended into international life. Limited contact was maintained with the Japanese. In Pusan there was a small colony of Japanese, and Tsushima Island provided an intermediary stop for the dozen or so official missions sent by Seoul to Japan after 1600.

Korea had only negligible contacts with the Occident. In the second half of the eighteenth century, Christianity ("Western Learning" to Koreans) began to penetrate the peninsula with Korean envoys returning from Peking. Chinese and French missionaries later spread the Gospel. But there were few conversions to the new doctrine, and the government endeavored to halt its spread. Persecutions broke out as early as 1801 and continued sporadically through later decades. At the same time, Western ships, including American, began to visit the Korean coast to make demands for trade and diplomatic representation. The Yi dynasty remained unreceptive to foreign pressures. In the midst of dynastic disintegration, the "Hermit Kingdom," absorbed in factional struggles, pursued its traditional ways.

FEUDAL JAPAN (1185–1603)

In feudal Japan, rearrangements of social and economic life proceeded, and new political forces became prominent. Militarism played a particularly conspicuous role in local and central leadership. Military families, replacing the Fujiwara, became shogunal powers, exercising indirect authority through the emperor. The warriors and their retainers assumed importance. As militarism grew, Japan fell apart politically. Yet while rule was decentralized, it was effective on a smaller scale. Because of near incessant warfare and civil strife, economic and social divisions between city and country, noble and commoners, became less marked. Agriculture, transportation, and trade improved. Buddhism won many converts. Reaching its political nadir, Japan in the latter half of the sixteenth century was then reunited in successive steps by three strong men.

The Minamoto Shogunate. After defeating the Taira family and its allies in 1185, Yoritomo of the Minamoto family established his government at Kamakura, near modern Tokyo. Thus for the first time in Japanese history, the real political center (1185–1333) was removed from emperor and court at Heian. In 1192 a retired emperor bestowed on Yoritomo the title of *shogun,* with which went control of the central military forces. His administration became known as the shogunate, or *bakufu* ("Tent Government"). It kept much of the traditional structure, including the imperial house, the provincial governors, and the local administrators, which dated from the Taika Reforms of the mid-seventh century.

However, Yoritomo added to tradition. He streamlined bureaucracy into three main organs: a central policy-making body, a board to administer affairs of his retainers, and a court of appeals to rule on traditional feudal law. In an attempt to regulate land distribution, he appointed in each estate a steward who was directly responsible to him. He also appointed in each province one retainer as protector, essentially a military position. Protectors were also responsible to Yoritomo. Feudal subordinates followed his lead in appointing similar positions in their fiefs. The system, with only minor modifications, persisted into the nineteenth century. (From steward and protector ranks later evolved the samurai warriors and the daimyo or "great lords.") The resulting domination of military authority had lasting effects. Japan had rejected the Chinese example of the educated civilian bureaucrat and, like medieval European countries, turned to a hereditary and landed aristocratic rule based on military strength.

The Hojo Interim. Yoritomo died in 1199. His successors were too weak to stay in power. Rule passed into the hands of the Hojo, a family related to the defeated Taira and also to Yoritomo's widow Lady Masa, who sided with them. The Hojo did not themselves want to become shoguns but set up princes in the position and acted as regents to these nominal rulers. Because of superimposed and sometimes conflicting duties, complex patterns of political power arose. In Kyoto there was a titular emperor, who had been supplanted by a Fujiwara regent or a cloistered emperor. These imperial persons were in theory directed from Kamakura by a shogun, who, however, now took orders from a Hojo regent. In 1221 Toba II, a retired emperor, tried to overthrow the system but failed. The Hojo regents then ringed the imperial position with more restrictions. Meanwhile, rural life continued as usual. Peasants had few property rights and were liable to military conscription. However, because of the economic and military conditions of the time, the lower classes gradually participated in a broadening social system.

End of the Kamakura Government. Eventually, Hojo power declined. The ruling line weakened. Succession disputes arose and factional strife intensified as emperors came and went. At one time five ex-emperors lived in Kyoto. Warriors were corrupted by luxurious court life. Retainer loyalty, strong to Yoritomo, weakened to his figurehead successors. Confidence in government broke down. The Mongol invasions of 1274 and 1281 further weakened Kamakura rule, especially as retainers who fought off the invaders were not rewarded. The events that finally caused the Hojo downfall originated in Kyoto. Daigo II, the titular emperor, aspired to actual political power and in 1331 began a rebellion. Ashikaga Takauji, the Kamakura general sent against him, went over to the royal cause and seized Kyoto for the emperor. The rebellion spread, and anti-Hojo forces captured and burned Kamakura. In 1333 the Hojo regency came to an end.

The Ashikaga Shogunate. With newfound help, Daigo II sought to re-establish imperial rule. But the opportunistic Ashikaga general instead seized Kyoto and drove the monarch into southern exile, where he set up court at Yoshino in the mountains near Nara. For five decades Japan had two rival courts at two capitals. In 1338 Ashikaga Takauji appointed himself shogun, and his line maintained the position in Kyoto until 1573. But unlike the Minamoto and early Hojo regents, the Ashikaga never established control over the warrior class. They maintained the Kamakura structure of stewards and protectors, but beyond the capital it was ineffectual. A half-century of political and military turmoil ensued. In 1382 the third Ashikaga shogun, Yoshimitsu, achieved the return to Kyoto of the Southern court, but no descendant of Daigo ever occupied the throne. The later Ashikaga-sponsored emperors were impoverished and powerless.

Feudal warfare was continuous. Shoguns fought provincial nobles and feudal lords, who were despots or petty kings in their domains. As a result of famine and oppressive taxation, peasants rose in revolt. Large Buddhist temples and monasteries with their own forces fought each other, the court, and feudal lords. A nadir was reached during the Onin War (so-called after the reign name of the emperor) when fighting became a regular feature in the streets of the capital.

Reunification. Oda Nobunaga (1534–1582) was the first of the three great men involved in the reunification of Japan. The son of a minor provincial lord, Nobunaga achieved military and political success in his own region and was then asked by the titular emperor to restore order in Kyoto. He controlled the Ashikaga figureheads but did not assume the shogunate when the position became vacant in 1573. Nobunaga ruled the capital and its surrounding territory from Azuchi, a castle town near Kyoto. After containing his political enemies, he directed his forces against the militant Buddhist orders and broke their power. Taking strong measures against both religious and secular enemies, Nobunaga gained ascendancy over half Japan. In 1582 he was assassinated by one of his men.

After an ineffectual interim regency, Toyotomo Hideyoshi (1536–1598), who had begun as a foot soldier and risen to become one of Nobunaga's lieutenants, came to the fore. In great campaigns with up to 250,000 troops, Hideyoshi conquered northern Honshu, Shikoku, and Kyushu. Though he did not accede as shogun, he assumed the title of dictator, *Kampaku.* Restoring prestige to the imperial court, he rebuilt royal palaces and erected others, including Momoyama near Kyoto. Reflecting his military background, he ruled through the old feudal system of vassalage. Like Yoritomo, he centralized actual authority but permitted the daimyo vassals to enjoy local autonomy. As had been done in acts dating to the Taika reforms, he conducted a land survey of all Japan and kept census records up to date. In 1588 the "sword hunt" law ordered the disarming of all but military men. Other feudal edicts attempted to stabilize class distinctions, occupations, and places of residence.

In his later years, Hideyoshi tended toward megalomania. Aiming to conquer China, he launched invasions on Korea as a prelude. He wanted to incorporate Southeast Asia as well into a

Japanese empire. None of these dreams was realized, but posterity bestowed on Hideyoshi a high place in Japanese history. Because his policies were based more on his personal dominance than on institutions, some of these did not last long after him. After his death another regency was formed for his son, but Tokugawa Ieyasu (1542–1616) won out in the struggle for power. In 1600 he defeated his rivals in the Battle of Sekigahara (in a pass near Lake Biwa). Three years later he assumed the title of shogun but located, as had Yoritomo, outside the capital in his home territory, the Kanto plain. Japan then began the Tokugawa period, the last traditional epoch in Japanese history, with *de facto* rule centered at Edo (old Tokyo).

Growth of Buddhism. The feudal era witnessed major developments in Japanese Buddhism. The Mahayana faith became popularized and took on Japanese forms. The common people and the military elite accepted the new schools for various reasons, including the desires to escape the perennial warfare and to find easy paths to salvation. The keystone of the new doctrines was salvation by faith, similar to the bhakti of Indian philosophy. In 1175 the monk Honen (1133–1212) founded the *Jodo* (in Chinese, Ching-t'u or "Pure Land") sect, which stressed faith in the western paradise of the Buddha Amida. Following the Chinese school, it held that salvation could be achieved by a repetitious *nembutsu* of Amida's name. One of Honen's disciples, Shinran (1173–1262), carried this concept further in his *Jodo Shinshu* ("True Pure Land") sect, which maintained that *one* true invocation of Amida would suffice for salvation. Another major school was named after its founder, Nichiren (1122–1282), who held that salvation could be achieved by invoking the Lotus sutra. A religious fanatic, Nichiren was intolerant of other schools, an unusual trait in Asian Buddhist history. A distinct school was Zen Buddhism, which emphasized meditation as the means to discover salvation and believed in sudden enlightenment through inner experience. This concept in Buddhistic thought arose in India and was accepted by the Chinese Ch'an sect. It was brought into Japan by monks who had studied in China.

Culture. The Buddhist faith was manifested in art and architecture. The 52-foot bronze Daibutsu ("Great Buddha"), representing Amida at Kamakura, was a monumental creation of sculpture. Some of the larger temples were decorated with secular picture scrolls or *nise-e* ("likenesses"). The feudal age left no outstanding literature, though at court, poetry anthologies, travel diaries, and military stories were composed. An innovation in poetry was the *renga* ("chain poem"), in which the traditional thirty-one-syllable tanka was split in alternating three- and two-unit lines of 5-7-5 and 7-7 syllables. Zen monks developed, though they did not originate, Japan's first great dramatic form, the *No* ("Ability") drama. They also imported from China the arts of landscape gardening, flower arrangement, and the tea ceremony.

In the later feudal period, the Ashikaga shoguns provided a cultural center at Kyoto. Upon Yoshimitsu's retirement to Buddhist orders in 1397, he built as his residence the *Kinkakuji* ("Golden Pavilion"), which was burned in 1950 and as yet has not been completely restored. Yoshimasa, the eighth shogun, upon his retirement in 1473, constructed the *Ginkakuji* ("Silver Pavilion"). In the Sung dynastic style, impressionistic landscape painting flourished. Ashikaga painters attempted, like the Chinese, to suggest the essence of nature in a few brush strokes. Sesshu (1420–1506) was probably the greatest Japanese artist of this line painting. The Kano school made landscape painting into a stereotyped art monopolized by hereditary traditions. The Tosa school, also a hereditary one, painted historical scenes.

Economy. Domestic trade flourished, and a money economy augmented the barter system. Commercial centers included castle towns, such as Osaka and Edo, which were built around daimyo capitals; port towns, such as Sakai, the port for Osaka; and temple towns near important Buddhist or Shinto shrines and monasteries. A merchant class arose, and guilds (*Za*) became prominent. Overseas trade, mainly with China, revived. In 1404 Yoshimitsu reinstigated official missions to China (which had been stopped by the Heian court in 894). Trade was carried on through private and official missions as well as by illegal channels. Despite depredations of pirates, the trade (mainly in luxury items) was profitable. Among those who participated in it were the shogun and court, feudal families, and Buddhist monasteries, particularly the Zen orders.

Advent of the West. Foreigners shared in Japanese trade. The Portuguese were the first Westerners to arrive in Japan. The traditional account is that in 1542 Portuguese sailors landed at Tanegashima, an island off south Kyushu. Other Portuguese ships followed, and the southern feudal lords adopted foreign trade and weapons. Missionaries soon arrived. In 1549 the Jesuit Francis Xavier landed in southern Kyushu, and he spent two years in the country preaching the faith. The Spanish followed the Portuguese into Japan, but they sent only a few missionaries. When Hideyoshi had gained control of western Japan, in 1587, he issued a decree ordering all Christian missionaries to leave the country. A decade later, he began the first major persecution. However, Westerners continued to filter into Japan. The Dutch followed the Portuguese and Spanish, but by 1600 none of the alien groups had made significant impact.

TOKUGAWA JAPAN (1603–1868)

After the reunification of Japan, the Tokugawa shogunate chose as its overriding policy that of stability and isolation. Remembering the past periods of disunity and civil war, the shoguns resisted change, tried to freeze society at home, and aimed to keep foreign contacts at bay. This policy was immediately successful, for Japan had two and a half centuries of stability and isolation. But the price was high. The shoguns retained feudal institutions during the centuries when the Occidental countries were entering the modern age. After Perry helped to force open its doors in 1854, Japan experienced serious policy debates, which resolved themselves forcibly, through domestic and external factors, in favor of accepting the West and modernization.

The State. From their great fortress complex at Edo (part of which is now the imperial palace), the Tokugawa ruled Japan. They kept up a feudal structure involving vassals, political hierarchies, and ranks of society. In their capital, the Tokugawa developed a centralized bureaucracy, including a prime minister, a top advisory council of half a dozen elders, a similar number of junior elders to supervise petty vassals, and a corps of *metsuke* (secret police). The shogunate maintained strict control over the emperor and Kyoto court three hundred miles away. The emperors, in or out of office, continued to be weak.

Social Classes. The daimyo, or feudal lords, were divided into three categories. First were the branch families of the Tokugawa itself, who were strategically located at Mito east of Tokyo, Nagoya in central Honshu, and Wakayama near Osaka. Second were the so-called *fudai* ("inside") lords, who had been allies or vassals of Ieyasu before the Battle of Sekigahara. Last were the *tozama* ("outside") lords, who had been enemies of the Tokugawa before this battle. Through the principle of alternate attendance, all daimyo spent time at Edo. The daimyo were also ranked according to their rice production. To become a daimyo, a lord was required to possess lands with an annual yield of at least 10,000 *koku* (about 50,000 bushels) of rice. The size and number of estates varied from time to time as family lines ended or as fiefs increased, divided, or were appropriated by the shoguns.

In addition to ranking the lords, the Tokugawa stratified society on the basis of occupation. They established four classes which were designated as hereditary. The highest class comprised military administrators who were drawn from the daimyo and their samurai (a term now applied to the entire military class). The peasants came second as primary producers; they probably made up about 85 percent of the populace. The third rank consisted of artisans and the fourth of merchants, who according to time-honored Confucian theory were parasites. Like previous Japanese political eras, Tokugawa was regulated by numerous codes and laws. Some related to royal affairs; some were directed toward feudal nobility, others concerned the public; and a few were comprehensive in scope. The shoguns continually preached and exhorted the people to behave and to work hard.

Isolationism. The Tokugawa sealed off the country from abroad. After initial gains, early Western contacts were not allowed to continue. In 1600 the the first Dutch ship reached Japan with an English pilot, Will Adams, whose ability and ingenuity gained him a position with Ieyasu. Other Dutch ships followed, and a Dutch factory was established at Hirado, an island near Nagasaki. The English came late to Japan and did not remain long; after some years on Hirado, they gave up the venture to concentrate on India and Southeast Asia.

Though Ieyasu tolerated the Dutch, in 1613 he began to persecute Christians, as had Hideyoshi, in order to ferret out possible political subversion. This campaign suddenly intensified in 1637–1638, when peasants of Shimabara near Nagasaki, who had early converted to Christianity, revolted against economic and religious oppression. Under leadership of some *ronin* (masterless samurai), 30,000 peasants held out in an old fortress for almost three months against 100,000 government troops supported by Dutch ships. The rebels were finally massacred. Thereafter, Christianity, which at its height had an estimated half a million Japanese converts, ceased to exist as an organized religion in Japan.

Allied with the proscription of Christianity was the termination of foreign trade outlets. Commerce was closed to most foreign contacts, and alien traders for the most part departed voluntarily or were expelled. Some Chinese and the Dutch trading post at Deshima (an island in Nagasaki Bay to which the Dutch had moved from Hirado) were tolerated. But the Dutch East India Company merchants were kept in virtual imprisonment. As foreigners were not permitted to enter the country, so the Japanese were not allowed to leave it. Those who had gone abroad were forbidden to return lest they bring in undesirable ideas. Construction of large vessels was prohibited. The expansion of Japanese trade abroad ceased. The relatively many Japanese residing abroad, particularly in Southeast Asia, were absorbed into the populations of those areas.

The Economy. Though the Tokugawa shoguns could control foreign contacts, they could not stifle indigenous social, economic, and cultural changes. One development was the growth of cities. With samurai and warriors grouping in or near their lords, castle towns increased in size. The processions of daimyo trains on alternate attendance to and from Edo stimulated trade along the routes, especially the Tokaido. The merchant class, though placed in a low social rank, gained influence through its financial and economic power. Class distinctions broke down because of interclass contacts and marriages. Town guilds fragmented into smaller trade units. Wholesale and retail family firms became more prominent. (The Mitsui, one of the largest private enterprises in the world today, began during this period.)

As the merchants became richer, the military class declined. Daimyo and samurai fell into debt because of increased urban expenses and luxury living. The peasant class also experienced changes. Village industries developed in silk production, textile weaving, and *sake* brewing. In every village there was at least one farming family of more wealth and prominence than the rest. Other villagers lived marginal existences or were dispossessed and drifted to the cities, to become unskilled or semiskilled laborers. By the end of the Tokugawa, all major classes had problems. Peasants were generally overtaxed; military-administrators inherited hollow prestige and increasing debts; merchants and artisans lacked political and economic status.

Culture. The great cities of Edo, Osaka, and Kyoto became Tokugawa cultural centers. Reflecting prosperity, Tokugawa architecture became more garish. Elaborate palaces and public buildings were erected, including the Nikko shrines which were the mausoleums for Ieyasu and his grandson. Sculpture was secondrate. In art, *ukiyo-e* ("floating world") pictures, portraying daily secular life, became prominent, particularly in wood-block prints. Among the best-known of the later wood-block artists were Katsushika Hokusai (1760–1849), who made a series of "Thirty-six Views of Mount Fuji," and Ando Hiroshige (1797–1858), who produced two editions of "Fifty-three Stations on the Tokaido."

In literature puppet drama developed. Called *bunraku* after the puppets, *joruri* after the texts, or *gidayu* after the name of an early playwright, it centered at Osaka, where it still flourishes today. The major figure in early puppetry was Chikamatsu Monzaemon (1653–1724), whose librettos were derived from historical drama and contemporary domestic themes. Another dramatic form which arose during the Tokugawa period was the *Kabuki,* which took its themes from various religious and secular sources. Like the No, the Kabuki often used a chorus to chant the narrative parts. The Kabuki survived through family lines of great performers, and the Kabukiza theater in Tokyo maintains the tradition today. In poetry, the tanka and renga were refined to the terse *haiku,* three lines arranged in a 5–7–5 syllabic sequence. Probably the greatest haiku poet was Batsuo Basho (1644–1694), a former Edo samurai. Printing by wood-block method gave impetus to secular literature, including the novel, which reflected contemporary urbanization. Ihara Saikaku (1642–1693), a major novelist of the period, depicted the city life of his native Osaka.

Tokugawa Japan also experienced a changing intellectual climate. In the later years of the era, some intellectuals became dissatisfied with the existing governmental structure and idealized the periods of imperial power before the shogunate. In order not to appear subversive, the historians did not discuss the Tokugawa period, but the implication was clear that they wanted to restore power to the emperor. However, because of government restrictions and their own lack of organization, these nationalistic ideologists did not develop cohesive leadership.

Foreign influences advocating modernization also seeped into Japan, chiefly through the Dutch at Deshima. In 1720 the shogunate removed its ban on the study of Western subjects and books, excepting those on Christianity. A small but inquiring group began to study European scientific works. Certain men were assigned to learn Dutch, though close watch was kept over them as well as the Dutch. By the middle of the nineteenth century, Japanese had become skilled in some Western sciences and techniques, including gunnery, smelting, ship-building, cartography, and medicine. Such men and ideas helped to end the shogunate and begin the modernization of Japan.

The Opening of Japan. By the mid-nineteenth century, there were varying factors ready to change Japan. Western efforts to open the country were finally successful in the person of Commodore Matthew C. Perry. (Earlier Russians, British, and Americans had tried and failed.) As a Pacific power, the United States was especially interested in Japan, for commercial, strategic, and political reasons. In July, 1853, Perry with four ships sailed directly into Edo Bay. His arrival, forewarned by the Dutch, was unwelcomed. He presented to shogunate officials a letter from President Millard Fillmore requesting terms of peace, friendship, and free trade. Then he left, with the firm announcement that he would return within a year to sign a treaty along such lines.

The American presence posed a dilemma for the shogunate. The shogun was ill (he died before Perry returned), and his advisers were divided in opinion. Finally they decided on drastic steps. They lifted all restrictions on ship-building; they solicited opinions of the daimyo, who were also divided on the question of opening the country; and they consulted the emperor. This was the first time in six and a half centuries that the imperial advice had been sought by the shogunate on an important matter of state. The problem was still unsettled when Perry returned ahead of schedule in February, 1854, with seven ships. Under this pressure, the Tokugawa concluded a treaty (the Treaty of Kanagawa) the following month. Its provisions included most ideas outlined in the presidential letter: humane treatment for shipwrecked American sailors; some trade, supply bases for Americans at Shimoda in central Honshu and Hakodate in Hokkaido, with consular residence at the former port; and the most-favored-nation clause. Within two years, other settlements were concluded between the Japanese and the major European powers.

To implement the provisions of the American treaty, in August, 1856, Townsend Harris, a New York merchant who had traded in Asia, was sent to Shimoda as the first American consul-general in Japan. Harris arrived in Japan alone and was promptly isolated in Shimoda, not the most pleasant post. But he was patient. In 1857 he concluded a convention with the shogunate that allowed Americans to reside in Shimoda and Hakodate, to obtain maritime supplies at Nagasaki, and to have extraterritoriality in criminal cases. Harris then went to Edo to seek a full commercial treaty. Without a show of force, he concluded a new treaty which was signed in July, 1858, on an American ship in Tokyo Bay. This treaty opened to trade four additional ports: Nagasaki, Kanagawa, Niigata, and Kyogo (Kobe); granted the right of American residence at Osaka and at Edo; and extended extraterritoriality to civil cases. It also provided freedom of worship for American residents, regulated customs duties, and contained the usual most-favored-nation clause. The shogunate, taking note of Western demands in China at the same time, seemed satisfied with the terms, though the emperor did not ratify either the convention or the treaty, as he had the Perry one. Yet in spite of divided home counsels, the shogunate sent a mission of ratification to Washington in 1860.

The End of the Shogunate. The shogunate was caught between domestic pressures. Many daimyo resented the presence of an increasing number of foreigners. They pressed for an adamant exclusion policy tinged with *kokutai,* the Japanese brand of nationalism. Others compromised by advocating self-strengthening with selective adoption of Western ideas. One advocate of this policy was Yoshida Shoin (1830–1859), from the tozama Choshu clan in western Honshu, who advocated the abolition of feudalism, emancipation of peasants, and creation of a modern army. A few Japanese opted for complete Westernization. Among them was Fukuzawa Yukichi (1834–1901), a versatile man who advanced utilitarian and liberal ideas, edited a newspaper, and founded Keio University.

The final decade of the Tokugawa shogunate witnessed a struggle between daimyo supporting the isolationist emperor and those backing the shogunate, which under pressure had admitted the Westerners. As the latter faction's influence waned, the former's grew. Supporting the emperor were two particularly strong daimyo, Satsuma in Kyushu and Choshu, who linked the shogunate and foreigner in the slogan, "Revere the emperor and expel the barbarian." Japan verged on civil war and the lives of foreigners were in danger. In 1862 the emperor on his own authority cancelled the policy of daimyo attendance at Edo and set June 25, 1863, as the date to reclose the country. Thereupon, the Choshu clan began shelling foreign ships from their capital of Shimonoseki, which guarded the strait between Honshu and Kyushu, a major shipping lane to China. Foreign commercial vessels, including an American one, were damaged. In retaliation, the United States and France dispatched warships to the scene. Meanwhile, a British diplomat had been killed near Yokohama when he did not dismount as a Satsuma lord passed by. The English demanded an apology and an indemnity. Receiving no satisfaction, in August, 1863, they bombarded Kagoshima, the capital of the Satsuma fief.

The following year, in September, 1864, an allied expedition of seventeen Western ships (British, Dutch, French, and American) defeated the Choshu and demanded from them a $3 million indemnity. The Choshu and Satsuma clans thereupon dropped their opposition to foreigners and concentrated single-mindedly on terminating the Tokugawa shogunate. The emperor also capitulated to Western force and, after another allied show of force off Osaka (in which American vessels did not participate), agreed late in 1865 to ratification of the Harris and other Western treaties.

By early 1867, the times were propitious for change, because a new shogun and a young emperor had arrived on the scene. The daimyo backing the emperor sent an ultimatum to the Tokugawa shogun demanding that he surrender his shogunal powers. Already of a mind to do so, he readily agreed. On January 3, 1868, the imperial court issued a rescript restoring to the emperor political power (which emperors had never enjoyed in their historic role). The ex-shogun was then asked to surrender his extensive lands, but he refused. Not until after some months of fighting did he give up his territory. He was then accorded princely rank, and the family turned its energies to successful commercial enterprises. With the end of the old backward-looking Tokugawa, came a new forward-looking regime in Japan associated with the young emperor.

PART FOUR
MODERNIZING ASIA
(Mid-Nineteenth to Mid-Twentieth Century)

The introduction of Asia to the modern world was the most fundamental phenomenon of this century. Initial selective Western contacts were now transformed into basic erupting forces. But the West itself was undergoing transformation as it forced its ways on Asia. And so the continent was exposed to double pressures—its own changes in the midst of ongoing Western revolutions. The Far East came under partial or complete political control of the Western world, which brought material and technical progress. While the political and economic aspects of change were visibly recorded, those relating to the social and psychological were less apparent.

A major Asian reaction to the West in this century was the rise and intensification of nationalism, which was due in part to Western education and the impact of Western doctrines. Asians formed political parties; their leaders rose to prominence on the platform of independence; they demanded equality with Westerners. In the period between the First and Second World Wars nationalism waxed particularly strong as Western European powers maintained their colonial grip. Communism, concentrating on the Far East, added complexity to national movements. As Soviet Russian presence increased over the years, so did that of the United States.

The Asian countries and regions which were subjected to Westernization reacted in differing paces and intensity. The core of ancient civilizations proved resistant. Protected by a Pax Britannica, large populous India, with a basic Hinduism that was at once flexible and intransigent, continued in great measure with old ways. In Southeast Asian colonies and independent Thailand,

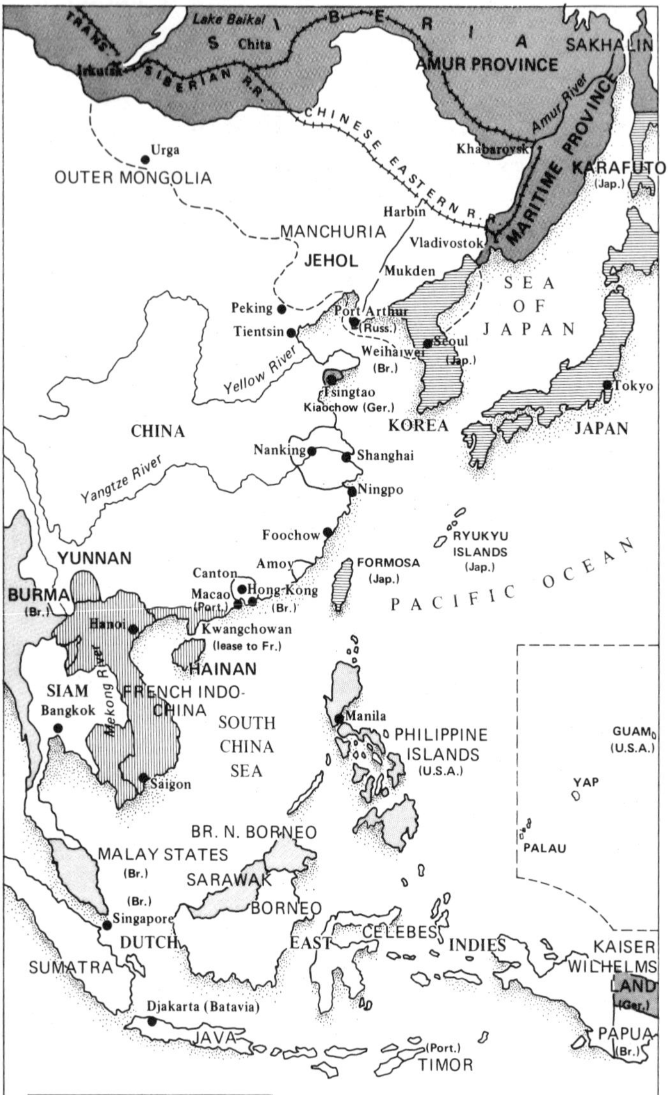

THE WEST IN EAST ASIA
c. 1900

Westernization affected village masses only superficially. China, the heart of the Confucian world, resisted the longest and suffered the most. The Middle Kingdom was already in dynastic decline, but cultural stability glossed over problems of state. And when, in the first decades of the twentieth century, political changes were forced, they erupted in staggering and dislocating proportions. Neighboring Korea similarly experienced dynastic decline behind a facade of cultural stability, which was particularly stultifying.

It was Japan that recorded the wonder story of Westernization. It modernized in part to preserve political independence, but the country in the mid-nineteenth century was already moving in the same general direction of the Western world. Its class structure was breaking down; a rudimentary capitalist and commercial system was developing; a receptivity to new ideas existed. The Japanese, though earlier deriving much from China and later much from the West, always retained an innate sense of national consciousness and distinctiveness.

Over the years as large China became a world problem, small Japan became a world power. In the course of the Second World War it created the largest empire known to Asia. And whereas a squadron of a few American ships could open Japan in the mid-nineteenth century, a century later it took massed American, and Allied, might to defeat Japan. The Second World War brought a catastrophic but historic conclusion to the Asian century of modernization.

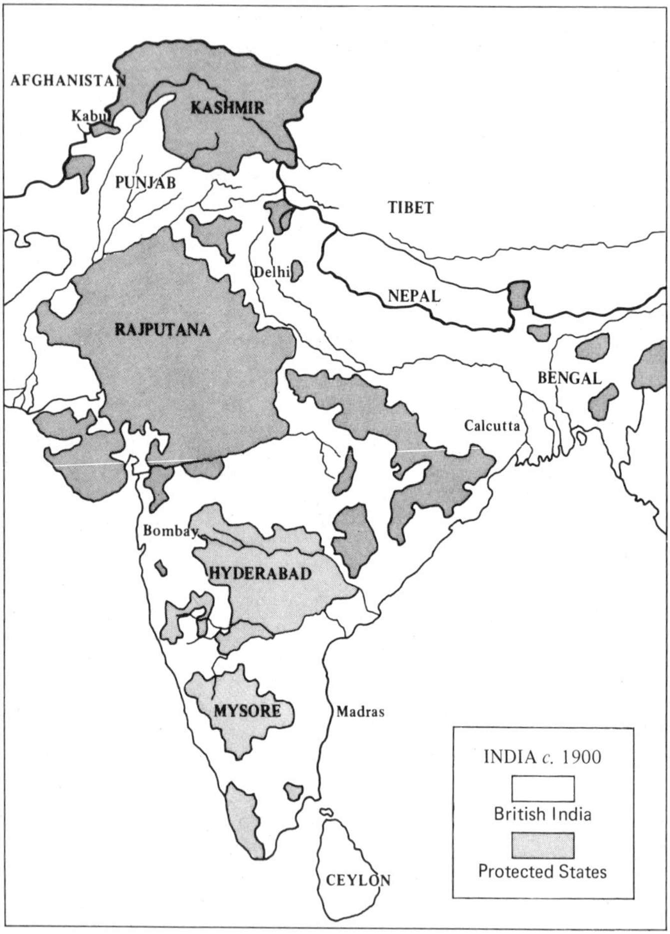
AFGHANISTAN
Kabul
KASHMIR
PUNJAB
TIBET
Delhi
NEPAL
RAJPUTANA
BENGAL
Calcutta
Bombay
HYDERABAD
MYSORE
Madras
CEYLON
INDIA c. 1900
British India
Protected States

12
SOUTH ASIA
1858–1937

In India, the world's largest colony, the years between 1858 and 1937 were formative. Under the crown, modernization proceeded through diverse but allied channels: British government and administration, higher education that emphasized the use of the English language, missionary schools, and rapid and comprehensive transportation systems. But these developments touched only a fringe of the over-all population in a crowded, large land. Village India continued as in traditional eras. Protected by British power abroad and at home, the subcontinent continued with old ways the longer.

For the British the burden of empire was mixed. India afforded extensive markets for their products, particularly textiles. It was an outlet for British capital investments and a source of raw materials. Many Britishers found occupation in the civil service and private companies. India provided needed troops at home and abroad. But to keep imperial lines open required the presence of British fleets and way stations. For India remained the keystone of British strategic policy in Asia. Though they had extensive interests in Southeast Asia, China, and Japan, it was India that provided the core of British concern. India might have been the brightest jewel in the British imperial crown, but it was one that warranted also the most serious consideration.

IMPERIAL RULE AND THE RISE OF NATIONALISM (1858–1914)

While in the decades following the Sepoy Mutiny, modernization of the subcontinent proceeded, the British authority continued to spread into border areas. Concurrently, there came extensions of limited political rights to Indians. The years between

1858 and 1900 witnessed the initial reform steps, as well as the beginnings of Indian nationalist parties, including the chief one, the Indian Congress Party. From 1900 to 1914 a more radical Hindu wing emerged, and Muslim political thinkers also came to the fore. By the outbreak of the First World War, nationalist movement was more than ever guided by the Congress Party. Those reforms granted by the British failed to placate some of the party's leaders, who were already demanding independence. Muslims formulated their own programs, which the princely states generally kept aloof from political problems. The cool, somewhat inflexible British approach to conflicting Indian nationalist desires proved too little and too late in solving the India problem.

Initial Crown Policies (1858–1900). The crown administered India through the Parliament; the Secretary of State for India, who was a member of the cabinet; the Council of India composed of expert officials; and the India Office. In Calcutta, the colonial capital, was the viceroy presiding over British India, or those areas under direct rule. Assisting him were two advisory bodies created by the Act of 1861: the Executive Council of five Europeans, all of whom were appointed by the crown and each of whom had a special portfolio; and the Legislative Council, composed of the full Executive Council along with additional members appointed by the viceroy. Depending on their size and importance, provinces, which also had councils, were ruled by governors, lieutenant-governors, or commissioners. Provinces were further divided into districts, each headed by a deputy commissioner and district magistrates. The judicial structure embraced both central and the local organs. The Indian Civil Service, numbering several thousand, was recruited through examinations given in England.

Over five hundred indirectly ruled "protected" native princely states existed in varying sizes and importance. They consisted in the aggregate of one-third of India's land area and one-fifth of the population. The states were subject through treaties and precedents to British control and residents. Largest among them were Kashmir and Hyderabad, each equivalent in size to a large European country. Finally there were a handful of minuscule Portuguese or French possessions, whose presence the British, and the native princes, tolerated.

The crown continued Company territorial expansion along India's peripheral areas. In 1865 Bhutan in the northeast ceded some 4,000 miles of territory along the mutual frontier. In the west the protected state of Baluchistan gave to the crown the district of Quetta, which extended the full length of that frontier. In the course of the Second Afghan War of 1878–1880, troubles continued with the Afghan ruler, who, after playing off British and Russian interests, was displaced by an emir more amicably disposed toward the British. To help control the unruly Pathan tribes who lived on the Afghan-Indian border, the British created the separate Northwest Frontier Province in 1901.

Modernization. The British continued to modernize India. Under the long-standing policy of Westernizing education rather than incorporating indigenous thought, the government promoted education on all levels. In 1857 the first three major universities, in Calcutta, Bombay, and Madras, were opened. All educated Indians throughout the country learned the English language. Upper social classes and professionals came to draw on that langauge for their livelihood, and nationalists used it to further their cause. Education was one of the most potent forces for Westernization in the land.

In economic activities the British followed the contemporary principles of free enterprise and free trade. No fixed plans or programs created the modern commercial or industrial base in India. Indian markets were unified and brought closer to the European continent. In 1865 the first overland telegraph line was completed between Calcutta and London. Four years later, the opening of the Suez Canal provided easier and faster transport between India and Europe. A modern internal transport system developed and the railroads expanded rapidly under state aegis. British investments came to India in sizable figures and helped to spur industrial projects. In the mid-nineteenth century, in Calcutta the first jute mills were established; textile production, centered in Bombay, followed. In agriculture the British expanded irrigation systems. Plantation crops such as tea, coffee, indigo, and cotton became chief export items.

Advances were also made in other areas. Persistent efforts were made to prevent starvation and to care for the sick in hospitals and dispensaries; but better health meant more people and more pressures on the land. In finance the government put currency on a silver standard. The rupee became the unit of currency, closely tied to sterling. Budgets were formulated. Law codes, incorporating much of native customary practice, were framed. A structure of courts was established. The military arm was expanded and partially Indianized. In 1858 there were some 15,000 European troops; by the end of the century British troops numbered 75,000 and Indians twice that, though no Indians filled commissioned ranks.

Through such measures India was gradually and partially modernized. A small middle class emerged, comprising merchants, lesser government officials, professional men, and military leaders. But even the Westernized minority was divided as to what course the country should take. Hinduism embodied concepts associated with old and traditional India, though some Hindu leaders from professional and business classes were receptive to foreign ideas. Muslims had their own claims. The princes for the most part remained indifferent to nationalistic struggles.

Development of Political Consciousness. Following the assumption of sovereignty by the crown, Indians were granted some limited political rights. They gradually participated in central executive and legislative organs as well as in provincial counterparts. Spurred by the vernacular nationalist press, Indians demanded more voice in political affairs. The establishment of the Indian National Congress in 1885 was the first sign of nationalism on a country-wide basis. The leader in the founding of the Congress was an Englishman, Alan Hume, who had served in the Indian Civil Service. The first session was held at Poona. Reforms called for by the Congress included elected provincial legislative councils; civil service examinations to be held in India as well as in England; reduced military budgets; the abolition of the Council of India in London; and the inclusion in the army of Indian commissioned officers.

Over the first two decades of its existence, the Congress gained prestige, though Muslims, who comprised one-quarter of its membership, remained in subordinate position. During the early years, moderate leaders retained control of the body; but by the turn of the century a militant minority was demanding self-rule. By 1900, the only significant reform had been the Indian

Councils Act of 1892, which enlarged the viceroy's Legislative Council to include some Indians nominated by Indian groups. The provincial legislative councils were similarly structured. Indians asked for more rights.

Developments in Border Lands. In the border lands of the Indian subcontinent, British presence was also manifested. Under British administration, Ceylon developed, particularly in agriculture. Plantations growing tea, rubber, spices, and coconuts flourished. Population rapidly increased. Western schools, some founded by missionaries, were established, and English became the main language. In Afghanistan, under the Anglophile emir, order was restored to the land. In 1893 most of the border (known as the Durand Line after its demarcator, Sir Mortimer Durand) was defined between the Northwest Frontier Province and Afghanistan; but the status of some tribal areas, notably that of the Pathans, remained unclear.

Indians Abroad. Overseas Indians watched home political developments with interest. By the turn of the century, there were more than two and a half million of them spread throughout the British Empire. They were concentrated in sizable numbers in Ceylon, Burma, Malaya, Mauritius, East and South Africa, in the Caribbean, and Pacific islands. Most of them derived from the lower castes and went abroad as indentured servants for a given number of years. When their contract terms expired, they remained abroad. Some prospered; others were discriminated against. It was among such a group of his own people in South Africa that Gandhi, who was to become the most famous name in Indian political history, was already at work.

Initial Nationalism (1900–1914). At the turn of the century, Lord Curzon came into the viceregal office (1899–1905). He was the last of the strong colonial personalities. An able, arrogant, hard-working man, he defined the good of the Indians as he saw fit. While in service Curzon accomplished much and alienated many. During his tour of duty, in 1903, a unified Indian army was created. His interference in domestic university affairs antagonized Indians, but more important was his partition of Bengal (along with Bihar and Orissa). The large unwieldy province, containing almost 80 million people, was divided into West Bengal and East Bengal, the latter united with Assam. The partition increased religious separatism, because Hindus were the majority in the West Bengal and the Muslims in East Bengal. Hindu nationalists began a *swadeshi* ("Buy Indian") campaign, and in 1906 *swaraj* (self-rule) was proclaimed as the objective of the Congress. In the same year, the Muslim League was founded in Dacca.

During Curzon's tenure the British also concerned themselves with Tibetan events. In 1904 a British expedition went into Tibet to contain Russian advances. Through a treaty that year the Tibetans were forced to pay a small indemnity, while the British received the right to trade and to send a representative to Lhasa, the capital.

Political Reforms. In 1907, almost half a century after its assumption of sovereignty, the British government announced the principle of increased Indian representation in political life. That year two Indians were appointed to the Council of India in London. With Lord Morley as Secretary of State for India and Lord Minto as viceroy, Parliament granted more rights. The Morley-Minto Reforms of 1909 included the appointment of the first Indian to the viceroy's Executive Council and enlarged the Legislative Council to include Indians elected from certain groups. Indians were also appointed to provincial executive councils. Fifty members each were elected to legislative councils in Bombay, Bengal, Madras, and the United Provinces by Indian voters who met property qualifications. Significantly, the reforms recognized Muslim demands by providing for separate Muslim electorates. In 1911 King George V and Queen Mary came to Delhi to personalize the empire for their Indian subjects. There they announced the reversal of the Bengal partition and the transfer of the capital from Calcutta, a British-made city, to Delhi, the longtime Mogul capital. The Indian Congress Party meanwhile had broadened its targets and tactics. One of its early leaders was Bal Gangadhar Tilak (1856–1920), the "Father of Indian Unrest," who called for non-co-operation with the British. Another leader, more conciliatory in tone was Gopal Krishna Gokhale (1866–1915), mentor of Gandhi.

Hindu Culture. In these years, along with growing political awareness, ideological movements produced a Hindu renaissance. The ascetic Ramakrishna (1836–1886) sought to incorporate principles of each great world religion. His most important disciple, Vivekananda (1863–1902) combined a program of social action with the meditative life and founded the Ramakrishnan Mission, a monastic order. Another Hindu group was the militant *Arya Samaj*, founded in 1875, which emphasized Vedic knowledge. Still another school was the Theosophical Society, founded also in 1875, in the United States by a Russian lady, Mme. Helena Blavatsky. The movement spread to India, where it was led by an Englishwoman, Mrs. Annie Besant, who was also associated with the Indian nationalist movement and founded the Home Rule League. Another intellectual leader was the great poet Rabindranath Tagore (1861–1941), who won international repute and a Nobel Prize. He wrote in a self-assertive tone that praised Indian culture and criticized the West.

Muslim Leaders. The Muslim nationalist cause also covered varying personalities and ideologies. The conservative Wahhabiism attacked Western learning and promoted the "holy war" concept. More moderate in tone was Sir Syed Ahmad Khan (1817–1898), who, though a devout Muslim, advocated toleration for all faiths. He sought to combine Islamic and Western ideas and founded a college at Aligarh near Delhi. Muhammed Ali (1878–1930) was an intellectual leader of a pan-Muslim movement during the early twentieth century.

NON-CO-OPERATION AND STRUGGLE TOWARD INDEPENDENCE (1914–1937)

In the course of the First World War, Indian nationalism grew stronger. The Act of 1919 permitted more Indian participation in central and provincial organs. But Indian demands were greater than British concessions, and new indigenous leaders came to the fore. Most prominent among them was Gandhi, whose nonviolent non-co-operation movement was the word of the day. Muslims in their separate electorates intensified communal interests. The Sikhs advanced theirs in the Punjab. But other minority groups, including Parsees and Christians, did not push communal ends. Princes still kept aloof from the nationalist struggles. Leftist movements, embracing Socialists and Communists, arose. As a result of political re-examination of the situation in the 1920's and "Round Table" discussions of the early 1930's, the Act of 1935 was formulated. This last organic law affecting India was wide-ranging, but still fell short of independence for Indians. As war clouds once again descended in Europe and Asia, the Indian problem seemed insoluble.

***Unrest* (*1914–1930*).** During the First World War, the Indian Congress Party set its immediate politics aside in order to co-operate with the British, hoping thereby to gain favor for their cause. Indians participated in European and in Middle Eastern campaigns. Some 800,000 volunteer Indian troops and 500,000 noncombatants joined the Allied effort. There was also temporary co-operation between Hindus and Muslims who in the Lucknow Pact of December, 1916, agreed to pool forces in working toward Indian self-government. The move was prompted in part by India's overriding anti-British sentiment that resulted from British attacks on Turkey, a Muslim country which fought on the German side. In August, 1917, Lord Montagu, secretary of state for India, and Lord Chelmsford, viceroy of India, announced a policy of providing for the gradual development of self-governing Indian institutions. Hinting at some type of Commonwealth arrangement, they promised more Indian participation in every branch of the administration.

Reforms of 1919. The India Act of 1919, based on the Montagu-Chelmsford Report, provided for greater participation of Indians in central and provincial organs. The viceroy's Executive Council was enlarged from five to seven members, now to include three Indians. The central Legislative Council became a bicameral national parliament. The upper house, the Council of State, included 60 members (26 appointed, 34 elected), serving five-year terms. The lower house, the Legislative Assembly, had 146 members (one-third appointed, two-thirds elected), serving three-year terms. The elected members were apportioned on communal bases (e.g., Hindus, Muslims, Sikhs, and landlords). A Chamber of Princes provided a forum for consultation among the princely states. Eight governor's provinces were created, each with executive and legislative councils (60 percent elective). High property qualifications determined the franchise. At the provincial level, dyarchy was established. Under this system, councillors responsible to the British governor handled important "reserved" matters, including finance, public works, and law and order. Indian ministers were delegated "transferred" functions, including agriculture, education, and health. The governor and the viceroy maintained the power to veto any measure. Communal electorates continued. The India Act provided for a review of its terms after a decade.

Repressive Measures. On the one hand, the British gave concessions; on the other they constricted rights. In 1918, during the war, the Rowlatt bills provided for trial without jury and in some cases internment without trial of persons considered subversive. In April, 1919, the Amritsar incident further exacerbated Indian feelings. In that city in the Punjab the British commanding officer ordered a political gathering of Indians, mostly Sikhs, to disperse. When they did not immediately do so, the general ordered his troops to open fire. Almost four hundred Indians were killed and twelve hundred wounded. The incident resulted in bitterness and militancy throughout India. Thereafter little ground for conciliation existed. Protests, boycotts, and non-co-operation campaigns became commonplace, as Indian demands became increasingly strident.

Growth of The Nationalistic Movement. Most prominent among the political names to emerge in the nationalistic movement was Mohandas Karamchand Gandhi (1869–1948), called *Mahatma* ("Great Soul"). From West Indian and of Vaisya background, Gandhi studied law in England and on his return to India, became involved in politics. In 1893 he went to South Africa, where for over two decades he espoused the Indian cause against racial prejudice. In India during the interwar period, whether in or out of Congress Party office, he was the acknowledged political leader. He began his first civil disobedience movement in 1920. He espoused the cause of the untouchables, whom he called *harijans* ("children of God"). He developed his philosophy of *ahimsa* (nonviolent non-co-operation). Through *satyagraha* ("soul force"), he mingled religious ideas with politics. A pacifist, he desired equitable relations between the English and the Indians and among the Indians themselves.

Gandhi's protégé was Jawaharlal Nehru (1889–1964). Of Kashmiri Brahman background, Nehru also studied law in

England. He became involved in Indian politics through the Congress Party but in its more radical wing, while his father Motilal was a spokesman for the moderates. The former demanded complete independence; the latter, Dominion status. The younger Nehru remained ideologically apart not only from his father but also from Gandhi. He was a secularist who had little place for religion and who advocated nonviolence as a means, rather than a principle. A modern man, he desired a centralized, socialized, and industrialized state, whereas Gandhi dreamed of self-supporting villages with cottage industries.

In the 1920's the schism deepened between Hindus and Muslims, whose League demanded provincial autonomy, separate electorates, and weighted representation. To promote their own cause, Hindu extremists within the Congress formed the Mahasabha. Meanwhile, Socialist and Communist movements arose. Within the Congress, the All-India Independence League called for independence, elimination of landlords, and establishment of a Socialist state. The Communists in 1925 convoked the first All-India Communist Conference at Cawnpore, but their leaders were imprisoned. Three years later, a Communist conference, held in Calcutta, joined the Comintern (Communist International). Communists organized a militant labor movement and fomented strikes. Again the leaders (including M. N. Roy, the best-known) were arrested, and in the 1930's the movement went underground.

The Economy. Meanwhile, economic life in the interwar period progressed. In 1919 India fixed its own tariffs and benefited from the system of imperial preferences adopted by Britain in 1927. The textile industry, basically the spinning and weaving of cotton, was most important. Second were jute mills. The steel industry sprouted. From estates came tea, coffee, indigo, and spices. Some new consumer industries appeared; airlines were established; railroad trunk lines nationalized; and road systems elaborated. A trade union movement appeared. In agriculture more lands came under cultivation through the continued extension of irrigation canals. India's population continued to grow at a dizzying rate; the interwar period saw a rise from 319 million to 389 million.

Confrontation (1930–1937). As noted previously, the terms of the Act of 1919 had provided for its review after a decade. In 1927 an all-English Simon Commission of seven, including Clement Attlee, was appointed to consider the Indian government. The commission encountered Indian hostility because of its lack of indigenous membership and its advocacy of less than full independence. In October, 1929, the viceroy announced a goal of Dominion status, as implied in the 1917 declaration. But this fell far short of nationalist independence aims. In December, 1929, the Congress resolved to sever all connections with the British. The Party members proclaimed this purpose again on January 26, 1930, a date observed after Indian independence as Republic Day.

Returning to active politics by 1930 after a period of retreat, Gandhi threatened a civil disobedience campaign if Indian demands for full home rule and a constituent assembly were not met. After an unsuccessful conference with the viceroy, he began the campaign by an attack on the government's salt monopoly. The campaign lasted four years. Government officials resigned; foreign businesses were boycotted; *hartals* (work stoppages) occurred; and violence erupted. After a symbolic salt march, Gandhi was again imprisoned, as were many thousands of his supporters.

Meanwhile, new Muslim leaders emerged. Muhammad Iqbal (1873–1938), president of the Muslim League in 1930, proclaimed the unique Muslim way of life, which he felt could be realized only in an independent Muslim homeland. Also a major Urdu poet, he wrote mystical works in the Islamic tradition. Toward the end of his life, he designated as his successor Muhammad Ali Jinnah (1876–1948). Jinnah, the founder of Pakistan, was born in Karachi of a wealthy family and educated in England. On his return to India, he practiced law in Bombay. He later entered politics and, in order to work for national unity, joined both the Congress and the Muslim League in 1913. He subsequently resigned from the Congress in protest against Gandhian policies. In 1934 he was elected president of the Muslim League, a position which he held until his death.

Round Table Conferences. The Simon Report recommended the enlargement of provincial legislatures, the extension of dyarchy in the provinces, the election of the central legislature by the provincial councils, the broadening of the franchise, and the ultimate establishment of an Indian Federal State. The British government announced the convening in London of an all-India conference to act on the recommendations. The first Round Table Conference (November, 1930, to January, 1931) included all Indian political groups except the Congress, which boycotted the sessions. Then changing its stand on non-co-operation, in late 1931 the Congress Party sent Gandhi to the second conference. But divisions persisted among Indians and between the British and Indians. The conference again broke up, and London announced the Communal Award, establishing separate electorates for minorities, including the untouchables. In protest against this plan to perpetuate social cleavages, Gandhi vowed a fast unto death. Eventually, however, he and Dr. B. R. Ambedkar, leader of the untouchables, made an arrangement to eliminate separate electorates at least among the Hindus. In 1932 from the third and last session of the Round Table Conferences came a white paper which helped form the India Act of 1935.

India Act of 1935. As the last major law to direct affairs of state in British India, this act established a federal union for India. It extended autonomy in the provinces, continued separate communal electorates, and promulgated a new constitution. It contemplated an all-India federation to be created out of the governor's provinces and consenting princely states. It provided for a bicameral federal legislature. The lower chamber, the Federal Assembly, with 250 members from British India and 125 from princely states, was to be elected for five-year terms by provincial legislative assemblies. The upper house, the Council of State, with 156 members from British India and 104 from princely states, comprised members, some elected and others appointed, who served nine-year terms. Provincial legislatures were enlarged. Representation continued on communal lines. Dyarchy, abandoned in the provinces, was adopted in the central government, where defense and external affairs were kept as "reserved" matters.

In 1937 provincial assemblies were elected in accordance with the Act, and the Congress won a clear majority of seats in eight of eleven provinces. But central federation proved impossible to effect, and the viceroy continued with his Executive Council. Princes declined to federate. The members of the Congress who demanded full independence had little rapport with those who were willing to settle for Dominion status and co-operation with the British. Muslims agitated for a separatist arrangement, wherein they would be the majority in given areas. Since this was unacceptable to the Congress, conflict intensified between Hindus and Muslims.

Border Lands. The British meanwhile kept a watchful eye on neighboring countries. They continued to exercise authority directly over Sikkim and Bhutan and indirectly over Nepal. In Ceylon during the First World War there arose a movement for independence. A constitution of 1931 provided for universal adult suffrage, but Ceylonese nationalists demanded full independence. With Afghanistan the British experienced problems. During the First World War, the neutral Afghans' sympathy for the Muslim Turks in part caused the Third Afghan War (1919). The emir negotiated a peace treaty with the British and then turned his attention to the modernization of the country. In 1921 the Soviet Union opened diplomatic relations and sent technicians to help construct the country's economy. In 1926 a kingdom replaced the emirate and more reforms were introduced. Westernization alienated zealous Muslims, and after a revolt in 1929 the king was forced to abdicate. A more moderate successor was assassinated in 1933. That year the young Mohammad Zahir Shah ascended the throne, but over the decades remained in the background while working through prime ministers. In 1936 the United States extended diplomatic recognition to Afghanistan. Wedged in among stronger powers, the mountain kingdom played its classic role of a buffer state.

13
SOUTHEAST ASIA
1850–1937

It was during the last half of the nineteenth century that colonial empires, other than the Philippines, were fashioned in Southeast Asia. After centuries of gradual expansion, European countries burst on the scene. On mainland Southeast Asia, Thailand, through a combination of internal policies and external colonial rivalries, kept its sovereignty, but Indochina went under French rule, as did all Burma under the British. The latter also consolidated hold over the insular Malayan world, while the Dutch rounded out Indonesian borders. And by 1900, Americans had inherited the Philippine archipelago from the Spanish. With Western contact came a degree of modernization in all lands. The first decades of the twentieth century in Southeast Asia, as in India, witnessed a growing expression of national consciousness. Indigenous leaders demanded political reforms that were quite beyond the willingness of colonial powers to concede. But though nationalists were united in the policy of ending Western rule, they developed no common regional bonds in their mutual struggle. Each was concerned with his own country. Despite unrest, by 1937, when conflict broke out in Asia, only the Philippines had been promised, by the United States, a definite independence date.

MAINLAND SOUTHEAST ASIA

In the latter half of the nineteenth century, Thailand was fortunate in having two monarchs who "bent with the wind" in trying to keep the country politically solvent. In part because of this and in part because of Anglo-French rivalry in the land, the policy was successful, though unequal treaties were imposed and some border areas confiscated. In Indochina, the French by degrees built up their "balcony on the Pacific." First appropriating as a colony Cochin China with its rich Mekong Delta, they then established protectorates over Annam, Tonkin, Cambodia, and Laos. A heavy-handed rule was imposed, which inhibited the expression of national self-consciousness. The Vietnamese led a one-sided struggle; but by 1937, the Communist movement had taken root in Vietnam. The British, already possessing coastal provinces of Lower Burma, won Upper Burma as well. Unlike the French, they extended political reforms to such an extent that by 1937 the Burmese, though they had not been promised independence, enjoyed political autonomy.

***Thailand* (*Siam*).** King Mongkut (Rama IV), who ruled from 1851 to 1868, brought Siam into the modern world. Before assuming the throne, he had been a Buddhist monk but had also studied with foreign teachers. On the throne, he invited Western advisers to his country. Best known of these was Mrs. Anna Leonowens, who described her experiences as a royal tutor in a book which a hundred years later was dramatized as *Anna and the King of Siam*. Mongkut made many reforms in the governmental structure. He introduced new coinage, encouraged instruction in foreign languages, and built public works. He updated treaties, in 1855 with the British and the following year with the Americans, who now received extraterritorial and consular rights. Mongkut encountered difficulties with the French, who under Napoleon III began to impinge on Thailand's borders from the east. In 1867, in a Thai-French treaty, the king was forced to recognize a French protectorate (replacing that of Thailand) over Cambodia.

Mongkut's son Chulalongkorn (Rama V) was also a mixture of East and West. On the throne from 1868 to 1910, he continued his father's reforms. He modernized the educational system; adopted the Western calendar; replaced tax farming with direct government collection; abolished debt slavery; promulgated new codes of law; introduced budgetary and auditing practices; and inaugurated public health measures. He attempted to modernize the military arm, improved transport, and reformed the judicial system. He overhauled the local government bureaucracy by replacing hereditary provincial governors with appointed officials. He maintained Hinayana Buddhism as the state religion but tolerated Catholic and Buddhist sects. Because of political stability and economic improvement, during his reign Thailand attracted overseas Chinese as immigrants.

Chulalongkorn was less effective in his foreign relations. In 1893 he ceded some Laotian territory to the French. In 1896 a treaty between France and England divided Thailand into three spheres of influences: an eastern third for the French, a western third for the British, and a neutral central one in the Chao Phraya Valley. In a 1904 treaty, the Thai gave up additional territory in Laos to the French, who in turn surrendered extraterritoriality in Thailand. In 1907 Thailand ceded to France Cambodian territory where the Angkor temple complex was located. As the British consolidated rule over Malaya, they similarly whittled away at Thai territory to the south. In 1909 they received four peninsular Thai states of Kedah, Perlis, Kelantan, and Trengganu, but at the same time gave up almost all rights of extraterritoriality in Thailand.

Thai nationalism continued to direct itself toward terminating the unequal treaties, though the monarchy remained autocratic. Adhering to the Westernizing but authoritarian tactics of his father Chulalongkorn, Wachirawut (Rama VI) ruled from 1910 to 1925. In the hope of eliminating the unequal treaties, he espoused a number of Westernizing reforms, though he made no moves toward a constitutional government. Despite the country's strong anti-French feeling, he aligned Thailand with the Allies during the First World War. This move brought rewards at the Versailles Conference. Thailand was allowed to confiscate German shipping and railways; it received membership in the League of Nations; and by 1922 the unequal treaties were ended.

Wachirawut died without heirs, and his youngest brother, Prajadhipok (Rama VII), ascended the throne. The early years of his reign (1925–1935) were characterized by further modernization. A national library and museum were established; a currency act linked the *tical* with gold; a radio service was inaugurated; and the Bangkok international airport was constructed. But the depression of the 1930's reduced Thailand's rice exports, and the national budget registered deficits. Attempts by the king's advisers to draft a constitution came to naught, and in June, 1932, there was a coup d'état.

Disaffected Thai leaders had formed a People's Party. Its ranks included a civilian, Pridi Banomyong, who had studied law in Paris and was a professor at Chulalongkorn University, and a young military man, Phibun Songgram. After taking over the government, they promulgated a constitution, providing for a unicameral legislative assembly of 156 members (half elected and half appointed by the king). But ideological differences soon developed among the ruling clique. Pridi, who had drawn up thorough nationalization plans, was attacked as communistic and exiled for a year, during which Phibun gained power. After Pridi returned to official life in 1934, Thai politics essentially revolved around the two men into the period following the Second World War.

A delayed aftermath of the 1932 coup was King Prajadhipok's abdication in 1935. He was succeeded by his ten-year-old nephew Ananda Mahidol. The new state leadership was strongly nationalistic. It imposed heavy taxes on the merchant class, particularly those (mostly Chinese) of foreign extraction. Thailand's increasing nationalism and anti-Chinese drives coincided with the expansion of Japan in Asia. Fearing China more, Thailand did not join the League of Nations majority that in 1933 condemned Japanese aggression in Manchuria. Caught amidst conflicting external pressures, the Thai monarchs and party leaders tried to adapt to changing situations.

Indochina. With Emperor Napoleon III's reign in France in the mid-nineteenth century, came a French imperial burst of conquest abroad. Capitalizing on earlier missionary and commercial interests in Vietnam, the French returned in force to build up an empire. First getting a toehold in rich Cochin China, they then expanded west into central Cambodia, north into Annam and Tonkin, then finally in western and northwestern peripheral areas of Laos and Cambodia. In the course of their expansion, they met and surmounted traditional Thai pressures in the west and Chinese in the north.

FRENCH EXPANSION. In the mid-nineteenth century the Vietnamese imperial line, reversing the pro-French outlook of Gia Long, reinstituted hard policies. Emperor Tu Duc (r. 1848–1883) suppressed and persecuted Christian groups, both native and foreign. In 1857 the Spanish bishop of Tonkin was put to death.

The French, who had forces in China at the time, joined the Spanish from the Philippines in a retaliatory expedition that occupied Tourane, and then Saigon. But bogged down in Chinese wars, the French took no decisive action until 1862 (by which time the Spanish had returned to the Philippines). In that year, Tu Duc ceded to the French three Cochin China delta provinces which they had occupied. Treaty terms included the freedom of worship, opening of three ports to trade, and payment of an indemnity.

In 1863 the Cambodian emperor Norodom put his kingdom under French protection. In South Vietnam the French continued to meet resistance. To consolidate their rule, in 1867 they occupied three additional western delta provinces and created the colony of Cochin China. In control of the lower Mekong, the French probed the river route through Cambodia into Laos and South China. Meeting Chinese resistance and finding much of the river unnavigable, the French turned their attention to central Annam and northern Tonkin. In 1873 the governor of Cochin China sent an expedition north to negotiate on a Red River route into South China, where the French were creating a sphere of influence. Its leader was killed and Emperor Tu Duc, alarmed, concluded a treaty with the French .

In 1874 a treaty between France and Annam gave to the French the right to trade in Hanoi and to develop the Red River route upstream into southwest China. They also received extraterritorial rights and protection for their missionaries. By this treaty Annam and Tonkin virtually became French protectorates. Taking advantage of a disintegrating royal Annamese line, the French occupied central and northern Vietnam, interfered in succession disputes, and put residents into adviser's offices. As they had to the Thai in Cambodia, so the Chinese protested to the French in Annam these moves into what they considered their sphere of influence. But in 1885 they were finally compelled by superior French force to renounce their claims in Annam and Tonkin.

At the same time the French increased their hold on Cambodia and Laos. In 1884 all real power was transferred to the French chief resident in Phnom Penh. Some local resistance developed but was put down in a few years. The French permitted the Cambodian king to keep ceremonial power and, as protector of the Buddhist religion, he continued to be a strong stabilizing force. Laos, facing the French in the east and south, also soon fell to the Western power. In 1884 the Vietnamese emperor delegated to the French all rights in territory not actually under his administration; under this understanding the French annexed western portions of North Vietnam adjoining Laos. From the north and the south, through Champassak, by degrees, central and riverine Laos fell to the French. In 1893 Thailand gave up all claims to the east of the Mekong, in 1904 to the west of the river, and finally in 1907 over the two Cambodian provinces. After assigning certain peripheral areas to Cambodia, the French declared Laos a protectorate. The capital remained at Luang Prabang, but was controlled by the French resident-general in Vientiane.

French Administration. A centralized French colonial administration was established in Indochina. In 1887 the Indochinese Union was created. The chief colonial official was the governor-general in Saigon. Early governors-general, Paul Donner (1897–1902), Paul Beau (1902–1907), and Albert Sarraut (1911–1914), were strong-willed men with quasi-absolute powers. A privy council composed of French officials and native princes assisted the governor-general; a colonial council elected by French citizens and companies handled financial matters. There was also a governor in Saigon who administered the colony of Cochin China and its provinces. Residents-general supervised the four protectorates and their provinces. Though some elite Indochinese (termed mandarins) held legal and provincial posts, the French provided for only limited Indochinese political participation. In the mid-1920's elected administrative councils were established in several thousand Vietnamese villages. In 1929 the colonial council of Cochin China had twenty of its two-dozen members elected, half by French colonial residents and half by narrowly franchised Vietnamese.

In economic life, the French monopolized finance and trade. The Chinese immigrants staked out rubber estates, owned rice mills, and conducted export trade. Cholon, Saigon's twin city, became next to Singapore the most prosperous Chinese center in Southeast Asia. Most Indochinese continued their existence as before without resistance to their colonial masters. The French generally were tolerant of local customs, but imposed their own culture on those who wished to advance under their regime. In 1906 the educational system was reorganized to provide instruction in French, Chinese, or the romanized vernacular. Some of the higher French institutions (notably the *École Française d'Extrême Orient,* established at Hanoi in 1899) were of excellent academic standing.

Rise of Nationalism. Self-government was never a keystone of French colonial policy; much less was independence its goal. Some of the native elite, after education in the French system, were assimilated into the political structure; others became nationalist leaders. The nationalist movement consisted almost entirely of Vietnamese, who made up three-fourths of the Indochinese population. But the leaders, divided by rival personalities and ideologies, had no unified program and made little progress against French dominance. Early leaders were primarily reformers who called for broader educational opportunities. Later ones turned revolutionary. In 1912 a nationalist party appropriated the name of Vietnam (for Annam). During the First World War, some hundred thousand Vietnamese soldiers and workers served in Europe, where they acquired new ideas and skills. Toward the end of the 1920's, the Vietnamese Nationalist Party was formed with the aim to oust the French militarily and establish a republic. The French cracked down, and the party was forced to go underground, where it died out.

Another nationalistic stream was essentially Communist. It was spearheaded by Nguyen Tat Thanh (1894–1969), known by various aliases, including Ho Chi Minh. Ho went to high school in Hué; shipped out as a cabin boy on a merchant vessel; and became politically active in Paris during the First World War. As a member of the French Communist Party, he denounced imperialism. His Association of Vietnamese Patriots petitioned the French government for more civil rights. Ho was attracted to the Comintern, and in the 1920's his platform became more revolutionary. He wanted to eject the French from his home territory in two stages: first through a temporary democratic bourgeois regime, and then a Communist one. His wide-ranging programs included land redistribution and the abolition of native conscription for labor and foreign wars.

In the interwar period, Ho promoted his ideas through his writings. He also traveled widely in Russia, Central Asia, and China. He was part of a Soviet mission sent to assist the Nationalist *Kuomintang* (under Chiang Kai-shek) to reorganize the Chinese party and army. In 1925 Ho organized his second party, the Association of Vietnamese Revolutionary Youth. Five years later, this was replaced by the Vietnamese Communist Party, which organized strikes and demonstrations; touched off an army mutiny; and sparked an abortive peasant rising in Tonkin. For a time soviet-type councils of workers and peasants were established in two northern provinces.

In 1931 the British arrested Ho Chi Minh and imprisoned him for two years in Hong Kong, while in Vietnam the French clamped down on his followers. Thereafter, the Communist movement lost momentum. Simultaneously, the right wing of the nationalist movement was suppressed. In 1932 Emperor Bao Dai announced his intention to establish a constitutional monarchy, but not much progress was made toward that goal. The French did not widen indigenous political participation. They did, however, improve the economy in a mercantilistic fashion, partly by the flight of French capital from the depreciating franc to the stable piastere. The depression years affected Indochina, but rubber, the main plantation crop, recovered. While French, Chinese, and some Vietnamese shared in the increased wealth, its distribution was lopsided. The impact of modernization in Indochina remained narrow and selective.

Burma. The Burmese kings continued to resent the 1826 cessions to the British, disliked the presence of British traders in Burmese towns, and in general were hostile to foreigners. In 1830 the British resident at Ava was recalled. In early 1852 the energetic Lord Dalhousie, governor-general of the East India Company, sent a naval squadron to Rangoon to investigate complaints of British businessmen. Local conflict spiraled into the Second Anglo-Burmese War. British and Indian forces occupied Rangoon, overran the Irrawaddy delta country, and penetrated north beyond Prome and Toungoo. In December, 1852, Dalhousie declared the annexation of occupied areas, which were then grouped into the province of Pegu.

In 1862, after the British crown assumed Company sovereignty, the three Burmese provinces (Arakan, Tenasserim, and

Pegu) were united into British Burma and put under a chief commissioner responsible to Calcutta. British Burma prospered. Many Indians immigrated and some Chinese arrived. Rice acreage increased in the delta areas; the teak industry developed; steamships plied the Irrawaddy; and roads and rail lines were constructed.

As a result of Burmese defeat in the 1852 war, the king was deposed and his brother Mindon came to the throne (1853–1878). A humane monarch and a devout Buddhist, he ruled from his new capital, Mandalay. Concerned about British inroads, the king, like his Thai counterparts, effected some reforms. He gave his realm peace and order, sound taxation, coinage rather than barter for trade, and the telegraph (using a type of Burmese Morse code). He pursued friendly relations with China, into which he wanted to extend railroads, and maintained friendship with Thailand. He concluded two commercial treaties with the British in 1862 and 1867; the latter re-established British residency at the capital and provided for extraterritorialty.

British Conquest. Mindon died without designating a successor, and Thibaw, a junior son came to the throne (1878–1885). A weakling, the monarch attempted to play British interests off with French in Upper Burma. The British resident was once again withdrawn. The French were granted the right to build a railway from Mandalay to Toungoo and given commercial privileges. The Burmese levied a fine on a British firm for an alleged breach of contract. Reacting strongly, the British in 1885 presented Thibaw with an ultimatum to exonerate the company, reopen the residency, and put Burma's foreign relations under British control. When the Burmese rejected the demands, the British took the capital in a two weeks' campaign. Thibaw was exiled to India; and on January 1, 1886, independent Burma was annexed to the British crown, united with Lower Burma as a province within the Indian Empire. It took another decade to exert control over restive hill tribes and Burmese guerrillas. In 1895 Burma's traditional decennial tribute to China, allowed by the 1885 treaty between China and the British, lapsed. In Burma, as in Vietnam, China was momentarily out of the political picture.

Under British rule, Burma was administered from India with a chief commissioner resident in Rangoon. Through direct rule, a British civil service administered some of the functions of state. Through indirect rule, British control was maintained by passing edicts to district and village chiefs in lower political echelons and to native princes in semi-independent states, such as that of the Shan hill tribes. Burma achieved peace and prosperity. Agricultural production increased; the Irrawaddy Delta became the world's largest rice producer. British capital developed shipping, the extractive industries, and transportation. Indian immigrants engaged in various professions, money-lending, and manual labor. Chinese immigrants were active in retail trade, rice-milling, and light industry. Modern law, the English language, and secular schools helped undermine some traditional aspects of Burmese society. Burmans were restive; but native minorities, including the Karens and Kachins, progressed under foreign domination.

Political Reforms. Unlike the French, who granted next to no concessions in Indochina, the British prepared Burma for self-government. As early as 1874, nominated municipal committees were allowed in seven Lower Burma towns. In 1882 some of these became elective; two years later rural districts were formed. In 1897 the post of chief commissioner for Burma was elevated to that of a lieutenant-governor, with a nine-member appointive legislative council. In 1909 the legislative council was expanded to seventeen members, two of them elected, and in 1915, to thirty, two elected. The Burmese made more demands as time went on. The Young Men's Buddhist Association, formed in 1908, entered politics during the First World War. Students became activist, having as their aim to "purify country customs and expel foreigners."

In 1923, partly as a result of the Montagu-Chelmsford Reforms in India, the Legislative Council was again greatly enlarged, to 103, of whom 79 were elected by all householders eighteen years old and over (including women). Dyarchy was introduced in the governor's executive council; two of its four members were responsible for reserved matters involving defense, law, and finance; the other two were responsible to the legislative council for transferred subjects such as education, health, and forestry. Burma was given five seats in the new Indian legislature that dealt with central subjects. A majority of municipal and district committees were elected, while minorities and hill tribes were, under their headmen, ultimately responsible to the governor.

Divided among themselves, the Burmese could not control the government. The extreme nationalists associated with the Grand Council of Buddhist Associations boycotted the Legislative Council, though a handful of other, more moderate, parties co-operated. Political restiveness continued in the course of the 1920's. Burmans demanded more rights, and ones separate from India. Economic conditions resulting from depression years aggravated political matters. Rice prices fell and peasants sold lands. The Simon Commission of 1928, investigating Indian problems, extended its scope to include Burma. Its report came out for separation of the two countries. Some Burmese, who thought that separation would slow reforms, objected. After a Burma Round Table Conference in London (November, 1931, to January, 1932), they did an about-face when the British stated that the antiseparationists, none of whom wanted permanent union with India, would not be able to terminate the union at their own desire.

As a result of the provisions of the India Act of 1935 applicable to Burma, the country was separated from India. In the colony a British governor headed administration. He was assisted by a Burmese prime minister and a cabinet of ten. The legislative council was replaced by a bicameral legislature that included an upper house of 36 members, half appointed by the governor and half elected by the lower house, and a lower house of 132 members, 92 elected by territorial constituencies and the remainder by special interests. The franchise approximated adult suffrage. Nearly all internal subjects were turned over to ministers responsible to the parliament. When the provisions of the Act took effect in 1937, Burma had achieved a wide measure of self-government.

INSULAR SOUTHEAST ASIA

Unlike their situation in Burma, the British in Malaya faced no nationalist demands. In their unhurried absorption of the peninsula, they continued with the three Straits Settlements as their main base. To these in time were added the Federated and Unfederated States on the peninsula. British interests were also expanded on Borneo. In the Philippines the Spanish met a mounting nationalist movement, which by the time of American occupation had declared its independence. But such was not to be, and the archipelago came under American rule. To the greatest degree of any colonial power in Southeast Asia, the United States prepared the indigenous inhabitants for independence, though along lines the mother country deemed propitious. The Dutch in Indonesia, like the French in Indochina, were more cautious. Nationalism based on varying grounds proceeded, but the Dutch made haste slowly.

The Malay Peninsula. On the Malay Peninsula, Singapore, Penang, and Malacca (as the Straits Settlements) formed the cornerstone of British interests in Southeast Asia. When in 1858 the East India Company was abolished, authority was assumed by the crown, first through the India Office and then, after 1867, through the Colonial Office. In the last quarter of the nineteenth century, a time of warfare and disorders on the peninsula, the British interfered in the political affairs of several Malayan states. Between 1874 and 1888, the four central states of Perak, Selangor, Negri Sembilan, and Pahang came under British protection. In 1895 these states were amalgamated as the Federated States, responsible to a British resident-general at Kuala Lumpur. With the acquisition from Thailand in 1909 of the Kedah, Perlis, Kelantan, and Trengganu States, and with Johore in 1914 placing itself under British protection, advisers were also sent to these five states, which, however, remained unfederated.

The political structure of the Straits Settlements, Federated States, and Unfederated States continued into the Second World War. Under British watchfulness, Muslim Malays, Confucian Chinese, and Hindu Indians coexisted in peace. Economically, Malaya was the greatest earner of American dollars for the British Empire principally through exports of rubber and tin. Rubber plantations occupied most of the arable land, so that rice needs had to be met by two-thirds imports.

In the communal society, Malayans put up with the British, but the Chinese registered some opposition. In China, the antiforeign riots and the growth of communism in the first decades of the twentieth century had some repercussions in Singapore with its overwhelming (80 percent) Chinese population. In 1921 an underground Communist Party was established there. In 1928 organized communism made its appearance with the South Seas Communist Party in Singapore; two years later this was transformed into the Malayan Communist Party, founded at Hong Kong. Despite the name, in essence it was a Chinese-directed movement. By 1937 when conflict broke out in Asia, it was small in numbers but ready for action.

Borneo. The British were also active in Borneo. In the eighteenth century, the English East India Company had founded a post on Labuan, an island off Brunei. In 1847, after the sultan of Brunei ceded the island, Labuan became a crown colony. Brunei itself came under increasing British influence until 1888, when it became a protectorate. By that time, the sultanate had experienced a progressive shrinkage of territory. Earlier, in 1841, the sultan had ceded his southern domain of Sarawak to an English adventurer, James Brooke, who had helped him to quell a rebellion there. Thereafter, three "white rajahs" of the Brooke family in succession ruled Sarawak, which became a British protectorate in 1888 and then a crown colony in 1946. North Borneo was similarly incorporated by the British, first as a protectorate, then as a colony in the same years.

The Philippines. After leading a relatively isolated life for most of the colonial period, in the last half of the nineteenth century the Philippines began to receive liberal political and economic ideas filtered in from Europe. Filipinos became restive and a nationalistic movement arose.

Early Nationalism. Among early nationalist leaders was José Rizal (1861–1896), the "Father of His Country." He was a man of wide interests, a linguist, surgeon, artist, and writer. He wrote two novels critical of Spanish rule, *Noli Me Tanger* (*Social Cancer* or *The Lost Eden*) and *El Filibusterismo* (*Reign of Greed*). He was charged by the Spanish with instigating rebellion, and on December 30, 1896, was executed. Filipinos commemorated the date, setting it as the one for presidential inaugurations after the Republic was established.

More unrest ensued. But divisions among insurrectionists led to a truce with the Spanish in 1897. Rebels who gave up their arms were granted amnesty; some, including Emilio Aguinaldo, went into exile. Then in 1898 the Spanish-American War broke out. At first, American plans were not definite as to the disposition of the Philippines after the war. Congress debated the issue, while President William McKinley struggled and prayed over it. The upshot of the arguments and counterarguments was to retain the archipelago, to "uplift and civilize and Christianize" the already civilized and Christianized Filipinos.

After the American Admiral George Dewey defeated the Spanish navy in May, 1898, Aguinaldo returned to the islands and proclaimed an independent Philippine Republic on June 12. (The date was adopted later by the Philippines Republic as its independence date instead of July 4, earlier decreed by Americans.) But following the occupation of Manila by Americans, on August 13, 1898, conflict developed between them and leaders of the Philippine Revolutionary Government, located in nearby Malolos. There a convention ratified the earlier declaration of independence and adopted a constitution.

American Rule. On February 4, 1899, two days before the United States Senate (by a one-vote margin) ratified the Spanish-American treaty, hostilities broke out between the Filipinos and Americans. Refusing to recognize American sovereignty, Filipinos continued guerrilla warfare under Aguinaldo for three years before United States military forces were able to "pacify" the country.

Before the outbreak of guerrilla warfare, President McKinley had appointed a special commission to secure on-the-spot information upon which to base policy. After the group returned with its report, in June, 1900, a permanent Philippine Commission, headed by Judge William Howard Taft, went to the Philippines for the purpose of gradually replacing military with civilian rule. The Commission created a judiciary and a department of education and reorganized local administration. Provincial and municipal governments were elected by literate male property-owners. On July 4, 1901, the central military administration was replaced by a civilian one. Taft became the first governor-general of the islands, with the Philippine Commission as an advisory council.

The new government laid the groundwork for social and economic reform. It instituted public health measures and put currency on the gold standard. With papal approval, it redistributed 430,000 acres of friar lands. It organized a system of primary and secondary schools. In 1908 the University of the Philippines was established.

The peace treaty had provided for a ten-year period in which no legislation could exclude economic rights of third parties in the islands. At the end of this time, in 1909, Congress brought the Philippines inside the American tariff system. Philippine exports —chiefly sugar, coconut products, hemp, and tobacco—were tied to American markets. The islands had assured markets and a budget balanced through the levying of local taxes.

Political Reforms and Preparation for Independence. In its initial years of rule, the American government did not grant Filipinos any appreciable degree of self-government. The Cooper Act of 1902 authorized the taking of a Philippine census after which a national elective assembly would be constituted. The *Nacionalista* Party was formed, under the leadership of Manuel Quezon and Sergio Osmeña, to take part in the elections. In October, 1907, the first Philippine Assembly met with 81 members. The Philippine Commission, which eventually was expanded to include five Filipinos and four Americans, all appointed, became the upper house of the legislature. In 1908 the first Filipino was appointed to cabinet rank.

Under the administration of President Woodrow Wilson, the Democrats implemented their promise of moving the Philippines toward independence. Many Filipinos, some replacing Americans, were made government officials. In 1916 Congress passed the Jones Act, which promised independence for the Philippines as soon as a "stable government" was established. The Philippine Commission, then acting as an upper house, was transformed into a 24-member (22 elected) Senate and the Assembly was enlarged to 93 (84 elected). The governor-general, however, retained veto power over all legislation. In 1918 the Council of State, or cabinet, was established. The following year the governor-general reported that a stable government had been achieved, but by then the Democrats had lost their majority in the Congress, and no action was taken.

During the Republican administrations of the 1920's, the Filipinization policy was halted. In the 1930's, however, the Democratic administration of President Franklin Roosevelt reconsidered the situation. American interests were divided on the issue of independence. Farm and labor groups protested the competition of duty-free Philippine products and considered the islands a liability. Other groups, including manufacturers, shippers, and missionaries, favored American retention. After two unsuccessful attempts to enact legislation acceptable to both Filipinos and Americans, in 1934, the Tydings-McDuffie Act was passed. The Act provided for Philippine independence on the first fourth of July after a ten-year transitional Commonwealth status, during which United States authority would continue in external affairs.

In early 1935 a constituent assembly met in Manila to establish the Commonwealth government. The new constitution provided for a president elected for one term of six years and a unicameral assembly of 120 members. After the constitution was ratified, elections for national office were held. Quezon was elected president and Osmeña vice-president. On November 15, 1935, the Philippine Commonwealth government was inaugurated in Manila.

Economic Problems. The new government had to face long-festering economic and agrarian problems. In the mid-1930's, a peasant movement called the *Sakdalistas* demanded reforms in Central Luzon. Peasants destroyed land records and seized estates. The government suppressed this uprising, but economic unrest continued. A Philippine Communist Party was founded in 1931, but was soon dissolved. When it was again legalized in 1938, it followed a united-front policy, and Communist leaders took part later in guerrilla activity against the Japanese.

During the decades of the American occupation, Filipinos enjoyed improved educational and health facilities. Peace and order prevailed; the currency was stablized; humane penal laws and prisons were established; an independent judiciary functioned; and a relatively speedy—for Southeast Asia—path to autonomy was pursued. Less successful were American efforts in promoting economic welfare. The gap between rich and poor remained, if it was not widened. Economic exploitation by both foreign and native interests continued. Americans and Chinese controlled investments in banking, shipping, and industry; aristocratic Filipinos and mestizos were landlords. Despite a comparatively high degree of literacy and education in the archipelago, the selective benefits of modernization were to plague future regimes.

Indonesia. During the last half of the nineteenth century

Dutch expansion and consolidation in Indonesia were completed. Between 1850 and 1870, Celebes and non-British Borneo, as well as the Moluccas and other small eastern island groups, came under Dutch rule. In Sumatra fighting persisted, but all of the island, including the militant Acheh territory, was finally conquered. Western New Guinea came under Dutch control; the eastern half of the island was divided between the British and the Germans.

Political Reforms. With the spread of liberalism in mid-nineteenth-century Europe, the Dutch instituted reforms in their colonial policies. In 1848 the Dutch Parliament requested annual reports on conditions in the islands, and six years later it adopted a constitution promulgating colonial policies, including abolition of slavery, establishment of native schools, and regulation of compulsory labor. The reform movement was furthered in 1860 when a retired civil servant, Douwes Dekker, published a novel (*Max Havelaar*) portraying evils of the Dutch colonial system.

Additional reforms in Indonesia included a civil service law, an auditing act, and a modest educational program. Royal economic monopolies were abolished, and the culture system was phased out. The Agricultural Act of 1870 allowed free enterprise for Dutch investors. Private interests took over government plantations on lease from communities. They were not, however, allowed to buy land, and peasant tracts were protected. The resultant mixture of large estates and small holdings lasted into modern times. Extractive industries, notably tin and oil, developed. Various social classes participated in the plural economy. Dutch and other Europeans managed estates and finances; Chinese constituted the middle men; Indonesians, below the aristocracy, provided the labor force.

In Indonesia, the Dutch proceeded faster than the French in Indochina but slower than the British in Burma and the Americans in the Philippines toward the goal of home rule. The Dutch promoted what they defined as Indonesian welfare, expressed in 1901 as the "ethical policy," an extension of the earlier liberal policy. This included economic development, expanded social welfare services, a wider educational system, and political decentralization. A policy of "unhurried adjustment" initiated reforms. As yet, Indonesian nationalism had not appeared to demand more indigenous rights, though the beautiful Javanese princess, Raden

Adjang Kartini (1879–1904), who died in childbirth, worked for the emancipation of Indonesian women. Implementing the ethical policy, the Decentralization Act of 1903 and subsequent decrees established in selected areas advisory municipal and district councils composed of Europeans, Indonesians, and Chinese. The Village Act of 1906 provided for indigenous local administrations. In some provinces and residencies, indirect rule continued, with self-government by local rulers proceeding under Dutch residents.

The Dutch initiated educational reforms, mainly in the elementary stage. Beginning in 1907, village schools were constructed, with villagers providing the labor and the government the materials, teachers, and texts. Secondary and higher education was slower in coming. In the 1920's, general middle schools that taught Western learning were created, and professional schools were established at Batavia, though there was no university until 1941.

Foreign investments grew in the early decades of the twentieth century. Western capital was encouraged, and Indonesian natural resources, unhindered by any closed-door policy, were integrated with world markets. The Dutch East Indies registered gains in financial, production, and marketing operations. However, as in other Southeast Asian colonies, few natives shared in the accumulation of wealth.

Rise of Nationalism. The emerging Indonesian nationalist movement was kept strictly controlled by the Dutch. The *Budi Utomo* (Beautiful Endeavor Society), founded in 1908, was a cultural association headed by Javanese aristocrats. Dutch Eurasians organized several parties. In 1912 a militant organization known as *Sarekat Islam* (Islamic Association) was formed. Its announced aims were to promote Indonesian commerce, Indonesian economic co-operation, and the Islamic faith. Led by merchants and the Western-educated elite, the Association developed broadening programs aimed not only against the Chinese but also against the Dutch and the Indonesian aristocracy. Committed to economic and religious particularism, it became increasingly nationalistic.

The interwar period in Indonesia, as elsewhere, witnessed economic prosperity in the 1920's and a slump in the early 1930's. The initial boom years brought more Dutch to the archipelago in both official and private capacities, increased foreign investments, and augmented markets for diversified estate products. But in the course of the following depression the Dutch, additionally faced with the influx of cheap Japanese goods, tried to establish quotas not only on imports but on exports. As the country weathered the adverse years, the Dutch developed a sense of partnership with Indonesia. They also changed their governmental attitudes from one emphasizing social welfare to a program of gradual administrative reforms.

In 1918, reacting to nationalistic forces produced by the First World War, the Minister of Colonies declared as Dutch policy the development of Indonesia's resources and the education of Indonesians toward self-rule. Shortly thereafter the *Volksraad* (People's Council) convened in Batavia. With a Dutch majority, it was an advisory body of 48 members, half appointed by the governor-general and half elected by city and local councils (those created in 1903 in selected areas). In the course of the 1920's, Indonesians gradually achieved the majority in the Volksraad. The governor-general retained the right of veto, but the council received some legislative powers. It passed the annual budget, subject to parliamentary review in the Netherlands. Its members could and did criticize official policy, and this became their main function.

In 1927 a decree divided Java into three provinces, each with a governor and partly elected councils with an Indonesian majority. Parts of provinces were designated as autonomous regencies; by 1930, there were some fifty of these, all with regency councils. These councils, along with the local and provincial ones, elected the Volksraad. The Outer Islands were later organized into the three provinces of Sumatra, Borneo, and the Great East. In 1936 the Volksraad called for a conference to discuss Indonesian self-government or independence under the Dutch constitution. Queen Wilhelmina did not consider the request.

Several nationalist strands were in evidence in the interwar period outside of the officially sponsored and approved Volksraad. The Muslim-oriented one was most prominent. Declining in the 1920's, Sarekat Islam was replaced by two other Islamic-based parties: the urban and reformist *Muhammadijah,* and the rural and conservative *Nahdatul Ulama* (Muslim Scholars). These parties were primarily interested in religious and social issues, but they also furthered the growth of nationalism. In 1927 the Indonesian Nationalist Party, led by an eloquent young engineer, Sukarno, was founded in Bandung. Sukarno advocated Indonesian independence through combined efforts and non-co-operation with the Dutch, who reacted promply and predictably to dissolve the party. Sukarno and other nationalist leaders, including Mohammed Hatta and Sutan Sjahrir, were exiled.

A third nationalist strand was Communist. The 1917 Russian revolution encouraged the Indonesian revolutionary movement, which that year affiliated with the Sarekat Islam. In 1920, this group became the Indonesian Communist Party, the first Communist Party in Asia. Rifts soon developed with the Party because of violent Communist tactics. The following year, members of the Communist Party were expelled from the Sarekat Islam. Continuing to instigate strikes and disorders, the party was banned in 1926 by the Dutch. Many of its members were exiled, and the movement went underground.

In or out of the government the opportunities for Indonesians to participate in the democratic process had been limited. The role of the Volksraad was constricted; that of the parties negligible. The few educated indigenous elite were relegated to permanent opposition roles at national and local levels. Nor had there been any substantial place for Indonesians in the country's economy. By 1937, the Dutch, like the French in Indochina, had contained the festering nationalist movement. But the very fact of its repression was to constitute a future source of great strife between the parties involved.

14
CHINA AND INNER ASIA 1844–1937

In a slowly modernizing China the years between 1844 and 1937 witnessed the decline of an alien Manchu dynasty, the impact of the West, and the growth of Chinese national consciousness. Western presence and ideas not only helped to undermine Manchu authority but also dislocated traditional Chinese cultural patterns. Over the years China was wracked by political, economic, and social revolutions. Contending factions sought to unite the country. In time the disparate schools narrowed down to a contest and political struggle between the Nationalists under Chiang Kai-shek and the Communists under Mao Tse-tung. Then in 1937 came the outbreak of conflict between Japan and China, which added new dimensions not only to the domestic Chinese scene but to the Far East as a whole.

IMPERIAL DECLINE (1844–1912)

As a result of the first treaty settlement of the 1840's, Westerners acquired toehold bases in south coastal China. They expanded from these areas, receiving more rights and privileges over the decades. Through subsequent treaty provisions they penetrated all of China. Manchu rulers and Chinese intellectuals varied in reaction to Western encroachments. Some accommodated themselves; some ignored the alien presence; others compromised with foreign ideas. Those who favored Westernization were themselves divided as to what to adopt and how to adopt fresh ideologies and institutions. Thus China was modernized in a wrenching process that involved divided Chinese, disintegrating Manchus, and forceful Westerners.

***Initial Modernization** (1844–1874)*. As a result of the first treaty settlement, foreigners flocked to the open ports. Traders and missionaries came there to reside. Few Chinese or treaty-port Westerners knew the language of the other party, and a type of "pidgin," or corrupt, English arose as a medium of communication. Scholars of China were rare, though an American Protestant, S. Wells Williams, compiled a dictionary and the first general account of China, *The Middle Kingdom* (1848), available to Americans. In the midst of minimal contact, misunderstandings arose at all levels. In the wake of the treaties and enforced foreign presence, some Chinese sought ways to graft onto Chinese life some of the more desirable imported concepts. Some in the south continued, in the earlier tradition of the Manchu school of statecraft, to examine what caused Chinese weaknesses and seek ways to invigorate decaying institutions. Lin Tse-hsü composed a book on maritime history that included updated naval tactics. But the official line generally subscribed to by the Manchu was to ignore the foreigners. The situation simmered along until the outbreak of the Taiping ("Heavenly Peace") Rebellion.

The Taiping Rebellion. Lasting over two decades, this rebellion was a major event of nineteenth-century Chinese history; because of it at least twenty million perished directly or indirectly. Its leader was Hung Hsiu-ch'üan (1814–1864). A peasant who belonged to the minority group called Hakka, he was a poor student who failed the traditional Confucian examinations repeatedly. Converted in Canton to Christianity, he began to preach his own brand and attracted a following. He predicted a millennium for China in which he would rule the state in good Confucian hierarchy with Christ as the "Heavenly Elder Brother." Amassing followers in the south, in the early 1850's he moved up to the Yangtze Valley. In addition to the planned overthrow of Manchu rule, he promised land redistribution to peasants and other social reforms. Westerners, initially sympathetic to the movement, withdrew moral support because of its violence and its perversion of Christian theology. Hung died, and with no successors but divided leadership, the rebellion faded by 1865. As a typical Chinese agrarian-religious revolt, the uprising unfolded according to historical form. But the Taiping phenomenon was also revolutionary because it was spawned in part by modern factors, including the humiliation of China by Western powers and the introduction of Christian ideas.

The Taiping threat was the greatest of many mid-century

rebellions. Bandit groups roamed at will throughout the land. The *Nien* groups in North China were particularly destructive. Two serious Muslims revolts occurred, one in the south and another in the west.

Western Inroads. In the midst of internal strife, the Manchu faced renewed Western aggression. In 1856 war once more erupted between Peking and the British, now allied with the French. The immediate causes for war were the British charge that the Chinese had poisoned Hong Kong bread and the Chinese boarding of a British-owned ship, the *Arrow,* in Canton where its cargo was confiscated. The French excuse for war was the murder of a French priest in southern China, far beyond treaty boundaries. Though invited to join as allies, Russians and Americans stayed on the sidelines. The conflict was easily won by the British and French. They retook Canton, pushed into North China, and occupied Tientsin. Treaties there were once again negotiated with the Chinese. But before ratifications could be exchanged, fighting again broke out, and British-French forces moved on Peking, where they burned the summer palace as a punitive move.

The second settlement consisted of a series of new treaties. Because of the most-favored-nation clauses, the Americans and Russians in later treaties received similar rights. The Tientsin Treaties (as they were called) with the British and French ceded a part of Kowloon opposite Hong Kong to the British in perpetuity. New indemnities were imposed. The Chinese were to create a foreign affairs bureau and permit alien diplomatic residence in Peking. The term "barbarian" was dropped in official communications. The treaties added ten more ports to trade and residence, while the supplementary Treaty of Peking in turn opened Tientsin to trade. The Yangtze was made accessible to Western merchant ships. Foreigners were allowed to travel in the interior, and missionaries received added protection. Tariff schedules were revised, and the opium trade was legalized.

Russia, through two special treaties, received additional consideration. In the Aigun Treaty of 1858, China ceded to Russia the territory north of the Amur River to the watershed but kept joint occupation of the territory east of the Ussuri River in Siberia. Two years later, Russia received full title to the latter territory, known as the Maritime Province. Manchu rulers, through pledges of aid, concluded these treaties because Russia had promised them help against British and French forces. But the Russians never aided the Chinese; instead, Anglo-French forces occupied the capital; and so the Chinese lost all around. Without committing manpower Russia won out. Yet several times again in later decades the Chinese turned to the Russians for help.

Modernizing Measures. The Taiping Rebellion and the second treaty settlement spurred at Peking a program of limited reform known as the T'ung-chih Restoration, termed after the reign name of the Manchu emperor (1861–1874). Some new leadership emerged in this interim. Prince Kung, a man in his late twenties, stayed behind to negotiate with the Western powers after the court fled south in 1858. A few Chinese generals also rose to prominence through platforms of reforms and efficiency. Of these probably the most important was Tseng Kuo-fan. In the process of defeating the Taiping he organized the first modern army in China. His tactics of restoration were to re-establish civilian morale, reinstitute the examination system, rebuild libraries, and return pacified areas to normalcy. Li Hung-chang, his disciple, operated in the Shanghai area, where he established arsenals. He also founded a Chinese navigation company, a coal mine, and a textile mill. Developing into a statesman-diplomat, he later negotiated for China some of its chief treaties.

With a few top men promoting some Westernization, Peking embarked on a limited reform program under the T'ung-chih emperor. It restored peace and order by quelling not only the Taiping but also the Nien and Muslims. In the latter campaigns, Tso Tsung-t'ang, another strong Chinese general in the employ of the Manchu, was particularly effective. The Manchu government also reduced the land tax, initiated a more effective collection, instituted economy measures at court, and sent the first Chinese abroad to learn various technological skills. The conduct of foreign relations was modernized with the establishment of the Tsungli Yamen, an office to deal with the West. The T'ung-chih measures also included the modernization of the military, the promotion of industry, and the construction of short railroad and telegraph lines.

Some of the court protested even a program of limited

modernization. Heading the opposition was Tz'u-hsi (Empress Dowager), who in effect directed the political fortunes of China from the mid-1870's until her death in 1908. A Manchu concubine of the emperor, she presented him with a son who became the T'ung-chih emperor. Throughout the period of his minority, she was the actual ruler of China. When he died the year after attaining majority, the empress chose to succeed him a nephew four years of age, known as the Kuang-hsü emperor. In 1884 she ousted Prince Kung and his clique. She misappropriated naval funds to rebuild the summer palace. She had little concept of important state matters and underestimated the strength of the West.

***Reform and Reaction** (1874–1900)*. Some Chinese in the post T'ung-chih period continued to opt for modernization. Tso Tsung-t'ang and Chang Chih-tung, another bureaucrat, showed interest in constructing railroads financed by consortiums, or groups of foreign powers. But while China needed general reorganization on a broad basis, the measures taken tended to be piecemeal, halting, and ineffective. K'ang Yu-wei (1858–1927) was one of the few Chinese who came to grips with the problem of total modernization. A scholar in the traditional Confucian system, he studied Western subjects and wrote several books, including *Confucius as a Reformer* and the *Ta T'ung Shu* (*Book of the Great Unity*), in which he envisioned universalism and social harmony as China's contribution to world civilization.

K'ang's ideas soon reached the youthful Kuang-hsü emperor, who, during a temporary retirement of the Empress Dowager, called the philosopher to effect reforms. In the spring of 1898, during the so-called One Hundred Days of reform, K'ang Yu-wei drafted edicts, which rained down upon the country from Peking. A multitude of measures were promulgated relating to constitutional monarchy, education, literacy, industrialization, military training, formulation of a budget, and the abolition of the banners (the traditional Manchu military units). Factionalism split the court, and the Old Buddha, as the Empress Dowager was familiarly known, came out of retirement to reassume command. Yüan Shih-k'ai, the commander of the only modernized army in the Peking area, sided with the conservatives rather than with the reformers, whose programs were abruptly squelched. K'ang escaped, and the reforms ground to a halt.

Relations with the West. As a result of the terms of the second treaty settlement, foreigners were now residing in Peking, along the China coast from Canton to Manchuria, and in the interior. Commercial and missionary interests expanded. Unique among the treaty ports, Shanghai grew phenomenally. There foreign settlements and concessions burgeoned. Chinese studied at home and abroad. The Tsungli Yamen founded a College of Foreign Studies to train young diplomats. In 1877 the first resident Chinese minister abroad took up his post in London. Within two years, other diplomatic posts were established in the United States, Japan, and Western Europe. Chinese students went to the United States, England, and France. Other Chinese who went abroad were the work emigrants and coolies (unskilled laborers), who fanned out over Southeast Asia and countries farther afield, including the United States.

By the end of the century, foreign interests in China had expanded further. In 1870 the French, as a result of mission persecution in the north, retaliated with extensive diplomatic demands. In the south they clashed over Vietnam with the Chinese. In 1885, with Li Hung-chang as negotiator, a treaty was concluded which ended Chinese suzerainty there. After a member of the British consular service was murdered in southwest China, the Chefoo Convention of 1876 gave the British, in addition to the usual indemnity and apology, more open ports on the Yangtze and official residence in Yunnan Province in the southwest. In 1887, after annexing the last of Burma, the British eliminated Chinese political influence there. That same year, the Portuguese received in perpetuity Macao, a colony they had leased since the mid-sixteenth century. Meanwhile, Russia in the 1881 Treaty of St. Petersburg had settled western China borders, established consulates in Turkestan and Mongolia, and received permission to trade in border areas without the payment of duties.

The United States also escalated interests. After the first treaty settlement, in 1845 representatives in Canton were upgraded from consuls to commissioners. In 1857 the rank again jumped to that of envoy extraordinary and minister, with residence at Peking. The most famous name in Chinese-American diplomatic relations of these years was that of Anson Burlingame (1862–1867), who was sent to Peking by President Abraham Lincoln. Counseling restraint in Western demands on the Chinese, he won favor in the host country. Upon his resignation from the United States diplomatic service, Peking requested his services to negotiate new and more equitable treaties for China. In 1868 Burlingame in Washington concluded a treaty with Secretary of State William Seward. The agreement provided for Chinese sovereignty in treaty ports over areas not already ceded; granted the right to station Chinese consuls in American ports; and extended reciprocal freedom of religion. Its terms provided for immigration of coolie labor into the United States. The provisions stipulated the most-favored-nation treatment for Americans in China and for Chinese in the United States except in naturalization cases. They proclaimed equal educational opportunity and reconfirmed American noninterference in Chinese affairs. Burlingame proceeded to European capitals in an attempt to wring similar concessions of equality for the Chinese government, but he died before completing his task.

War with Japan. Japan concurrently advanced interests in China and peripheral areas. In 1894 war broke out over Chinese and Japanese rights in Korea, where both neighbors had long historic affiliations. The conflict was short-lived and one-sided; the modernized Japanese fleets and troops easily defeated the Chinese. The next year, a treaty concluded at Shimonoseki imposed harsh terms on the Chinese. Among them, China renounced its suzerainty in Korea, recognized Korean independence, paid an indemnity, and opened four new treaty ports to Japan (which through the most-favored-nation clause became available to other powers). China ceded to Japan the Liaotung Peninsula in southern Manchuria, Formosa, and the Pescadores, an island group off Formosa. But within a week after the treaty was signed, Russia, France, and Germany, in the so-called Triple Intervention, forced Japan to retrocede the Liaotung Peninsula to China because it threatened sea approaches to Peking. The Japanese, bowing to superior force, complied, but received an additional indemnity from China for the territory lost.

Cessions to the West. As a result of the Sino-Japanese War, Westerners moved in to demand additional rights. Foreign powers sought to obtain additional cessions of territory and to create spheres of influence. They forced loans on the hapless Chinese and practiced financial imperialism. In the south the French asked for railway and mine concessions and the adjustment of the North Vietnam border. The Germans procured Kiaochow Bay in Shantung under a ninety-nine-year lease. The British, concentrating in the rich and vast Yangtze Valley, extracted other economic concessions, and obtained in 1898 the New Territories, extending behind Kowloon opposite Hong Kong on the mainland, on a ninety-nine-year lease. The Russians at the coronation of the czar at St. Petersburg in 1896 persuaded Li Hung-chang to sign a fifteen-year treaty of alliance directed against Japan. They also received the right to construct the Chinese Eastern Railway across North Manchuria as a short-cut to Vladivostok. In 1898 in the Liaotung Peninsula, from which they had three years earlier helped to eject the Japanese, they now received twenty-five-year leases for Port Arthur and Dairen. The Russians also built the South Manchurian Railway, a southern spur from the Chinese Eastern Railway to link up with the newly acquired coastal leaseholds.

As the dismemberment of China proceeded, the United States, concerned for its own rights and for those remaining to the Chinese, reformulated the Open-Door policy. In September and November of 1899, Secretary of State John Hay instructed American ambassadors in the chief European capitals and Japan to seek assurances from their accredited governments that they would freeze the spheres of influences, apply the Chinese treaty tariff equally in all spheres, and charge equal harbor and railway costs. Foreign replies gave only conditioned acceptance at best.

The Boxer Rebellion and Its Aftermath (1900–1905). After the third treaty settlement and with growing Chinese unrest, in 1900–1901 the Boxer Rebellion broke out in North China. An offshoot of an eighteenth-century secret society, the Boxers (so-called because of their closed-fist signal) initially revolted against the Manchu, but Tz'u-hsi redirected their energies against the foreigners. Encouraged by the Empress Dowager and court conservatives, they besieged the capital's Legation Quarter, where the foreign diplomats lived and worked. They killed several diplomats and a number of missionaries and desecrated foreign cemeteries. In the course of the rebellion (in July, 1900), Secretary of State John Hay in Washington circularized another round of Open-Door notes in ten European capitals and Tokyo giving the official position. American policy was to preserve Chinese territorial and administrative integrity, while at the same time to seek peace, protect treaty rights, and adhere to international law. More immediate American aims were to rescue Americans in danger, protect American lives and property, and stop the spread of disorders.

The Hay Notes did not prevent American military intervention in China. American troops participated in the joint allied action to lift the siege in Peking, which was finally retaken, looted, and burned as the court temporarily relocated southwest in Sian. In 1901 China signed with the Western powers the Boxer Protocol, the last extensive groups of demands imposed on imperial China. China tendered apologies to those countries whose ministers had been murdered and erected monuments in foreign cemeteries that had been desecrated. To undercut the Confucian basis of Chinese political life, the allies demanded the suspension of civil service examinations for five years in all places where foreigners had been manhandled or killed. The Chinese government posted edicts in all district towns discouraging antiforeign activities. The Tsungli Yamen was transformed into a full-fledged Ministry of Foreign Affairs. China was prohibited from manufacturing munitions. An indemnity of $333.9 million was paid to thirteen powers. (The United States later returned its share, which was used for Chinese education.) The powers occupied strategic posts in North China and moved the Legation Quarter in Peking to a better defensive location. Using the Protocol as a cover to improve commercial relations, the foreign states amended the existing treaties of commerce and navigation.

China emerged from the Boxer experience with increased debt, in greater humiliation, and in effect a subject nation. Large-scale contingents of foreign troops were stationed in the country. Following the Russo-Japanese War of 1904–1905, China, though not a belligerent, had to acquiesce in Japan's assumption of Russian rights, railroads, and ports in South Manchuria, where concessions once again changed hands. The Protocol and allied events impressed on some Chinese more than ever the urgency of creating a strong China. To carry on the work initiated by Tseng Kuo-fan, Tso Tsung-t'ang, Li Hung-chang, and K'ang Yu-wei, other reformers came to the fore. Among their ranks was

Liang Ch'i-ch'ao, who came into prominence during the Hundred Days of Reform. A pupil of K'ang Yu-wei, he advocated nationalism but in moderate guise. A leading editor and journalist, he was influential until around 1905, when his evolutionary tactics lost favor among the revolutionary-minded youth.

Revolution and the End of the Empire (1905–1912). Some Chinese wanted to take direct action in the political arena. Of these the most prominent was Sun Yat-sen (1866–1925), called the father of the modern Chinese political revolution. A southerner, he traveled widely in his country and abroad to get financial and personal backing for his programs. His original revolutionary organization was the *Hsing Chung Hui* (Prosper China Society), active for a decade (1894–1905), whose aim was to establish a republic. He then created another society, the *T'ung Meng Hui* (League of Common Alliance). The League's political manifesto and early publications embraced the "Three People's Principles" (*San Min Chu I*): people's rule (nationalism), people's authority (democracy), and people's livelihood (socialism). He also outlined the three stages in the revolutionary process to achieve these ends: the first one of military control, the second of political tutelage, and the final one of democratic, constitutional government. These ideas were later elaborated in books and subscribed to by the Nationalist government of Chiang Kai-shek.

As the revolutionaries embarked on extremism, the Manchu effected last-minute reforms. In 1905 the civil service examinations, already suspended, were abolished. In effect over some two millennia, the system came to an abrupt end, with nothing to replace it. The Empress Dowager also ordered the provincial governors to modernize their troops. Some concessions were made toward representative government. In 1906 an edict pledged the formation of a constitutional monarchy. Three years later, after the Empress Dowager's death, provincial assemblies were elected by a limited franchise with high property qualifications. The assemblies convened but displayed an independence of mind. In a second step, in 1910, a national assembly was formed. Also not docile, it openly discussed in Peking political issues of the day.

The last-minute Manchu reform program helped to terminate dynastic rule rather than prolong it. The program did not satisfy the Chinese revolutionaries. On October 10, 1911, in Wuhan, the militant League of Common Alliance precipitated an uprising, which spread to other cities and provinces to become national in movement. (The date—"Double Ten"—was later appropriated by the Nationalists as a national holiday commemorating the start of the Chinese Revolution.) Before the end of the year a nationalist council representing revolutionaries assembled at Nanking and elected Sun Yat-sen provisional president. Yüan Shih-k'ai tried to save the situation for the dynasty, but Manchu days were numbered. On February 12, 1912, the throne was abdicated on behalf of the six-year-old emperor, Pu-yi. Yüan then threw his military arm behind the revolutionaries. Sun bowed out of office while Yüan stepped in to become president of the new Republic of China. Thus ended abruptly the ancient Chinese dynastic structure.

REPUBLIC OF CHINA (1912–1937)

The Republic of China was in fact a hollow shell. For two and a half decades after 1912, the country was divided into politically warring factions. The years were strife-filled because no effective national political structure replaced the late empire. Regionalism increased; economic distress compounded; Western and Japanese political demands compromised Chinese sovereignty. Philosophies from left and right competed for the ideological mantle of Sun Yat-sen, though all indigenous parties sought as their ultimate aims Chinese unity and the termination of the unequal treaties. Despite manifold problems, the growth of Chinese nationalism during this interim was significant in both its positive, or pro-China, stance and in its negative, or anti-West, expression.

***Political Disunity** (1912–1928)*. The Republic began with Yüan Shih-k'ai as president in Peking. Essentially a military regime and one recognized by foreign powers, it claimed to speak for the whole country, though it was effective only in North China. After Yüan's death in 1916, other presidents and prime ministers came and went in rapid succession at the capital. In opposition to the northern republic was a rival party and government centered in the south, the *Kuomintang* (National People's

Party), Sun Yat-sen's third party, founded in 1912. Then there were warlords who set up their independent military entities throughout the land which were based generally on provincial strength. They played an important role in modern Chinese history, but they lacked any appealing or popular ideological foundations.

Effects of the First World War. In the First World War, Japan once again entered a weak and politically divided China. Allying itself with the West, Japan appropriated German rights in China. These were concentrated mainly in Shantung Province with the newly built port city of Tsingtao, its surrounding territory, railroads, and economic concessions. Going further, the Japanese in 1915 pressed on Yüan Shih-k'ai's government the Twenty-One Demands in which the Japanese sought possession of the German rights in occupied Shantung, the extension of southern Manchurian leaseholds and acquisitions, more economic concessions in the Central Yangtze, the nonalienation of territory along coastal China opposite Taiwan (which, as previously noted, Japan acquired in 1895), and various miscellaneous privileges and rights, such as joint Sino-Japanese ventures in administration and military affairs. After these terms leaked out, Secretary of State William Jennings Bryan of the Wilson administration informed China and Japan that the United States would not recognize any agreement that impaired American treaty rights in China. The Japanese backtracked on some demands, but the Chinese acquired greater national consciousness and more distrust of their Asian neighbor.

The Republic of China also joined the Allied wartime cause but played only a negligible role in the First World War. At Versailles the Chinese wanted to terminate the unequal treaties but met with little success. The Japanese kept Shantung rights and over-all Western privileges were not ended. After learning of the diplomatic defeats, on May 4, 1919, several thousand Chinese students demonstrated in Peking. They directed their particular ire against the Japanese and held anti-Japanese rallies. Student unrest spread throughout the country and extended to the treaty ports, where Japanese goods were boycotted. The May Fourth movement remained significant in modern Chinese history, in part because groups, including merchants and laborers, not historically noted for political activism participated in issues of the day. Non-Marxists agreed that the outburst was the first strong indication of broadly based Chinese nationalism; Chinese Communists interpreted the phenomenon as the beginning of their movement.

Communism and the Kuomintang. By 1919 Communist doctrine had entered China in both Marxist and Leninist garb. From Marxism the Chinese Communists adopted such scientific socialist theories as an economic interpretation of history that emphasized control of modes of production; the five stages of history (primitive, slave, feudal, capitalist, and socialist); and class struggles. Leninism's legacy was as profound. It emphasized the importance of Communist parties as the vanguard of the political revolution to hasten the socialist (read communist) millennium. It dwelt on the negative aspects of imperialism and predicted its inevitable downfall. After 1919, Russians, representing both the new state and the Comintern, went out to China in search of converts; some Chinese, particularly in Peking, formed study groups and were won over. In July, 1921, the first congress of the Chinese Communist Party, with representatives from already formed provincial cells, convened at Shanghai. Twelve delegates and Maring (or Sneevliet) from Moscow were in attendance. Ch'en Tu-hsiu, a scholar from Peking National University, though not present, was elected secretary-general. Among the original founders of the Party was Mao Tse-tung. The Party affiliated with the Comintern.

The following year, Party members were authorized as individuals to join the Kuomintang Party, which the Russians realized was the most potent force for change at the time. Adolf Joffe was dispatched to China to initiate Soviet co-operation with Chinese nationalists. At Shanghai, in 1923, he signed an agreement with Sun Yat-sen, in which the Russians agreed to provide help in reorganizing the Kuomintang into a tightly knit party structure but without the Communist ideology. Reorganized the next year, the Kuomintang spearheaded a united front aimed against the warlords, the Republic at Peking, and the Westerners. Michael Borodin (born Grusenberg) became the most prominent of the civilian Russian advisers; General Galens (born Vassily Bleucher) was the principal military adviser. The Kuomintang army was also restructured under Russian guidance, with young Chiang Kai-shek as the chief Chinese general. As president of the newly established military academy at Whampoa, Chiang came from a military background. To Whampoa, he brought his former classmates and built up in traditional personalized Chinese style a group of army leaders loyal to him. Soviet advisers resented this, but they could do little about it. Coalescing several groups, the academy grew and the Kuomintang extended its influence in the south.

After helping to found the Chinese Communist Party and reshape the Kuomintang, the Russians proceeded to re-establish diplomatic relations (ruptured in 1917) with the Peking government. In 1924 Leo Karakhan of the Soviet Foreign Office went to China to negotiate a definitive agreement. This cancelled or replaced some former treaties, stipulated that Russia was not to engage in subversive activities in China, recognized Outer Mongolia as an integral part of China, and ended some Russian rights in China. But it kept a joint Sino-Russian management of the important Manchurian railroads.

The first united front (1924–1927) was a period of nominal co-operation among the Kuomintang, the Chinese Communist Party, and the Russians. Despite common aims, disparate groups competed for over-all power. The Kuomintang itself was rent with factions, and Chiang had a difficult task to keep the party viable after 1925, when Sun Yat-sen died. Military cliques worked at cross purposes with civilians, who themselves were split into left- and right-wing groups. The former wanted a greater degree of unity with the Communists and emphasis on land and social reforms, while the latter wanted less or none of this. The most important of the non-Communist Kuomintang left faction was Wang Ching-wei, a rival of Chiang's, to whom Sun Yat-sen dictated his last will shortly before his death. After a jockeying of forces, Chiang slowly improved his position in the party and vis-à-vis the Communists and planned a move north to subdue recalcitrant warlords and conquer Peking.

Reunification under Chiang Kai-shek. In the summer of 1926, the campaign to reunify China under the Kuomintang commenced its northward march in two columns, one with Chiang, most of his army, and the civilian right-wing Kuomintang faction; the other with the Russians, Chinese Communists, and the Kuomintang's left wing. Some warlords in the south gave in as the columns progressed north, and the British, impressed with newfound Kuomintang strength, promised to give up certain rights and privileges. But converging on initial success, the Chinese cause then divided. Upon reaching the Yangtze area, the two columns refused to coalesce. For added strength, Chiang turned to Chinese business leaders in nearby Shanghai and to Western powers. He combatted the antiforeign spirit which had surged once again from an incident of the year before, when Chinese police under British command had fired on demonstrating Chinese students and workers in Shanghai.

The left wing at Hankow, in the midst of a sprawling industrial complex, endeavored to effect socialist doctrines. It also provoked antiforeign incidents, such as those which broke out in Nanking in March, 1927, and which brought allied gunboats, including American, to the scene. But Chiang settled Western claims, and the next month in Shanghai he conducted an anti-Communist purge. Now that he was securely in control of the Kuomintang's right wing, Chiang's next step was to assume control of the whole party. In this move he was aided by swift-moving events in Hankow. There the non-Communist left faction of the Kuomintang under Wang Ching-wei on its own initiative expelled the Russians and the Chinese Communists because it had taken issue with their drastic land-reform measures and attempted nationalization of Hankow industries. Non-Communist left-wing leaders, moreover, feared that the Chinese might be subordinate to foreign interests, a possibility indicated in Stalin's communications to Chinese Communists working at Hankow along with the Russians.

The departure of the Russians, who returned home, and of the Chinese Communists, who went underground, eased the path for Kuomintang reunification under Chiang. In January, 1928, he was confirmed commander-in-chief of the army and chairman of the party's Central Executive Committee. With South and Central China partially reunited, Chiang then continued his march northward to subdue Peking and the northern warlords, who paid him token allegiance. The seat of the Republic of China was then relocated at Nanking ("Southern Capital") and the former northern capital was renamed Peiping ("Northern Peace"). Chiang considered that he had now implemented Sun Yat-sen's first stage of the Chinese revolution, that of military control.

Border Lands. Chinese peripheral land borders in these years were caught up in developments as they affected the Chinese scene. In Manchuria the warlord Chang Tso-lin, "the Old Marshal," operated independently of both the Peking regime and the Kuomintang, but he met rising Japanese military pressures. In the Liaotung Peninsula, where they had appropriated Russian economic rights in 1905, the Japanese had built up their security forces over the years into a veritable army. The Japanese, watching Chiang Kai-shek's move north and fearing a rapprochement between Chiang and the Old Marshal, in 1928 eliminated the latter and hoped his son, Chang Hsüeh-liang, "the Young Marshal," would be more amenable. In Sinkiang, with the outbreak of the Chinese revolution, the Chinese grip became weaker. Warlords there also acted independently or gave their allegiance to Chinese or Russian interests as they saw fit.

In Mongolia, in 1911, the Hutukhtu, the religious head of Mongolia, was proclaimed chief of an independent Mongolian state. Czarist Russia recognized the new regime and dispatched arms. But the Mongolian political position remained nebulous, because in 1913 Russia signed a treaty with the new Republic of China that recognized the latter's suzerainty while safeguarding Russian rights. In June, 1915, Russia convened at Kiakhta a conference of the three involved parties that in effect transferred Mongolia into a joint Sino-Russian protectorate. With the subsequent Soviet consolidation of Siberia, in 1921 a revolutionary government, spearheaded by the newly created Mongolian (Communist) People's Revolutionary Party, came into power at Urga, the capital (later renamed Ulan Bator). In 1924 it proclaimed the Mongolian People's Republic, the world's second Communist state. But in a Sino-Soviet treaty also concluded that year in Peking, the Soviet Union recognized Mongolia as an integral part of China. Over the years, under Marshal Choibalsan, a Stalin-like dictator, the Mongolian People's Republic pursued the Communist path. With Chinese attention diverted elsewhere, the Soviets came into paramount position.

***Nationalist China** (**1928–1937**)*. Now relocated at Nanking, the Republic of China under the Kuomintang, popularly called the Nationalist government, functioned and received international recognition. The United States recognized Chiang's government by concluding a treaty of commerce in July, 1928. But the Republic was far from unifying China because Nationalist power was still based primarily in the lower Yangtze area. In North China and Manchuria, as well as in some southern provinces, warlords continued to rule independently. Kuomintang factional struggles persisted. Personal rivalries continued among Nationalist leaders who were subordinate to Chiang. At Nanking, Wang Ching-wei remained in the left-wing faction, which urged more rapid policies toward representative government while the right wing wanted the consolidation of national power as the first order of priority. Over the years, despite obstacles the Kuomintang effected Sun Yat-sen's second period, that of political tutelage. In the Nationalist structure party, army, and government positions were interlaced; Chiang presided over all three components in top but complementary offices. The Organic Law of 1928 created the national bureaucratic structure but did not provide for mass participation. Attempts were made to promulgate provisional constitutions, but these were curtailed by Japanese invasions of North and Central China in the mid-1930's. In 1930 the Kuomintang formulated a basic land rent law stipulating that rent was not to exceed 37½ percent of the main crop. The Nationalist government recorded limited gains in establishing banks and a managed currency, in improving transportation lines, and in developing postal services.

Foreign Relations. In foreign affairs, the Nationalists concentrated their efforts on the "rights recovery" program, which was aimed at the termination of the unequal treaties with the West. Rebuffed at Versailles, the Chinese met with some later success. In 1928 they regained tariff rights, and in the following year they put into effect a native import tariff schedule, their first since 1843. At the Washington Conference (1921–1922), the signatories agreed to relinquish their post offices on Chinese soil. Some leaseholds were terminated in the ensuing years, but the powers remained in Shanghai, the most important and populous city. The Boxer indemnities were for the most part remitted, and the chief powers used the payments mainly for Chinese educational purposes, as had the United States. Little headway was made on abolishing extraterritoriality. (Not until 1943, in the midst of the Second World War did the United States surrender extraterritoriality in China, ninety-nine years after it had acquired the unequal right.)

MAO TSE-TUNG AND THE COMMUNIST MOVEMENT. Chiang and the Kuomintang were also concerned with the growth of the Chinese Communist movement. After its expulsion in July, 1927, from the Kuomintang left wing at Hankow, the Chinese Communist Party reorganized itself on Comintern orders. It created a scapegoat in Ch'en Tu-hsiu, who was later expelled from the Party for a variety of ideological crimes. The Party subscribed to Stalin's line that in spite of failures the Chinese revolution was entering a higher phase, one which was to be marked by insurrections and communes. In the face of overwhelming odds, the Chinese Communists between late 1927 and 1930 embarked on a series of rural and urban uprisings, all disastrous to them. While blame for failures was fixed on other Chinese Communists (Stalin was never criticized), some went to Russia for re-indoctrination, but Mao Tse-tung in home territory slowly and surely started his climb to the top.

From Central Hunan Province, Mao Tse-tung, born in 1893, in his youth had turned to communism. He helped to initiate the Chinese Communist Party and built up the Hunan provincial cell. During the first united front, he worked in the executive committees of both Communist and Kuomintang parties. After the split-up in 1927, he directed political efforts in his home province toward the peasants, his main force for the Chinese revolution. Over the years, he consolidated his gains, and attracted others to him, including Chu Teh, a military commander who on August 1, 1927, defected with some of his troops from the Nanchang branch of the Whampoa Academy. (The Chinese Communists mark the day as the establishment of their People's Liberation Army.) Maoism in early form emerged in the mountains of southwest China where it benefited from peasant support, Red Army strength, and a territorial base in a strategic location but with assured food supplies.

In November, 1931, Mao proclaimed the Chinese Soviet

Republic (known either as the Juichin Republic after the town in which it was proclaimed or the Kiangsi Republic after the province). There the Chinese Soviet issued its own constitution and laws. It received no substantial foreign aid as no foreign advisers or personnel were present to perform major roles. Alarmed by the growth of the Communist movement in the south, Chiang Kai-shek dispatched expeditions there. Applying ever increasing pressures through blockades, his troops ringed the Communist stronghold. Holding out for some time, the Chinese Communists then decided, whether on Moscow prodding or their own initiative, to evacuate and re-establish a new base of power to the north in the Yenan area of Shensi Province, closer to Mongolia and Russian territory, and where another Communist center was also located.

The "Long March" was an epic in Chinese Communist history. In October, 1934, in several columns and groups (and from other Communist pockets in China), they broke out of the Kuomintang encirclement and trekked their way toward the Yenan region. Over the ensuing year, the main bulk proceeded by circuitous routes through western to northern China. Initially numbering some 80,000, the marchers lived off the countryside. They marched through a dozen provinces, across mountain ranges, and fought major battles with opposition forces, usually local provincial warlord armies. Along the routes the soldiers continually propagandized the peasants. When they finally arrived at their destination and took command from the local Communist faction at Yenan, the Communist movement had been considerably weakened. Perhaps only a quarter survived the ordeal. But the Long March strengthened Mao's position. On the way in January, 1935, at a conference of Party leaders, and in the absence of any Russian advisers, he was formally elected chairman of the Central Committee. Simultaneously, Chiang's hand was also strengthened by the Long March because in its course local warlords and provincial armies assumed much of the brunt of the fighting. By weakening non-Communist opposition, the Kuomintang gained greater control of South and Central China.

Eventually the Chinese Communist factions coalesced and created the Yenan Border Government (1935–1949). Under Mao they initiated new tactics and revived old ones, with little or no outside aid. Under pressures generated by Japanese expansion and Kuomintang containment, the Yenan government assumed form. Mao was the chief power in the one-party government. His tactics were to harness peasant discontent and promise much to most groups, at least those with grievances in the class struggles as defined by Marxism-Leninism. As in the south, his regime in the north emphasized the role of the peasant and his participation in village councils. Cadres of workers and activists pushing Party aims were also organized. They accompanied Red Army units into "liberated" villages and indoctrinated the peasants. They initiated the administration of newly incorporated territory, proclaimed land reforms, and effected redistribution programs. They eliminated the age-old curse of foot-binding and promoted education and literacy.

Japanese Expansion and United-Front Efforts. As Chiang Kai-shek consolidated his power in Central China and the Communists entrenched themselves in the north, the Japanese in Manchuria were expanding their base of operations. Aided by developments in Japan that were leading to fascism and militarism, they were ready to take over the land. After an incident of September 18, 1931, when a train was blown up near Mukden, their Manchurian capital (an incident it turned out later that they had created), they forced Chang Hsüeh-liang and his army to evacuate into North China. The Japanese then established the puppet state of Manchukuo, from which they pushed toward and across the Great Wall. Chiang Kai-shek, more concerned in containing the Chinese Communists and involved in immediate problems in Central and South China, could not stem the Japanese advance in the northeast, where the invaders also set up puppet regimes.

The Japanese presence on the Asian mainland left repercussions on the Chinese scene. The two chief domestic parties initiated moves toward a second united front, this time to contain the growing foreign menace. As early as 1932, the Chinese Communists from the Juichin Republic had declared war on Japan, and they appealed for co-operation against enemy encroachments in Manchuria. From Yenan four years later, they reiterated the appeal, now backed by Russian support. The Comintern line opted for the united-front tactic in order to stop the rise of Hitler in

Germany and of fascism in Japan, both threats to the Russian state. Chiang at the time did not go along with the priority of stemming Japanese advances, for he put the containment of domestic communism as a more urgent goal. To this end he urged Chang Hsüeh-liang's troops in North China to eradicate the Communist neighbor. The warlord demurred; he assigned a greater priority to taking action against the foreign enemy, who had displaced him from his home base. In December, 1936, Chiang flew to Sian, near the Communist stronghold, to persuade the reluctant Chang to change his mind. Instead, the warlord placed him under arrest. The Chinese Communists (possibly on Moscow orders) acted as mediators. The triangular talks resulted in Chiang's release and warlord declarations pledging support to the Kuomintang Party in the foreground of another united front directed against the Japanese.

By 1937, China verged on a second united front. But the political pattern was not so clear cut. The Kuomintang and Chinese Communists competed for over-all power and recognition, but warlords were sprinkled throughout the country. Yet each protagonist had his own disparate prescription for national salvation. Negligible third parties advanced some liberal and centrists programs, but these left little impact in the times. With China divided, it seemed peculiar that the two main rival factions would again fashion a united front, this time to contain Japanese advances. But such was the case that year. Modern Chinese political history has been documented by surprising twists and turns.

15
NORTHEAST ASIA
1868–1937

Korea entered the last third of the nineteenth century with a faction-ridden court, politically dependent on China. Successful in holding the West back, it could not stop Japan, which took the lead in opening up the country. In so doing, Japan came into conflict first with China and then with Russia. Eventually, Korea became a Japanese colony, and the peninsula, long a scene of contending foreign powers and invasions, went down once again under another master. As Korea faded out of the Asian international scene, Japan's role rose phenomenally. The Meiji period was one of initial modernization and expansion, while the ensuing Imperial period witnessed Japan as Asia's first modern state and a world power poised to create one of the largest empires in history.

KOREA
(1868–1910)

Into the mid-nineteenth century, Korea continued to be a cultural and political dependency of China, which was itself falling to Western encroachments. But it was the modernizing Japanese who after the Meiji Restoration forced the opening of the country with its first treaty in 1876. Russia, Britain, and the United States followed Japan's lead, while the Koreans and their Chinese mentors tried to stem the tide of Westernization. Japan's stake was pre-eminent, and in successive degrees the Japanese assimilated the country. As a result of the Sino-Japanese War, China was evicted from Korea; and following the Russo-Japanese War, the Russians bowed out. Britain and the United States acquiesced in Japan's gain. In 1910 Korea came into a colonial status under Japan.

Korea and the Powers (***1868–1894***). As Western powers became entrenched in Peking and North China after the second treaty settlement, they turned their attention to problems of Korea, a "ceremonial" dependency of China. They complained to the newly created Tsungli Yamen of religious persecution and commercial restrictions in Korea, but the Chinese disavowed any responsibility. In 1855 the first Americans set foot in Korea; they were four deserters from a ship and spent a month in the country. When in 1866 the United States schooner *General Sherman* ran aground off Pyongyang, Koreans burned the ship and killed the crew, which included three Americans. After getting no satisfaction from the Chinese, in 1871 the United States sent its minister in Peking, with five warships, to Korea. Meeting resistance at the Han River, leading to Seoul, the expedition withdrew after bloody but indecisive battles. The American "retreat" made the Yi all the more seclusionist; in 1868 they also refused to establish diplomatic relations with the new Meiji regime in Japan.

Pressures built up in Japan for the relaxation of Korean rigidity in international conduct. In 1875 a Japanese survey ship and Korean shore batteries near Kanghwa were involved in an exchange of fire, and the Japanese government decided to use the incident to obtain a Korean treaty. Working through the Chinese and Li Hung-chang as intermediaries, they received their treaty the following year. Terms of the Kanghwa Treaty established diplomatic relations, opened three ports, acknowledged Korean independence, and allowed coastal surveys. After delays the Japanese established a legation in Seoul and developed commercial bases in the opened ports of Pusan, Inchon, and Wonsan.

Treaties with other powers also resulted. After their initial rebuff, the Americans, also working through Li Hung-chang, concluded in 1882 a treaty with the Koreans negotiated by Commodore Shufeldt. But Yi court factions were divided over the early open-door policy, and in the same year the Japanese legation was burned by an anti-West faction headed by the regent. The Japanese sent an expedition and amends were made. Legations of other states were established, and some young Koreans began to study Western subjects. In 1884 there was another confrontation at court between progressives and conservatives; the Japanese legation once again was destroyed. Neither the Japanese nor the Chinese, who maintained troops in Korea, wanted an embroiled country. In the Tientsin Convention of 1885 they agreed that neither nation would keep troops in Korea, nor return them if deemed necessary, without notifying the other party. However, the Chinese, though they had through Li Hung-chang encouraged Korea to open up, maintained their suzerainty status. Despite treaty inroads, they were determined to maintain effective control. Through their resident Yüan Shih-k'ai, they prescribed Korean policy and foreign affairs. Other powers complained of the special Chinese position which violated treaty most-favored-nation clauses. Augmenting problems was the persistence in Korea of an antiforeign strain, which during the mid-1890's was evidenced most noticeably in the Tonghak ("Eastern Learning") movement.

Korea and Japan (1894–1910). Japanese interests were most directly involved, and Tokyo resolved to oust Chinese influence. Concerned also over Russian presence in neighboring Manchuria, it sought to bring Korea into its sphere. In July, 1894, the Japanese attacked a Chinese troopship. Hostilities broke out and lasted over some eight months. The victorious Japanese occupied not only Seoul and Korean strategic areas but also South Manchuria and the Shantung Peninsula. Forces also landed on Formosa, another area of dispute. The Chinese sued for peace, and Li Hung-chang came to Shimoneseki to conclude a treaty. As noted in the previous chapter, China now recognized Korean independence; paid an indemnity (with the Japanese occupying Shantung until it was paid); and ceded Formosa with the nearby Pescadores and the Liaotung Peninsula. The Triple Intervention (Russia, Germany, and France) forced the retrocession of the Liaotung Peninsula to China, which then paid an additional indemnity. China was now out of the Korean picture, but another power, Russia, came to plague the pre-eminent Japanese position there.

In the course of their temporary wartime occupation of Seoul, the Japanese tried to effect reforms. The resisting Korean king sought refuge from his Japanese advisers and moved into the Russian legation. He granted the Russians economic and political concessions at a time (1896–1898) when the Chinese were granting similar concessions to the Russians in Manchuria. The Japanese, alarmed, twice in those years pressed for accommodation with Russia in Korea; but these steps were only temporizing in nature. From another quarter, the British were also alarmed at Russian incursions affecting their interests not only in

East Asia but elsewhere. The Anglo-Japanese Alliance of 1902 was the result of a coincidence of anti-Russian spirit, which was one of the factors that emboldened the Japanese to take stronger action in Korea.

With British diplomatic support, over the next two years the Japanese tried to persuade Russia to effect a Korea-for-Manchuria swap of spheres of influence. When this proved unsuccessful the Japanese, after long-drawn-out policy debates, resolved on conflict. In February, 1904, war broke out. Japanese troops once more occupied Korea and moved into South Manchuria and Russian leaseholds there, where land campaigns over the next year were bloody and extended. The main Russian fleet from the Baltic Sea, which had steamed around Africa and via Southeast Asia to Korean waters, was destroyed by Japanese naval forces in the Tsushima Strait. But with resources strained in both countries, the enemies sought a negotiated peace through United States President Theodore Roosevelt. The terms of peace were concluded in August, 1905, in Portsmouth, New Hampshire. (Neither China nor Korea, the two most directly affected noncombatant nations was present.) In the treaty, Russia acknowledged Japan's "paramount" position in Korea. This special Japanese status was also acknowledged by Britain that year in a revision of the Anglo-Japanese Alliance, as well as by the United States in an exchange of notes.

After the war, Japan continued military control and political tutelage over Korea. Koreans became increasingly restive as more Japanese called for annexation. In 1909 the Japanese resident-general in South Manchuria was assassinated by a Korean. The event added weight to the argument for complete control, and in August, 1910, Korea was formally annexed to Japan as the colony of Chosen. For the next three and a half decades it remained under authoritarian Japanese colonial rule.

MEIJI JAPAN (1868–1912)

During the first half of the Meiji period, until around 1890, the Japanese were primarily concerned with domestic matters. Their chief international endeavors were toward terminating the unequal treaties and expanding their boundaries to include offshore islands and archipelagoes. In the later half of the Meiji period, after establishing a strong domestic base, Japan became a world power. It embarked on wars with China and Russia; annexed Korea; and came into diplomatic accommodation with the major European powers and the United States. By the end of the period all the unequal treaties were terminated and replaced by new ones based on equality; Japan was the first state in Asia to achieve this goal.

***Consolidating* (*1868–1890*).** After the restoration of the Meiji ("Enlightened") emperor, his advisers, mainly samurai from Choshu and Satsuma, drew up the brief Charter Oath, which vaguely promised constitutional processes. This was promulgated in April, 1868, and two months later a more extended document outlined similar ends. The capital was moved from Kyoto to Tokyo, where the imperial family appropriated the former Tokugawa fortress. Over the years, the city grew in scope and importance and became the symbol of a modernizing Japan. The oligarchy, speaking in the name of the young emperor, instituted centralized government controls and modernized financial, postal, police, and juridical systems. They adopted the Western calendar in place of the lunar one and provided for religious toleration. They abolished the ranks of daimyo and samurai, who were pensioned off and given lump sum payments. There was some opposition to all these changes, and from Satsuma, in 1877, an ex-samurai, Saigo Takamori, led an abortive rebellion.

THE STATE. An outstanding figure in Japan's new civilian leadership was Ito Hirobumi (1841–1909). Of Choshu background, Ito studied in Europe and rose to high positions that included cabinet posts and eventually the prime ministership. He was impressed with the need to adopt Western knowledge, but he hesitated to accept a full-fledged parliamentary government in Japan. Another notable figure was Yamagata Aritomo (1838–1922), who also came from Choshu and studied abroad. Yamagata helped create the new conscript armies, one of which defeated Saigo's rebels. In later years Yamagata filled not only top military but also civilian offices: he was minister of war, chief of general staff, field marshal, home minister, prime minister, and president of the privy council. Later men from the Satsuma clan also became prominent in early Meiji politics.

The inner Satsuma-Choshu clique met its chief rivals in the

Tosa clan of Shikoku and the Hizen in Kyushu, who as former tozama lords had helped to overthrow the shogunate. After the restoration they found themselves relegated to the background, and their leaders founded Japan's first political parties to promote their interests. Itagaki Taisuke (1837–1919) of Tosa formed the first one, the Public Society of Patriots, in 1874. Within a few years it had become national in scope. It extracted some political concessions from Tokyo, including elected prefectural assemblies in 1878 and, two years later, similar assemblies in smaller administrative units. With Itagaki in the opposition was Okuma Shigenobu (1838–1922) of Hizen, who in 1881 forced a showdown in the cabinet over corruption in the Hokkaido Colonization Office and other issues. He lost office, but as a compromise move the throne promised to promulgate a constitution by 1890. In order to share in the constitution-making, in 1881, Itagaki formed the Liberal Party, and the next year Okuma organized the Progressive Party.

The emperor, however, commissioned Ito to draw up a constitution without party consultation. Working with an exclusivistic privy council, in the 1880's Ito hammered out a document. On February 11, 1889, the anniversary date of the founding of the ancient Yamato state, the emperor bestowed a constitution upon the people as a royal favor. Its provisions kept the political authority of the emperor, whose traditional divine status was reaffirmed. The bicameral parliament, or Diet, consisted of the upper House of Peers, comprising members of aristocratic standing and former daimyo, and the lower House of Representatives, elected by males over twenty-five who paid an annual tax of fifteen *yen* or more. The Diet had the right to initiate legislation, though most bills were presented by the government. It did not enjoy the power of the purse; fixed expenditures, including bureaucratic salaries and imperial household expenses, were beyond its regulation. The Diet never enjoyed real power, which remained in the emperor and his advisers, including the so-called *genro*, or elder statesmen, like Ito and Yamagata.

Economic Progress. In the first half of the Meiji period Japan's leaders also turned their energies toward the shaping of an industrial revolution, in line with a general policy to "enrich the nation and strengthen its arms." Observing the contemporaneous situation in China, where foreign loans incurred foreign interference, the Japanese did not seek loans abroad. The state initiated the economic programs, because they were of great scope and extended financing. The government controlled and operated basic industries, but it extended considerable subsidies to encourage the development of certain specified private industries. In 1872 it completed the first Japanese railway, between Tokyo and the port of Yokohama (a distance of only eighteen miles). It developed paper mills, textile plants, and other light industrial enterprises. After getting them off to a paying start, the government in the 1880's sold many of these businesses to private interests, who developed them further. The government practiced deficit financing until a centralized fiscal system could be established. Over the years agriculture remained the early chief source of wealth, with most of official revenue of the Meiji period derived from land.

Culture. In another area, the Meiji leaders discerned the importance of education. Drawing greatly on Western ideas but hiring few foreign advisers, they developed a modern universal education system. In 1871 the Ministry of Education was instituted, and it centralized control over thousands of schoolhouses and tens of thousands of teachers. The Imperial Rescript of 1890, however, emphasized the traditional arms of morality, social order, and loyalty. The press flourished. In 1870 in Yokohama the *Mainichi*, the first regular Japanese daily, began publishing, and in 1879, the *Asahi* chain was established. Into contemporary times these were the largest Japanese newspapers. To help rid the country of unequal treaties, the government initiated legal reforms with the adoption of basic criminal, civil, and commercial law codes. Meiji literature was also influenced by the West. American and European classics were translated, and the novel was developed.

Beginning of Expansion. The energies devoted to domestic affairs were also reflected in the creation of imperial foundations. The government enacted universal conscription and built up an army patterned after Prussian methods and a navy inspired by British model. With growing military might, Japan assumed growing territorial commitments. Japanese expeditions landed on Sakhalin and the Kurile chain, where they encountered Russian rivalry. In an 1875 treaty with Russia Japan gave up its claims to Sakhalin while Russia in turn relinquished claims to the Kuriles. In 1878 the Bonins, lying offshore in the Pacific, were annexed. To the south, the Ryukyus were incorporated. Curiously, these islands were claimed by China; paid tribute to the Satsuma clan; but acted independently by concluding a treaty with Perry. In 1871 some shipwrecked Ryukyuans were killed by aborigines on Taiwan, which was also claimed by China. Japan protested the act by formally annexing the Ryukyus the next year and later (in 1874) by dispatching a punitive expedition to Taiwan. The Chinese finally agreed to pay Japan an indemnity for the costs of the expedition as well as for murdered islanders.

Expanding (1890–1912). Under Satsuma and Choshu civilian and military leadership, constitutional government began after the emperor's promulgation of the document. Strong personalities dominated Japanese politics, and factions formed around leaders rather than around political programs or ideological issues. In the first parliamentary election (July, 1890), Itagaki's Liberal Party and Okuma's Progressive Party won a combined total of 171 out of 300 seats in the lower house of the Diet. However, despite their popular mandate, the parties had tough sledding in the Diet because government oligarchs worked against them. With Ito, Yamagata, and Matsukata Masayoshi of Satsuma as early prime ministers, the government intended to keep the status quo.

The State. Between 1896 and 1900, the government oligarchs, represented by the same three prime ministers, modified their opposition. They co-operated to some extent with Itagaki and Okuma, who in 1898 united in a coalition Constitutional Party. The new party won a resounding victory in that year's election, and Okuma became prime minister. However, the coalition soon fell apart over a division of cabinet spoils. The oligarchy reasserted rule; Yamagata stepped back in the prime-ministerial post, while Ito headed a new *Seiyukai Party* (Association of Friends of Constitutional Government). Between 1901 and 1913, two genro, Prince Saionji Kimmochi and General Katsura Taro, protégés of Ito and Yamagata respectively, alternated as heads of parties in premiership. But the country finally tired of political maneuvering and with the Emperor Meiji's death in 1912, a new period began in the Japanese political scene.

The Socialist Movement. Marxism also came to Japan in

these years. With a slow growth of the social conscience in the country, books with Marxist flavor were translated into Japanese and socialist magazines were circulated. A small group of individuals, including some Christians, established the Society for the Study of Socialism in 1898. Labor unions were organized in railroads and iron works. In 1901 the Social Democratic Party was formed, but the government promptly dissolved it. Three years later the *Heimin Shimbun* (*Common People's Newspaper*) was founded, and it managed to survive six years. Political protest was something novel to Japan, and the government took action against what it considered subversion. By 1911, twenty-three leading Socialists had been tried and twelve executed. Thereafter the movement temporarily disappeared from the Japanese scene.

The Economy. In economics, as in politics, Japan by 1890 was ready for a "break-through," at least in certain key industrial areas. Textile mills started the trend and other fields followed. The transfer of many government enterprises to private hands resulted in the first Japanese industrial boom. In the mid-1890's, another surge in industrial output occurred. Light industry became more diversified, and heavy industry became extensive in scope. Coal and steel factories, the manufacture of machine tools, electrical industries, chemical fertilizer plants, sugar refining, and cotton-weaving mills were among the more important. The Sino-Japanese War and the Russo-Japanese conflict further accelerated industrial development. However, rural life continued in traditional patterns. Farm acreage remained small. The conservative, rural, self-sufficient society emphasized time-honored and authoritarian values. On the other hand, cities grew in population and importance. There resided the zaibatsu, the urban middle class, and the mass of unskilled industrial laborers. Increasing urbanization and growing wealth helped to promote potential liberal political trends.

Imperialist Expansion. With politics and economics placed on firm domestic bases, Japanese embarked on imperialistic schemes much like those of the Western powers. Korea was its first chief target. Over the years, as noted above, Japanese control over that country increased. During the years between 1868 and 1876, the Meiji leaders established the fact of Korean independence and eliminated Chinese suzerainty. But since China refused to concede the growing Japanese role in Korea, over the next two decades (1876–1894), tense coexistence continued between the Chinese and Japanese there. The Sino-Japanese War resolved the issue in Japan's favor; the peace terms included the acknowledgment by China of Korea's independence. A subsequent growing Russian presence (1895–1904) was terminated by the Russo-Japanese War, which eliminated Russian influence not only in Korea but in South Manchuria, where the Japanese also stepped in. The Japanese position in Korea was aided by United States noninvolvement and by terms of the Anglo-Japanese Alliance.

Free from foreign intervention in Korea, Japan consolidated hold there until annexation in 1910. As the colony of Chosen, Korea played a key role in the Japanese movement into China, as did Taiwan in its southward expansion. The Japanese improved the Korean economy, though they did so for their own benefit as a colonial power. Having confirmed its supremacy also in South Manchuria, Japan next came to accommodation with the leading European powers. With Britain and France, there were no political conflicts. Between 1907 and 1916, Japan concluded four agreements with Russia to define spheres of influence in East Asia. By the time of the First World War, three of the great powers, Russia, England, and France, were favorable to Japanese expansion on the Asian continent.

The situation was different with the United States, as earlier friendly feelings between Japanese and Americans cooled after 1905. Basic problems between the two powers included Japanese immigration into the United States, commercial rivalry, and power politics in the Pacific. Protecting treaty rights in China and territorial presence in the Philippines, the United States was concerned with real or potential Japanese thrusts toward both countries. United States policies vis-à-vis Japan were somewhat contradictory. On the one hand, in an attempt to contain Japanese expansion, Secretary of State Frank Knox in 1909 proposed the neutralization of Japanese (and Russian) railroads in Manchuria and their operation by an international board. Both Japan and Russia opposed this proposal, and in fact it brought the two ex-enemies closer together. On the other hand, American policy seemed to accommodate to Japanese expansion. The Taft-Katsura Agreement signed in 1905 by Secretary of War William Howard

Taft and Prime Minister Katsura and the agreement signed in 1908 by Secretary of State Elihu Root and the Japanese Ambassador Baron Takahira recognized Japan's control of Korea. In turn, Japan disavowed interest in the Philippines. These agreements temporarily alleviated tensions, but in the post-Meiji period others were to arise.

IMPERIAL JAPAN (1912–1937)

After the passing of the Emperor Meiji from the scene, under two subsequent emperors Japan achieved international status. At home a more diverse leadership replaced the earlier oligarchy to include military men, bureaucrats, political parties, the zaibatsu, and middle classes. A growing liberal movement in the 1920's implied that the emperor was only the highest organ of the state and not an absolute independent entity. But many continued to subscribe to *kokutai*, or the national essence of Japan, which emphasized the country's uniqueness. In the 1930's this more extreme and particularistic position won out as Japan continued its imperial expansion.

Liberalism (1912–1930). Upon the death of the Emperor Meiji in 1912, his son succeeded him and began the Taisho ("Great Righteousness") era, which lasted until 1926. Along with a new emperor, other men came to high posts. The alternating premierships of Saionji and Katsura ended the following year, as politicians supported by mass rallies demanded the termination of oligarchical genro rule. An admiral was appointed prime minister, but after budgetary problems with the Diet he resigned. In 1914 the eighty-year-old Okuma, now heading the *Kenseikai* coalition party, received the office. Though in his younger days Okuma had supported representative government, his administration was characterized by nationalistic and imperialistic policies, including the presentation of the Twenty-One Demands to China. After two years in office, Okuma was replaced by a general, but this cabinet fell in 1918. In that year, Hara Kei, head of the Seiyukai, then the majority party in the Diet, was appointed prime minister. With the exception of the 1898 interim of the Okuma-Itagaki party coalition, Hara Kei was the first party leader and the first commoner to become prime minister. His appointment marked the end of genro rule and the inauguration of party government that lasted until 1932 (except for a hiatus between 1922 and 1924).

Relations with the West. Despite the establishment of party governments, cabinets continued to press for pre-eminent Japanese rights in East Asia and the Pacific. After the First World War, Japan sought rewards at the Versailles Conference. There it met with compromises. Japan, having occupied the former German Pacific possessions (Marshalls, Carolines, and Marianas), wanted them as colonies but got them only as League-mandated areas. It wanted clear title to former German rights in Shantung but had to give up some of them. It insisted on a declaration of racial equality in the League's Covenant, but was denied this because of adverse reaction in the United States and parts of the British Empire. However, Japan did make substantial territorial and political gains from its limited participation in the First World War.

At the end of the war, the Russian Revolution caused complications in Manchuria and Siberia. In the vacuum left by the collapse of czarist authority, Japan appropriated the Russian-administered Chinese Eastern Railroad in North Manchuria. The United States protested the direct Japanese action and created an inter-allied board to administer the railroad on an interim basis. The situation in Siberia was more difficult. In July, 1918, President Wilson reluctantly agreed to American participation in the Allied Siberian intervention. Its purpose was ostensibly to save the Czech troops (former prisoners of war or deserters from the Austrian army who were trying to make their way back to Europe); but actually it was to prevent Japan from taking over eastern Siberia. Some 9,000 American troops were sent; Japanese troops totaled 72,000. However by 1922, the Bolsheviks had gradually consolidated their hold over Siberia. The American troops were withdrawn in April, 1920, but the Japanese left only under pressures generated by the Washington Conference.

The Washington Conference (November, 1921, to February, 1922), was called to consider Far Eastern issues generally and Japanese-American problems particularly, including the immigration issue, commercial rivalry, and naval escalation. Previously, there had been some American acquiescence in Japan's pre-eminent interests in China. In 1917 Secretary of State Robert Lansing and Japanese Ambassador Viscount Ishii Kikujiro in an exchange of notes acknowledged that "territorial propinquity creates special relations." However, most American policies in Asia had been directed at curbing Japanese expansion. On several occasions between 1911 and 1920, the United States joined consortiums to finance railways in China in an attempt to thwart unilateral Japanese railroad schemes. In 1915 Secretary of State William Jennings Bryan expressed American disapproval of Japan's Twenty-One Demands on China. At Versailles, President Wilson did not back Japanese claims to the former German colonies in the Pacfic, their Shantung demands, or their proposed racial equality clause. The inter-allied board to manage the Chinese Eastern Railroad and the Siberian intervention in the aftermath of the First World War were also moves toward containing Japan.

In an attempt at peaceful settlement of Far Eastern issues, the Washington Conference drew up many agreements, of which three were the more important. The Five Power Naval Treaty (United States, Great Britain, Japan, France, and Italy) limited capital ships (battleships and aircraft carriers) to an over-all tonnage ratio of 5 : 5 : 3 : 1.75 : 1.75 respectively and prohibited the construction by signatories of additional fortifications of certain Pacific islands (excepting Singapore and Hawaii). The Four Power Treaty (United States, Great Britain, Japan, and France) bound the parties to respect each other's Pacific possessions and to take common action against any aggression in the area. The Nine Power Treaty, relating primarily to China, internationalized the Open Door. It was signed by the five powers plus four other nations (China, Belgium, Netherlands, and Portugal) with interests in the Pacific. These nations agreed to respect the territorial and administrative integrity of China. At the Washington Conference the Japanese also agreed to pull out of Tsingtao, the chief port on the Shantung Peninsula, but they retained control of the main railroad in the province for another fifteen years.

Party Government. Japan's signing of the Washington treaties was an indication that for the first time, its civilian-oriented party leaders were helping shape foreign policy. During the 1920's, two conservative parties, the *Seiyukai* and the *Kenseikai* (renamed the *Minseito* in 1927), were predominant. Both represented groups of landlords, agrarian capitalists, zaibatsu, and the urban middle class. Though it was Japan's most democratic period to date, Japanese democracy was still limited. In 1925 universal manhood suffrage (for those twenty-five years old or over) was enacted, and the property tax qualification was abolished. But the same year the Diet enacted the Peace Preservation Law that provided for the imprisonment of persons considered subversive by the government. Neither parties nor individuals were allowed to attack the status quo.

Despite restrictions, the leftist movement continued to grow, outside the law. Japanese attended international Communist conferences in Russia, and the Japanese Communist Party was founded in July, 1922. Police repression helped to keep the Party down, and Communist ideological idiosyncracies also handicapped its development in Japan. In the 1920's Party leaders directed their efforts against both agrarian and urban capitalists but with little success. Because the Communist Party was illegal, Communists operated through the Farmers and Workers Party in the general elections of 1928, the first since the 1925 suffrage law. The front party received a quarter of a million votes, but shortly after the election the police cracked down again. By the early 1930's, Communist leaders had gone into hiding at home or abroad.

Foreign Relations under Party Leaders. Throughout the 1920's Japanese foreign policies remained basically unchanged with its primary goal of hegemony in Asia. But whereas military spokesmen had advocated direct action to this end, civilian party leaders used diplomacy. The latter prevailed, and Japanese foreign policy in the twenties was nonaggressive. Japan was an active participant in the League of Nations and in international conferences. At the Geneva Conference in 1927, the United States, Great Britain, and Japan attempted to extend the Washington 5 : 5 : 3 ratio to auxiliary ships (cruisers, destroyers, and submarines), but no agreement was then reached. In 1930 a more successful effort was made in London relating to over-all tonnages and numbers of ships in these categories. The acceptance by Japan of the London Naval Agreement was a victory for the nation's civilian leaders in their progress in constitutional government.

Toward the divided China of the 1920's, Japan's policies

varied. Baron Shidehara Kijuro, foreign minister (1924–1927 and 1929–1931) in both the Kenseikai and the Minseito cabinets, pledged Japanese respect of China's sovereignty and territorial integrity. The country "hard" policy was advocated by a general, Baron Tanaka Giichi, prime minister from 1927 to 1929, who reasserted special Japanese interests in Manchuria and eastern Mongolia.

Though the Japanese government repressed the Communist movement at home, it moved to restore diplomatic relations with Moscow that had been broken by the Russian Revolution. In 1925 a treaty of recognition provided for the exchange of diplomatic representatives and regulated fishing rights and other matters of mutual concern.

With the United States the immigration issue was a sore one. In 1924 the United States Congress considered a new immigration law. Some Congressmen advocated Asian exclusion, while others opposed it. Harding's Secretary of State, Charles Evans Hughes, warned that such discrimination would negate much of the success of the Washington Conference. The Japanese ambassador in Washington informed the State Department that "grave consequences" would result if the law excluded Asians. In part because of what was considered unwarranted Japanese interference, the Congress approved an exclusivistic immigration bill. (Had the exclusion feature not been adopted, the law would have provided for an annual total of only 250 Japanese under its general national origins quota.)

Authoritarianism (1930–1937). The relative liberalism of the 1920's obscured the rise in Japan of militaristic groups. Militarism gained varying degrees of support not only from the bureaucracy and middle classes but also from right-wing civilian organizations that had been gathering strength in Japan since shortly after the First World War. These groups propounded a fascistic way of life with its connotations of the glory of war, extreme nationalism, and an authoritarian one-party system. The right-wing civilian movement, which had held in check during the 1920's, in the ensuing decade joined forces with some of the military to advocate militant fascism and practice violent tactics.

Take-over of Manchuria. The immediate events that brought the military into power began in South Manchuria. As noted in the previous chapter, by 1932 the Japanese military command had occupied the land and created the state of Manchukuo. The Hoover administration of the United States protested Japanese absorption of Manchuria. Washington never recognized Manchukuo, though it permitted American businessmen to reside and travel there. In Tokyo, discontent among the younger and lower-ranking army and navy officers led to direct military action in Manchuria. On May 15, 1932, a group of these officers, claiming to free from evil influences the Showa emperor (Hirohito, the "Enlightened Peace" emperor), assassinated the prime minister and demanded the end of party government. The bureaucrats were forced to compromise, and a nationalist, military-oriented government came into office. Meanwhile, the League of Nations dispatched a commission under Lord Lytton to investigate the course of events in Manchuria. Its report in effect condemned Japan for aggression, and in March, 1933, Japan walked out of the League. Manchuria became a Japanese possession, with Henry Pu-yi, the last of the Manchu emperors, installed as head of a puppet state.

Militarization. On February 26, 1936, young army officers again took direct action in Tokyo. They made attempts on the lives of leading statesmen, including the old genro Saionji, and killed a former prime minister. After holding out for three days in government buildings, the rebels were subdued by the higher military command. But in the process, the government had contributed to the growth of authoritarianism by fighting force with force.

Economic developments of the mid-1930's contributed to the trend toward centralized and military government. Depression years affected Japan, whose economy was so dependent on international trade. In part because of conquests in Manchuria and North China, Japanese economic activity increasingly turned in that direction. Associated with army interests, the zaibatsu at home effectively implemented military expansion. Domestic economic affairs were also characterized by increased state intervention. The government envisioned military expenditures as one solution to domestic problems caused by the depression.

By 1937, Japan was industrially self-sufficient and prepared for war. Control boards for each major industry were established.

Increased armaments put now strains on foreign relations. When the Washington and London naval agreements lapsed at the end of 1936, the army had emerged as top policy-maker in foreign relations. After consolidating gains in Manchuria, Japan by degrees extended control over North China until its troops were in the vicinity of Peking. It sought to secure its northern flank from Russian advances, and in 1937 Russia sold the Chinese Eastern Railroad to Japan. Japan also aligned itself with the Axis powers of Germany and Italy to contain Soviet Russia. In the Anti-Comintern Pact of November, 1936, Japan and Germany pledged to oppose international communism; a secret protocol promised that if either signatory were attacked by Russia, the other would not act to help Russia. The following year, Italy joined the pact. By 1937, when Japan moved into China Proper, it had come into direct confrontation with Western powers, including the United States.

16

CONFLICT IN ASIA (1937–1945)

Japan's march to imperial heights was a transitory but phenomenal story. The Japanese created the largest empire Asia had ever known, but it was built on hollow foundations. Problems compounded at home. The Japanese-enunciated Asian Co-Prosperity Sphere seemed to be all in favor of Japan, rather than a concept shared abroad. The Chinese offered resistance—some in occupied territory, some in free inland China, some in Communist-dominated areas, some in warlord-ruled provinces. Southeast Asians, though divided among themselves, also came to dislike the new overlords. While not directly experiencing a Japanese occupation, the Indian subcontinent had perplexing political problems. Outside powers, not only Britain in India, but Russia, the United States, and other Western states had vital stakes in the outcome of the Asian conflict that was to shape the future course of events. The settlements following the Second World War not only called for a new Japan, but hastened to rearrange the over-all Asian power structure.

JAPAN AND CHINA (1937–1945)

With a firm base at home and in Manchuria, Japan invaded China Proper in force in 1937. In the course of the four years' undeclared war, its forces occupied the most productive and populous area of the land. But it came into growing conflict with Western powers, including the United States. By the time Japan reached into Southeast Asia, conflict became inevitable. In the Pacific War, Japan initially registered great military gains but then came under Allied attacks, eventually going down to defeat. In the wartime Chinese scene difficulties compounded. Chiang

Kai-shek's siege government at inland Chungking was beset with problems, while Mao Tse-tung's regime in Yenan expanded. International conferences provided for Japan's postwar status, but they were less successful in calling the China tune.

***Undeclared War* (*1937–1941*).** Under a militaristic government and with a highly industrialized economy, Japan prepared for war. Hastened by the turn of events in China toward the formation of a united front, the Japanese embarked on their conquest of that country. In an incident on July 7, 1937, at the Marco Polo Bridge near Peiping, Japanese forces exchanged shots with the Chinese. In the tense situation, aggravations were compounded. Though the Chinese government apologized, the Japanese proceeded to occupy North China. After making initial gains, they encountered Communist forces, who put up formidable resistance. As a result, much of northwest China (at least that area west of the Yellow River bend) stayed in Chinese, but Chinese Communist, hands. Simultaneously, the Japanese came in force to protect their extensive Shanghai interests and pushed the Chinese army out of central coastal areas. Campaigns moved up the Yangtze, but before the fall of Nanking, Chiang evacuated to Chungking, up in the river gorges and safe from surface attacks (though not immune from continual Japanese aerial bombings). Also moving up southern river valleys, the Japanese occupied strategic cities and coastal areas in South China. Between mid-1937 and late 1938, the Japanese had occupied most of China, the richest part. After 1941 they acquired little additional territory.

EFFECTS IN CHINA. Occupied China was only one part, though a major part, of the Chinese political scene. Searching for a national figure to head a puppet Republic of China at Nanking, the Japanese obtained the services of Wang Ching-wei, who defected from the Kuomintang. Under him, a state was declared at Nanking in March, 1940, and recognized by the Axis powers. Economic reorganization accompanied political control in occupied China, and Japanese companies and corporations took over the economic sector. Cultural redirection was also ordered. Farther inland from Chungking, Chiang Kai-shek after 1938 ruled over what was called Free China. Numerous Chinese evacuated to the interior, and schools and offices were re-established in new rural locations in western and southwestern provinces. But much of northwest China remained in Communist hands. Centered at Yenan, the Communists maintained guerrilla warfare behind Japanese lines. And on the fringes of the country, independent warlords operated. They ruled over some provinces in a high-handed manner.

In the course of the undeclared war, the Kuomintang and the Communists took some measures, at least on paper, of political and military co-operation to implement the second united front. In March, 1938, Chiang formed a People's Political Council, consisting of two hundred members appointed from various political organs, including Communists and third parties, as an advisory body. The Council was not effective. Military clashes between the Communists and Nationalists continued, even behind Japanese lines. The most critical one occurred in January, 1941, where in the lower Yangtze region the Communist Fourth Route Army, disobeying Chiang's orders to attack Japanese troops, were set upon from the rear by Nationalist forces. This clash strained even the nominal co-operation of the second united front.

International Repercussions. As the Nationalists and Communists coexisted uneasily, and as the Japanese consolidated gains, the aggressors took note of the international situation. Time and again, between 1937 and 1939, large-scale fighting occurred on Japanese-Russian border areas in the Amur River vicinity, Korea, and Inner Mongolia. With the conclusion of the unexpected German-Russian pact in July, 1939, these conflicts came to a halt. In September, 1940, with the fall of France and new German military successes, the Axis states—Japan, Italy, and Germany—concluded the Tripartite Pact, aimed against the United States. Its terms provided that if one of the three powers were attacked by a country not then involved in the European war or the Sino-Japanese conflict, the other two would come to the assistance of the beleaguered party. Only the United States and Soviet Russia, among the major powers, were then neutral; and another article of the treaty stated that the terms did not affect the then existing status between each of the three parties and Soviet Russia. In mid-1941, when Hitler attacked Russia, Japan felt safer and redirected efforts southward. (Japanese military leaders refrained from moving into the relatively barren eastern Siberia.) Japan concluded a five-year neutrality pact with Russia in April, 1941.

In China, Japanese expansion impinged on Western treaty rights, particularly those of the British, who retained extensive economic interests in occupied China. Their subjects were maltreated and suffered indignities. As it had done on previous occasions, the United States protested infringement of its rights, individual and collective, in China. Washington participated in collective security measures to restore peace on the Asian mainland, such as the 1937 Brussels Conference called by Belgium but not attended by Japan. Though not a member of the League, the United States co-operated unofficially with the Lytton Commission, on which it had an observer.

The United States extended supplies and loans to Chiang Kai-shek and, more importantly, applied economic sanctions against Japan. Initially, acts of Congress, such as the 1935 and 1937 laws regulating sale and transportation of arms to belligerents, were directed mainly toward keeping the United States out of European wars. But in the late 1930's other laws were directed specifically against Japan. In July, 1938, the United States placed an embargo on the export of airplanes to Japan. In December, 1939, the embargoes were extended to shipments of petroleum products. Earlier that year, Washington had announced its intention to terminate the 1911 treaty of commerce, which was due to expire. This action left the United States free to restrict any trade with Japan. In July and December, 1940, embargoes were imposed on the export to Japan of scrap iron, aviation gas, munitions, and other war material. In July, 1941, after the occupation of Saigon by Japanese troops, Japanese financial assets in the United States were frozen. Despite negotiations over issues, Japanese and American positions had become irreconcilable vis-à-vis treaty rights and privileges in China and East Asia.

War in the Pacific (1941–1945). In 1941 Japan decided to go to war in the Pacific. On July 2, 1941, an imperial conference made plans to move into Southeast Asia, where valuable natural resources lay. On October 18, General Tojo Hideki became prime minister of Japan. On November 1, Admiral Yamamoto Isoroku issued the orders for a Pearl Harbor attack, designed to immobilize the American Pacific fleet while the Japanese gained control of Southeast Asia. The date of December 7 was chosen on November 17. Nine days later, a striking force left the Kuriles for Hawaii. On the same day in Washington, Secretary of State

Cordell Hull repeated to a Japanese delegation his final proposals for a negotiated settlement. On Sunday, December 7, the first Japanese air attack at 7:55 A.M. caught American forces in Hawaii unprepared. Within two hours, six United States battleships had been sunk, 120 planes disabled, and 2,400 personnel killed.

After these heavy losses, the United States gradually recovered military might. The Japanese began to encounter reverses as early as mid-1942. In the Battle of the Coral Sea (May 4–8, 1942) off Australia, and at Midway the next month (June 4–6), the Japanese failed to take any additional territory. In the Guadalcanal operations (August, 1942, through February, 1943), they sought to maintain an anchorhold for their extended Pacific lines; but the island was reconquered by Allied forces. The tide of war turned in 1943 and 1944, as the Allied cause under General Douglas MacArthur, who had withdrawn from the Philippines to Australia, slowly advanced through island-hopping campaigns back into the Philippines. Complementing the southwest Pacific operations were the northern and central Pacific campaigns which retook the Aleutian Islands in March, 1943, and the central Solomons in the Battle of the Bismarck Sea (March 2–3, 1943). Within another year, Allied operations had advanced through the Marshalls to the Marianas, where the fall of Saipan in July, 1944, made Japan accessible to American bombers. Tojo's cabinet fell, and in Tokyo muted talk of a negotiated peace commenced.

By 1945, combined operations of land, sea, and air forces had turned the war decisively against Japan. The end of the war was hastened by the dropping of atomic bombs on Hiroshima and Nagasaki, on August 6 and 9 respectively, and by the entrance of Russia into the Pacific War on August 8. Following an imperial decision, the Japanese surrendered on August 15, over the opposition of the military. In the years since 1937, 3.1 million Japanese had lost their lives in the imperialist ventures.

A Divided China. Meanwhile, in wartime Chungking, the Nationalist government had to wrestle with numerous problems. Leadership was aging, and no new blood replenished the ranks. Cabinets were reconstituted, but the same men occupied different positions over time. The situation necessitated military priorities, but it was difficult to sustain in the technologically backward areas of southwestern China an infrastructure including industry for a

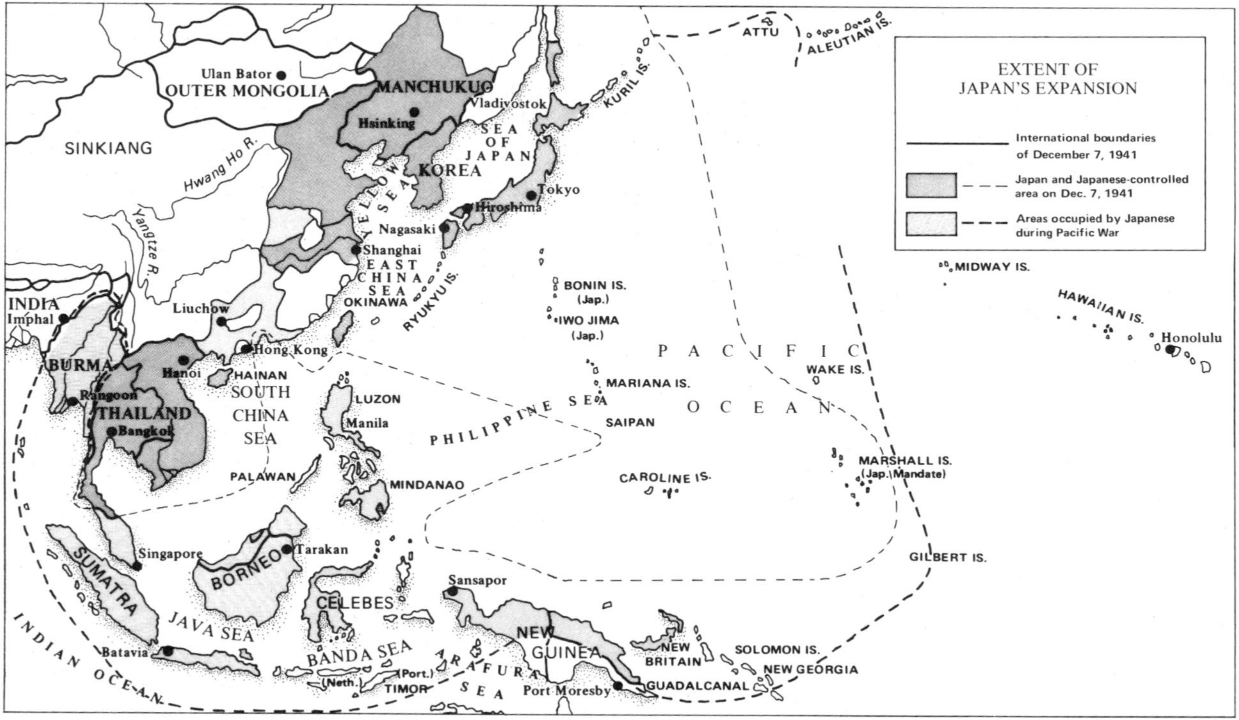
EXTENT OF
JAPAN'S EXPANSION
International boundaries of December 7, 1941
Japan and Japanese-controlled area on Dec. 7, 1941
Areas occupied by Japanese during Pacific War
OUTER MONGOLIA
Ulan Bator
SINKIANG
MANCHUKUO
Hsinking
Vladivostok
SEA OF JAPAN
KOREA
YELLOW SEA
Tokyo
Hiroshima
Nagasaki
Shanghai
EAST CHINA SEA
OKINAWA
RYUKYU IS.
KURIL IS.
ATTU
ALEUTIAN IS.
MIDWAY IS.
HAWAIIAN IS.
Honolulu
Hwang Ho R.
Yangtze R.
INDIA
Imphal
Liuchow
Hong Kong
HAINAN
BURMA
Hanoi
Rangoon
THAILAND
Bangkok
SOUTH CHINA SEA
LUZON
Manila
PALAWAN
MINDANAO
PHILIPPINE SEA
BONIN IS.
(Jap.)
IWO JIMA
(Jap.)
MARIANA IS.
SAIPAN
PACIFIC OCEAN
WAKE IS.
CAROLINE IS.
MARSHALL IS.
(Jap. Mandate)
GILBERT IS.
Singapore
SUMATRA
BORNEO
Tarakan
CELEBES
JAVA SEA
Batavia
BANDA SEA
(Neth.)
(Port.)
TIMOR
ARAFURA SEA
Sansapor
NEW GUINEA
Port Moresby
NEW BRITAIN
SOLOMON IS.
NEW GEORGIA
GUADALCANAL
INDIAN OCEAN

modern war machine. Moreover, with the scarcity of consumer goods and the excess printing of currency, inflation became rampant. The usual charges of graft and corruption were hurled at the government. Kuomintang politics increasingly centered on Chiang Kai-shek, whose monolithic titles included generalissimo of the army, president of the government (after 1943) and chairman of its Executive Yüan, and chairman of the party's Central Executive Committee. In 1943 he wrote two books whose theses blamed Westerners for China's basic ills. *China's Economic Theory* stressed the traditional Chinese official policy of state control over economic life, emphasized industrial goals, but paid little attention to agricultural problems. *China's Destiny* marked the end of a century of unequal treaties, which the work indicated had caused China's humiliation and distressing conditions.

While the Kuomintang as a "siege government" held out in the interior, the Communists expanded in the northwest. Recouping from losses incurred during the Long March, Party membership grew spectacularly. By 1945, according to Mao himself, it had skyrocketed to 1.2 million. Through guerrilla activities the Party expanded its territorial hold behind Japanese lines in North China. In the midst of membership and territorial gains for the Communists, Mao secured his top position by composing definitive Party literature. In these war years he devoted much time to studying Marxism-Leninism-Stalinism. Among his most important works were two composed in late 1939 and early 1940. The earlier one, entitled *The Chinese Revolution and the Chinese Communist Party,* developed the two aspects of the political revolution: an internal one that ranged the masses against the feudal class and an external one that pitted the Chinese nation against the imperialists. Mao's later work, *On New Democracy,* outlined two stages to realize the goals of the Chinese revolution. The first temporary period was to be marked by a coalition government, the second and final stage would result after the Party led the nation into socialism.

By 1945, these and other basic volumes of Mao had defined and refined his ideology. They were significant because his thought and programs were to carry over as guidelines for the Communist state which was to rule all of mainland China in 1949. As Mao wrote, so he tightened control over the party structure throughout the war years. He pursued rectification programs and reindoctrination measures, the most important of which was the *cheng feng* ("correct the wind") program in 1942 and 1943. By the end of the Second World War, communism in China had become Chinese to the core, and Maoism was grafted onto Marxism and Leninism as party dogma.

Wartime Diplomacy. Events after Pearl Harbor complicated the international scene as it related to China. The Chungking government declared war on Japan and became an ally of the United States. Most of the wartime Allied conferences concerned Europe as Japan, but two affected China.

In late 1943, at Cairo, Chiang Kai-shek, Franklin Roosevelt, and Winston Churchill (Stalin was not present because Russia was not in conflict at the time with Japan) convened to discuss postwar Pacific problems. In the Cairo Declaration of December 1, the three leaders promised the return of all territories that Japan had "stolen" from China to the Republic of China, and that these territories would specifically include Manchuria, Formosa, and the Pescadores.

The Yalta Conference, held in the Crimea in February, 1945, was attended by Roosevelt, Churchill, and Stalin. In order to involve Russia in the final campaigns against Japan and to save American lives in the projected invasion of that island country, Roosevelt in a secret protocol with the Russians promised to restore certain pre-1904 rights they had enjoyed in Manchuria. Among these rights were "pre-eminent" interests in Dairen, Port Arthur, and the management of Manchurian railroads. Chiang Kai-shek was not informed of the terms for four months and then only by the United States president, Harry S. Truman. Chiang reluctantly sent his foreign minister to Moscow in August, 1945, to confirm details in a treaty.

In wartime China, diplomatic representatives of Roosevelt and Truman sought to sustain Chiang's claim as the leading and legitimate Chinese government. No official aid was channeled to Yenan, whereas, in the course of the Second World War, Chungking received some $1.5 billion worth of grants and loans from Washington. Subsequent to the outbreak of the Pacific War, several military missions went to China to co-ordinate Chinese and Allied efforts against Japan. But as the war entered its final phases, China was bypassed. Japan was eventually defeated not from the mainland but by sea and land campaigns from eastern and southern Pacific island chains. As was the case in international conferences, so in military strategy, China, at war with Japan longer than any other party, was relegated to a subordinate role. Concerned with the necessity of immediate victory against Japan, and anticipating political problems that could result from a divided China, the United States endeavored to cement the second united front. Roosevelt dispatched several civilian missions to Chungking to heal Chinese political breaches. In late 1944 General Patrick Hurley, the American ambassador, endeavored to unify Nationalist and Communist military and political stands. Welcomed by both factions, he commuted between Chungking and Yenan. But claiming obstruction from Department of State representatives in the field, he cut short in a huff his difficult mediating task. Hurley left, but Americans were now all the more committed to the China problem. Yet the requested American intercession soon turned into Chinese charges of unwanted intervention.

In July, 1945, at Potsdam, following conclusion of the European War, Harry S. Truman, the incoming American president; Clement Attlee, who succeeded Churchill as British prime minister; and Marshal Stalin outlined zones of occupation in Asia (some of which jelled into political boundaries). The Americans were to receive the Japanese surrender in the Philippines, Japan, the Pacific islands, and Korea south of the 38th parallel; the Russians in the northern Japanese islands, North Korea, and Manchuria; the Chinese under Chiang Kai-shek in China and Indochina to the 16th parallel; the British, in Southeast Asia. The Potsdam Conference also called for the demilitarization of Japan, the occupation of the country, and restriction of Japanese territory to its four main islands and some adjacent minor ones. After two atomic bombs and the Russian entry into war (which involved scrapping its neutrality pact with Japan) the Japanese signed a surrender document in the emperor's name at 9:08 A.M on September 2, 1945, aboard the United States battleship *Missouri* in Tokyo Bay.

By the end of the Second World War in August, 1945, political and military affairs in China were confusing. As stipulated in the Yalta Agreement, the Russians entered the Pacific War against Japan and occupied Manchuria to accept the Japanese surrender. They received back their old rights. In North China, the Communists were extended but growing in numbers. The Nationalists remained the stronger of the two main Chinese domestic factions. They received international diplomatic recognition (even from the Russians) and had the military advantages. Their troops reoccupied the important coastal cities (with American help) after the Japanese surrender. In contrast, the Communists had no sea coast, limited agricultural lands, few industrial complexes, a mediocre air force, tenuous logistical lines, and little Russian support or aid (until the Russians evacuated most of Manchuria by spring, 1946, and left behind Japanese war booty to them). Yet in the course of the next few years, they emerged victorious on the Chinese mainland.

JAPAN AND SOUTHERN REGIONS (1937–1945)

In Southeast Asia, Japan's initial war years were ones of military success and political consolidation. But after some time of subjection to an occupation, Southeast Asian leaders generally developed an antipathy to the new overlords who showed themselves to be no more amenable to independence movements than had the earlier Westerners. At the end of the war, some colonials co-operated with the returning masters, while others did not. Though the Japanese never invaded India, that land was rent in these years with a high degree of political turmoil.

Southeast Asia. The initial Japanese successes left great psychological impacts on Southeast Asian peoples. The myth of the white men's invincibility had again been exploded (as in the Russo-Japanese War), and they were paraded as prisoners through Asian streets. The war toppled colonial regimes and gave impetus to native nationalism. The Japanese set up autonomous governments which claimed independence from their colonial powers. But as the war progressed, Southeast Asians became increasingly disenchanted with the new Japanese masters because of their many brutal and tactless actions. The slogan "Asia for Asians" meant instead "Asia for the Japanese."

INDOCHINA. After the fall of France in spring 1940, the

Japanese pushed into Indochina. There they met with little resistance. That year in the Hanoi Convention, from the hard-pressed French colonial regime, Japan received the right to station troops in northern Indochina. In 1941 troops fanned south into Saigon and Cochin China. To all intents and purposes, Japan had occupied Indochina prior to Pearl Harbor; afterward, as in China, it added little territory. But the Japanese worked through French officials until the last months of the Pacific war. Under the Japanese occupation, Communist activity revived. In South China, Ho Chi Minh had established yet another party, the Vietnam Independence League (Vietminh for short). In a manifesto directed against both the French and Japanese, he called for help from all Vietnamese. The Vietminh organized guerrilla forces under General Vo Nguyen Giap, which with some Allied support, became highly skilled. They were under Communist control and were spread throughout Vietnam by 1945. The non-Communist indigenous movement centered on Emperor Bao Dai. Under Japanese prompting, in March, 1945, at Hué, this monarch issued a proclamation of independence from the French and abrogated the 1874 French-Annamese treaty. The kings of Laos and Cambodia issued similar statements of independence. Taking no heed of the indigenous royal regimes, the Vietminh continued to entrench itself throughout Vietnam. On September 2, 1945, as the Japanese cause collapsed, it proclaimed the Democratic Republic of Vietnam and five days later declared its independence from the French. Following the Japanese surrender, the Vietminh moved to Hanoi and temporarily occupied Saigon.

Thailand. The outbreak of the Pacific War found Thailand not as an occupied country but as one with Japanese "guests." Phibun, as prime minister, signed a treaty of alliance in December, 1941, and shortly therafter declared war on Great Britain and the United States. The United States ignored the declaration, but Britain declared war on Thailand. Japan gave to Thailand two Shan states in Burma, two Cambodian provinces, and four northern Malay states. Japanese came to Thailand as advisers and concluded economic and cultural agreements. Despite the alliance, the Thais disliked the enforced guests, who monopolized their rice exports, debased their currency, and established prisoner of war camps in their country. Phibun co-operated with the Japanese.

Pridi, as regent for the young king still in Switzerland, supported the Free Thai resistance movement. As Japan's cause waned, Phibun's cabinet fell and Pridi once more had a turn as top leader. With Japanese defeat, Thailand agreed to restore the Burmese and Malayan territories to the British and the Cambodian provinces to the French, and in 1946 it joined the United Nations.

Burma. After the separation of Burma from India in 1937, three Burmese prime ministers successively assumed office. When war broke out, the Burmese had had some experience in political autonomy, but wanted more. Aided by the disenchanted Burmese as well as by superior tactics in jungle warfare, the Japanese overran Burma in the course of the first half of 1942. The Burmese were at first friendly toward the new conquerors, who established a puppet government. However, because of harsh Japanese treatment, their friendliness gave way to resistance. In 1943 the Communist Party of Burma was founded. The next year witnessed the formation by a secret youth organization of the Anti-Fascist People's Freedom League. Under General Aung San, the League was armed by the Japanese to subdue local uprisings, but it later rebelled against the Japanese occupation. When the British returned after the war, the Burmese were willing to co-operate with them.

Malaya. With only few local forces in Malaya, the British there also found themselves unprepared for the Japanese. Expecting attacks from the straits, they had directed Singapore's guns toward the sea. But the thrust of Japanese attack came from the peninsula. In February, 1942, Singapore fell. The Japanese placed strict controls on the island and on the Malay Peninsula because tin and rubber were essential to their military machine. There was no puppet government during the occupation. An underground resistance movement, the Malayan People's Anti-Japanese Army, was organized. With British help and Malayan leadership, of Chinese extraction and Communist persuasion, it pursued effective jungle guerrilla warfare against the temporary common enemy. In a 1943 agreement with the British, this force accepted British military command in exchange for arms. When the British returned to the peninsula in September, 1945, the Communist problem was the main issue of colonial concern.

The Philippines. The Philippine Commonwealth government under President Quezon and Vice President Osmeña made commendable strides in political and economic matters. In 1940 a constitutional amendment changed the one six-year presidential term to four years, with the possibility of a second term. A bicameral legislature was adopted and the twenty-four-man Senate reinstated. Only half of the projected Commonwealth period had been realized when the Japanese invaded the Philippines in Decembre, 1941. Under General Douglas MacArthur, formerly military adviser to the Commonwealth and since the previous July, commander-in-chief of the United States Armed Forces in the Far East, Filipino and American forces fought valiantly against great odds. But military resistance proved hopeless. Fil-American troops surrendered on the Bataan Peninsula in April, 1942, and on the nearby island of Corregidor in Manila Bay the next month. From Australia, MacArthur continued to direct war operations. Quezon and Osmeña evacuated to the United States. Some Filipino leaders in Manila collaborated with the Japanese. Others escaped to the hills or organized guerrilla forces. One such group, established early in 1942 in Luzon, was the *Hukbalahaps,* who during the course of the war became infiltrated by Communists.

As the Japanese consolidated their hold on the archipelago, they formed a mass political organ, the *Kalibapi.* Filipinos were urged to abandon Western culture and acquire the Japanese one. The Filipinos, however, turned out to be unwilling students. In mid-1943 the Kalibapi formed a Preparatory Commission for Philippine Independence. In October of that year, the puppet republic was announced under a former Philippine senator, José Laurel. It declared war on the United States, which ignored the act. MacArthur's forces landed on Leyte Island late in 1944, beginning the arduous reconquest of the islands. Laurel evacuated to Tokyo, and Osmeña, who had assumed the presidency after Quezon's death in the United States, returned with MacArthur to re-establish the Commonwealth in Manila in February, 1945.

Indonesia. After the Second World War erupted in Europe, the Dutch government in exile in London still made no definite political commitments to Indonesians. In 1940 the Volksraad requested an imperial conference to establish a representative form of government, but the request was denied. The Dutch regime at

Batavia, cut off from London, was increasingly thrown more on its own resources. However, the governor-general rejected Japanese demands for greater access to Indonesian oil, tin, and rubber. In March, 1942, the Japanese attacked and soon overran the archipelago. They imposed strong rule. Their army took over the administration of Java; the navy administered Borneo, Celebes, and the lesser islands. Sumatra was integrated with Malaya. In 1943 the Japanese set up the *Putera*, a mass political party, which they replaced the following year when it became too nationalistic. Some Indonesian leaders, notably Sukarno and Hatta, released from their exile, co-operated with the Japanese. Sukarno became president of the Central Advisory Council established in September, 1943. Sjahrir refused to collaborate and went into hiding.

As the tide of war turned against them, the Japanese in February, 1945, set up an advisory council for South Borneo, Celebes, and lesser Sundas. On July 17, Japan decided to grant Indonesian independence. An Independence Preparatory Committee was organized. It scheduled its first meeting for August 19, but Japan surrendered four days before that date. However, Sukarno and Hatta went ahead and on August 17 declared Indonesian independence. (The date has since been commemorated by the Indonesians.) Hence when the Dutch colonial administrators returned (the British preceded them to accept the Japanese surrender), they found an existing *de facto* native government, the Republic of Indonesia, which did not welcome them. As in Indochina, internal wartime developments laid the basis for future conflict.

South Asia. As war approached in Europe, the Indian Congress Party warned the mother country that India would not fight foreign wars. However, on September 3, 1939, when England declared war on Germany, the viceroy's proclamation brought India into the war. The princes affirmed their loyalty. The Muslim League offered support on the condition that no constitutional changes be made in the Act of 1935 without prior approval. In October, 1939, the British government reaffirmed its 1929 pledge to grant India Dominion status. The next month, the Congress provincial ministries resigned to signify their opposition to the circumstances under which the British brought India into the Second World War without its consent.

In March, 1940, the Congress reiterated its decision of non-co-operation in the war effort. The same month, at Lahore the Muslim League under Jinnah demanded partition. In the fall of 1940, the British promised a purely Indian assembly to frame the postwar constitution. Neither the Congress nor the League accepted the proposal, and the Congress began a civil disobedience campaign in September, 1940. The viceroy took steps to enlarge the Executive Council to twelve, with seven Indian representatives, but the British government still hesitated to grant independence. When the Atlantic Charter was drawn up in August, 1941, by President Franklin D. Roosevelt and Prime Minister Winston Churchill, the provision which called for the right of peoples to choose their form of government did not apply to India (or to Burma), as Churchill later made clear.

As the Pacific War began, the British remained fixed in their policy toward India. The princes continued aloof from national struggles. The Congress demanded independence, the Muslim League partition. There were more efforts to find solutions to the knotty Indian problem. In March, 1942, a mission was dispatched from England under Sir Stafford Cripps. The Cripps mission sought to create an Indian Union, which was to be associated with the United Kingdom and other Dominions through a common allegiance to the crown. The mission recommended the British retention of the defense power during the war and the complete Indianization of the viceroy's Executive Council (which was implemented). It called for the convening of a postwar constituent assembly and the revision of treaties with the Indian states. It proposed to extend Indian Union Dominion status to those provinces and princes desiring it, and to give separate Dominion status to those provinces wishing to secede from India. Minority rights were to be guaranteed in all cases. Most of the Cripps provisions were rejected. Gandhi went into another fast, but the Muslim League was encouraged by the British acceptance of the concept of an independent Pakistan. In August, 1942, the Congress demanded that the British get out of India. The British in reply outlawed the Congress and jailed Gandhi and other leaders.

Despite these political conflicts, the Second World War resulted in some measure of Indian unity and in the country's economic expansion. An Indian army of some two million volunteers was recruited. Some of the troops served in the Anglo-American Southeast Asian Command, established in 1943 with headquarters in Ceylon under Lord Louis Mountbatten. India, particularly in the Assam area, provided bases for American operations in China and Allied ones in Burma. Indian industrial production spurted and supplied nearly all the military equipment for the home army. Because of extensive British wartime purchases, India reversed its role as debtor to creditor nation. But political problems remained to plague the Indian subcontinent in immediate postwar years.

PART FIVE

POSTWAR ASIA

(Since 1945)

The aftermath of the Second World War in Asia brought new political patterns and realigned international relations. India received independence but was partitioned in the process. Southeast Asian colonial dependencies achieved statehood. From a China rent with civil war there emerged a victorious Communist regime, while Japan reasserted an important position in Asia but in a nonmilitary manner. Western European states declined in power, while the power of Soviet Russia and the United States continued to increase. The ideological and political confrontations between the Communist and anti-Communist worlds, augmented by the presence of Communist China, was focused on the Asian continent. A divided Korea, as well as divided Indochinese states, similarly experiencing warfare, were dramatic manifestations of the confrontation. Confronted by impinging international powers, Asian states sought to achieve political stability and economic viability. The millennium did not arrive with independence or the termination of subordinate colonial status. On the contrary, for most Asian countries, domestic and foreign problems compounded over the postwar decades.

17
SOUTH ASIA
Since 1945

After the defeat of Germany in the Second World War, Britain once again focused on the Indian problem. In June, 1945, a constituent assembly was called. Nothing was accomplished; spokesmen for the Muslim League and the Congress clashed over their respective communal interests. The following February, a British mission of three was sent to draw up a plan for orderly British withdrawal from India. Nehru asked the British to leave and let the Indians settle their own conflicts. Jinnah demanded that the British partition the country before leaving it. In order to force a conclusion, the Labour government of Prime Minister Attlee in February, 1947, scheduled British withdrawal from India by June, 1948. The new viceroy, Lord Louis Mountbatten, in June, 1947, announced India agreement to partition and a separate state for predominantly Muslim territories. A partition council and a boundary commission were established; Parliament ratified the partition and confirmed Dominion status for India and Pakistan. The princely states were given the options to join either or neither Dominion. On August 15, 1947, Pakistan and the Union of India came into existence. India thus achieved sovereignty but lost unity.

INDIA

India, the world's most populous democracy, is a racially, linguistically, socially, economically, and politically complex country. A group of families rather than a state, since independence it has registered a modicum of progress and a plethora of problems. Under Nehru's leadership, political balance was fairly well maintained, but his successors were buffeted by cross currents. Varying dogmas, both within the Indian Congress Party and from other parties, competed for official acceptance. In foreign affairs, estrangement ensued with Communist China, but relations remained correct with the Soviet Union. Toward the United States, from which it received most foreign aid, Indian approaches varied.

The Constitution. During the early years of independence, India, under Nehru defined the nature of its state. Over a three-year period, a constituent assembly prepared a document which promulgated on January 26, 1950. The Union of India then became the Republic of India, a member of the British Commonwealth. The constitution included a bill of rights; abolished untouchability; and forbade religious instruction in state-supported institutions. It provided for an independent judiciary, a president, a vice-president, and a bicameral central legislature. The upper house, *Rajya Sabha* (Council of States), comprised 250 members, of whom 12 were nominated by the president and the rest elected for six-year terms by members of the state legislative assemblies. The lower house, the *Lok Sabha* (House of the People), comprised 500 members, of whom 20 represented Union territories and the rest were elected for five-year terms by universal suffrage. A president was elected for a five-year term by an electoral college composed of members of both houses of Parliament and elected members of state assemblies. The vice-president, who presided over the Rajya Subha, was elected for a five-year term by members of both houses. Actual power was in the hands of the prime minister, who headed a cabinet, or council of ministers, and was responsible to the Lok Sabha.

Native States. The fate of the princely states was a problem of partition. The Indian Independence Act of 1947 provided that states could accede to either India or Pakistan. Most of the states, because of largely Hindu populations, acceded to India, which pensioned off their rulers. India forcefully incorporated others, including Junaghad and Hyderabad. Kashmir, which had a Hindu ruler but a predominantly Muslim population, constituted the most serious problem. The monarch did not announce an accession decision. During the political chaos of late 1947 that resulted from partition, not only large numbers of refugees but also armed Muslim tribesmen from Pakistan entered Kashmir. The invaders occupied the northern part of the state, where they proclaimed Azad (Free) Kashmir. The monarch thereupon decided to accede to India, and India sent troops to support him. Pakistan refused to recognize the act of accession and called for a plebiscite on the issue. The Kashmir problem was brought to the United Nations, which inconclusively debated the matter over the years. In time, the part of Kashmir occupied by India became a state within the Union of India. Pakistan forces remained in control of the northern part of the state.

At the state level, which incorporated the princely domains, 27 political entities were at first established in four categories. In 1956 the States Reorganization Act abolished this system and grouped state boundaries to correspond more closely with major language divisions; the number of states was about halved. However, more states were later added. In 1960 Bombay was partitioned into two states, Maharashtra and Gujarat. In 1963 the state of Nagaland was created on the Burma border. In 1966 Punjab was divided into Punjabi Suba with a Sikh majority and Hariana with a Hindu majority.

Social and Economic Changes. The vast scope of problems handicapped India's social revolution. Much was changing; much remained unchanged. Nationalists wanted to eliminate English as the official language, but there was dissension about what would replace it. North Indians advocated Hindi, while those from the Deccan and the South advanced their own languages. British reforms had brought about changes in ancient Hindu patterns. In an independent India, the caste system was not recognized by the constitution, though it was impossible to abolish it overnight. Improvements in education and transportation further undermined traditional ways. Social reforms were accomplished in marriage, minority, succession, and adoption acts. Marriage was recognized as contractual; women were allowed to obtain divorces. In inheritance daughters were given rights equal to those of sons. Educational challenges were great. By the early 1960's, India recorded almost 50 million students in primary and secondary schools, with another million in colleges and universities. It was impossible to provide jobs for all graduates, and the problem of the unemployed intellectual was acute. Yet most of India, at least three-fourths of the population, was illiterate.

Large-scale efforts were required to relieve pressing economic problems. A vast gap existed between the "haves" and the "have nots"; 5 percent of India's population controlled one-third of the wealth. Much of the country was disease-ridden; public health problems were enormous. Many Indians were undernourished, and diets were marginal. Few communities enjoyed a safe water supply or adequate sewage facilities. Doctors and nurses were scarce; nevertheless, attacks on major diseases strikingly reduced deaths from malaria, cholera, and tuberculosis.

Population increased at a greater rate than development of natural or food resources, though the government experimented with birth-control projects at national and state levels. Most of the people lived in rural areas, had a twenty-six-year life expectancy, and received an annual income much below $100. Agriculture was mainstay of 70 percent of the population; yet productivity, limited by outmoded farming practices, poor seed, and seasonal monsoons, was among the world's lowest. Moreover, the average farm size was small and uneconomical, with usually less than five acres, sometimes scattered in strips. To ameliorate conditions, the Indian government abolished the middleman function, reduced rents, fixed land-holding ceilings, redistributed land, and promoted co-operative systems. It also launched the Community Development Program to improve village life throughout the country.

In the industrial sector, India aimed at a mixed economy, in which the basic industries were state-owned but private ownership was allowed in consumer sectors. Private enterprise, foreign and native, contributed to Indian industrial development within limits defined by the state. Industrial output included aircraft, railway equipment, telephone equipment, and automobiles. The Indian government also broadened commerce, transportation, and communications systems. The railway system, as the single largest employer, had over a million workers, paid out one-third of a billion dollars in annual wages, and had about four million daily passengers. In international trade, India's major imports were foodstuffs, industrial products; exports were tea, sugar, jute, cotton, fabrics, hides, and manganese ore. The government initiated programs for the peaceful use of atomic energy. Its Atomic Energy Commission established projects at Trombay and Tarapur near Bombay and others near Madras and in Rajasthan. A succession of five-year plans embraced wide-ranging projects to spur economic productivity.

Political Development. In political life, the Congress Party remained predominant. Its candidates won the vast majority of national and state elections. Through an All-India Congress Committee and a Working Committee, it formulated social and economic programs. Nehru led the party until his death in 1964. His successor as prime minister was Lal Bahadur Shastri, who served for a year and a half until his death in 1966. He was succeeded by Mrs. Indira Gandhi, the daughter of Nehru (but no relation to the Mahatma).

The Congress Party itself encompassed a wide range of competing personalities and factions. In 1969 it split into two wings. Minor right-wing Indian political parties included the Mahasabha; the R.S.S. (Rashtriya Swayamsevak Sangh, or National Volunteer Association); the Bharatiya Jan Sangh (Indian People's Party); and the Swatantra (Freedom Party). The All-India Scheduled Castes Federation represented those who by the caste system were regarded as untouchables. Parties of the left also developed. After independence, the left wing of the Congress split off to form an independent Socialist Party of India. In 1952 it merged with another Socialist group, the Praja Party (Peasants, Workers, and People's Party), formed the preceding year. The coalition Praja Socialist Party operated until 1956, when it divided into the Praja Socialist Party and the Socialist Party. The Socialist movement was not significant, in large part because the dominant Congress Party had similar programs of state socialism. At the extreme left was the Indian Communist Party. For several years after independence, it promoted violence (among the results of which was the establishment of a soviet in Hyderabad). The Communists then changed tactics and through coalition groups gained control of state governments from time to time. But their internal divisions and split into pro-Moscow and pro-Peking factions vitiated party strength.

The Republic of India held its first national and state elections between October, 1951, and February, 1952. The Congress Party gained 363 of the 489 Lok Sabha seats and the majority of all but one of the state assemblies. In the second elections, held in early 1957, the voters returned to the Lok Sabha a plurality (48 percent) of the Congress candidates. The Congress Party lost the state of Kerala to a coalition government headed by Communists.

In the third national election (February, 1962), the Congress Party captured 45 percent of the Lok Sabha seats and won control of twelve state assemblies. In the fourth national elections (February, 1967), Congress Party seats were reduced to a bare plurality in the Lok Sabha, while the party was defeated in half the sixteen state assemblies (Nagaland at the time had no assembly). By the time of the fifth national election (March, 1971), called by Prime Minister Indira Gandhi a year ahead of schedule, political fragmentation was evident. Both wings of the Congress Party ran candidates. Also in the field were another seven national parties, including two Communist, two Socialist, and two right-wing groups. Regional parties and independents also participated, but Mrs. Gandhi's Congress faction came out ahead.

Foreign Relations. India's foreign policy was defined most clearly in the Five Principles of *Panchshila,* first set forth in a 1954 India-Chinese treaty on Tibet. These principles included mutual respect for the other's sovereignty, nonaggression, noninterference in the other's internal affairs, equality, and peaceful coexistence. Nehru himself personalized the principle of nonalignment, which he interpreted to mean freedom from military alliances rather than avoidance of political, economic, or ideological commitments. The Indian government was necessarily more concerned with major domestic issues and priorities than with foreign affairs. Moreover, it was aware that it could exert little actual power in world politics. But India took keen interest in regional problems. Before their own independence, in the spring of 1946, Indians convoked in New Delhi the unofficial Asian Relations Conference, which was attended by delegates from twenty-eight countries.

Relations with Communist China. The principles of coexistence were hard pressed in Indian dealings with Communist China. After the Communists took over mainland China in 1949, India withdrew recognition from Chiang Kai-shek and extended it to Mao Tse-tung. India voted to admit the Chinese Communists to United Nations organs. Nehru visited Peking and Chinese leaders came to India. However, border problems remained. India protested the Chinese invasion of Tibet in 1950, but four years later made a trade treaty with Peking over Tibetan rights. In 1959 a conflict erupted. The Chinese Communists occupied 5,000 square miles of territory claimed by India in the Aksai Chin region of Kashmir, and built a road through the area to connect Chinese border regions of Tibet and Sinkiang. In 1962 Indian-Chinese hostilities broke out again in that area and also in the North East Frontier Agency on the Assam border, where the Chinese squatted for some weeks. Chinese disputed the validity of sections of the so-called MacMahon Line (drawn up in 1914 in India and agreed to by representatives of India, Tibet, and China, which, however, never ratified it). Indians felt freer with the more distant Soviet Union. Relations with that country became closer in the mid-1950's, when Pakistan turned toward the West and commenced to accept military aid from the United States. Between 1955 and 1965, over $1 billion worth of Russian aid was extended to India.

Relations with Other Asian Powers. With the non-Communist world, Indian relations varied. France voluntarily gave up its colonial enclaves in India, but the Portuguese in 1961 were forced by India to withdraw from Goa, Diu, and Daman. India's main concern was with Pakistan. Partition bequeathed a multitude of problems to the subcontinent. Substantial minority groups existed in each country; boundaries were disputed along extensive areas in east and west; trade wars erupted; the distribution of Indus and Ganges river waters was a subject of bitter debate. With Japan there was little trouble; trade ties were close. With the Republic of China and Taiwan, India had minor trading contacts. Correct though not cordial diplomatic relations were maintained with Thailand and the Philippines. India did not participate in the Korean War but co-operated in the work of the postwar commissions. Nehru felt affinity for Prime Minister U Nu of Burma and President Sukarno of Indonesia, both of whom were also neutralists. A representative of the Indian government was chairman of the three International Control Commissions established for Vietnam, Laos, and Cambodia by the Geneva Conference of 1954 relating to Indochina.

Relations with the United States. Because of the importance of India as a nonaligned state, the United States had proposed long-range economic help. American programs commenced in June, 1951, and within two decades some $9 billion had been committed. The aid included technical assistance, commodity exports, and, most important, surplus food. In 1960 a four-year surplus food agreement provided for the shipment and use of 17 million tons of grain valued at $1.2 billion. (This was the first comprehensive and long-range agreement of its kind and the largest trade agreement in history.) Others followed. Usually part of the grain was donated and part paid for in Indian currency, which the United States returned to Indian development projects. After 1958 the United States, along with nine other countries and United Nations agencies extended aid through the Aid-India Consortium. Despite these extensive aid measures, Indians raised points of issue with the United States. These included the American government's alleged insensitivity to colonial struggles, its growing rapprochement with Communist China, its emphasis on military solutions to political and economic problems, its bilateral and multilateral defense arrangements, its nuclear tests, and its military aid to Pakistan.

PAKISTAN

Pakistan was a new independent entity on the Indian subcontinent, where India enjoyed the position as successor state to the British. During its first decade various political and economic problems plagued the nation. In 1958 General Ayub Khan assumed top office, and he kept the country on a more even keel. After a decade in power, he bowed out and other names came to the fore. In foreign affairs, relations with India consumed most effort. With other major powers Pakistan's record was remarkable; it received military and economic aid from such disparate countries as Communist China, Soviet Russia, and the United States.

Political Developments. The largest and most populous Islamic nation in the world, Pakistan was split into eastern and western wings. The smaller but more populous eastern section felt discriminated against, and the lack of national leadership handicapped administration. Jinnah, the first governor-general of Pakistan, was the outstanding political leader. After his death in 1948, less prominent figures assumed top posts. Following ten years of rapidly changing leadership, the army chief-of-staff, General Mohammad Ayub Khan, took over the presidency in a coup. For the next decade he dominated the country's politics.

Pakistan encountered difficulties in formulating a constitution. National and provincial bodies which had been elected in colonial India acted as interim parliaments. Jinnah convened a constituent assembly, which also served as a temporary legislature. In 1949 the assembly declared Pakistan to be an Islamic state and proposed Urdu as the national language as against Bengali which was preferred by East Pakistanis. Disputes arose between orthodox and liberal Muslims over the constitution's provisions on religion. In 1954 the governor-general dissolved the assembly because of his differences with it, and the following year his successor convened a second constituent assembly. In 1956 this assembly effected a constitution, but two years later when Ayub Khan seized office he abolished it and initiated administrative reforms under martial law. He moved the capital from Karachi to Islamabad, a new city in the northwest. He formulated the "Basic Democracies," which established five levels of councils from local committees through regional committees up to national organs. East and West Pakistan were each divided into 40,000 local constituencies as the "Basic Democrats." In December, 1959, the first councils were elected. In February, 1960, the "Basic Democrats" confirmed Ayub Khan as president and gave the mandate to effect another constitution.

President Ayub Khan set up a third constituent commission. Its document provided for a Republic of Pakistan with an indirectly elected president (who had to be a Muslim) and a unicameral national assembly of 156, elected by the 80,000 Basic Democrats. Bengali and Urdu were proclaimed national languages, but English was to be continued as the official one for another decade. The political structure of East and West Pakistan, each with a governor appointed by the president, was confirmed. Two provincial assemblies, each with 155 elective members plus the provincial governor, were to be elected by the Basic Democrats. In April, 1962, the first national assembly was elected. The next month, the provincial governments elected their assemblies. In late 1964 a second national election was held for the 80,000 Basic Democrats. These representatives returned Ayub Khan to office for another five-year term. (His opponent for the position was Jinnah's sister.) In 1968, because of the increase in population, the number of Basic Democrats was raised to 120,000. In March,

1969, as a result of national unrest stemming from labor problems, student agitation, and political opposition to his authoritarian measures, Ayub Khan stepped down from the presidency. Army commander-in-chief Yahya Khan then assumed the office. The new president reimposed martial law and re-examined Pakistan's basic constitutional and electoral framework. But fresh moves toward redefining Pakistan's political structure were clouded by regional issues existing between the eastern and western wings. In early 1971 a secessionist movement appeared in East Pakistan, but it was contained through military force by the national government.

Social and Economic Changes. Pakistani social policy was aimed at improving the living standards for all the people. The government established a social security system, provided medical benefits, and sought free and compulsory primary edeucation (the literacy rate was about 15 percent). School facilities were greatly increased. The educational system included Islamic studies, which were for the most part privately financed. Rights were extended to women and polygamy was restricted. Freedom of the press was limited; the government was empowered to appropriate newspapers which it considered objectionable. Major health problems existed, and medical facilities were inadequate.

Agrarian development was essential. Three-fourths of Pakistan's population depended for a livelihood on agriculture, which accounted for half the national income. In 1959 the government limited landowners to 500 acres of irrigated land or 1,000 acres of dry land. About 3.5 million acres of farmland were redistributed to peasants on easy terms. A Village Agricultural and Industrial Development program similar to the Indian program was begun, but it lost momentum after the Basic Democracies superseded it in the reform movement.

Pakistan's main exports were raw jute, cotton, rice, leather, and footwear. Imports were food grains, capital goods, and raw materials. With government aid industry made great gains, starting almost from scratch. Pakistan became self-sufficient in textiles, jute goods, and electric wire and cable production. Various consumer goods were manufactured. Domestic and foreign private investments were encouraged. The country imported half its coal supply and possessed only low-grade iron ore resources. Natural gas was produced from reserves in West and East Pakistan. Power projects, including multipurpose dams, were developed. The government owned and operated the railway systems in both wings. Inland waterways were also used for transportation, particularly in the eastern delta lands. Karachi was the main seaport in the west, Chittagong in the east. Overseas and domestic air service was developed. Atomic reactors were located at Islamabad, Karachi, and Raropur in East Pakistan. In 1955 Pakistan began five-year economic plans.

Foreign Relations. Pakistani relations were generally friendly with other Muslim countries, though boundary disputes erupted with Afghanistan. Pakistan maintained its long-standing close relations with Iran. Its relations with secular Turkey were also friendly. In 1964 the Pakistani president initiated the Regional Co-operation for Development among Pakistan, Iran, and Turkey. President Ayub Khan traveled throughout Arab and Muslim lands but refrained from participating in any regional organization based on religious bonds.

In early 1950 Pakistan followed Burma and India in recognizing the Chinese Communist regime. Western China had a large Muslim population, and Peking encouraged visits between Muslim organizations in the two nations. Though Pakistan joined the Southeast Asia Treaty Organization (SEATO), both Pakistan and China interpreted the move as aimed against India more than the Communists. In the Kashmir dispute, Peking called for a negotiated settlement. In March, 1963, a treaty delineated boundaries between China and the Pakistani-controlled part of Kashmir. In 1964 Pakistan International Airways, using American jets, inaugurated service to China. The same year, Pakistan received from Communist China a $60 million interest-free loan. The Soviet Union at first favored India in the Kashmir dispute, but during the 1960's, Pakistan-Russian relations improved. In three agreements concluded between 1961 and 1966, the Soviet Union promised a total of $128 million in credits; Russian military aid was also given. In January, 1966, Moscow convened the Tashkent Conference, at which India and Pakistan agreed to a limited settlement of the Kashmir conflict.

At first Pakistani leaders appeared open-minded on cold-war issues. Only in the early 1950's, when it appeared that Russia was siding with India in the Kashmir dispute, did Pakistan orient noticeably toward the West. In 1954, upon signing a mutual defense assistance pact with the United States, Pakistan joined SEATO and it also adhered to the Middle East Central Treaty Organization (CENTO). Between 1951 and the early 1970's, the United States supplied military and economic aid amounting to over $750 million and $3.5 billion respectively. American economic aid ran the usual gamut of dollar grants, counterpart funds, technical assistance, commodity programs, and food-surplus shipments. During the three weeks' undeclared war between India and Pakistan over Kashmir, in September, 1965, troops of each country invaded the other. The United States thereupon suspended all aid programs to both Pakistan and India. In the spring of the following year economic aid was resumed; however, only limited military assistance was reinstituted. In turn, Pakistan reexamined the status of American military bases within its borders.

BORDER LANDS

South Asia border lands, though small in size, were important because of their strategic location. The entities of Sikkim, Bhutan, Nepal, and Afghanistan were wedged in between India, Pakistan, China, and Russia. The insular border lands—Ceylon and scattered Indian Ocean archipelagoes—lay athwart important sea lanes. With the passing from the scene of the colonial rule, realigned power patterns emerged.

Sikkim and Bhutan. India succeeded to the British position in Sikkim. A 1950 treaty allowed it to control foreign affairs and defense and to station troops in the country. As a constitutional monarchy, Sikkim had a Buddhist maharajah. Domestic affairs were administered by a cabinet of three members and a state council of seventeen (twelve elected and five appointed). Elections were held in 1953, 1959, and 1967, for state council seats, but no constitution was effected. In 1967, 213 village councils were also elected. Indian-financed plans helped to shore Sikkim's economy.

Bhutan was also a protectorate of India through a 1949 treaty. A king was the constitutional monarch, and a prime minister was actual head of the government that included an assembly of 130 members and an eight-member advisory council. An Indian-financed economic program was put into effect in 1961. Both Bhutan and Sikkim had border problems with Communist China, which did not recognize this segment of the MacMahon line.

Nepal. Nepal, though politically independent, was caught between Indian and Chinese power plays. In 1951 the royal line overturned the century-old *de facto* rule of the Rana family, restored the power of the monarchy, and appointed a cabinet. An advisory assembly was established the following year. In 1959 King Mahendra promulgated a constitution. However, it was abrogated by the king the following year, and Nepali Congress Party leaders went into exile. In 1962 Mahendra began (as Ayub Khan had in Pakistan) a system of guided democracy. In the so-called Nepali *panchayat* system of government, four levels were established from the villages through the districts and zones to the national assembly. A constitution promulgated in 1962 confirmed the governmental structure. It prohibited political parties, gave the king executive power, and provided for a council of ministers. In 1963 the national panchayat of 125 members (six nominated by the king and the rest elected by zonal councils) was inaugurated. Nepal implemented the usual over-all economic development plans.

In foreign affairs, Nepal's relations with India were close but not cordial. The government sought the reduction or elimination of India's military presence but welcomed its economic help. In 1956 diplomatic relations were established with Communist China and Soviet Russia. The Soviet Union extended some aid, and Communist China contributed substantially to Nepali aid programs, with $62.6 million extended between 1956 and 1966. In October, 1961, Nepal and Communist China signed a border agreement, defining 650 miles, including the alignment of Mount Everest, the world's highest mountain. With the United States, Nepal concluded a treaty of friendship and commerce in 1947. American economic aid by the early 1970's exceeded $100 million. It was channeled into low-keyed projects, such as education, forest development, malaria control, and school construction. Some of it was for co-operative projects with India, such as joint road-building programs.

Afghanistan. As one of the few landlocked Asian states,

Afghanistan was continually aware of its more powerful neighbors. In 1964 King Mohammad Zahir Shah promulgated a new constitution. It provided for a lower house of 216 members, elected by universal suffrage, and an upper house of 84 members (one-third directly elected, one-third elected by provincial councils, and one-third appointed by the king). The constitution guaranteed basic rights, a free press, and an independent judiciary, and permitted political parties. Except for the king, members of the royal family were barred from political power. In 1965 and again in 1969 elections were held for the parliament.

The country was poor and had a low literacy rate. Chief exports were karakul sheepskins, wool carpets, timber products, fruits, nuts, and vegetables. Chief imports were textiles, machinery, vehicles, construction materials, oil, sugar, and tea.

In foreign affairs, Afghanistan profited from its strategic location. It accepted aid from Communist countries, including Russia and China, and non-Communist countries, including the United States and West Germany. Postwar military and economic Soviet aid by 1970 was estimated at about $1 billion. Russians built the Kabul airport (but Americans installed the navigation facilities). The Soviet Union was active in gas and oil exploration, irrigation projects, highway construction, and the building of technical schools. A large part of Afghanistan's international trade was with the Soviet Union, with which it had a common boundary along the Oxus River. The Afghans developed a seaport on this river, and the Russians built a road to connect the port with Kabul. In order to reach the Persian Gulf, Afghans had to traverse difficult roads through Iran.

With Communist China Afghanistan established diplomatic relations in 1955; a treaty of friendship was signed in 1960; and a boundary treaty in 1963 settled some 80 miles of common borders. Two years later, the Chinese extended to Afghanistan $28 million of credit. Between 1950 and 1970, United States aid totaled $400 million, almost all of it economic, including surplus food shipments, technical assistance, bank loans, and agricultural and educational exchanges. The largest economic development, aided by the United States and other countries, was the Helmand Valley reclamation and settlement project. Begun in 1946 as part of a five-year economic plan, the project included dams providing hydroelectric power, water reservoirs, and irrigation ditches.

Ceylon. The British pulled out of Ceylon as they did out of India. In 1946 a constitution was promulgated, and the next year Parliament passed the Ceylon Independence Bill. On February 4, 1948, Ceylon became a self-governing Dominion within the British Commonwealth. A governor-general was appointed by the crown as nominal head of the state. The parliament was bicameral. The upper house comprised 30 members, half appointed by the cabinet and half elected by the lower house. The lower house at first consisted of 101 members, 95 elected by popular vote and 6 appointed by the governor-general. In 1960 its number was raised to 151 and all seats were made elective.

Following independence, Ceylon maintained close relations with Great Britian, partly through apprehension of India and of the sizable Indian minority (Tamils) on the island. The British retained most of the tea and half the coconut plantations in Ceylon, and the United Kingdom was Ceylon's major export market. Between 1947 and 1962, the British were allowed the use of bases and the fine eastern harbor of Trincomalee. The first major postwar party, the United National Party, founded in 1946 as a coalition of various groups, governed Ceylon for a decade with a policy of friendliness toward the West and opposition to communism. But nationalistic and anticolonial forces were too strong for it. The 1956 elections were won by the Sri Lanka (Ceylon) Freedom Party, under Oxford-educated Solomon West Ridgeway Dias Bandaranaike.

The new government pledged itself to reforms and was inclined toward neutralism. It aimed to cancel the British defense agreements, replace English with Sinhalese as the national language, and nationalize basic industries and services. The Tamil minority strongly objected to some of these measures, and violence erupted between the Sinhalese and the Tamils. In 1957 the Tamils formed the Federal Party; began civil disobedience campaigns; and demanded that Tamil be made a second official language and that the government be decentralized. Rioting ensued between the two groups. In 1959 the prime minister was assassinated by a Buddhist fanatic. After an interim period, the April, 1960, elections brought to office the late leader's widow, Mrs. Sirimavo Bandaranaike, who became the world's first woman prime minister. At the head of the Freedom Party, she came into conflict not only with the Tamils but also with rightist political groups, religious elements, journalists, and economic interests. However, she remained in office for five years, after which the United National Party reassumed power. That regime lasted five years until the Freedom Party in 1970 once again returned in strength, with Mrs. Bandaranaike reinstated as prime minister.

The chief problem for Ceylon's governments was economic development. The population was expanding too rapidly to maintain itself on a plantation economy. The island produced less than half of its own food and had to import rice and other staples. Only one-fourth of the country was under cultivation, and much of the remaining land was marginal. Tea was the main export, but it was subject to vagaries of world market prices. Industrialization was limited; the island had little iron and no coal or petroleum resources. The most profitable enterprises were food-processing, plywood, cement, ceramics, and paper factories. Ceylon had the usual economic development plans.

In foreign affairs, Ceylon proposed neutrality of varying shades. Relations with India were of greatest concern. The existence in Ceylon of an Indian ethnic minority, numbering about a million, was a major problem in Indo-Ceylonese relations. With the Bandaranaikes as prime ministers, Ceylon improved relations with Communist countries. In 1955, when Soviet Russia relaxed its opposition, Ceylon entered the United Nations. Two years later, it exchanged diplomatic missions with and began to sell tea to the Russians. Trade agreements were later concluded, and the Soviets extended a modicum of aid. With Communist China, Ceylon had trade ties dating to 1952, when the two countries made rice-for-rubber barter agreements. In the decade following 1957, Communist China made available to Ceylon $41 million for economic programs. In 1962, during the Chinese-Indian border conflict, Mrs. Bandaranaike convened a conference of neutrals in Colombo to mediate the dispute but the effort was unsuccessful.

The United States sent diplomatic representatives to Ceylon after independence. Through 1962, the United States gave economic aid to the island totaling $85 million, two-thirds of which was in the form of food supplies. In 1963 this aid was stopped because of Ceylonese nationalization of the petroleum industry, which affected the interests of two American oil companies. Agreement on compensation was reached when the United National Party government returned to power, and in 1966 American aid programs were resumed. Though it had differences with the United States, Ceylon continued to look to both West and East as sources of aid to help solve basic economic problems.

Other Indian Ocean Islands. The Maldive Islands, 400 miles to the southwest of Ceylon in the Indian Ocean had also been a British colony. In July, 1965, independence was granted, but the British stayed on for a time to settle their defense arrangements in the archipelago. A military agreement was reached that allowed the British to keep the Royal Air Force base and other facilities at Gan, on one of the southern atolls. Maldive Islands subsequently entered the United Nations. The nearby Laccadive Islands continued under Indian control, as did the Andaman and Nicobar island groups in the Bay of Bengal.

In the southwest Indian Ocean, lying some 500 miles to the east of the island of Malagasy (Madagascar), Mauritius was granted independence by the British in March, 1968. In its capital, Port Louis, a mutual defense treaty was signed permitting the British army to retain forces to help maintain order on the island. Mauritius had a long colonial history. Originally discovered by the Portuguese in 1507, it was later occupied by the Dutch and the French. In 1810 the British took the island. After the abolition of the slave trade in the British Empire (1834), Indian laborers emigrated to man the sugar plantations, the mainstay of the insular economy. The island was important also to trade between America and the Far East; it provided cargoes and provisions for clipper ships from East Coast cities on the way to Asian ports. Over time various races came to settle in Mauritius. Racial conflict arose among the 800,000 inhabitants, who included Negroes, Indians, Chinese, Europeans, and Creoles (descendants of Europeans and African slaves). These problems were acerbated by religious conflicts among Christians, Muslims, and Hindus (who composed half the population). The first days of independence were marked by bloodshed and strife among the varying groups.

Other Indian Ocean islands remained in colonial status. The

French controlled Reunion, near Mauritius, and Amsterdam and St. Paul Islands far to the south near Antarctica. To the east, the Cocos (Keeling) and Christmas islands were administered by Australia. Scattered across the ocean were islands formerly governed from Mauritius but retained by the British: the St. Brandon Group, Rodrigues Island, and Diego Garcia, as well as the British Indian Ocean Territories (the Chagos Archipelago and the Seychelles group, the latter with its satellite-tracking station on the main island of Mahe). The widely dispersed and thinly populated islands were re-evaluated as military bastions in Western defense considerations as British retrenched interests while the Russians and Americans increased theirs.

18
MAINLAND SOUTHEAST ASIA
Since 1945

At the conclusion of the Second World War, the countries of Southeast Asia suddenly entered world politics as new factors. Each Southeast Asian state had its own particular problems of independence. While some attitudes and issues had area relevance, no leader could claim a unique status as spokesman for Southeast Asia. Each country resolved issues in its own fashion. Thailand carried on in an outward form of stability. Burma had centrifugal forces pulling apart the national fabric. The Indochinese states of Cambodia, Laos, North and South Vietnam over the decades became involved in a confrontation between Communist and non-Communist forces.

THAILAND (SIAM)

Postwar Thailand seemed relatively stable—a fortuitous condition that resulted partly from its heritage of political independence. The Thais did not have the nationalistic drive that helped to shape policies of most other Southeast Asian states. Domestic natural and food resources were in good supply; rice production was more than adequate for food needs. Military leaders led strong regimes that restricted the role of political opposition. Governments came and went, but political life continued (between 1932 and mid-1968 there were twenty-six coups, thirty-one government changes, and eight constitutions). Though relegated to a secondary political role, the monarchy continued to be a national unifying factor. In foreign affairs, Thailand continued to "bend with the wind" and make the most out of changing international situations.

Political Developments. After the defeat of Japan, politics continued for several years to revolve around familiar names.

Marshal Phibun Songgram, who had been associated with the Japanese occupation, was replaced as prime minister by Regent Pridi Banomyong. But Phibun remained in the background, ready to take over should the opportunity arise. In 1946 a new constitution changed the unicameral (since 1932) house to a bicameral one, with the upper house chosen by the elected lower house. But several months later, a new crisis arose. King Ananda Mahidol (Rama VIII) was found shot to death in his bed. The circumstances were never explained, but criticism mounted against Pridi. As a result of events over the next two years, Pridi was forced out of the country, eventually going to Communist China. In 1948 Phibun returned to office and remained in power for another ten years, albeit uneasily.

In 1949 another constitution was promulgated. It continued the bicameral structure but with the upper chamber appointed by the king rather than chosen by the lower house. This arrangement lasted two years, until in 1951 still another constitutional change was effected, restoring the 1932 unicameral structure, with half the members appointed by the king and the other half elected. But Phibun's position continued insecure as various factions jockyed for political advantage. By 1951, two military men had become contenders for top power. They were General Phao Sriyanon, chief of police, and General Sarit Thanarat, commander-in-chief of the army. In the February, 1957, elections for the national assembly, the government party was defeated. A coup the following September brought Sarit to power. Both Phibun and Phao went into exile.

In December, 1957, new elections were held for the assembly. Sarit, who had formed his own party, won. Having selected one of his deputy generals, Thanom Kittikachon, as prime minister, he then went to the United States for prolonged medical treatment. But in October, 1958, he returned to Thailand and took over the government until his death in 1963. The new regime was authoritarian. Sarit dissolved the national assembly, abrogated the constitution, and in 1959 inaugurated an all-appointive concurrent legislative and constituent assembly to prepare a new constitution. He outlawed political parties and labor unions and effected newspaper censorship. After Sarit's death in 1963,

Thanom Kittikachon once again became prime minister, assuming office through peaceful succession rather than through a coup. He proved efficient but not so domineering as his predecessor had been. After a decade of preparation and debate, in mid-1968, he announced a new constitution. The Thai political structure reverted to a bicameral system with an appointive upper house of 162 members and an elected lower house of 219 members. Elections (the first in eleven years) for the lower chamber were held in February, 1969. The military-dominated United Thai People's Party gained the majority of seats, but the opposition Democrat Party made a respectable showing.

Social and Economic Changes. The Thai regimes faced minority problems, but not to the same extent as neighboring countries. A million Chinese lived in the country; half of them in the capital. Other ethnic groups included Thais or Malay, Shan, and Lao extraction.

The Thai economic scene was fairly favorable, for most of the land was productive. A majority of the peasants owned their land. Much of Thai industry related to food-processing; but heavy industry began to develop, with steel mills, automotive assembly plants, and transport companies. Factories except for rice mills were centered in the Bangkok area. Rice, rubber, and tin exports predominated. Cottage industries supplemented factories. Thai silk was internationally famous. To encourage foreign investors, the government guaranteed them the remission of profits earned abroad and the exemption of necessary machinery from import duties. Economic planning was implemented in the usual stages.

Foreign Relations. The Thai government aimed at realistic diplomatic goals in the changing Asian scene. Searching for security, its leaders formulated policies that reflected the shifting alignments of global as well as Asian power. Its statesmen argued that strength lay in flexibility, and ideology seemed to play negligible parts in their formulation of policy. This adaptive approach, particularly to the containment of communism, seemed effective in the early postwar decades. Though aligned with Japan during the war, Thailand shortly thereafter resumed friendly relations with the winning side, and in 1946 it was admitted to the United Nations. By then it had concluded treaties or agreements with the United States, Great Britain, Soviet Russia, France, and China. The boundaries were rectified, with peripheral areas returned to Burma, Malaya, and Cambodia.

Relations with Asian Countries. Regarding Communist countries, Thailand was primarily apprehensive of China. Communism in Thailand was essentially Chinese in derivation and membership. The party was organized during the 1930's, but it made no headway until after the Second World War. It was permitted to operate legally in 1946, but was again outlawed after the Phibun coup in 1947. In 1953 Peking announced the formation of the Thai Autonomous People's Government in the southern Chinese province of Yunnan, whose inhabitants were mostly Thais. In the 1960's, Communist guerrilla activity in the northeast of Thailand was accelerated with the escalation of the Indochina war. In 1946 Thailand signed a treaty with the Soviet Union which began diplomatic relations between the two countries, though it was not until two years later that a Soviet minister was sent to Bangkok. Trade negotiations were undertaken from time to time but without significant results. Toward Japan there was some hostility resulting from the war, though the two countries had been nominal allies. However, over the years, Japan became Thailand's major trade source. Thailand's relations with neutralist Burma were strained but formally correct. With an independent Malaya, there were problems of Communist guerrilla border crossings. Communist infiltration and advances in bordering Laos were continual causes for concern. With Cambodia also, there were periodic disputes, chiefly over alignments and territorial boundaries. Toward the Vietnamese, the Thais were sympathetic in the early resistance to French colonialism, and Thailand provided bases of operations for the Communist Vietminh. However, after the Communist take-over of China, Thai policy changed direction. As the Vietnam War escalated in the mid-1960's, Bangkok dispatched troops to help the South Vietnamese cause. Thailand took an active interest in American-Vietnamese peace talks and prepared for the day when United States military presence in Southeast Asia might be diminished.

Relations with Western Countries. In respect to the United States and other Western countries, about 1950 Phibun turned from the traditional Thai aim of maintaining a balance of power in Southeast Asia. The increasing power of the Chinese Communists and the outbreak of the Korean War helped move Thailand toward the West. In 1950 American aid programs began with the signing of both economic and military assistance agreements. Subsequently, numerous American programs operated in the country. Within two decades, Thailand had received some $500 million of economic aid and $600 million of military assistance from the United States. The latter program had two purposes: to support and aid the Thai in their containment of Communist subversion within their borders, and to provide bases for American flights into Laos and Vietnam after the Indochina war escalated. By 1970 some 50,000 American military personnel were stationed in half a dozen bases in Thailand.

REGIONAL INTERESTS. Thailand took interest in regional affairs. It dispatched troops to Korea in the course of the conflict there, and sent others to South Vietnam. In 1954 it became a charter member of the Southeast Asia Treaty Organization (SEATO). Bangkok provided SEATO's secretariat site, and that of the Economic Commission for Asia and the Far East (ECAFE), a United Nations regional commission. Along with the Philippines and Malaysia, it sponsored the short-lived Association for Southeast Asia (ASA) and joined its successor, the Association of Southeast Asian Nations (ASEAN), to which Singapore and Indonesia also subscribed. In the early 1970's Thai spokesmen advocated strong indigenous regional co-operation as the United States indicated intention to re-examine its Asian priorities.

BURMA

Postwar Burma had serious domestic problems. Minorities constituted one-fifth of the population, including large groups of Shans, Karens, Chins, Kachins, Kayahs, and Arakanese. Partly as a result of minority issues and partly of military versus civilian polarization, Burmese political life was divided and troubled. In foreign affairs Burma, like India, subscribed to a policy of neutrality or nonalignment.

Political Developments. The period immediately after the war was especially difficult for Burma. In July, 1947, General Aung San, considered the father of his country, was assassinated by a political enemy. After a chaotic period, U Nu, a founder of the Anti-Fascist People's Freedom League (AFPFL), assumed leadership. In October, 1947, he concluded with Britain a treaty granting Burmese independence. A constitution provided for a president, indirectly elected for a five-year-term by a joint session of Parliament. Actual power was in the hands of the prime minister, appointed by the president from the majority party. The legislature was bicameral, with a popularly elected lower house (the Chamber of Deputies) of 250 members, and an upper house (the Chamber of Nationalities), comprising 125 representatives of Burma's various states. In the Chamber of Nationalities the Burmans had 63 seats and the minority groups a total of 62. The Union of Burma government was a federation, consisting of six main states, plus other divisions and districts.

Burma received independence on January 4, 1948. For the following decade U Nu was prime minister. In the first elections (1951), the AFPFL, under U Nu, won 95 percent of the Chamber of Deputies seats; in the second elections (1956), it won 85 percent of the seats. U Nu then left office for nine months in order, as he said, to purge party corruption. But the effort was not successful, and in September, 1958, he invited his old friend General Ne Win, commander-in-chief of the army, to take over temporarily as prime minister. For the next year and a half, the caretaker prime minister continued the Burmese policy of neutralism. He accommodated Communist China but cracked down on Communists at home. He improved security, established order, and eliminated corruption. The elections of February, 1960, returned U Nu to office as prime minister. He served another two years, during which factionalism in the AFPFL increased.

In March, 1962, Ne Win returned, this time to take over the government in a coup. He abolished the constitution; established a revolutionary council of military and civilian advisers; and whittled down the political parties until only his own, the Burma Socialist Program Party, was left. He jailed some civilian leaders, including U Nu, who languished four years in prison. Sweeping widely with a clean broom, Ne Win embarked on a program even more neutralistic and socialistic than that of the previous civilian administration. He increased nationalization of economic life, and eliminated not only foreign but also domestic private enterprises in the "Burmese way to socialism." However, because of his drastic measures, the over-all distribution system broke down; prices spiraled; and a black market developed. In the late 1960's, Ne Win relaxed some of the restrictions on consumer goods and permitted a modicum of private enterprise.

Foreign Relations. In foreign relations, Burmese leaders aimed at neutralism, a policy interpreted as one not of noninvolvement but of selective judgment on particular issues. Burma endeavored to remain aloof from its large neighbors, Pakistan, India, and China. Upon independence, Burma declined to maintain any political links with Britain. But it kept defense ties until 1953; remained in the sterling bloc; and signed air transport, tariff, and taxation agreements. Under Ne Win, it measured out neutrality in doses of equal consideration for equal parties, and was remarkably successful in its working international relations in the initial decades of independence.

Relations with Communist Countries. Communism gave rise to problems. Burma had some 1,300 miles of common boundaries with China that made Chinese Communist infiltration difficult to spot or to control. Some 300,000 Chinese lived in Burma. The Burmese domestic Communist movement, however, was not Chinese led. It was split into several native factions: the Communist Party of Burma (or the Trotskyist Red Flag Communists); the Burma Communist Party (or the Stalinist White Flag Communists); and the White Band of the People's Volunteer Organization, a semimilitary wartime organ. Burma was the first non-Communist Asian state to recognize and exchange diplomatic missions with Communist China. The Chinese Communists extended aid to Burma, in 1958 a $4 million loan and in 1961 a six-year $84 million one. In 1960 a twelve-year Chinese-Burman boundary dispute was settle peacefully. With the Soviet Union, which it recognized in 1948, the Union of Burma also concluded trade and aid agreements.

Relations with Non-Communist Asian Countries. Among non-Communist Asian states, India was the most important concern. U Nu was a close friend of Nehru, with whom he exchanged visits. There were more Indian immigrants (some 700,000) to Burma than to any other Southeast Asian country. After the war, Burma appropriated land held by Indians, and compensation for it became an issue. Nehru provided arms loans to help keep U Nu in power, and India imported Burmese rice. The two countries had a boundary problem, arising from the Nagas and Mizos hill peoples, who spilled over into Burma from India. In the early 1960's, increasingly stringent measures were taken on resident Indians by Ne Win, who nationalized their trades and forcibly repatriated to India over 100,000 of them. The Burmese were bitter toward Japan following the war. Burma ended the state of war in 1952 but refused to sign a peace treaty until there was an adequate reparations agreement. In April, 1955, settlement provided for $200 million of Japanese goods and services over a ten-year period. A supplementary agreement, effective in 1965, provided for an additional $140 million over a twelve-year interim. Burmese relations with other non-Communist Asian states were relatively unimportant.

Relations with the United States. Burma's relations with the United States were varied. In 1950 Burma began receiving American economic aid. But this aid was terminated in March, 1953, by the Burmese because they blamed the United States for the continued presence in Burma of about ten thousand armed Chinese Nationalist soldiers, who in 1949 had fled from the Communists over the South China border to Burma. In the Shan region, these forces accentuated acute minority and security problems. Since they belonged to an American-supported government, the Burmese argued that it was an American responsibility to evacuate them. By 1956 the United States, in co-operation with Thailand, had evacuated most of the Chinese soldiers out of Burma. The Burmese then requested the resumption of economic aid, which was granted. By 1970, despite the three-year hiatus, the aid totaled over $100 million. An American military aid program augmented the economic aid. In a mid-1958 agreement, an $85.5 million ten-year program, aimed at maintaining internal security and checking Communist threats, was effected. Additionally, a thousand Burmese military officials were trained in United States schools.

INDOCHINA

Indochina's regional difficulties were great. In the course of the postwar decades, the two Vietnams, Cambodia, and Laos had interrelated problems. Between 1945 and 1954, the French tried to reimpose their rule, but increasing opposition from both Communist and non-Communist sources led to the Geneva Conference of the latter year, in which the four political entities gained international recognition. The second regional period, 1954 to 1965, witnessed the growth of both Communist interests and the American presence. After 1965, regional security problems increased and held the center of the stage as the successor states in Indochina attempted with great difficulty to establish viable governments.

French Return and Withdrawal (1945–1954). When the French came back to Indochina after the Second World War, their policy generally was directed toward reasserting their colonial rule. But in no country did they succeed.

Vietnam. Political divisions were already apparent in Vietman. The leftist forces centered on Ho Chi Minh, the rightist ones on Bao Dai. Lesser native groups of varying ideologies existed; temporary foreign presence of the British in the south and the Chinese in the north complicated matters. When the French came back in late 1945, in the south, they reoccupied their former colony with relative ease. In the north, they experienced considerable difficulty. In January, 1946, Ho Chi Minh's regime conducted its first election and later that year promulgated a constitution. That March, France signed an agreement recognizing the Democratic Republic of Vietnam as a free state within the Indochinese Federation and the French Union. However, as the French grew stronger in Indochina, their policy hardened. In November, 1946, French forces bombarded the port city of Haiphong, killing more than six thousand Vietnamese. The next month the Vietnamese in retaliation attacked the French in Hanoi. Fighting spread, beginning a war which was to last seven and a half years.

To bolster their position, the French set up Bao Dai in the south as a rallying point for anti-Communists. In June, 1948, they signed a treaty with him, recognizing an independent Vietnam. In March, 1949, Bao Dai signed an agreement to bring Vietnam into the French Union as an Associated State and the following December, he proclaimed in Saigon the State of Vietnam. While the Democratic Republic of Vietnam received diplomatic recognition from Communist countries, Bao Dai's regime was recognized as the government of all Vietnam by the United States, the United Kingdom, and other Western powers. The French offered independence to this government within the French Union; however, Vietnamese nationalists sought total separation from France.

As the military situation escalated in Vietnam between 1950 and 1954, the United States gave increasing aid, up to 80 percent of expenses, or some $500 million annually. While the United States bolstered Bao Dai through the French, Communist countries, principally China, helped the Vietminh. Ho Chi Minh moved to strengthen his supremacy in the north by a united-front effort. In late 1951 the former Vietnamese Communist Party was reconstituted as the Lao Dong (Workers) Party. With military aid from Communist China, the Vietminh attacked the last French post, Dien Bien Phu, near the Laos border. There in May, 1954, the French troops surrendered as the Geneva Conference was in progress. These events marked the end of the French colonial rule in Indochina.

Cambodia. Whereas in Vietnam differing personalities shared the political limelight, postwar Cambodian politics were dominated by one individual, Norodom Sihanouk, whom the French had put on the throne in 1941. In October, 1945, the French returned to Phnom Penh to find that Sihanouk had declared Cambodian independence. When the French arrived, however, the king repudiated this act and reaffirmed his loyalty. In September, 1946, elections were held for a constituent assembly, and a constitution was promulgated in May, 1947. The following December, the first elections were held for the National Assembly, the supreme legislative body. In 1949 the king dissolved the Assembly, and in the 1951 elections his hand-picked delegates won. Meanwhile, he was extracting political concessions from the French. In a treaty of November 8, 1949, he confirmed the status of Cambodia as an Associate State within the French Union. In 1953 the French gave *de jure* recognition to Cambodia, but they still controlled some aspects of domestic life. The Communist movement, in both domestic and international forms, was negligible in these years.

Laos. As they did to other ports of Indochina, the French after the Second World War returned to Laos with the intention of reasserting their rule. In April, 1945, the king had declared his country's independence, but upon the return of the French, he again accepted their sovereignty. However, the domestic political situation was riddled with political factions, family loyalties, and regional ties. In December, 1946, elections were held for a constituent assembly; the following May the document was promulgated. It established an upper house (the Council of Ministers, or the King's Council) of 12 members, appointed by the king, and a lower house (the National Assembly), of 40 to 60 members, elected for four-year terms. On July 19, 1949, by the terms of a treaty with France, Laos received self-government within the French Union.

Meanwhile, the Communist movement increased in strength. During the war the Lao Issarak (Free Lao) had resisted the Japanese; after the war it resisted the French. In August, 1950, the leftist party was renamed the Pathet Lao (State of Lao). It was headed by Prince Souphanouvong (a son of the king), who had long-time ties with Hanoi. The Pathet Lao contested the neutralist forces under Souphanouvong's half-brother Prince Souvanna Phouma, who had several terms as prime minister. It also strengthened links with neighboring North Vietnam, whose troops conducted major campaigns in North Laos. As the leftist forces became stronger, in October, 1953, the French signed additional treaties with the government. By 1954, the Pathet Lao controlled the two northern provinces of Phong Saly and Sam Neua.

The Geneva Conference (1954). At the height of the Communist military victories in North Vietnam and Laos, the Geneva Conference on Indochina met in mid-1954. It had been convened by Great Britain and the Soviet Union. The Chinese Communists sent a delegation under Chou En-lai, concurrently their prime minister and foreign minister. Both North and South Vietnam were represented, though Bao Dai's delegation did not sign the agreements. United States president Dwight D. Eisenhower, who had vetoed direct military intervention in North Vietnam despite urgent French requests, declined full American participation in the conference but sent an observer. The United States did not sign the agreements.

The Geneva Conference concluded agreements relating to

Vietnam, Cambodia, and Laos. One set related to cease-fire arrangements. Vietnam was partitioned at the 17th parallel into two independent entities: the Democratic Republic of (North) Vietnam and the State of (South) Vietnam. All troops were to be withdrawn to their respective zones; civilians could repatriate themselves if they wished. The Cambodian agreement provided for the withdrawal of French and any Vietminh forces within three months. The Laotian agreement similarly provided for the withdrawal of Vietminh and French forces, but allowed Pathet Lao military units, temporarily, in Phong Saly and Sam Neua as well as French military presence. Another set of agreements related to political matters. In Vietnam, national elections were to be held within two years on the issue of reunification. (This provision was not effected.) The Cambodian and Laotian governments similarly promised (and effected) elections. To supervise provisions in Vietnam, Cambodia, and Laos, three International Control Commissions consisting of India as chairman, and Poland and Canada as members, were established.

Conflicting Interests (1954–1965). During the decade following the Geneva Conference, tensions in Indochina erupted into full-scale hostilities in which the United States became increasingly involved.

North Vietnam. Following the Geneva Conference, the French position in the Democratic Republic of Vietnam was phased out. For a year, the United States maintained a consulate in Hanoi, which the Vietminh did not recognize. Ho Chi Minh as president continued as the dominant figure, though he shared power with Premier and Foreign Minister Pham Van Dong and General Vo Nguyen Giap. With non-Communist Asian neighbors Hanoi had some trade but few diplomatic ties. Trade agreements were concluded with India and Japan (which, however, paid reparations to Saigon). In January, 1960, a communistic constitution was promulgated. It centered power in Ho but continued the forms of presidential and prime ministerial posts, a unicameral legislature, and a standing committee to act when the legislature was not in session. In the May, 1960, elections, with four minor parties putting up candidates, the Workers' Party won most of the seats. Ho Chi Minh was re-elected president, as he was again four and eight years later. A politically indoctrinated army remained loyal to the regime.

Agriculture continued to be the mainstay of the economy. Rice, the main food crop, had traditionally been supplied from the south. By 1957, however, Hanoi claimed self-sufficiency in rice production. The Vietminh continued the experiments, begun during the war, with agricultural reform and land redistribution. Ho Chi Minh followed the Chinese Communists in dividing agricultural society into five classes: landlords, rich peasants, middle peasants, poor peasants, and landless peasants. The last two groups were allotted land from that of the first three. Co-operative projects, including production co-operatives and marketing associations, were undertaken, but communes were not developed as they were in China. Both industrial and agricultural economic plans were formulated. North Vietnam received substantial aid from other Communist countries.

SOUTH VIETNAM. While leadership stabilized in North Vietnam, it was the opposite in the south. In 1954 President Bao Dai appointed Ngo Dinh Diem as prime minister. In this position Ngo established his powers, and within two years, he deposed Bao Dai. In October, 1955, South Vietnam changed its name from the State of Vietnam to the Republic of Vietnam, with Ngo as president. The following March, elections with universal suffrage were held for a national constituent assembly. A constitution was promulgated on October 26, 1956. It provided for a president and a vice-president, directly elected for five-year terms. The constituent assembly then became a unicameral national assembly, whose members filled out a three-year term of office. In August, 1959, elections were held for the legislature of 125 members. In 1961 Ngo was re-elected president. Because of the worsening military situation, the 1962 legislative elections were postponed until September, 1963. Meanwhile, growing Buddhist, military, and Communist tensions caused problems for Ngo. In November, 1963, he was killed by a military junta, which came into power.

Overshadowing any domestic issue was the growing threat of the Communist Vietcong (an abbreviation of Viet Nam Cong Sam, meaning Vietnamese Communists). Its political counterpart, the National Liberation Front, established by Hanoi in 1960, embraced several organs and parties, including the People's Revolutionary Party. During the years following the Geneva Conference, the Communist movement, dating to war years and enhanced by refugee movements south, increased in strength. By the early 1960's, its military operations had become substantial. With thousands of professional troops and many more sympathizers, the Vietcong, aided by Vietminh contingents infiltrated through Laos from North Vietnam, operated in the central Vietnam highlands and the Mekong Delta. The resulting guerrilla warfare involved counterattacks by large numbers of South Vietnamese troops, as well as American military advisers.

As the Communist cause escalated, so did American presence in South Vietnam. American military, political, and economic commitments steadily increased following the Geneva Conference. Thousands of American advisers and soldiers came into the country. This aid was unilateral, as international pacts, such as SEATO, whose protocol extended defense commitments to South Vietnam (and Cambodia and Laos), proved impracticable in the situation. American military probes into North Vietnam also commenced. In August, 1964, two American destroyers in the Gulf of Tonkin were involved in incidents with North Vietnamese torpedo boats. President Lyndon Johnson, with a senatorial resolution sanctioning appropriate action, ordered retaliatory attacks on North Vietnamese naval and oil installations. The Vietnam War then entered a new phase.

Cambodia. In contrast to Vietnam, Cambodia seemed relatively stable and free from overt Communist activity. In March, 1955, king Norodom abdicated in favor of his father in order to himself become active in Cambodian politics. Now unencumbered by royal title, he founded his own party, the Sangkum Reastra Niyum (Popular Socialist Community). Elections were held in September, 1955, and Sihanouk's party won all 91 seats in the National Assembly. In April, 1960, when the king died, Sihanouk declined the succession. The queen mother became nominal ruler, while Norodom assumed the title of chief of state. In June of that year, a popular referendum approved the prince's policies by a 99.8 percent affirmative vote. In 1962 and 1966, legislative elections again returned in force the Sangkum Party representatives. Cambodian politics by then predictably reflected the hallmarks of a one-party state.

Economic stability matched its political counterpart. About 85 percent of the cultivated land was planted with rice, the highest percentage of rice production in the world. Rubber production was next in importance, followed by miscellaneous food crops. Food-processing was the most important of Cambodia's limited industries. Five-year economic plans outlined development programs. Fortunately for an agricultural country, Cambodia had no pressing problems of overpopulation, soil exhaustion, or lack of arable land.

In foreign affairs, Cambodia profited from its policy of neutralism. Aid poured into the country from Communists and non-Communist countries. Cambodia received no reparations from Japan, but the Japanese instead provided a grant of several million dollars. In 1956 the Chinese Communists gave a $22.4 million grant, their first to a neutralist state, and sent advisers to implement it. The Soviet Union also supplied aid, and in 1963 it delivered military aircraft. Prior to that time, Cambodia had accepted military assistance only from the Western world (principally the United States and France). Peking later also gave military aid.

Norodom Sihanouk similarly received aid from and criticized Western powers. Between 1955 and 1963, the United States extended $309.6 million in economic aid and $83.7 million in military assistance, the latter helping to sustian a great portion of Cambodia's 30,000-man army. Economic aid went to build hospitals, irrigation systems, and roads, including the so-called Friendship Highway from the capital to the new port of Sihanoukville on the Gulf of Siam. But in November, 1963, angered by the treatment toward the bordering United States allies—South Vietnam and Thailand—Sihanouk announced the termination of all United States aid programs in Cambodia by the end of the year. The final diplomatic break came in May, 1965, after border violations by the South Vietnam air force.

Laos. The Laotian situation was muddied by divided internal politics and growing Communist strength. After the Geneva cease-fire arrangements, the elections promised for 1955 were held, but the Communist Pathet Lao party did not participate. However, it then changed tactics in an attempt to gain seats in a coalition government. Following two years of negotiations, the two half-brothers, Souphanouvong and Souvanna Phouma, came to terms in November, 1957. The provinces of Phong Saly and Sam Neua were to be assimilated into the central authority; 1,500 men from the Pathet Lao's 9,000 troops were to be integrated into the national army and the rest demobilized. The Pathet Lao received legal status and organized a party called the Neo Lao Hak Xat (Lao Patriotic Front), which was given two cabinet posts. In the elections of 1958 for an enlarged National Assembly, the new party won the majority of the twenty additional seats. But the coalition soon disintegrated, and the situation was further complicated when a rightist bloc came to the fore.

In 1960 elections were held for the National Assembly. A strong rightist faction from the south under General Phoumi Nosavan and Prince Boun Oum then emerged and temporarily came out on top of the ideological heap. With Communists, neutralists, and rightists coexisting uneasily, the domestic situation worsened. In mid-1962, a major Communist campaign spread through the country, causing the United States, with Thai consent, to bring marines to northeast Thailand on a stand-by basis. In an attempt to stabilize the situation, another internal Laotian agreement was signed in June, 1962, this time among the three domestic parties. The next month in Geneva a conference of thirteen nations, including the United States, and Laos, guaranteed the neutrality of Laos and stipulated the withdrawal of all foreign troops. But in 1963 fighting again broke out among the rival forces, and the coalition government fell apart. After an unsuccessful attempt at a coup to force the situation in early 1965, Phoumi Nosavan retired to Bangkok. Boun Oum remained behind. The rightist cause collapsed; the neutralist persisted; the Communist gained.

In economy Laos was almost entirely agricultural, with little mining or industry. Rice was the chief crop. Transportation was primitive, and Laotians had to traverse neighboring countries in order to reach ports. The Mekong River was suitable for navigation of only small craft, but a railroad from Bangkok extended to a Mekong River border town opposite Vientiane. Economic planning could not be effectively realized in the midst of political uncertainty.

Foreign relations were similarly complicated by political factionalism. Despite the exchange of ambassadors with North Vietnam, problems still existed. Vietminh infiltration (reportedly up to 50,000 in the late 1960's to augment 30,000 Pathet Lao insurgents) was an issue. Relations were smooth with South Vietnam until the formation of the Laotian coalition government in 1962 to include Communists, whereupon Saigon recalled its diplomatic representative. With Cambodia relations were formal. Thailand was opposed to a Communist Laos. Relations with India were cordial; visits were exchanged with Nehru. With Japan, there was no reparations agreement, but Tokyo provided loans totaling several million dollars. The country established diplomatic relations with Soviet Russia, and the Russian ambassador in Bangkok was accredited to Laos. There was no boundary dispute with Communist China, which, however, completed several roads (employing 20,000 troops) pushing down into adjoining Laotian territory controlled by Communist factions.

***Escalation* (*since 1965*).** In the years following 1965, despite attempts at negotiation, the war in Indochina not only continued but spread.

THE VIETNAMS. Ho Chi Minh, until his death in 1969, not only directed Indochina's war efforts but endeavored to play off Russia and China, both of which gave him sizable aid. After his demise, second-rank leadership promised some new faces but not necessarily new policies. Leadership also was changing in South Vietnam. Amidst growing problems, in September, 1966, a constituent assembly was again elected; it completed its task the following March. Electoral laws were enacted in mid-1967. That September, voters elected a Senate, as well as General Nguyen Van Thieu, the chief of state, as president. Nguyen Cao Ky, former prime minister, was designated vice-president. In another round of elections in October, 137 members were returned to the lower house. South Vietnam thus finally received its first legally constituted government after almost four years and a dozen coups since the overthrow of the Diem regime. But political factionalism in domestic politics augured problems for the future.

In the latter half of the 1960's, military operations in South and North Vietnam spiraled as cautious probes for peace proceeded. There were at least three campaigns, cutting across lines of civil and external warfare: the land and the air war against the Communists in the south, and the air war in the north. Saigon-sponsored pacification programs and Hanoi domestic measures were relegated to secondary consideration. As the Gulf of Tonkin incident had provoked American retaliatory raids against North Vietnam targets, so Communists guerrilla attacks (in early February, 1965) against United States installations in South Vietnam elicited similar reaction. The next month, as first American ground combat troops, 3,500 marines landed at Danang (Tourane) to defend the air base. By the end of the year, some 175,000 troops were in South Vietnam. Over the next four years, a build-up to half a million American troops took place. As the South Vietnamese non-Communist and Communist strengths similarly grew, there were moves for peace. In April, 1965, President Johnson called for "unconditional discussions" on peace, urged Communists to cease their attacks in the south, and declared as United States policy the establishment of an independent South Vietnam regime free from outside interference.

The United States also authorized several moratoriums on bombing of North Vietnam targets. President Johnson reiterated American policy to the effect that the United States would stop bombing and troop build-up in the south if infiltration from the north ceased. Ho Chi Minh in turn announced his terms; peace talks would take place after bombing and other "acts of war" against the Democratic Republic of Vietnam were ended. Despite polarized views, moves were made toward negotiation of the issues. In May, 1968, Washington and Hanoi delegations met in Paris to conduct peace talks. As these dragged on, the Vietcong expanded its political and diplomatic role. It created the Provisional Revolutionary Government of the Republic of South Vietnam, which some two dozen countries shortly recognized. Over the years, the United States withdrew some troops and turned over more responsibilities for the conduct of the war to the South Vietnamese. As the 1970's dawned, American commitments to South Vietnam had been sizable—over $100 billion expended, over 40,000 lives lost, and 300,000 on the casualty lists—in pursuit of policy ends variously defined as supporting United States national interests, containing militant communism, honoring South Vietnamese agreements, and seeking a viable national government in Saigon. Despite American troop withdrawals, pressing Vietnamese political considerations remained.

Cambodia. The Vietnam War spilled over into Cambodia. Border bombing incidents by American planes after 1965 continued to occasion outbursts from Sihanouk, who demanded from the United States, as well as other countries, respect and recognition of his country's borders as they currently existed. As the United States moved to meet the prince's conditions, efforts were made to restore normal relations between the two countries. By 1970, an American mission was once again operating in Phnom Penh, but in March that year Sihanouk, while abroad, was deposed in a military coup led by the chief of staff, General Lon Nol. The following month, President Richard Nixon authorized American troops to flush Communists out of Cambodian sanctuaries bordering South Vietnam. Though the troops were withdrawn by mid-year, American aid poured into Phnom Penh. The war escalated in Cambodia with increased Communist and anti-Communist activity, while Sihanouk lived in exile in China.

Laos. In Laos, in 1965 elections were once again held, but the Pathet Lao did not participate. As in South Vietnam and more recently Cambodia, the United States poured aid into Laos, at the rate of some $250 million a year by the end of the 1960's. By mid-1969, economic aid had totaled $643 million. (Military aid from 1955 to 1962 was $128 million; figures since 1962 are undisclosed.) Aid programs were occasionally used to promote policy ends; twice, in 1958 and 1960, they were temporarily suspended because of Congressional irritation of their lack of proper implementation. Advisers included about a thousand resident Americans to administer the programs. Also present were two private United States air lines that serviced Laotian missions in the field and supplied remote areas. The role of the United States in Laos vis-à-vis the Vietnam War was reassessed, and the royal government permitted American military operations in and from its territory to this end. Increasingly, Communist presence and the American response involved Indochinese regional considerations. Problems and policy could not be broken down into component political subparts or neat geographical delimitations.

19
INSULAR SOUTHEAST ASIA
Since 1945

Malaysia, the Philippines, and Indonesia faced problems similar to those of mainland Asian entities—underdeveloped economies, expanding populations, social divisions, communal tensions, Communist presence. The British possessions in the insular world gave way to Malaysia, which for some decades seemed outwardly stable but yet could not assimilate the sizable Chinese resident group. The Philippines routinely went through an established succession of administrations and despite nationalistic outbursts, established close ties with the United States. Indonesia, the most important of all Southeast Asian countries, was guided by Sukarno for two and a half decades. Its scope of problems warranted special consideration.

MALAYSIA

After the Second World War, the British returned to reimpose their rule over the Malay Peninsula and British Borneo. But the prewar peninsular pattern of Straits Settlements, four Federated States and five Unfederated States was altered. From 1946 to 1948, the five Federated and four Unfederated states, with Penang and Malacca, formed a Malayan Union. From 1948 to 1957, the Union reverted to an eleven-state Federation of Malaya. In the latter year, it received independence. Singapore remained a colony, as did Sarawak and British North Borneo, until in 1963 they were incorporated into an expanded, independent Malaysia. Singapore stayed in Malaysia for two years, but because of its unique status involving millions of Chinese, after 1965 it separated and became an independent entity. Brunei remained in British protectorate status.

Political Developments. For six months after the Japanese surrender in August, 1945, the British effected a military administration in Malaya and Borneo. In late 1945 they negotiated treaties with the sultans, who relinquished their sovereignty again to the British government. The nine Malay states, as well as the settlements of Penang and Malacca, were reconstructed politically to form the Malayan Union. Singapore kept its status as a separate crown colony.

Criticism was soon directed against the Union. The United Malay National Organization was formed to work toward the restoration of Malayan rights. Chinese and Indians felt excluded. As a result of this widespread opposition, on February 1, 1948, the British replaced the Union with the Federation of Malaya. The political structure was that of the prewar Federated States pattern, but now with eleven states instead of four. The Federation was governed by a British high commissioner and by an executive and legislative council. To advance their own communal causes, the Malayan Chinese Association and the Malayan Indian Congress were formed during this period. In 1955 elections were held for the 52 elective federal legislative seats. The Alliance Party, a coalition of the three main ethnic groups, received the great majority of votes. Singapore continued as a separate crown colony under a governor, a legislative council, and a municipal council. A commissioner-general stationed in Singapore represented over-all British interests in Southeast Asia. In the years between 1948 and 1960, the Communist problem, termed "the emergency," was most critical on the peninsula. After the war only part of the Communist-dominated Malayan People's Anti-Japanese Army surrendered to the British and gave up their arms. Several thousand others embarked upon a program of terrorism, which spread over a large part of the country until it was finally suppressed by the British.

In August 1957, the British granted the Federation of Malaya its independence. Its constitution provided a head of state called the Yang di-Pertuan Agong, who was chosen on a seniority basis from among the nine sultans (Malacca and Penang had no sultans). But effective power was in the hands of the prime minister. In the early years of independence (1963–1970) the prime minister was Tunku Abdul Rahman of the Alliance Party. A federal bicameral legislature was established.

British North Borneo and Sarawak continued as colonies and Brunei as a protectorate. Singapore as a separate state also remained under British jurisdiction. A Cambridge-trained lawyer, Lee Kuan Yew of the People's Action Party, became prime minister. The government of the State of Singapore was somewhat like that of Malaya. The state was headed by the Yang di-Pertuan Negara, who was required to be a Malay; the prime minister had the effective power. There was a unicameral legislature with four official languages: English, Chinese, Malay, and Tamil. An Internal Security Council was established, with three members each from the State and Britain plus a minister from the Federation.

In May, 1961, Tunku Abdul Rahman suggested to the prime minister of Singapore that a federation of Malaysia be formed as a political and economic co-operative endeavor to counteract renewed Communist influence in the area. Lee Kuan Yew agreed to the plan, which was then extended to include British Borneo. But the Philippines objected to the inclusion of portions of North Borneo, over which it claimed jurisdiction, and Sukarno of Indonesia objected to Malaysia on principle. A United Nations team polled North Borneo (Sabah) and Sarawak on the issue (the sultan of Brunei elected not to join the federation) and found a majority decision to join. On September 16, 1963, Malaysia came into existence. The Philippines and Indonesia thereupon broke diplomatic relations. For two years Singapore continued an uneasy partner, and Chinese under Lee Kuan Yew feared a position of perennial political minority in Malaysia. The union became increasingly impractical, and in August, 1965, the political divorce took place. With Singapore out, the former British Borneo colonies were incorporated more firmly when in 1967 the Federation was divided into two political subentities of West Malaysia (Malaya with the eleven states on the peninsula) and East Malaysia (Sarawak and Sabah on Borneo).

But communal problems persisted on the peninsula. After the May, 1969, elections in West Malaysia in which the Alliance Party's position, including that of participating Chinese, was seriously challenged by independent Chinese candidates, rioting erupted in Kuala Lumpur. The constitution was suspended; emergency measures were promulgated; and Deputy Prime

Minister Tun Abdul Razak was given wide powers. An uneasy peace was eventually restored, after which Tunku Abdul Rahman bowed out of office and his deputy replaced him. The constitution was restored and elections took place in East Malaysia. In Singapore, the ruling People's Action Party continued to dominate the political scene. Elections in 1963 and 1968 confirmed its primary position. In the protectorate of Brunei, the British high commissioner continued to control foreign and military policies. Brunei registered only one political party, the People's Independent Front, which was authorized by the sultan.

Economic Development. Racial strife clouded the Malaysian political picture, but the economy was relatively advanced. Rubber and tin continued to be the chief exports, earning respectively one-half and one-fourth of Malayan foreign exchange. Rice had to be imported because Malaysian crops were insufficient. Diversification of industry was encouraged. New industrial areas, notably Petaling Jaya near Kuala Lumpur, were established. The usual economic development plans were effected. Singapore continued to prosper as the third busiest port in the world (after Rotterdam and New York); but it also began some light industries. Less advanced Sabah and Sarawak exploited forest products. In the oil-rich land of Brunei, Shell Company developed fields that provided the protectorate with its main source of foreign exchange and wealth.

Foreign Relations. In foreign affairs, after independence Malaya (unlike Burma) joined the British Commonwealth. Malayan-British defense arrangements were formulated in the regional External Defense Mutual Assistance Agreement, with which Australia and New Zealand were affiliated. Cultural and educational exchanges also were effected with the three Commonwealth countries. In 1968 Britain gave notice that, in accordance with general retrenchments in military, political, and territorial interests in Asia, the crown would pull out of Malayan and Singapore defense arrangements by 1972. However, with the inauguration of a Conservative government in England in 1970, the situation was reviewed.

After taking office, Tunku Abdul Rahman exchanged visits with leaders of other non-Communist Asian countries. India took a hands-off attitude toward the Indian minority in Malaysia. Following changes of leadership in their respective countries, the Philippines and Indonesia normalized relations in the late 1960's. Malaya did not demand reparations from Japan. They had been previously waived for the country by Prime Minister Winston Churchill, and Japan claimed that the confiscation of Japanese property in Malaya had in effect paid them. Singapore, however, pressed for compensation. In late 1966 Japan agreed to pay Singapore $16,510,000, half in grants and the remainder as reparations. (Singapore had originally demanded twice the amount.) The United States role in Malaysia was minor compared to that of the Commonwealth. By the early 1970's American aid, all economic, approximated only $50 million. Because the past "emergency" and great numbers of resident Chinese, Malaysia and Singapore hesitated to deal with either Communist or Nationalist China and did not extend diplomatic recognition to either regime although carrying on some trade with both. However, in 1968, they recognized the Soviet Union.

THE PHILIPPINES

The Second World War and its aftermath cemented rather than loosened Philippine-American ties. Though independence came as scheduled, the Republic in its initial decades was particularly dependent on American military and economic aid programs. Its presidential administrations all subscribed to this end, which made the Philippine position unique. For its part, the United States Congress set precedents in postwar aid and trade programs in the Philippines. In effect, the Republic became a testing ground for American policies that were later applied on a worldwide basis. Domestic problems continued, and only slowly did the Republic enter into international life. As nowhere else in Southeast Asia, independence was followed by a proscribed succession of national and provincial elections and administrations.

Formative Years (1945–1953). In February, 1945, the Philippine Commonwealth government in exile returned to Manila. The next year presidential and congressional elections were held. Sergio Osmeña of the Nacionalistas lost to Manuel Roxas, lawyer, economist, and prewar politician from the Visayans, who founded the Liberal Party in late 1945. Independence was effected without difficulty on July 4, 1946. The structure and offices of the Commonwealth government were continued.

After two years in office, Roxas died. His vice-president, Elpidio Quirino, took office to complete the unexpired term, and was re-elected in his own right in November, 1949, for another four years.

Political Developments. The Liberal Party administrations of Roxas and Quirino (1946–1953) were precedent-setting. The first president had a difficult time in stabilizing economic affairs, in rehabilitating the islands, and in containing dissidence. Quirinio's years of office were also difficult. The government was charged with corruption, waste, and inefficiency. Guerrilla warfare occurred in Central Luzon, where the Communist Hukbalahaps (Huks), who had been armed during the war, led an agrarian rebellion. Quirino appointed as secretary of defense fast-rising Congressman Ramon Magsaysay, who took strong action against the rebels. The direct Magsaysay tactics, effectively utilizing American aid, dampened the internal Communist problems and skyrocketed Magsaysay to the presidency in 1953 when he ran against Quirino.

Relations with the United States. The Roxas-Quirino administrations established the bases of Philippine-American economic programs. Responding to Philippine petition, the United States Congress in 1946 passed a Rehabilitation Act that authorized aid totaling $620 million: $400 million as compensation for private-property war damage, $120 million to rebuild government buildings, and $100 million transfer of surplus American supplies left in the country after the war. The Rehabilitation Act was tied to a Trade Act, which provided for eight years of mutual free trade, followed by twenty years of gradually declining duty-free quotas or increasing tariff duties on a reciprocal basis. But the United States Congress stipulated that for the duration of the Act, American businessmen were to receive parity rights with Filipinos in the Philippines' public utilities and natural resources. To effect these provisions, the Filipinos had to amend their constitution, which had reserved to them primary rights in these economic areas. In September, 1946, a surplus agreement was signed. Since American surplus material in the Philippines was valued at $137 million, the excess of $37 million over the $100 million provided for in the Rehabilitation Act was allocated for two purposes: $5 million for Filipino education programs and $32 million to discharge the United States responsibility to redeem guerrilla currency that it had authorized during the war.

After the outbreak of the Korean War the United States began to consider Philippine aid as part of its policy to contain communism throughout the world. The United States Congress also insisted on self-help measures to improve domestic conditions. Filipinos, however, continued to press for preferential treatment from the United States on the bases of past colonial ties and devastating effects of the war in the islands. In mid-1950, an American mission examined the Philippine economy and specified social reforms as prerequisites for an American loan of up to $250 million. The Philippine government under Quirino reluctantly enacted the reform measures but got only a portion of the proffered loan.

Other arrangements were effected with regard to military matters. In March, 1947, a military bases agreement was signed that listed 27 Philippine sites as possible American leaseholds. The agreement skirted questions such as boundaries and ownership of bases and jurisdiction over military personnel. United States military assistance was extended to the Republic, beginning with the gift of $100 million worth of arms upon independence. In March, 1947, the first of several agreements on military assistance was signed. There were differences between the two countries on veterans' benefits, another war legacy. Filipino veterans, both of the United States Armed Forces in the Far East and of officially recognized guerrilla groups, were officially entitled to rights and privilages of American veterans. But President Truman declared that it was "impractical" to extend to Filipinos those G.I. rights relating to housing, education, and unemployment benefits. Hence initially Filipino veterans received only limited benefits, hospitalization costs and up to $75 to cover burial expenses.

Relations with Other Countries. In addition to the historic American orientation, the Philippines emphasized Spanish affinities. (It was the only Southeast Asian country with two colonial heritages.) Because of geographic factors, the Republic was also involved in Asian problems. Japan was an important consideration. Due to their bitter wartime experiences, many Filipinos did not welcome relations with Japan. The Republic at first demanded reparations totaling $8 billion from Japan (in addition to American rehabilitation programs). In 1951 the Philippines attended the Japanese Peace Conference in San Francisco but signed the treaty only after a Philippine-United States mutual defense treaty had been concluded. However the Philippine Senate refused to ratify the treaty until reparations were provided for.

The Republic made halting steps toward regional co-operation. In 1950 Quirino convened a conference at Baguio (the Philippine summer capital in the central Luzon mountains) of six countries to discuss regional questions, but nothing material resulted. With Indonesia, relations varied. In UN councils, the Philippines supported the Indonesian cause against the Dutch. After Indonesia won independence in 1949, differences between the two states developed over cold war issues. Ties were formal with United States allies in Asia: Taiwan, South Korea, Thailand, and South Vietnam. Filipino troops joined the Allied cause in the Korean War. With Western Europe, both diplomatic and trade bonds existed. With the Arab world, the Muslim minority in the islands pledged friendship. The Republic did not establish relationships with Communist China or the Soviet Union. Filipinos actively participated in the United Nations. General Carlos Romulo, former journalist, wartime propagandist, and ambassador to the United States, was the first Asian to serve as General Assembly president (1949–1950).

Personalities and Policies (since 1953). Ramon Magsaysay, formerly of the Liberal Party (party-hopping was common in Philippine politics), ran on the Nacionalist ticket in the 1953 elections and easily defeated Quirino. The Nacionalistas returned to power for the next eight years through Magsaysay and his successor, and, after a four-year interim of Liberal Party rule, came back again in 1965.

POLITICAL DEVELOPMENTS. Magsaysay, of humble background, was quite popular with both Filipinos and Americans. As president, he traveled throughout the country, concerning himself mainly with social reforms and economic development. He had held office only three years, when he died in a plane crash in March, 1957. He was succeeded by his vice-president, Carlos Garcia, who continued his policies. In November that year Garcia was re-elected in his own right for another four years. He emphasized a "Filipino First" economic policy, aimed primarily against Chinese economic interests. In the 1961 election he was defeated by his vice-president, Diosdado Macapagal, of the Liberal Party.

The Liberal Party lasted in power only four years. The Macapagal administration extended transport systems, promoted the usual reform measures, and spurred rice production. A nationalistic move changed the independence date of July 4 to the more meaningful one of June 12, when in 1898 General Emilio Aguinaldo of the Philippine Insurrection Army had proclaimed the Philippine Republic. In 1965 the Nacionalistas won the elections and put into the presidency Senator Ferdinand Marcos, a former Liberal. Four years later, Marcos was re-elected for a second term. But party affiliation meant less than personalities. Presidents of both parties advanced similar programs relating to civil projects, land reform, economic development plans, foreign policies, and into the early 1970's, continued emphasis on the "special relations" with the United States.

Relations with the United States. Philippine administrations continued to opt for American ties. Magsaysay won an eighteen-month extension of the free-trade period, but the Laurel-Langley revised trade agreement of 1954 kept the 1974 terminal date for all privileges. Manila continually urged some type of post-1974 trade preferentials, if only on a commodity-for-commodity basis. Concurrent with the redefinition of trade ties came a re-examination of aid programs. The Rehabilitation Act had authorized payments by the War Damage Commission of up to 75 percent on approved claims above $500. (Authorized claims up to $500 were paid in full.) However, appropriations were exhausted after 52.5 percent of claims over $500 had been met. To help cover the remaining authorized 22.5 percent, the United States Congress in 1963 appropriated an additional $73 million (of which $40 million was to underwrite educational exchanges). In 1967 Filipino veterans received an additional $31.1 million to represent the final settlement of claims affecting some 75,000 men. Filipino leaders, including Magsaysay, pressed further claims, ranging up to $3 billion against the United States government, which recognized only a fraction of them.

Some progress was made toward defining military base terms. In 1966 the leaseholds were reduced from ninety-nine years to another twenty-five years. The United States, which had never fully utilized all sites, restricted itself to three main bases. Joint boards with Filipinos were established to discuss mutual military problems. But jurisdiction over American service personnel remained unclear.

Over the years, American-Philippine relations had been close yet trying, because of varying interpretations and conflicting philosophies. The United States government claimed that Filipinos had been well provided for (postwar American aid by 1970 to the Philippines reached $1.3 billion). Filipinos maintained the contrary. They continued to press their claims to further aid, objected to tie-in programs, demanded cash payments, and pleaded for a sustained and unique place in American programs. There were indications, however, that the preferential treatment was losing force. The new postwar Philippine generation questioned the validity in changing conditions of agreements from earlier times.

Relations with Other Countries. A greater degree of flexibility came about in dealing with other countries. In 1956 a reparations agreement was reached with Japan; $550 million was to be paid over a twenty-year period with an additional $250 million extended in loans. Diplomatic relations were then resumed, and trade rapidly increased between the two countries. In the face of phased-out trade preferentials with the United States, the Republic sought other markets, including Communist ones. But Filipinos continued to concern themselves with immediate problems: Indonesian ideological orientation, Malaysian incorporation of Sabah, the Chinese Communist position. Soviet Russian and Chinese Communist attitudes appeared to mellow in the latter half of the 1960's, but the Filipino thaw came slower. In the United Nations organs and Asian multilateral arrangements, the Philippine position changed from that of being in 1946 one of the few independent Asian countries to being one among many independent Asian states.

The Republic joined regional groupings, including the

Southeast Asia Treaty Organization (SEATO) and Maphilindo (Malaysia-Philippines-Indonesia), which foundered on the Malaysian crisis. In 1966 Filipinos helped form the Asian and Pacific Council (ASPAC), whose eight members ranged geographically from South Korea to New Zealand. In December that year, the headquarters of the thirty-one member Asian Development Bank, suggested by President Lyndon Johnson the previous year, were established in Manila. The Philippines dispatched several thousand noncombatant troops to South Vietnam. Like other United States military allies in Asia, it began to re-evaluate the international situation in the light of changing American policy objectives of the 1970's.

INDONESIA

Indonesia faced some of the most pressing postwar problems of all Southeast Asian states. The revolutionary period (which is defined in modern Indonesian history as those four years between the Indonesian declaration of independence in August, 1945, and the Dutch recognition of it in December, 1949) tended to be a unifying factor among the Javanese and some Sumatrans, but it seemed strained to other indigenous parties. Between 1949 and 1957, politics witnessed frequent cabinet changes, several temporary constitutions, one national election, increased army and Communist influences, and chronic economic problems centered on underproduction and spiraling inflation. The years between 1957 and 1965 were Sukarno's "guided democracy." After Sukarno's fall from top office, new leadership redirected policies.

Revolutionary Period (1945–1949). On August 17, 1945, the Independence Preparatory Committee proclaimed the Republic of Indonesia in Djakarta. The committee confirmed Sukarno as president and Hatta as vice-president. It prepared a constitution, established a cabinet, and created an advisory Central National Committee of 135 members. The *Pantjasila* (Five Principles, not related to the Indian set) of faith in God, nationalism, humanity, democracy, and social justice were proclaimed as Indonesian political doctrines. Six weeks after the founding of the Republic, British troops arrived to accept the Japanese surrender and to release the interned Dutch. The British recognized the Djakarta government.

When the Dutch returned in late 1945, conflict ensued. Like the French in Indochina, the former colonial masters desired to reimpose the prewar political structure, which at best would allow Indonesia to become a member of a Dutch Commonwealth. As the Dutch strengthened their forces, the Republican government established itself. The Central National Committee was converted into a legislature, and the cabinet was made responsible to the legislature. Four main political parties emerged: the Masjumi (Consultative Council of Indonesian Muslims), the Indonesian Nationalist Party, the Socialist Party, and the Communist Party.

Indigenous support for the Republic was evidenced on Java and some areas of Sumatra, where the Dutch encountered resistance. On the other islands the Dutch were more successful. During this uneasy coexistence, Republican leaders signed with the Dutch, in March, 1947 the Linggadjati (or Cheribon) Agreement, which recognized the Republic of Indonesia, having authority over Java and Sumatra, as part of a United States of Indonesia that would also include Borneo and the so-called Great East. The federated United States of Indonesia was to be part of a worldwide Dutch Commonwealth. However, this agreement was never effected. The Dutch in July, 1947, began a "police action" in Republic territory. The matter was brought before the United Nations Security Council, which called for a cease-fire. In January, 1948, a truce between the Dutch and Indonesians was signed on the *Renville*, a United Sates naval vessel. Its provisions were similar to those of the Cheribon Agreement. While the Republic did not wish federated status, it did not have sufficient forces to take on the Dutch. It was also faced, in September, 1948, with a Communist uprising at Madiun in Central Java, which it managed to subdue despite its own political divisions.

In December, 1948, the Dutch launched a second "police action" against the Republic. Their military success was greater this time, but world opinion turned against them and United Nations resolutions on Indonesia were worded in stronger terms. In January, 1949, Nehru convoked in New Delhi an Asian conference, which called for the transfer of sovereignty to a United

States of Indonesia by January 1, 1950. The Security Council proposed the same solution. The United States withheld some Marshall Aid money to the Netherlands. Under these pressures, the Dutch government gave way. A conference was held at The Hague in late 1949 among the Dutch, the Republic leaders, and the Dutch-sponsored Indonesian federal states. A Republic of the United States of Indonesia (RUSI) was created, and, on December 27, 1949, the Dutch recognized the independence of this federation.

Increasing Problems (1949–1957). Following independence, the Indonesian leaders soon accomplished the transformation of the federal government into a unitary republic. This was proclaimed on August 17, 1950, with another constitution and as president the charismatic Sukarno, who personified the cause of the Indonesian revolution. Between the creation of the unitary state in 1950 and the holding of national elections in 1955, the two major political parties were the Masjumi and the Nationalist. In September, 1955, elections were held for seats in the national assembly. Of the 38 million votes cast, the Nationalist Party received 30 percent, the Nahdatul Ulama (Muslim Scholars) 25 percent, the Masjumi and Communists each 20 percent. That December an election was held for 520 members of a constituent assembly. After several years of inconclusive deliberations on a new constitution, the assembly was abolished in 1959 by Sukarno, who revived the 1945 constitution.

Domestic Unrest. National elections did not improve the political situation. States' rights issues built up, instigated in part by dissident army leaders outside of Java. At the heart of the unrest was the imbalance between Java and the rest of the islands on political, military, and economic roles. In late 1956 regional commanders in Sumatra proclaimed its independence. Discontent spread to Borneo and Celebes. Sukarno took several steps to counter the secessionist movement. In February, 1957, he announced his program of "Guided Democracy." This meant increasing authoritarianism in all areas of national life. The next month, he proclaimed martial law, and from then on, took increasingly drastic and dictatorial measures.

Foreign Relations. In foreign affairs, from its inception

Republic leaders, like the Burmese leaders, followed an independent policy, aimed at avoiding involvement with any military power bloc. Immediately following independence, the policy tended toward moderation on world issues. Not able as a new state to implement strong foreign policies or shape international decisions, Indonesia proceeded cautiously maintaining bonds with the West. In the years 1951–1953, relations were developed also with Communist nations. In the following four years, nationalism increased despite domestic problems.

Asian problems received top priority. In April, 1955, with the other "Colombo powers"—India, Pakistan, Ceylon, and Burma —Indonesia convoked at Bandung a conference of 29 Asian and African nations. Sukarno was an old friend of Nehru's, and India had strongly supported Indonesian independence. On the other hand, despite the Islamic affinity, Indonesia was alienated by Pakistan's pro-West orientation. Indonesian neutralism was similar to Burma's, and relations were friendly with that country. Relations were formal toward United States Asian allies, Thailand and the Philippines. From Japan, reparations were demanded; the first Indonesian claim was $18 billion. Indonesian representatives attended the Japanese Peace Conference, but like the Filipinos, they signed the treaty with reservations on this issue. Diplomatic relations with Communist China were established slowly. An ambassador arrived in 1951 from Peking, but it was some time before one was sent in exchange. The Bandung Conference resulted in a treaty on dual citizenship between Indonesia and Communist China. Despite periodic crises resulting from nationalistic Indonesian domestic measures aimed principally against the Chinese, visits were exchanged by leaders of the two countries. In 1955 diplomatic missions were exchanged with Soviet Russia.

Indonesian relations with the United States were also subject to change. The United States supported the Indonesian struggle for independence from the Dutch. But after independence, relations varied. One Indonesian cabinet fell in 1952 over the wording of an American aid agreement. The United States did not back the Indonesian stand on West New Guinea, the most aggravating of the immediate Dutch legacy. As a result of indecision at The Hague talks in 1949, Dutch sovereignty continued in the territory, but the question was to be re-examined after a year. At the end of 1950, no solution had been reached as the Dutch kept possession of the area but the Indonesians claimed it.

Guided Democracy (1957–1965). In the midst of growing problems, Sukarno embarked on his program of Guided Democracy. In May, 1957, he increased executive authority over bureaucratic organs, while limiting political party activities. He appropriated Dutch property and took other measures to end Dutch interests in Indonesia. The military rebellion reached its climax in February, 1958, when the Revolutionary Government of the Republic of Indonesia was proclaimed in Central Sumatra. Some civilian leaders defected to the rebels. The revolutionary government (which was not recognized by any foreign state) was crushed by the central government, and by 1961 the rebel cause had collapsed.

The most marked trend in Indonesian politics after the suppression of the rebellion was the increase of presidential power. Sukarno had been proclaimed president of the Republic in 1945 and appointed himself prime minister in 1957. He was never elected by the people. By skillful tactics, he held the opposition in check. He tried to keep ahead of the game, but as he strengthened his position, so did the military. Indonesia became a paramilitary police state, with the army steadily increasing in power. The Communist movement grew simultaneously. Encouraged in part by Sukarno as a counterweight to army ambitions, Communists supported Sukarno's Guided Democracy.

Meanwhile, to replace the declining political parties, Sukarno promoted mass movements by means of staged parades and demonstrations. National councils, particularly as constituted in 1945, continued to replace normal executive and legislative organs. Sukarno abrogated the Parliament in 1960, and in its place he established a Council of People's Representatives with 280 members from various parties and functional groups. A People's Consultative Congress of some six hundred members was also formed. It included all members of the Council of People's Representatives plus members from outlying regions and functional groups and was scheduled to meet at five-year intervals. In November, 1960, this body proclaimed Sukarno president for another five years.

Economic and Social Problems. Wrapped up in political matters, the president concerned himself less with serious economic problems. Subsistence agriculture based on rice continued to be the mainstay of employment. But population growth outran production. Fortunate in raw materials, Indonesia had probably the largest petroleum reserves in the Far East. Crude oil production, mainly on Sumatra and Borneo, increased after the war. Oil accounted for one-fourth the value of Indonesia's exports. Tin and rubber were other major exports. There was less progress in industry and commerce. Petroleum-refining, sugar-milling, and the processing of estate products were undertaken. But political instability, technical backwardness, lack of industrial experience, and investment uncertaintities were handicaps. The period of Guided Democracy established state trading companies, while the state appropriated economic management, as in Ne Win's Burma. The government's economic development plans, however, proved abortive.

Sukarno's Indonesia was also faced with social needs. There were a number of indigenous ethnic groups, who differed in language, culture, and religion. Alien minorities also existed, including three million Chinese, who played an important role in Indonesian economic life, though they were discriminated against by nationalization measures. Village life changed, but some of its aspects remained the same. Into peasant communities came new ideas, more schools, and greater literacy. But traditions, including the authority of the village headman, remained. The great majority of the population adhered to the Muslim faith. Rural living standards did not appreciably rise, though indebtedness was not a serious problem. Population increased rapidly, particularly on Java, which accounted for some 60 percent of Indonesia's 115 million. In government, bureaucratic positions multiplied; many were filled by military veterans. Education lagged behind needs, but there was as increase of teaching facilities on the primary level. Bahasa Indonesia, derived from Malaysian, was made the official language.

Foreign Relations. In foreign affairs, from mid-1957 to late 1965, in line with Guided Democracy, Sukarno through world travels and sensational speeches voiced Indonesian policy. The West New Guinea issue caused a diplomatic break with the

Netherlands in 1966. After extended negotiations proceeding through the United Nations, in October 1962, the Dutch evacuated and entrusted the territory to the UN, which administered it for an interim of seven months. The Indonesians were awarded the territory, now called West Irian, in 1963 with a plebiscite on its future to be held by 1969. Other Asian issues simmered. In March, 1958, the Indonesian Parliament agreed to a greatly reduced figure, $223 million, in reparations from Japan, payable in goods and services over twelve years. The treaty advanced $400 million in loans for private economic projects and cancelled $117 million owed Japan by Indonesians because of an adverse balance. Diplomats were exchanged, and some tourism resulted between the two countries. Indonesia also established diplomatic relations with North Korea and North Vietnam. It broke relations with Malaysia in 1963 and quit the United Nations—the first country to do so—when Malaysia was named to the Security Council as a non-permanent member.

From the Communist bloc, Indonesia received aid and support. In 1958, Communist China extended a $11.2 million loan, and in 1963, Liu Shao-ch'i, then president of Communist China, visited Indonesia. During the last years of his leadership, Sukarno advanced the notion of a Djakarta-Peking axis that would also include Cambodia, North Vietnam, and North Korea. Diplomatic relations were established with Soviet Russia, which had extended by the mid-1960's up to a billion dollars worth of military and economic aid. As in Burma and Cambodia, so in Indonesia the United States received variable treatment. In the course of the civil war, it seemed to the Indonesians that the United States was favoring the military rebels because of their anti-Communist stance. Through 1963, American economic aid figures to Indonesia totaled some $680 million in grants and loans. In the mid-1960's, during Sukarno's confrontation policies toward Malaysia, relations with the United States dipped to an all-time low. Indonesian confiscatory policies turned against the Americans. Sukarno told aid programs to "go to hell," and American projects ground to a halt.

Redirection (*since 1965*). The Sukarno years produced some growth and much conflict. After two decades in top office, he was phased out of political leadership by a series of events. On

September 30, 1965, a coup, attributed to Communists, was attempted, and several top-ranking military men were killed. In the following weeks, military and popular reaction to the Communist-infiltrated and possibly Communist-inspired event resulted in a national bloodbath with up to 400,000 killed. Sukarno tried to stop the massacres, but his own equivocal position and unexplained actions during the coup put him under a cloud of doubt. The next two and a half years witnessed a sparring round between the president and his army, in which General Suharto, commander of the strategic forces, rose to the top. The army continued to fill more offices, while civilian power constricted. In mid-1966, the People's Consultative Congress confirmed Suharto as executive head of the government, called for national elections within two years, and stripped Sukarno of his prime ministerial position and title, "great leader of the revolution." The following March, the Congress designated Suharto as acting president. In March, 1968, it confirmed him in presidential office for five years but postponed parliamentary elections. Sukarno was eased out of national life; in 1970 he died. New leadership sought to recoup Indonesian domestic stability. 1971 elections confirmed Suharto's position.

Foreign Relations. After 1965, moderation returned to foreign affairs with army spokesmen and civilian colleagues in the Foreign Ministry taking the helm. After the 1965 uprising, relations deteriorated with Communist China, because the Indonesian government officially took the stand that the People's Republic of China had directly or indirectly supported the attempted coup. Embassies of the other country were stormed in Peking and Djakarta; diplomats were humiliated and beaten. In October, 1967, the respective embassies were closed and diplomats repatriated; neither capital seemed in a hurry to re-establish relations. On the other hand, conditions improved with the United States, though Washington assumed a cautious stand in renewing bilateral aid programs. In 1966 Indonesia returned to the United Nations, and in the following year relations were normalized with Malaysia. In 1969 in West New Guinea a thousand Papuan tribal chiefs opted for Indonesian sovereignty. Meanwhile, the Dutch came back into Indonesian favor, and The Hague extended loans and economic aid to Djakarta. Toward the small enclave of Portuguese Timor, no claim was made because the policy was to claim only those territories, including West New Guinea, or West Irian, that had formerly been part of the Dutch East Indies.

Economic Planning. In its attempt to restore the shattered economy, Indonesia faced great problems. Sukarno left a $2.4 billion over-all external debt, the repayment of which the Suharto administration tried to reschedule. As party to the Inter-Governmental Group on Indonesia, the United States since the late 1960's provided one-third of annual economic aid (over $600 million) received by Indonesia, Japanese and Western European sources rounded out the figure. In 1969 a new five-year development plan was effected, predicated not so much on growth as on getting the economy back to where it was before Sukarno despoiled it. Though temporizing with adverse but pressing budgetary situations, the government sought at the same time to establish a revitalized Indonesia on firm, long-range bases.

20

MAINLAND CHINA
Since 1945

At the end of the Pacific War, a race ensued between the Nationalists and Communists to obtain control of as much of mainland China as possible. The Nationalists returned to Nanking and consolidated Central and South China under their rule, while the Communists made headway in the north and Manchuria. By 1949, the latter won out and conquered the mainland as the Nationalists set up a government in exile in Taiwan. During their first decade in power, the Communists under Mao Tse-tung imposed their hold over the country, initiated policies, commenced economic programs, and confirmed military might. After 1958 they experimented with mixed policies in various sectors of national life. China became a world power and entered international life in force for the first time in modern history.

A HOUSE DIVIDED (1945–1949)

The end of the war found the Communists, with their capital in Yenan, spread throughout North China pockets and into Manchuria, temporarily occupied by the favorably disposed Russians. Returning to Nanking, the Nationalists, with American aid and support, endeavored to recover as much territory as possible. Several American missions tried to effect without success a Nationalist-Communist rapprochement, but each protagonist went his own way. By 1948 the tide had turned in favor of the Communists; within a year they had mastered the mainland.

Uneasy Coexistence (1945–1947). With the surrender of the Japanese in August, 1945, Nationalists and Communists jockeyed for mastery of the mainland. Warlords were gradually eliminated or absorbed into one camp or the other. But despite the fighting, negotiations continued, particularly after the Sino-Soviet treaty of August, 1945, in which the Russians continued aid and recognition to Nationalist China and left the Chinese Communists out on a limb. Late that month, Mao himself came to Chungking through the good offices of Ambassador Hurley, but the fragile united front remained a touch-and-go situation. After Hurley resigned, General George Marshall arrived as President Harry Truman's special envoy with instructions that reiterated long-time United States policies toward China. These included the desirability of establishing a strong, united, and democratic China, previously required to help defeat Japan, but now essential to maintain peace and advance the United Nations, according to official United States rationale. A strong China could be achieved only with the termination of the civil war. And to help end the conflict a national conference of all major political elements was to convene.

In January, 1946, soon after Marshall's arrival, the Political Consultative Conference met in Chungking. It firmed three basic agreements. In a military truce, both sides were to freeze troops in their respective occupied areas, which were to be policed by truce teams, each consisting of a Nationalist, a Communist, and an American officer. A second agreement concerned the division of territory between the Nationalists and Communists, an elected legislature, and the creation of a forty-man State Council with membership divided between twenty for the Kuomintang and twenty for all other parties. A third agreement sought the integration of Communist armies into the national Chinese military command. The three argreements soon broke down, for neither Chinese party wanted to implement effective co-operation. Under some American prodding, the Nationalists effected limited reforms. In November, 1946, a constituent assembly convened at Nanking, but Communist delegates refused to attend. Under Chiang's guidance, the assembly adopted a constitution that called for a parliamentary system with a cabinet responsible to an elected legislature. Two subsequent elections were conducted in Nationalist-held territory, one to elect Chiang president and the other to form a unicameral legislative body. Few third parties co-operated; the Communists did not participate; and the Kuomintang dominated the electoral processes. Despite drawbacks, the constitution, effected in 1948, theoretically ended Sun Yat-sen's second stage of political tutelage and ushered in the last stage, that of democracy and constitutionalism.

Resumption of Civil War (1947–1948). Over the months, Marshall experienced an increasingly difficult time in reconciling Nationalist and Communist aims, and he departed in January, 1947. The following month, the Nationalists expelled the Communists from Nanking, once again the capital site. Full-scale civil war resumed. American aid to Nationalist China after the Marshall mission reflected more the domestic American political scene than developments in China. (As it was, the United States extended some $2 billion in aid between August, 1945, and early 1948 to the Nationalists.) After the Communist-Nationalist split, the Kuomintang continued to face spiraling economic and political problems. Inflation continued; the national budget was hopelessly imbalanced; civilian morale declined; and corruption was evident. With growing expenses, the Nanking government had fewer sources of revenue. The government embarked on a widespread policy of the socialization of industry. Key plants were appropriated as government monopolies by leading officials and families.

Communist Victory (1948–1949). Last-minute Kuomintang political reforms proved too late and too little. The campaigns for the mastery of mainland China mounted in Communist favor. When Manchuria fell to the Communists late in 1949, the Nationalist house on the mainland collapsed like a stack of cards. In Manchuria the Nationalists fought a stationary war from city bastions, while the Communists, aided by Russian-left munitions, captured the countryside. Growing Communist strength isolated Nationalist troops, who eventually withdrew to Mukden, which was captured in November, 1948. The Nationalist position in North China was no longer tenable. Peiping soon fell. The Communists consolidated their gains in the North China plain. They confronted the Nationalists in late 1948 and early 1949 in a massive pitched battle at Hsuchow, between the Yellow River and the Yangtze. Each side threw in a million troops, but superior mobile Communist strategy helped turn the tide in their favor. As a result of increasing Communist military successes, Mao Tse-tung announced to Chiang Kai-shek surrender terms, which were comprehensive. Chiang asked Western powers for aid, but none came. He then temporarily retired from the presidency, while the Communists crossed the Yangtze in April, 1949, and spread southward. Chiang soon returned to the presidency, but the Kuomintang was eventually forced to evacuate to Formosa, where on December 8, 1949, the Republic of China was set up in exile.

As the Nationalist cause collapsed, the Communists busily organized their political and ideological machines. Mao promoted conferences of various kinds, such as all-China students and women's and youth conferences. In June, 1949, the Party convened a preparatory committee to create the Chinese People's Political Consultative Conference as a multiparty and interclass organ to establish a base for the new China. In September in Peiping, the Conference adopted an Organic Law and a Common Program, which became the administrative structure and philosophy for the Central People's Government of the People's Republic of China, established on October 1, 1949. Two months before Chiang evacuated to Taiwan, the Communist regime had been proclaimed in Peking, once again termed the "Northern Capital."

The victory of the Chinese Communists encompassed military organization, strategy, and tactics. It was a total approach, one in which political, social, economic, and military matters were interrelated. The Communists were never voted into power, nor were the Nationalists voted out. As in the traditional manner of establishing new dynasties, the Chinese people were never consulted on the issues or the choices.

COMMUNIST CHINA: CONSOLIDATING (1949–1958)

During the first decade of Communist rule on the mainland, basic development programs were initiated. The first few years witnessed the consolidation of power over a country wracked by external invasion and civil strife since 1937. By 1953, the regime felt secure enough to establish solid foundations of state. That year the first five-year plan was formulated and the first census was held. The latter formed the basis for the first national parliamentary elections which took place in late 1953 and 1954. A constitution was then adopted to replace the provisional 1949 Common Program and Organic Law. As the state structure strengthened, so Party hierarchy was redefined in the 1956 Party constitution. Assured control in domestic life, Mao Tse-tung in 1957 permitted some loosening up with the "Hundred Flowers Bloom" campaign, allowing criticism. But criticism of the government got out of hand and restrictions were soon reimposed.

In foreign affairs, with the establishment of the People's Republic on the mainland, China became a world power, whose interests had to be considered in international deliberations. Foreign policies of Communist China evolved through several periods, as did domestic policies. For the first three years or so after 1949, the regime advocated a type of revolutionary adventurism that looked to the spread of Maoism abroad. Feeling the fruits of victory at home, it urged Asians to similar ideological victories. In the ensuing five years (1953–1958), the ebullient spirit modified to one of "sweet reasonableness." Peking appeared more conservative, adopted the five principles of peaceful coexistence, and broadened diplomatic representation. Moderation abroad resulted in part from the inception of energy-consuming domestic long-range political and economic programs, including the first five-year plan.

Domestic Affairs. For its first five years (1949–1954) the Communist regime was based on the 1949 Organic Law, which called for several main councils at top executive levels: the Government Council, the State Administrative Council, and the People's Revolutionary Military Council. For military and political convenience, China was divided into six regional administrations. But in late 1952 the Chinese Communists felt ready to legitimatize the government. They initiated steps to draft a constitution and to hold national elections. After a national census determined the population in China (583 million), elections were held for the first National People's Congress. In these elections some six million were elected to village, town, and municipal congresses and councils. Over the ensuing months, the elected officials in the lowest tiers of offices elected from their ranks 16,807 deputies to the provincial congresses, who in turn elected 1,226 delegates to the National People's Congress at Peking. Reflecting a Marxist orientation, the Election Law of 1953, through a process of ideological gerrymandering, heavily favored urban and industrial areas over rural in representation.

In September, 1954, the First National People's Congress

met in Peking. In a two-week session it approved the new constitution promulgated by party leaders that created new government organs and elective offices of government. The constitution outlined the general principles of the road to socialism, described the organizational framework of the new state structure, and noted fundamental rights and duties of citizens. It disregarded the principle of the separations of powers, never strong in China. The rights of citizens were hedged by many stipulations.

The National People's Congress also elected the main officials of the central apparatus, including the president (or chairman), the vice-presidents, and cabinet ranking members. The president of the People's Republic enjoyed wide powers. He commanded the armed forces. Elected for four years, he was eligible for reelection. He was the ceremonial and procedural chief of the nation; he nominated the prime minister; and he served in an ex-officio capacity on various bodies. Prior to 1954, there had been six vice-presidents (or vice-chairmen) of the People's Republic, but that year the constitution reduced the number to two. As a type of super-cabinet, the State Council was the highest executive and administrative organ. Premier Chou En-lai, a long-time Party member, headed the body, which supervised day-to-day operations of the vast bureaucracy and implemented party and government directives. Other government organs included the Supreme State Conference, the Supreme People's Court, and the Supreme People's Procuratorate.

Administratively, China was divided into twenty-one provinces, two special municipalities, and a number of autonomous regions. The provinces, with varying numbers of county, subcounty, and village units, were under the direct jurisdiction of the central government. The two special municipalities of Peking, the capital, and Shanghai, the largest city, warranted special consideration as unique political entities within the national structure. The autonomous regions were established to relate to China's national minorities, who numbered some 10 percent of the total population. These areas were given types of "paper" rights, including limited powers to direct their financial affairs, draw up statutes, and train their people for local government positions. Over three hundred of the areas existed, of which the five at the provincial level were the most important.

Party Control. Behind the government was the Communist Party structure, a state within a state, with little relation or resemblance to Western-type political parties. Top Party members were also at the helm of governmental and military affairs. At the apex of power was the seven-man Standing Committee, with Mao Tse-tung as chairman, a position he had held in the hierarchy since January, 1935, when he was on the Long March. All Standing Committee members were included in the Politburo, of some two dozen members, and the Central Committee of almost a hundred. The Party structure also embraced the Central Control Committee, secretariat, various departments and regional bureaus. At lower levels were provincial and local congresses and cells in farms, factories, and schools. Each echelon elected members to the next higher rank.

The military arm augmented Party control. All formal military organizations in China were infiltrated at every level by Party members, who acted as political commissars with ranks equivalent to their counterpart military colleagues. The most important over-all military unit, the People's Liberation Army (PLA), comprised the army, navy, air force, and supporting service troops. With a total of around three million men, it ranked as the third largest military establishment in the world (after those of the United States and Soviet Russia). To ensure further control over the population of mainland China, the Communists organized mass organizations and institutions based on occupation, religion, and country or regional friendship interests. Other Party control organs included the uniformed police, the secret police, and the People's Procurator General's Office which enforced laws and policies. In working through all these bureaus, the Chinese Communists displayed a blend of coercion and persuasion toward the populace; it was difficult to distinguish the point where force replaced reason. On a mass basis the Chinese performed their appointed tasks "voluntarily" and "enthusiastically," as directed from above. To counteract flagging revolutionary spirits, the regime stirred up the people through the promotion of various slogans and campaigns. In the early 1950's, the Party embarked on the "3 anti" campaign against Party sluggards, and "5 anti" campaign against bureaucrats and the middle class. The Chinese Communists conducted "hate America" campaigns from the time of the Korean War. They promoted their versions of model men and women, who tended to be dull and stereotyped figures.

Economic Consolidation. In the first three years (1949–1952), Peking embarked on programs of rehabilitating the country's economy, which had been wracked by civil and foreign wars. It curbed inflation, restored production in key industries, and called for fiscal reforms. It began to rebuild the transport system; it redistributed land and stimulated agricultural production. In the next several years (1952–1958), the government began to collectivize agriculture and initiated grand-scale industrialization projects. It tightened economic controls, established a tax base, and embarked on a five-year plan (1953–1957), the first attempt at comprehensive economic planning. Peking continually manufactured economic slogans of one kind or another to spur production. The basic "general line" of 1952 was the policy the government proposed to take on the road to socialism. It had two aspects: socialization in agriculture and industrialization in urban areas.

The role of agriculture, despite its secondary position in economic planning, was most vital. About four-fifths of the Chinese were peasant families or others in rural areas. Agrarian problems were overwhelming. China had only a limited extent of reclaimable land. Yield increases on available land were also limited. Continuing natural disasters cut down production figures. Mao and other leaders faced agricultural problems with practical solutions and Marxist dogma. Drawing upon Juichin and Yenan experiments, Mao categorized five rural classes: the landlord, the rich peasant, the middle peasant, the poor peasant, and the tenant. An individual's status depended on the amount of land and tools he owned and the degree to which he exploited or was exploited by others. The first three classes lost land, which was distributed among the latter two classes. These programs of land redistribution were effected in the first three years (1949–1952) of the Communist regime. After the initial program had redistributed 22 million acres among 80 million peasants, the regime decried the inefficiency of small-scale ownership and the capitalistic tendencies of the new peasant owners. Between 1952 and 1955 it exhorted farmers to join together in mutual-aid teams and agricultural producer co-operatives. In the latter year, Mao announced the second phase of the land program, that of collectives. Over the next three years collectivization, which made land and tools the communal property of a collective private peasant group, became the keyword in agrarian policy. (Peking also had developed experimental state farms, while most of the collectives at this time were private.)

Despite the importance of agriculture, the Chinese Communists emphasized industry, commerce, and transport in general economic planning. In the early years factories were rehabilitated and confiscated from former Nationalist owners, "counterrevolutionaries," or foreigners. Private firms were converted to state-owned enterprises. With the inception of the first five-year plan, emphasis was placed on industrial development. This was part of an over-all master plan envisioned by Peking to catch up with Great Britain in absolute (but not per capita) output in certain commodities by 1973. The Chinese Communists utilized industrial areas that had been previously developed in south-central Manchuria, the Peking-Tientsin area, and the central Wuhan area in the Yangtze Valley. To these regions, they added new industrial centers all over China, particularly in the northwest. The industrial labor task force was recruited from off the land and paid in a wage-unit system or a "commodity-equivalent" practice, in which amounts of food and money were paid according to the type of job and hardship involved. The state controlled commerce, as it did industrial development. All important facets of domestic and international trade and commerce were placed under national direction. The regime manipulated goods and prices through various control schemes of rationing, compulsory buying, and allocation priorities. The Chinese Communists utilized great masses of people on public works projects and communications systems. They did not rely only on traditional waterways but extended roads, railroads, and the domestic air system.

Social Reforms. In social matters, the Chinese Communists capitalized on and hastened modernization trends. The Marriage Law of 1950 made consent mandatory to contract, a provision already stated in the Nationalist-formulated 1931 civil code. Again, building on precedent, the Chinese Communists effected certain reforms in the language to simplify its written and oral variants. In health programs they showed concern for public welfare and made headway against traditional diseases. Religion continued to be de-emphasized. Confucianism was dead and Taoism dying. Buddhism remained weak as an organized force; but Islam, associated with substantial minority groups, held its own in the border areas as a religious and political entity. The Christian churches were nationalized. The Chinese Communist leadership emphasized the necessity of education to create literate masses. The formal educational structure embraced kindergarten, primary grades, junior and senior middle (high) school, and higher education. In the curricula the Communists emphasized a blend of physical and mental work, a revolutionary concept in Chinese thought. Postgraduate schools existed, and scientific organizations conducted advanced research.

Cultural Orthodoxy. Despite the emphasis on education, the role of the intellectual was difficult. For one to be both "Red and expert" proved trying. Because of the double-barrelled policies of absorbing and reforming intellectuals, these were subjected to recurring stresses and strains. An ideological lid was placed on intellectual activity, though in 1957 Mao permitted a brief period of relaxation. He also set the orthodox line of socialist realism in literary and artistic work, which called for unity of art and politics, of life and ideology. To promote these ends, the regime utilized all media for popular dissemination of propaganda and culture. Official newspapers blanketed China. The *Jen Min Jih Pao* (*People's Daily*) was the mouthpiece of party and government, while other official organs had their own journals. The film industry was centralized; television stations were established; and radio networks spread from the capital. Short-wave services were maintained that beamed programs particularly directed to overseas Chinese.

Foreign Relations. The Common Program of 1949 and the Constitution of 1954 expressed some basic foreign policy statements, but Chinese national and ideological attitudes also kept up with the changing international environment. A Ministry of Foreign Affairs existed at the capital and dozens of embassies were established abroad. Augmenting formal diplomatic machinery were political, economic, and cultural ties that Peking participated in with Communist and non-Communist countries, recognized or not. But it refused to sit in any world organs or commissions in which Nationalist China was represented (an attitude reciprocated by the Nationalists). Foreign economic relations were formulated. Through extended trade and aid programs, Peking sought ties with over a hundred countries. But for the first decade or so after 1949, up to three-fourths and more of total trade was conducted with the Soviet bloc. In time-honored over-all international trade patterns, Chinese exported foodstuffs and raw materials and imported machinery and heavy equipment. On occasion, Peking separated the issues of practical economics and Communist ideology by trading with capitalist countries.

Relations with the Soviet Union. Soviet Russia recognized the People's Republic of China on October 1, 1949, the day it was proclaimed in Peking. Early the next year, the initial framework of Sino-Soviet relations was set in agreements signed in Moscow, where Mao, in his first known trip outside China, had gone. The most important of these was the thirty-year treaty of friendship, whose major clause related to military co-operation: If either party were attacked by Japan or any state allied with it (in effect the United States, which was then occupying Japan), the other signatory was to render military and other appropriate assistance by all means at its disposal. A second document promised up to $300 million in loans to the Chinese for industrial projects. A third agreement related to Manchurian railways and ports (Dairen and Port Arthur), all of which were to be evacuated upon the conclusion of a Japanese peace treaty but no later than 1952. (The Chinese later requested Russian presence in Port Arthur until 1955 because of the Korean War.) A fourth exchange of notes reaffirmed the independent status of the Mongolian People's Republic. A final agreement (terminated in 1954) established joint-stock companies in Sinkiang to exploit oil and nonferrous metals. It also outlined routes for airways between Peking and Central Russian Asian cities.

While Stalin was alive, the alliance seemed to operate smoothly. In late 1952, the Russians agreed to underwrite more projects. The following September, after the Korean armistice and death of Stalin, another technical-assistance program was announced. Under new leadership, the Russians paid more attention to their Chinese partner, who assumed greater independence and initiative in international communism. Mao continued his ideological and international rise to power in bloc politics, and the Chinese participated in Eastern European affairs. The Soviets provided more economic programs, and more top Russians came to Peking. But despite visitations and aid programs, as the 1950's progressed, stresses developed in Sino-Soviet relations.

Relations with Asian Nations. Among non-Communist nations in Asia, Japan remained a prime consideration in Chinese Communist policy. Though Tokyo recognized Taipei, it traded also with Peking after the occupation of Japan terminated in 1952. But with the recovery of Japanese independence, various issues arose between the two countries. Some were resolved successfully; others persisted. Tens of thousands of Japanese residents in China and prisoners of war on the mainland were repatriated. Several fishing conventions were concluded. Trade agreements were initiated. Among other non-Communist East Asian entities, Hong Kong had an anomalous position. Though it was Chinese territory, Peking made no immediate territorial demands, because the port was a great foreign-exchange earner for the mainland. Chinese Communists sold foodstuffs to the colony, which was also the transmitter of remittances from overseas Chinese to families back home on the mainland. They also tolerated in Portuguese hands the enclave of Macao. With South Korea there were no relations.

In Southeast and South Asia, Chinese Communist objectives related principally to securing frontiers and border areas. Peking aspired to include states in these regions within its sphere of political influence through the creation of friendly or at least nonhostile states. Southeast Asians reacted variously to the Chinese neighbor. Some states chose to align themselves with the West through military pacts; others preferred nonalignment and acted independently. The merits of either course of action could be argued, for both containment and accommodation seemed effective in given instances and in given times. At one time or another Peking was given diplomatic recognition by half the ten political entities of Southeast Asia: the Democratic Republic of Vietnam, Laos, Cambodia, Burma, and Indonesia. The other five —the Republic of Vietnam, Thailand, the Philippines, Singapore, and Malaysia—did not recognize Communist China. In South Asia the Peking regime developed official, formal, and diplomatic relations with five of the subcontinent's independent states: Ceylon, Afghanistan, Pakistan, India, and Nepal. The Chinese proved themselves accommodating to small powers such as Nepal and Afghanistan in the conclusion of treaties of friendship and boundary matters, as well as to large nations such as Pakistan. But they developed differences with India. Border issues were the most acerbating ones, and the Chinese related them to their conquest and occupation of restive Tibet.

Relations with the United States. Toward the United States, the Chinese Communists almost from the inception of their regime displayed hostility, an attitude that was reciprocated. The regime put out continual propaganda aimed at the United States, its allies, and their interests. Peking's attitude was shaped by several factors: by American bases ringing the land, by ideological dogma that precluded peaceful coexistence with capitalist countries, and by the security desire to eliminate or to lessen the American presence at least in East Asia. The People's Republic used American actions as catharsis for tensions within the country as well. The confrontations were broken by a few thaws, such as the Korean truce talks (1951–1953) and the Bandung Conference (1955), at which Chou En-lai claimed that China was ready to negotiate with the United States over Asian tensions. The Americans picked up the cue, and bilateral talks resulted sporadically over the years, first at Geneva at the consular level and later at Warsaw at an ambassadorial level.

Another stumbling block to improved relations was the detention of American nationals in China, who although few in number, suffered house arrest or were dying off in imprisonment. As a result of talks in Geneva, the United States and Communist China issued a joint statement on agreed measures for the return of American and Chinese civilians to their respective countries. Signed on September 10, 1955, it was the sole bilateral agreement concluded officially between Washington and Peking. It was not effectively realized. Many Chinese left the United States to return to China, but the State Department claimed that only a handful of Americans were permitted to leave China. Additional deterrents to friendly relations were the alleged territorial violations by American aircraft and vessels into Chinese air space and territorial waters (set at twelve miles). Peking served public notice of such violations, purportedly numbering hundreds, but Washington rarely acknowledged or refuted such claims.

Diplomatic recognition was a background issue. Under the circumstances, neither party asked for it, nor was it feasible to request it. The position of Taiwan constituted a special issue in the recognition problem. So long as Americans recognized Nationalist China and considered the island essential in their defense perimeter, diplomatic recognition of mainland China remained remote. There was, diplomatically speaking, only one China; Peking, Taipei, and Washington all agreed on this. The barring of the Chinese Communists from a seat in the United Nations was an issue. The offshore islands of Quemoy and Matsu constituted another problem. The Nationalists, with American support, kept up their defense postures on the island groups, which Washington related to the defense of Taiwan (though the United States by treaty with Chiang Kai-shek's government was not committed to their automatic defense). Another aspect of Chinese Communist-American relations included trade embargoes. In addition to the United Nations resolution on the matter in early 1951, the United States through domestic laws for several decades sought to freeze Peking out of international trading channels.

COMMUNIST CHINA: EXPERIMENTING (SINCE 1958)

In the course of the years after 1958, the Chinese Communists under Mao experimented. Sometimes they threw caution to the wind and formulated grandiose revolutionary plans; at other times they backtracked and implemented more realistic programs. The year 1958 was a particularly important one. Mao initiated the second five-year plan, created a people's militia to augment formal military ranks, announced the "Great Leap Forward" to stimulate industrial production, and proclaimed agricultural communes as the ultimate goal in rural collectivization programs. There was some retreat in the early 1960's from the overambitious scheme; a third five-year plan was never publicized. In what seemed to be a final paroxysm of revolutionary zeal, the aging Mao in the late 1960's was glorified with excessive praise by factions most loyal to him in the course of the Great Proletarian Cultural Revolution. What the post-Mao future would bring to Communist China was anyone's guess, for the succession problem was not fully resolved.

Domestic Affairs. Between late 1958 and early 1959, the Second National People's Congress was elected. Liu Shao-ch'i, a Party man of long standing, was elected the new chairman, or president, of the People's Republic after Mao bowed out. In late 1964, the third round of elections took place. By this time the number of deputies to the National People's Congress more than doubled in number to 3,040. Inasmuch as the National People's Congresses met infrequently, the elected Standing Committee (like the Party's counterpart but much larger in membership) took care of governmental affairs. Delayed by internal events, the fourth national elections were indefinitely postponed.

The Military Structure. In military affairs, China proceeded along various lines. It built up the People's Liberation Army; but in 1958, the people's militia was created in effect to make every able-bodied adult a part-time soldier. These millions augmented the formal PLA structure not only as a paramilitary force but also as a huge pool of available labor. Though Mao continued to emphasize the importance of manpower in military might, his regime developed nuclear weapons. In these years, Communist China entered the atomic age. It had the requisite engineers and research physicists, some of whom had trained in the United States. In October, 1957, a Sino-Soviet agreement was concluded to provide China with a sample atomic bomb and data on its manufacture, but two years later, the Russians tore up the agreement. On its own, Peking proceeded with experiments and tests on the Lop Nor area in desolate Sinkiang. On October 16, 1964, with the explosion of a first nuclear device, the equivalent of 20 kilotons (20,000 tons of TNT), China joined the exclusive nuclear club. Within the next three years, half a dozen other experiments and detonations took place, including a hydrogen explosion in mid-June, 1967. Around 1958, a short-range missile development program, utilizing ground-to-air missiles, was begun. The implications of nuclear energy and its potential military uses by Peking were not lost on neighboring Asians.

The Economy. In economic life, agricultural policy tightened when in 1958, collectives merged into communes, which were multipurpose units to manage agricultural, industrial, commercial, social, and military affairs. Generally the communes were formed from the pre-existing administrative boundaries of a district or group of villages. (Mao also tried to introduce urban communes in the cities to cover a certain number of blocks.) But because of climatic and administrative setbacks, in the 1960's many communes broke down into their smaller and more efficient component parts of production brigades and teams. The "Great Leap Forward" of 1958 in industry coincided with the commencement of the second five-year plan. But because of overambitious planning and poor harvests over a three-year period (1959–1961), adjustments had to be made. Heavy industrial priorities gave way to light industry, and, as a whole, industry was sidetracked to favor agricultural priorities. The fits and starts in general economic planning in the aftermath of the second plan revealed adverse conditions. The third plan, first broached in 1963, dropped out of sight for three years, was briefly resurrected in 1966, and then again lost from public view. A fourth plan was reportedly initiated in 1971.

Another economic difficulty that the Chinese faced was the overriding one of population growth. As the 1970's approached, the mainland was inhabited by more than 750 million Chinese, with an over-all increase rate of some 3 percent, a high one in a populous country. The Chinese Communists reacted variously to the dangers of overpopulation. Marxism stressed labor as the chief source of national wealth, an argument which seemed to justify a great labor force to guarantee economic development. But China had to face reality; it had limitations of land and food on which to support a burgeoning population. Top Party leaders came out quietly in the late 1950's for birth-control projects, which were advocated more openly later as problems persisted. Among other measures the regime promoted and advocated late marriages and the "happiness of the small family."

Changes in Party Leadership. After various programs over the years in which Mao sought to create the all-round Socialist man who was at once a peasant, worker, intellectual, and military figure, the final paroxysm of zeal came in the Great Proletarian Cultural Revolution (1966–1969). This probably originated from a combination of factors that stemmed from intra-Party power struggles and ideological differences. In the course of these three years, top Party heads, including Liu Shao-ch'i, lost office, while factions around Mao came in and out of favor. Formal Party operations were undercut by such temporary but publicized organs as Red Guards and Revolutionary Committees. Party purges, though not bloody, were extensive. The repercussions of uncertainty and extremism were reflected in economic life, and the educational field, and though Mao continued as top man, groups including some different names emerged.

Foreign Relations. As the revolution faded out, China ended the 1970's in an effort once again to restore normalcy to foreign as well as domestic affairs.

Relations with the Soviet Union. One of the most conspicuous trends in Chinese Communist foreign relations after 1958 was the open eruption of Sino-Soviet differences. As revealed in the Chinese version of the story, these developed as early as Khrushchev's 1956 de-Stalinization speech at the Twentieth Soviet Party Congress in Moscow. Yet the next year Mao went a second time to Moscow to help celebrate the fortieth anniversary of the Russian revolution. There he signed the Moscow Declaration that admitted the possibility of differing roads to socialism. Two years later, however, he publicly questioned the propriety of the Khrushchev-Eisenhower communiqué that pinned hopes of peace on peaceful coexistence of communism and capitalism. Late in 1959, more fuel was added to the fire, when in the course of Himalayan border warfare between China and India, Russia remained neutral instead of supporting a "fraternal" Socialist country. The following year, Soviet technicians began to leave China in large numbers. The 1960 Moscow statement issued by Communist leaders contained no reference to the Soviet Union as "head of the Socialist camp." The Chinese subsequently elaborated their side of the argument in ideological, political, military, and economic issues. They also raised the racial issue and branded Soviet leaders in the aggressive role of a "superior" nation lording over "inferior" ones. They claimed that mutual boundaries were inequitable and sought revisions of the four-thousand-mile borders. Fighting periodically erupted along the boundaries as the various Sino-Soviet issues simmered.

Relations with Asian Nations. Despite political differences, Japan became the largest non-Communist trading partner of Communist China. Some 13 percent of Peking's total trade was conducted with Japan, whose trade with mainland China, however, was only about 3 percent of its own total trade. Various Chinese Communist groups traveled to Japan, and Japanese descended by the thousands upon the mainland, when such visits were propitious and welcomed. In Southeast Asia, the escalation of the Indochinese War in the latter half of the 1960's saw Chinese involvement with military aid to Hanoi and presence at negotiating tables. When Sihanouk of Cambodia, in 1970, established himself in exile in Peking, China became even more involved. Prior to 1965 Chinese ties had been quite close with the Indonesian Communist Party, while Peking followed the underground activities of Communist parties of other lands and encouraged at least a pro-Peking, as against a pro-Moscow, orientation. Border disputes with India after 1958 acerbated feelings with that country but drew Pakistan closer to China. Peking showed interest in the neutralist-tinged administrations of Afghanistan, Nepal, and Ceylon.

Relations with Europe, the Middle East, and Africa. At the beginning of the 1970's, Communist China maintained diplomatic relations with nine Western European countries: the four Scandinavian ones, Switzerland, the Netherlands, France, Great Britain, and Italy. London early recognized Peking, which accepted the recognition but kept relations at a secondary level, with an exchange of chargés d'affaires rather than ambassadors. Despite Chinese disapproval of the historic British record in China, the Peking regime, especially after open differences with the Russians, turned to London for trade and commerce and invited British scientists and teachers to China. There the British sometimes represented American interests.

Despite the lack of formal diplomatic ties with other Western European nations and with the so-called white Commonwealth countries—Canada (which recognized it in 1970), Australia, and New Zealand—Communist China concluded trade agreements with their governments and business concerns. It sought to develop diplomatic, political, and commercial relations also with the Middle Eastern, Arab-African, and Sub-Saharan countries in Africa. Peking was interested in trade, particularly in the acquisition of crude oil supplies. It sought support for causes in international organs. It endeavored through long-range programs and almost insuperable obstacles to compete with Russian and American influence in some underdeveloped lands. It fished in muddied political waters to extend its national and Communist policies, promoting—to the concern of some established indigenous regimes—the export of revolution. The Chinese allied themselves with Middle Eastern and African guerrilla movements for national liberation, as well as with other causes and recognized governments dedicated to eradicating colonialism and neo-colonialism. They sought common cause with those African and Middle Eastern peoples who eschewed Western military pacts and promoted the goal of self-determination. They expanded trade with Latin American countries, though it was yet on a small scale.

Relations with the United States. The prospect of improving relations between the United States and Communist China was complex and multifaceted. In the United States, individual proposals called for the development of trade and exchanges and contacts along various lines. Though the prospects for increased mutual understanding appeared involved, in the early 1970's fresh approaches and re-examination of existing issues were indicated. American passports could be validated for travel to Communist China, which was selectively issuing visas for them. The Nixon administration relaxed restrictions on trade with Peking and permitted Americans to purchase Communist-made goods. The American public debated China policies, though the Chinese Communists remained more inflexible in their responses. The bamboo curtain opened partially in early 1971 when an American Ping-pong team was permitted to enter China for a week; selected American journalists and scientists were similarly allowed visits. After a visit to Peking in July, 1971, by President Nixon's adviser on security matters, the Chinese Communists extended, and Nixon accepted, an invitation to visit the People's Republic of China. Faced also with a plethora of domestic and international problems, some self-imposed, Peking pursued its own ways and policies. As heirs to the ancient, traditional, and modern eras, the Communists continued to shape China's destiny.

21
RIM LANDS
Since 1945

Communist China occupied the center of the Asian political scene, but rim lands of Inner and East Asia were also of importance. Japan in the course of an occupation and return to independent status surged to amazing economic growth and once again to international stature. Korea, like Vietnam, remained divided with a Communist regime in the north and anti-Communist government in the south. Mongolia continued in the Soviet Russian sphere of influence, while the National government in Taiwan remained staunchly anti-Communist.

JAPAN

From imperial tragedy to surprising recovery was the story of postwar Japan. After a period of Allied—in effect, American—occupation, Japan recovered independence. But for the next eight years it remained in a dependent status vis-à-vis relations with the United States. After 1960, its leaders indicated increasing independence of action. These years also witnessed not only the realization of far-flung economic interests but also a political re-awakening and renewed participation in the Asian scene.

***Occupied Japan* (*1945–1952*).** The occupation of Japan was chiefly planned and executed by the United States. The Potsdam Conference had enunciated broad objectives concerning the demilitarization and democratization of Japan; the Far Eastern Commission (FEC) in Washington and the Allied Council for Japan (ACJ) in Tokyo represented Allied interest. In effect, General Douglas MacArthur as Supreme Commander of the Allied Forces (SCAP), and his headquarters in Tokyo, directed the Occupation. For practical reasons, the Japanese political structure was generally maintained. The emperor continued at the head of the state, but he was stripped of his unique status. In a rescript issued on January 1, 1946, he renounced any concept of imperial divinity.

Reform Measures. The first years of the Occupation emphasized demilitarization and reform measures. Assuming that much in traditional Japan had contributed to the growth of militarism and fascism, the Occupation authorities tried to restructure Japanese political, economic, and social values. High-ranking military and civilian wartime officials were purged from office. An Allied International Military Tribunal for the Far East (IMTFE) in Tokyo tried some two-dozen Japanese leaders on three charges: conventional war crimes, crimes against peace, and crimes against humanity. Upon conviction, seven, including Tojo, were executed and the rest imprisoned. Individual Allied countries also tried some Japanese for war crimes against their own nationals. Many lesser civil service bureaucrats were dropped from office. SCAP also purged the zaibatsu and redistributed their assets. It encouraged the growth of labor unions. Proceeding also from the assumption that bigness in agrarian affairs contributed to authoritarian society, the Occupation redistributed large land estates and set limits on land holdings.

In political life, a constitution was promulgated in 1947 to replace the Meiji document. Drafted by Occupation authorities, this constitution democratized the political life of Japan, extending the franchise to all over the age of twenty. It included a bill of rights. It transformed the emperor's position from that of a divine ruler to a state symbol and created a bicameral Diet as the state legislative body. Membership in both houses of the Diet, 467 in the lower House of Representatives and 250 in the upper house of Councillors, became fully elective. Formerly subordinated to the Ministry of Justice, the judiciary was made independent. Local government was also democratized. The constitution renounced war as an instrument of national policy and prohibited domestic armed forces. Another political reform revised the centralized relations that had existed between Tokyo and local political units. Local governments were granted more powers in matters relating to taxation, education, police, and legislation. SCAP reforms also broadened educational opportunities. The academic structure came to resemble the American public school system with primary schools, junior and senior high schools, and junior and four-year colleges.

Recovery Measures and Treaties. By 1948 the Occupation had accomplished most of the basic reforms. Meanwhile, emphasis in the SCAP program changed from reform to recovery, partly because of internal developments in Japan and partly because of increasing confrontations in Europe and Asia between Communist and anti-Communist forces. Japan became important to the United States as a potential ally. The new policy at times conflicted with earlier SCAP policies of reform. The government launched a drive to reduce the budget. Labor union demands for higher wages and the right to collective bargaining went unheeded. Occupation authorities bore down on the left-wing movement, including Communists, who had been released after the war. Washington halted Japan's reparations shipments and plant-dismantling. SCAP also permitted some industrial leaders to return to their former positions. Finally, the United States began to formulate a peace treaty that would restore full sovereignty to Japan. These reconstruction measures were accelerated by the outbreak of the Korean conflict.

After making no headway in the Far Eastern Commission toward a peace treaty draft, the United States began bilateral negotiations with other involved nations. In September, 1950, President Harry Truman named Republican John Foster Dulles, as his special ambassador to negotiate the treaty. Within a year the final treaty text was drawn up by the British and the Americans, who jointly convened a peace conference in San Francisco in September, 1951. Fifty-two nations, including Soviet Russia, were invited to sign the treaty. Not invited were neutrals and the Allies' ex-enemies in Europe. Neither China was represented, since the British by 1951 had recognized the Communist regime in Peking while the United States continued diplomatic recognition to Chiang Kai-shek, now on Taiwan.

The peace treaty was one of reconciliation. The state of war was ended and Japan renounced its claims in China and Korea. The treaty, however, recognized Japan's right of individual or collective self-defense. It provided for the withdrawal of all Occupational troops except those invited to remain by the Japanese.

It begged the issue of reparations because the relevant terms implied voluntary reparations. (This issue caused the Philippine and Indonesian delegations to sign the treaty with reservations.) The treaty limited Japan to the four main home islands and some minor off-shore islands. Japan renounced all right, title, and claim to Formosa, the Pescadores, Kuriles, South Sakhalin, the former Pacific mandates, Antarctic areas, and the Spratly and Paracel Islands in the South China Sea. But the treaty did not specify what disposition would be made of these territories. In the special cases of the Ryukyus and Bonins island chains, Japan retained residual sovereignty, but the United States was given the sole right to administer them.

To effect security measures, the United States negotiated additional treaties with Japan. On the day the peace treaty was signed (September 8, 1951), the two countries also signed a security treaty, open-ended in duration, granting to the United States the sole right to maintain military bases in and about Japan. The stated purpose of this military presence was not only to preserve peace and security in the Far East but also to preserve the security of Japan, uniquely, from internal subversion. To implement this treaty, an administrative agreement of February 28, 1952, outlined in detail the disposition of such American forces and their rights and privileges.

Despite doubts, particularly concerning national rearmament, both houses of the Japanese Diet approved the treaty by great majorities. The United States Senate also consented to its ratification by a large majority. In an appended declaration, however, that body stated that its approval of treaty terms in no way constituted approval for the Russian occupation of, or title to, South Sakhalin, the Kuriles, and other former Japanese-owned islands occupied by the Soviet Union. On April 28, 1952, when the majority of signers, including Japan and the United States, had ratified the treaty, Japan regained independence. On the same day, Chiang Kai-shek concluded a separate peace treaty with Japan, which recognized Nationalist China as sovereign in those areas under its control, in effect, Taiwan and the Pescadores. Other nations which either did not sign the treaty or signed it with reservations later entered into negotiations with Japan: India in

1952, Burma in 1954, the Soviet Union in 1956, and the Philippines and Indonesia in 1956 and 1958 respectively (after reparations agreements had been concluded with these two countries).

Cautious Posture (1952–1960). After the recovery of independence, Japan experienced a transitional phase in which it displayed a cautious posture in domestic and international affairs. Prime ministers were mostly men of conservative background, who had gradually worked up through party ranks.

Political Developments. Continuing the prewar Seiyukai Party were the Liberals, while from the Minseito came the Progressives and Democrats. Yoshida Shigeru, who had opposed the war, was prime minister for seven and a half years (1946–1947, 1948–1954), during the transition stage from occupation to independence. Proceeding carefully in the early years, he had to honor treaty settlements and yet placate Japanese public opinion. Under him, in 1950 the parties of the right united as the Liberal Party, which three years later split into two conservative factions. Yoshida was succeeded in office by Hatoyama Ichiro (1954–1956), who in 1955 reunited the conservative cause as the Liberal Democratic Party. He followed a more nationalistic policy than had his predecessor. He sought treaty modifications with the United States, increased trade with Communist China, and peace with the Russians, who during his tenure withdrew their veto of Japanese admission to the United Nations. After the brief term of another conservative prime minister, Kishi Nobusuke held office from 1957 to 1960. He supported conservative tenets, including the return to Japan of the administration of Okinawa, the end of nuclear testing, and promoting trade with Communist China.

The conservative cause garnered most of the Japanese votes, but there was in the country a small right-wing movement which included extreme nationalists and militarists. They made headlines, but remained relatively weak. More significant was the *Soka Gakkai* (Value-Creating Association), a contemporary variant of Nichiren Buddhism, with a political branch, the *Komeito* (Clean Government Party). The left-wing groups, mostly Socialist, perennially included at least a third of Japanese voters. Socialist factions, like the conservatives, had right and left wings, though the differences were more of degree than of principle. From 1945 to 1951, the Socialists were united; in this period Japan had its only Socialist prime minister, Katayama Tetsu, a Christian who headed the Social Democrats. This coalition eventually disintegrated, and a period of disunity lasted until the elections of 1955. There was another uneasy coalition between 1955 and 1960, when once more a division occurred, with the majority forming the more leftist Japanese Socialist Party and the minority, the Democratic Socialist Party. Communism was not strong in postwar Japan. It was kept in check under the Occupation and after the recovery of independence it made only minor gains in the Diet.

The Economy. In economic life, growth was marked. Overall growth rates after the Occupation averaged 10 percent annually. Economic progress resulted from several factors. Agricultural production kept pace with the growing economy and population. Japan was ahead of other Asian states in modernization, with nearly a century of skills and experience. The people had adjusted to industrialism and accepted it. The government advanced the theory of free enterprise, but was ready to provide official help and large funds in areas of the economy which needed strengthening. Government, finance, and industry cooperated toward economic goals. Occupation aid programs, totaling $2 billion, as well as later American military procurements during the Korean War, also contributed greatly to the Japanese economy.

Foreign Relations. In foreign affairs, Japan concerned itself with a "low posture," which emphasized economic relations. It sought increased participation in the United Nations and other international programs, and more independence in foreign policy. Japan recognized the Republic of China on Taiwan, and carried on trade with Nationalist China, amounting to about $100 million annually. Chiang Kai-shek's government did not press for reparations. Similar normalization was effected with other Southeast Asian states. Reparations agreements were concluded with Burma, the Philippines, Indonesia, and South Vietnam. Cambodia, Laos, and Singapore received token amounts. Malaysia pressed for reparations but received none.

Japan also stressed economic factors in its relations with Communist countries. Soviet Russia did not sign the Japanese Peace Treaty at San Francisco, but a 1956 treaty between the two parties ended the state of war, provided for diplomatic exchanges, repatriated remaining Japanese prisoners of war, and reciprocally waived reparations claims. These accommodations resulted from the thaw in the Russian line under Khrushchev and the more neutralist policies of Prime Minister Hatoyama. However, Japan continued to protest Russian nuclear tests and sought extended fishing rights in the Japan Sea. With Communist China diplomatic relations were not considered, but trade arrangements were established. Between 1952 and 1958, four trade agreements were signed between Peking and private Japanese associations, though only three were effected and those incompletely. In other areas of bilateral concern, fishing conventions were signed and the Chinese Communists repatriated prisoners of war and former Japanese residents. Japan similarly had trade but not diplomatic relations with Outer Mongolia, North Korea, North Vietnam, and Eastern European countries.

***International Prestige* (*since 1960*).** With the revision of the United States security treaty and the gradual assumption by the Japanese government of worldwide interests, Japan entered into a new period of vitality and energy. It surged ahead in economic life, consolidated political reforms, and embarked on international programs. The revision in 1960 of the mutual security treaty removed the chief objections voiced by the Japanese to the treaty of 1951. The revised treaty was to be in effect for ten years and then indefinitely (subject to termination by either party on a year's notice). Japan was recognized as a partner with the United States in the preservation of Asian peace. The amended document stated that an armed attack on either signatory would constitute a common danger and that the two parties would consult on threats to peace. Japan was to be consulted on movement of American military personnel within or from territories under its administration (which then excluded American-administered Bonins and Ryukyus). No nuclear weapons were to be stored in Japan without Japanese consent. Japan could then receive military assistance from countries other than the United States.

Political Developments. Prime Minister Kishi rammed the revised United States security treaty through the Diet in the spring of 1960 but fell from office shortly thereafter. The ratification provoked riots and caused the cancellation of President Dwight Eisenhower's impending official visit to Japan. The new

Japanese prime minister, Ikeda Hayato (1960–1964), also a Liberal Democrat, proposed a "forward" look. Popular because of his engagingly plain manners, he accepted as permanent the Occupation reforms, worked toward harmony in domestic politics, and formulated a ten-year plan to double Japan's national income. He resigned because of illness in late 1964. Sato Eisaku, the next prime minister, sought solutions to keep the Japanese economy booming and to promote greater Japanese participation in world affairs. The Socialist parties continued as the perennial minority. The Communist Party, already in weakened condition, was further debilitated in the 1960's when Peking–Moscow differences resulted in Communist party cleavages abroad. On the other hand, the Komeito Party increased its showing at the polls and began to offer the conservatives real opposition.

Economic and Social Changes. Economic growth continued to soar in the early 1970's. With a gross national product of some $125 billion at the time, Japan became the third wealthiest country in the world (after the United States and the Soviet Union). It led the world in the production of spun rayon, cotton yarn, motorcycles, cameras, sewing machines, television and radio sets, and ships. It placed second in automotive vehicles and fishery; third in crude steel, fertilizer, and refined petroleum; and fourth in cement and electrical energy output. Prosperity brought about a great improvement in living standards throughout the country. The post-Occupation era brought changes to rural areas as a result of land reforms and mass education which attacked traditional myths and institutions. The Japanese farmer was better educated, lived better, and participated more in political life than did any of his Asian counterparts.

Social change paralleled economic growth. The imperial position became merely symbolic, as widespread pacifism and antimilitarism replaced worship of the emperor and state. The family system was often sundered between old and new generations. The formerly honored positions of bureaucracy and industrial entrepreneurs were diminished. Industry became more flexible in organization. While family connections still counted to a great extent, large companies selected executive trainees from promising college graduates. City workers moved into the lower-middle class and grew in political power. Nine million workers (about one-third of the total working force) belonged to unions. Many of the young Japanese belonged to leftist movements and engaged in direct political action. There was more college enrollment than in any other country except the United States and England. Extensive news media blanketed Japan with ideas. In the changing times, more Japanese shared in the ever expanding social and economic horizons.

Foreign Relations. In foreign affairs, the revised security treaty eliminated some problems with the United States, but others remained. The status of and jurisdiction over American forces stationed in Japan remained nebulous. The gradual cutback in American troops and installations helped to alleviate matters. In 1960 the United States paroled the remaining Japanese war criminals, numbering about one hundred. The Americans insisted that the Japanese pay the Occupation expenses; in 1962, Japan pledged $490 million (a fourth of the estimated Occupation costs) over a fifteen-year period. Japan's trade with both Communist and Nationalist China was contrary to the American policy of embargoes on Communist China. The Japanese objected to American nuclear tests in the Pacific, as they objected to all nuclear tests. Of vital importance was Japanese–American trade that by 1970 totaled $4.5 billion annually. Trade differences resulted from sporadic Japanese flooding of American markets with certain items and from domestic tariff and investment walls. Territorial problems were gradually resolved. On Christmas, 1953, the United States returned the Amami Islands south of Kyushu to Japanese jurisdiction. After Prime Minister Sato visited Washington in late 1967, President Johnson pledged the return of the Bonins, which were transferred back to Japanese administration in June of the following year. However, with over $1 billion invested in military projects, the United States was reluctant to return administrative rights over the Ryukyus to Japan. After years of Japanese agitation, in late 1969, President Richard Nixon and Prime Minister Sato confirmed the return of such rights to Japan by 1972. The provisions of the revised security treaty would then pertain to any American military presence on Okinawa.

The Soviet Union denounced Japan's revised security treaty with the United States. However, several weeks later, Moscow signed with Tokyo a three-year commercial and trade agreement, which was subsequently renewed for various interims. The Japanese laid claim to the Habomai and Shikotan islands lying immediately off of northern Hokkaido, as well as the Kunashiri and Etorofu islands, southernmost in the Kurile chain. The Russians promised to return the first two upon the completion of a full-fledged peace treaty with them, but they claimed the latter two as Soviet territory, by virtue of Allied wartime agreements. Bilateral talks periodically projected joint ventures in Siberia and resulted in establishing a Moscow–Tokyo air route. In January, 1966, reflecting improved relations, the Japanese foreign minister visited Moscow; the following July, the Soviet foreign minister returned the visit, the first such official ever to visit Japan. Trade continued with Communist China through official or informal arrangements. An agreement was concluded in 1962 providing for at least $100 million in trade each year over a five-year period. Under this arrangement Sino–Japanese trade spurted to a half a billion dollars annually. When the agreement ended in 1967, the Chinese Communists did not immediately replace it with another program, though through informal arrangements Japan became Communist China's most active trading partner. Japan also traded with other Asian Communist lands.

Toward non-Communist Asian nations, over the first two decades, through channels of war reparations and regular programs, Japan committed itself to over $1 billion in grants and loans. It supplemented reparation treaties by trade arrangements with Southeast Asian countries, which absorbed a third of Japanese exports. With South Asia it maintained some connections and extended financial aid to India and Pakistan. Tokyo developed a new and peaceful "Asian–Pacific concept" to replace the wartime Greater East Asia Co-Prosperity Sphere. It became a donor nation in the Colombo Plan for Asian economic development (which dated to 1950 and eventually included most non-Communist Asia states and some Western ones). In 1966 Japan convoked the Southeast Asia Ministerial Conference on Economic Development. The Asian Development Bank was planned in Tokyo, which, however, lost the site of headquarters to Manila. Japan contributed $200 million (as did the United States) to this agency's billion-dollar capitalization fund. Japan joined the Asian and Pacific Council (ASPAC), and Japanese firms participated in numerous development projects throughout Southeast Asia. Japan also showed active economic interest in all other areas of the world and left no stone unturned to promote commercial relations, so necessary to its national survival and growth.

THE KOREAS

Postwar Korea, by virtue of geographic location, continued to be caught in international power plays. The three and a half decades of Japanese occupation, as well as the wartime conferences of Cairo and Potsdam, left their historic heritage. The dividing parallel was artificial. The northern half of Korea was more industrialized and less populated than the agrarian overpopulated southern half. In the first postwar years an uneasy peace existed between the Soviet-sponsored regime in the north and the American-backed government in the south. Then the Korean War erupted. After its conclusion, the same 38th parallel was defined as a military demarcating line. But as in Vietnam, the line crystallized into a political boundary between the Communist North Korea and anti-Communist South Korea.

***Occupation* (*1945–1950*).** After the Russian army came into Korea on August 15, 1945, it exercised control through local committees that had sprung up in the north. The Soviets brought back as potential leaders from China and Russia several Korean Communists, including Kim Il Sung, who was to emerge later as top man in the north. Having spent the war years in Soviet Russia, he returned with the Russian army, won control of the Communist Party of Korea (organized in 1925), and in 1946 absorbed the New People's Party, which was composed of Chinese-trained leaders. In the south, the United States occupation troops (six weeks after the Russians in arriving), also brought back some well-known Korean leaders, notably Syngman Rhee. Coming from self-imposed exile in Hawaii and the United States during the decades of Japanese rule, he provided a focus for anti-Communist Korean leadership.

Indigenous names reappeared on the scene, but Korea was a big power consideration. Russians and Americans could not agree on reunification terms. In August, 1948, the Russians through their Communist spokesmen ordered elections for the Supreme People's Assembly and created the People's Democratic Republic of Korea at Pyongyang. Kim Il Sung was designated prime minister. His regime was recognized by the Communist bloc, including Russia, which then withdrew troops and entered into military and economic agreements with it. In the south the United States proceeded along parallel bilaterial lines, as well as through United Nations channels. In November, 1947, the General Assembly recognized the Korean right to independence and established a United Nations commission to formulate a national government. The Russians did not participate, and in May, 1948, the United States unilaterally proceeded to hold elections in the south for a national assembly. The assembly chose Rhee as president of the Republic of Korea, which was inaugurated the following August. The United States transferred authority to the new administration and prepared to withdraw troops. By mid-1948, the two Korean governments had emerged, each purporting to speak for the whole country.

In December, 1948, the General Assembly designated the South Korean government as the only lawful one and called for the withdrawal of foreign troops. On New Year's Day, 1949, the United States extended diplomatic recognition to the Republic of Korea. Within the next half year, Washington withdrew all tactical units. It left behind only a small military advisory group and began to extend economic assistance to Seoul, which faced great economic problems in rehabilitation programs. Through strong centralized rule and his People's Party, Rhee autocratically presided over South Korea and advocated forceful measures to reunify the country. The People's Democratic Republic in the north similarly called for reunification measures and a conference to settle the issue. Concurrently, the Russians began to help rebuild the North Korean economy. The Chinese Communists, at the time busy consolidating their regime at home, stayed out of the Korean scene. The United States implied a similar intention. In January, 1950, Dean Acheson, secretary of state in the Truman administration, made a policy statement which left Korea (and Taiwan) outside of the United States Asian defense perimeter.

He stated that any aggression in Korea would be considered a United Nations matter.

War (1950–1953). The Korean War broke out in mid-1950. Who triggered it has been a matter of debate. On June 25, tank columns in sizable force moved from the northern sector of Korea across the 38th parallel to Seoul. The United Nations Commission in Korea branded the act as aggression. The United States called for an emergency session of the Security Council. In the absence of a Russian delegation (which was then boycotting the United Nations Security Council and other organs for failure to seat the Chinese Communist regime as the legitimate representative of all China), the Security Council called on North Korea to stop hostilities and withdraw invasion troops. The next day, President Truman ordered Americans out of Seoul and directed General Douglas MacArthur, as commander-in-chief of all United States forces in the Pacific, to dispatch air and sea forces. On the third day, June 27, the president committed United States combat forces. He also ordered the Seventh Fleet into the Formosa Strait to prevent any attack on Taiwan. (It was not clear at the time whether the outbreak of the war was related to possible Communist military action elsewhere; Washington had in mind also the recently concluded thirty year Sino-Soviet mutual defense treaty.) The United States also stepped up military aid to the Indochinese area and reinforced Philippine bases.

Despite immediate unilateral American aid, Seoul fell to the enemy, and the South Korean army was routed. Branding North Korea as aggressor, the Security Council recommended assistance to the south. Working along United Nations and unilateral lines, the United States government appropriated $6 billion in emergency funds for the "police action" in Korea. By the end of June, the United States had committed sizable numbers of ground troops and had blockaded the entire coast. With MacArthur designated as head of the unified United Nations command, sixteen United Nations members provided contingents for the cause by the end of the year. The hostilities lasted one year and four months. In the initial months, the Communist momentum carried their troops far to the south. But in September, 1950, MacArthur directed a brilliant flank landing behind Communist lines at Inchon, near Seoul. United Nations troops liberated Seoul, counterattacked across the parallel, captured Pyongyang, and moved toward the Manchurian border. MacArthur assured President Truman, at a conference on Wake Island in October, that the troops would be home by Christmas.

The campaigns then changed their nature. Apprehensive at foreign forces poised on the Manchurian border, the Chinese Communists entered the war in force in November. They rolled back the United Nations forces and recaptured Seoul in January, 1951. MacArthur regrouped his troops, liberated Seoul, and advanced to the parallel. The Allied command dug in as the diplomats took over the matter of a cease-fire and armistice. Having already branded North Korea as an aggressor, the General Assembly in February, 1951, added Communist China to the category. That April, Truman fired MacArthur from all his posts because of the general's insubordination, stemming from policy differences in the conduct of the Korean War, which MacArthur wanted to escalate into China. Truman replaced MacArthur in all positions with General Matthew Ridgway, who also served out the remainder of the Occupation in Japan as SCAP. In May, 1951, the United Nations General Assembly further recommended an embargo on arms, ammunition, and implements of war to both North Korea and Communist China. In June, portents of peace appeared when the Soviet delegate in an American radio program stated that the armed conflict could be resolved. A cease-fire along the 38th parallel was shortly ordered. But it took two years of negotiations to confirm the provisions of an armistice.

Uneasy Co-existence (since 1953). Signed in 1953, the Korean truce provided for a demilitarized neutral zone, established supervisory and repatriation commissions, and called for a political conference on Korea. The conference convened at Geneva and in mid-1954 the conferees, who included all sixteen members of the United Nations forces and the directly involved Communist countries, confirmed previous arrangements. The Geneva Conference left Korea a divided country. Unilaterally, the United States continued to extend military and economic aid to Syngman Rhee, who had violently opposed any political arrangement leaving his country halved. In October, 1953, a United

States Korean Mutual Defense Treaty partially placated Rhee's sensibilities. It called for consultations on mutual issues but provided no obligation for American troops to be stationed in Korea. The United States also extended a five year $1 billion economic assistance program to rehabilitate once again the shattered South Korean economy.

North Korea. As a member of the Communist bloc, North Korea effected treaties with both Soviet Russia and Communist China. The leader of the Korean Worker's Party (the renamed Communist organ), Kim Il Sung, was perennial prime minister and chairman of the party. When the latter position was abolished in 1960, he remained as secretary-general. He collectivized agriculture, put industry and commerce under state ownership and control, and announced a seven-year plan (1961–1967, but extended three more years), with "flying horse teams" in industry and agriculture to spur production. In Pyongyang, the Supreme People's Assembly, which was elected every four years, periodically met to confirm laws handed down by the cabinet and top party men. After Chinese troops withdrew in 1958, Kim Il Sung announced plans for the reunification of the country in which neutral nations, rather than the United Nations, were to supervise elections.

The prime minister endeavored to steer North Korea between Communist China and the Soviet Union, though at times he seemed to lean to one side or the other. In December, 1948, he concluded military pacts with both parties. In the course of the Korean War, Pyongyang depended heavily on Chinese Communist manpower and the Soviet Russian military equipment. Following the war, in mid-1956, the North Koreans accepted $250 million in aid from Russia. Moscow cancelled $132 million in debts and extended an additional $75 million in aid and $45 million in credits. In 1960 the Soviet Union signed a new technical-assistance program, though that same year Peking extended a four-year $105 million loan. In 1961 the People's Democratic Republic again signed mutual defense pacts with both parties. Six years later, another one was signed with Russia.

North Korea was adamant against improving relations with the United States. Over the years, the Americans, representing the United Nations, met with the North Koreans at Panmunjon in the 150-mile long demilitarized zone, where charges and countercharges of border violations were hurled. Relations were further strained in early 1968, when the *Pueblo,* an American intelligence-gathering naval vessel, with its 83-man crew was seized by the North Koreans off their eastern coast, in international or territorial waters, as alleged variously by the respective parties. The men were eventually released, but other incidents clouded the scene.

South Korea. In South Korea, Syngman Rhee ruled through a heavy-handed regime. Re-elected president in 1952 and 1956, he seemed to be the indispensable man. Elected for a fourth term in March, 1960, at the age of eighty-four, he elicited student and national unrest that forced him out of office that spring. He retired from the presidency and spent his last years in exile in Hawaii, his former home. A caretaker government took over and called for new elections, which put John M. Chang in as prime minister. As a result of unstable policies, a military junta took over in May, 1961. Chang was ousted and in time General Park (Pak) Chung Hee emerged as the chairman of the Supreme Council for National Reconstruction. He pledged a return to civilian and parliamentary rule. The December, 1962, elections confirmed constitutional amendments to set up an American-type presidency. The November, 1963, elections elevated Park to presidency and his Democratic-Republic Party to majority position in the assembly. The presidential and parliamentary elections of May and June, 1967, confirmed the arrangement by handsome majorities. To permit a third four-year presidential term, the National Assembly in mid-1969 passed a constitutional amendment, which was approved in a plebiscite. Two years later Park was returned a third time to top office. In economic affairs, the Seoul government gradually recorded progress, resulting from the curbing of inflation, a rising volume of exports, and good harvests. The Park regime formulated the usual five-year plans.

In dealing with Japan, South Koreans initially took a hard line. After the Japanese defeat, they insisted that their former overlords leave, never to return. During the Korean War, they reacted unfavorably to any Japanese assistance to their country.

They were not present at the Japanese peace conference, but the treaty stipulated that bilateral talks be initiated regarding Japanese property and Korean claims. Economic stakes were huge, because Japanese nationals owned 80 percent of commercial and industrial property and over half of the farmland. Over the years, the parties argued the nature of compensation. They similarly debated the rights of 600,000 Koreans living in Japan and their rights of repatriation to either North or South Korea. An impasse was reached over the so-called Rhee line, named after the president, that prohibited all Japanese fishing vessels from entrance within its extended boundaries. Korean-Japanese relations noticeably improved after Rhee was forced out of office. In 1965 a Japanese-Korean agreement was concluded. It provided for joint fishing operations outside the twelve-mile territorial limits, granted permanent residence rights to Koreans in Japan, and extended to Korea $300 million in economic aid grants and $500 million in additional loans. Despite minority opposition in both countries, the ratified treaty re-established diplomatic relations and boded closer ties. Later economic agreements were firmed.

In foreign affairs, relations with the United States were paramount. Augmenting the mutual defense treaty of October, 1953, was a treaty of friendship, signed in late 1958. In mid-1960, President Dwight Eisenhower included the Republic of Korea in his swing through East Asia. In late 1966, President Lyndon Johnson visited Seoul. Massive American economic and military aid flowed to South Korea. In the course of the Korean War (which claimed the lives of 55,000 Americans), some $3.5 billion was expended. Between 1954 and mid-1966, an equivalent sum was spent, though grants were declining (to be phased out by 1972 because of the improved Korean domestic economic situation). The American military position was also retrenched, while the standing Korean army of over 500,000 soldiers maintained law and order. In early 1967, an agreement signed by Dean Rusk, secretary of state of the Johnson administration, and the Korean foreign minister gave to the Republic of Korea limited jurisdiction over criminal offenses of American troops (then estimated at some 50,000). Like his northern counterpart, General Park advanced plans for the reunification of the divided peninsula, but he included a role for the United Nations. Wending their separate ways but bound to common historic and geographic ties, the Koreas coexisted uneasily.

MONGOLIA

The Yalta agreement of February, 1945, preserved Outer Mongolian status quo, which in effect meant a Russian protectorate. A Sino-Soviet treaty of August, 1945, confirmed the Yalta arrangement but called for a Mongolian plebiscite on the issue of independence. This was effected and results confirmed independence. Following the conquest of the Chinese mainland by the Communists, Mao Tse-tung went to Moscow to negotiate treaties, one of which pledged Mongolian independence. After Choibalsan died in 1952, new leadership emerged in the person of Umzhagin Tsedenbal, premier and first secretary of the Party. Upon Stalin's death, the Russians handed over joint Soviet-Mongolian enterprises to Mongolians, and Ulan Bator began to seek international recognition. Sino-Soviet rivalry developed in aid programs, though Tsendenbal leaned more toward the Soviet camp.

Relations with Communist China had their ups and downs. In 1960 a treaty of friendship and mutual assistance was signed. Two years later, a border treaty defined the 2,700 miles of common boundary, with only minor territorial swaps. The Chinese contributed some $50 million to the third Mongolian five-year plan (1961–1965) and up to 13,000 workers on various projects, which had been initiated as early as 1955. But after 1964, Chinese workers were phased out of Mongolian plans, and pro-Chinese Party men in Ulan Bator were removed from office. In late 1965, the Chinese Communist foreign minister, Chen Yi, refuted allegations that China regarded Outer Mongolia as Chinese territory, though the next year the Chinese Communist New China News Agency reported Mongolian events under a "China" heading. In 1966 a Sino-Mongolian cultural co-operation agreement was signed, but that same year the excesses of the Great Proletariat Cultural Revolution spilled over into demonstrations before the Mongolian embassy in Peking.

Soviet Russia, on the other hand, enhanced ties with Mongolia. In early 1966, a twenty-year Soviet-Mongolian treaty of friendship was signed (updating the previous ones of 1936 and

1946). It renewed defense commitments and provided for consultations on matters of common interests. Soviet troops, possibly ten thousand in number, were stationed in Mongolia. Toward the third five-year plan costing $1 billion, the Russians extended some $156 million worth of aid and deferred payments of some $60 million of old debts. The Soviets underwrote about $725 million, or one-third of the total outlay, for 880 projects in the fourth five-year plan (1966–1970). Mongolian trade was chiefly directed toward Russia, with the rail link from Peking to Irkutsk via Ulan Bator, getting the bulk of traffic.

The Mongolian People's Republic, with outside aid, developed Ulan Bator into a showcase of international products and outlooks. It also created the new industrial city of Darhan, 120 miles north of Ulan Bator. It launched an international and domestic air service. It paid attention to education; in the late 1960's, out of a total population of just over a million, 165,000 children attended 462 schools in a seven-year compulsory education system. There were seven institutes of higher learning, all located at the capital. Political life was directed by the Mongolian People's Revolutionary Party, which ran the state. In 1966 it scheduled elections (the sixth) for the Great People's Hural (national assembly), which designated Tsedenbal as chairman of the Council of Ministers in the state and bureaucratic apparatus.

While modernizing at home, the Mongolian People's Republic broadened its diplomatic relations. By 1970, it enjoyed diplomatic relations with some forty countries. It exchanged diplomatic missions with Cuba and all Communist countries (except Albania). Britain and France maintained resident diplomatic missions at Ulan Bator, which in turn had resident diplomats in India, Guinea, and Mali. In 1961, over objections of the Nationalist Chinese (who, however, did not use their Security Council veto), the Mongolian People's Republic joined the United Nations in a package deal that included the contingent admission of Mauretania in West Africa. In 1966 Tsedenbal refused American aid for flood victims. He did not press for diplomatic recognition, nor did Washington seem ready to extend it. Ulan Bator's representatives attended international gatherings and, despite close Soviet ties, sought to establish Mongolia as an independent Communist political entity.

TAIWAN

As a result of wartime and postwar developments, Taiwan reverted to the Chinese fold. The Cairo and Potsdam conferences restored Taiwan and the Pescadores to the Republic of China, but these statements as declarations of intent did not constitute a legal transfer of title, which was the concern of a peace treaty. General Douglas MacArthur's order of August 15, 1945, bestowed upon Chiang Kai-shek control of Taiwan and the Pescadores to accept the surrender of Japanese forces. Nationalist generals and armies occupied the islands and the capital of Taipei. An initial period of harsh rule culminated in massacres of March, 1947, which decimated Formosan leadership. On December 8, 1949, Chiang Kai-shek arrived to set up a government in exile, which eventually included some two million military and Kuomintang adherents who had escaped the Communist regime on the mainland.

Relations with the United States. The United States policy of "Wait-until-the-dust-settles," previously pursued on the mainland carried over with the Republic of China on Taiwan. In January, 1950, both Secretary of State Dean Acheson and President Harry Truman indicated that Taiwan was not considered an essential link in the Western Pacific defense perimeter. But with the outbreak of the Korean War five months later, Taiwan catapulted into a prominent place in defense arrangements. On June 27, Truman ordered the Seventh Fleet into the Formosa Strait not only to prevent a Communist attack on the island but to deter any Nationalist ambitions to return to the mainland, which had been Chiang Kai-shek's primary aim. Concerned with the possible spread of Communist military activity in East Asia generally and with a possible renewed outbreak of the Chinese civil war specifically, Truman took this drastic decision, which in effect resulted in a two-China political policy for the United States and complicated Asian international relations for decades.

In foreign affairs, Taiwan's relations, like those of Japan and South Korea, were of paramount consideration regarding the United States. After the Korean War, American military and economic aid flowed to the island. In May, 1951, a military advisory group was established at Taipei. In December, 1954, a mutual defense treaty was concluded between Taiwan and the United States. Under terms of the treaty, in the event of an armed attack in the western Pacific against its territories, each party undertook to act in accordance with the constitutional processes of their respective countries. For the Republic of China, the pertinent territories were defined as Taiwan and the Pescadores; for the United States, those island territories in the western Pacific then under American administration (the Ryukyus and the strategic trust territories). In another note, the Nationalists pledged not to launch attacks on the mainland without American consent.

The Nationalist-held offshore islands of Quemoy, opposite the Chinese Communist port of Amoy, and Matsu, opposite Foochow, were not governed by these agreements. Subject to periodic bombardment (they lay only one to three miles off the mainland), they held an ambiguous position in treaty provisions. In January, 1955, in the course of another intensive round of Communist bombardment of the islands (and after the Nationalists and Americans had evacuated from the Tachens, another group of offshore islands, lying much farther to the north in the Yangtze estuary), President Eisenhower requested and received from the Congress a resolution which in effect left it up to presidential discretion to defend Quemoy and Matsu if such defense could be related to the defense of Taiwan. As other military priorities emerged in Asia and as the Taiwanese economy improved, American aid programs slowed down. Between 1951 and 1965, a total of approximately \$1.3 billion and \$2.7 billion of economic and military aid respectively had been extended. In the latter year, the economic programs were terminated (though some funds and surplus food arrangements remained in the pipeline for several years).

Political Structure. The Nationalists operated on Taiwan with a China-sized structure to implement Formosa-sized duties. The political organization was three-tiered in nature, consisting of national, provincial, and local governments. The dominant Kuomintang Party ruled the island according to the constitution adopted in 1946 in Nanking (and effected two years later). Initially elected for six-year terms, National Assembly members sat indefinitely because of the "emergency." As center of power, the president was similarly elected for a six-year term, with the possibility of a second term. Chiang Kai-shek was re-elected in 1954, but provisional amendments to the constitution sanctioned his re-election again in 1960, and, at the age of 79, to a fourth term in 1966. The traditional five yüan, or boards, continued to operate: the executive (headed by the chairman, who in effect was prime minister as well), legislative, judicial, control, and examination boards. The provincial capital was located at Taichung on the west coast. This level of government was concerned with matters of taxation, education, social welfare, and implementing land reforms. At the local level, district magistrates operated, as did mayors and urban legislative councils elected by the people. In this lowest rung of the political hierarchy Taiwanese participated.

The Economy. In economic life, agriculture was important; two-thirds of national income and 90 percent of foreign exchange derived from it. Intensive agriculture was practiced, with up to triple annual cropping for some products. Rice and sugarcane accounted for half the agricultural production. Lumber was an important commodity for export. Established on the mainland by the United States China Aid Act of 1948, the Joint Commission on Rural Reconstruction transferred operations to Taiwan. There it engaged in technical assistance, lent seeds and tools, and promoted irrigation projects. The Taipei regime embarked on a series of land-reform acts. In 1949 it put into effect measures (on the books since 1930) limiting rents to 37.5 percent of the main crop and guaranteeing tenants security of tenure. Two years later, the government began the sale of public lands. In 1953 it placed ceilings on land holdings of three hectares (about 7.4 acres). In part because of such measures, four out of five peasant families came to own their own land, a remarkable ratio in Asian agrarian life.

Improvements were also noted in industry. In 1949 the island was predominantly agricultural with little industry. Over the years, the industrial sector was developed. By 1952, industry had recovered to prewar levels, and then doubled in the ensuing decade. Food-processing was Taiwan's leading industry, with sugar-refining, pineapple-canning, and tea-packing among the other most important activities. Textile mills, aluminum plants, power projects, and fertilizer factories were established. In the early 1950's, three-fifths of industry was state-owned, but within a decade the private sector of the economy accounted for that ratio. Favorable investment laws attracted overseas Chinese and foreign capital. Taiwan embarked on the usual economic development, with four-year plans. Worldwide non-Communist foreign trade markets opened, with Japan accounting for a third of Taiwan's exports. Because of conditions favoring expansion, Taiwan in the 1960's registered an annual economic growth rate of 7 percent.

International Status. Though the Republic of China was recognized as the legal government of China by half the United Nations members, the question of Chinese representation perennially came up for debate in General Assembly sessions. The charter of the United Nations named the Republic of China as one of the "Big Five" permanent Security Council members with power of the veto; additionally its representatives sat on the specialized commissions and agencies. In 1949 the General Assembly passed a resolution calling on all states to respect Chinese political independence. Three years later, it passed a resolution condemning Russia's failure to implement the Sino-Russian 1945 treaty, in which Moscow pledged support to and continued recognition of the Nationalist government. With the consolidation of the Chinese Communist regime on the mainland, another contender appeared for the China seat. The General Assembly annually debated the problem. Solutions that advocated the seating of both Chinas in United Nations organs or the admission of Taiwan as a separate state appeared unacceptable to Taipei (and to Peking). So long as the bitter heritage of China's civil war days remained, the domestic and international status of Taiwan would remain a source of conflict.

COUNTRIES OF THE FAR EAST

Political Entity	*Administrative Capital*	*Size (Square Miles)*	*Population (Millions)*
Afghanistan	Kabul	250,000	15.4
Bhutan	Thimpu	16,000	.8
Brunei	Brunei	2,226	.1
Burma	Rangoon	262,000	27.0
Cambodia	Phnom Penh	71,000	7.0
Ceylon	Colombo	25,330	11.5
China	Peking	3,768,100	760.0
Hongkong	Victoria	400	3.8
India	New Delhi	1,262,275	554.0
Indonesia	Djakarta	575,450	121.0
Japan	Tokyo	143,000	103.0
Korea, North	Pyongyang	46,810	12.0
Korea, South	Seoul	38,450	32.0
Laos	Vientiane	88,780	3.0
Malaysia	Kuala Lumpur	127,000	10.0
Maldives	Male	115	.1
Mongolia	Ulan Bator	604,095	1.0
Nepal	Kathmandu	54,600	10.0
Pakistan	Islamabad	365,920	136.0
Philippines	Quezon City	116,000	38.0
Portuguese Timor	Dili	7,400	.6
Ryukyus	Naha	848	1.0
Sikkim	Gangtok	2,800	.2
Singapore	Singapore	225	2.0
Taiwan	Taipei	13,890	13.0
Thailand	Bangkok	198,250	36.0
Vietnam, North	Hanoi	63,350	21.0
Vietnam, South	Saigon	66,260	18.0

CHRONOLOGY

PART TWO: EARLY ASIA

B.C.	
3000	
3000–300	Jomon culture in Japan
c. 2500–*c.* 1500	Indus Valley civilization in India
c. 2500	Indonesians arrive in Southeast Asia
2205–1766 (or 1994–1523)	Hsia dynasty in China
2000	
1765–1123 (or *c.* 1500–1027)	Shang dynasty in China
c. 1500–1000	Vedic Age in India—Aryans
12th cent.	Chosen established in Korea—first traditional state
1122–221 (or 1027–221)	Chou dynasty in China
1000	
c. 1000–500	Epic Age in India—*Mahabharata* and *Ramayana*
c. 1000	Yüeh state in central China; people eventually move south to North Vietnam
722–481	Spring and Autumn Epoch of Chou dynasty in China
650–362	Saisunaga dynasty in Magadha, Gangetic plain
c. 567–487	Buddha
551–479	Confucius
c. 550–*c.* 400	Western Sind and Punjab part of Persian Achaemenian empire
c. 540–468	Vardhamana Mahavira, founder of Jainism
500	
6th cent.	Chinese philosopher Lao Tzu (?)
c. 500	Hinduism emerges as distinctive religion
470–391	Chinese philosopher Mo Ti
403–221	Warring States Epoch in Chou dynasty

4th cent.	Indians into Ceylon–Anuradhapura capital
372–289	Chinese philosopher Mencius
369–286	Chinese philosopher Chuang Tzu
362–322	Nanda dynasty in Magadha state, Gangetic plain
326	Alexander the Great in northwest India
322–184	Mauryan dynasty in North India—established by Chandragupta Mauyra
300–184	Yayoi Age in Japan
c. 300	Metal Age dawns in Southeast Asia
c. 300–237	Chinese philosopher Hsün Tzu
273–232	Reign of Indian emperor Asoka (Mauryan dynasty)
250	
221–206	Ch'in dynasty in China
214	North Vietnam incorporated into Chinese empire
208	North Vietnam becomes part of independent South China kingdom
206–A.D. 9	Early Han dynasty in China
190	New Korean state arises at Pyongyang—founded by Winman
185–73	Sunga dynasty, Gangetic plain
141–87	Reign of Chinese emperor Han Wu Ti
139–127	First mission of Chang Ch'ien to Central Asia
135	Scythians (Sakas) into Indus Valley
115	Second mission of Chang Ch'ien to Indus Valley
111	North Vietnam reannexed into Chinese empire (to A.D. 939)
108	Ch'ao-hsien colony in Korea part of Han empire
1st cent.	Tamil embassy to Rome
73–23	Kanva dynasty in Gangetic plain
57	Silla state founded in Korea
37	Koguryo state founded in South Manchuria
28–A.D. 225	Andhra dynasty in Deccan
18	Paekche state founded in Korea
End of period	Parthians (Pahlavas) into Indus Valley
A.D. **1–250**	
1st cent.	Champa founded
9–23	Wang Mang's reign in China
23–220	Later Han dynasty in China
57–75	Reign of Chinese emperor Ming Ti; Pan Ch'ao to Central Asian; Buddhism recorded in China
78 (to 144)	Accession dates of Kanishka, ruler of Kushans in Northwest India
99	Kushan ambassadors at Rome

c. 100	Two basic forms of Buddhism (Hinayana and Mahayana) recognizable in North India
c. 150–550	Funan state in Cambodia
3rd cent.	Hinduized kingdoms in lower Chao Phraya Valley and Lower Burma; Pyus in Central Burma
220–589	Six Dynasties—political division in China
220–265	Subperiod of Three Kingdoms in China
250–500	
265–420	Chin dynasty in China
300–600	Tomb culture period in Japan
320–480	Gupta empire in Gangetic plain—founded by Chandragupta I
330–375	Reign of Samudragupta in North India
372	Buddhism from China arrives at Koguryo in Korea
375–413	Reign of Chandragupta II in North India
384	Paekche adopts Buddhism in Korea
420–589	North and South kingdoms in China
4th–5th cent.	Indianization spurts in Southeast Asia Growth of Yamato state in Japan
427	Koguryo moves from South Manchuria to Pyonyang
mid-5th cent.	White Huns into Northwest India
500–750	
6th–8th cent.	Pallava dynasty in South India
528	Kingdom of Silla in Korea adopts Buddhism
c. 550	Chenla state replaces Funan in Cambodia
550–853	First Chalukya dynasty in Deccan
552	Introduction of Buddhism into Japan
570–632	Muhammad, founder of Islam
589–618	Sui dynasty in China
593–622	Regent Shotoku Taishi in Japan
7th cent.	Srivijaya rises in South Sumatra; acceleration of Sinification in Japan
604	Shotoku Taishi's 17-Article Constitution in Japan
606–647	Harsha Siladetya reign on Gangetic plain
618–907	T'ang dynasty in China
626–649	Reign of Chinese emperor T'ang T'ai Tsung
645–650	Taika Reforms in Japan
660's	Silla unifies Korea (to 936)
8th cent.	Haripunjaya founded in North Thailand Palas establish power in lower Gangetic plain
c. 700	Chenla in Cambodia divides into Upper (Land) Chenla and Lower (Water) Chenla
710–784	Nara capital of Japan
712	Muslim Arabs in lower Sind
712–756	Reign of Chinese emperor Hsüan
724–749	Reign of Emperor Shomu in Nara Japan

732	Rise of Saliendra dynasty in Java
750–1000	
Mid-8th cent.	Anuradhapura in Ceylon falls—Sinhalese relocate at Polonnaruwa (to 12th cent.)
c. 750	Nan-Chao rises in Southwest China
767–822	Buddhist monk Saicho (Tendai sect) in Japan
772	Borobodur erected in Central Java
774–835	Buddhist monk Kukai (Shingon sect) in Japan
794	Japanese court settles at Heian (Kyoto)—there until 1868
9th cent.	Burmans from South China into Burma
802	Kambuja begins to replace Chenla
c. 850	Sailendra and Srivijaya dynasties unite in South Sumatra
c. 850–*c.* 950	Rashtrakuta dynasty in Deccan
900–1050	Mataram state in Central Java (Airlangga, r. 1019–1049)
906–960	Five Dynasties period in China
936–1392	Koryo dynasty rules unified Korea
939	North Vietnam declares independence from China
960–1127	Northern Sung dynasty in China
973–1318	Second Chaluyka empire in Deccan
1000–1300	
10th–13th cent.	Chola the dominant power in South India
1018	Mahmud of Ghazni invades North India
1025	Cholas invade Sumatra
1044–1287	Pagan kingdom in Central Burma, founded by Anawrata
1050–1222	Kediri state in East Java
1113–1150	Reign of Suryavarman II in Cambodia—Angkor Wat
1125	Senas replace Palas in lower Gangetic plain
1127–1279	Southern Sung dynasty in China
1130–1279	Neo-Confucian scholar Chu Hsi
1175	Mohammad of Ghur into North India
1181–1219	Reign of Jayavarman VII in Cambodia—Angkor Thom
1185	Minamoto in Japan commence rule from new capital, Kamakura
1206	Slave Dynasty founded in Delhi by Aibak
1222	Singosari state in East Java (Kertanegara, r. 1268–1292)
1280's	Mongol incursions in North Vietnam, Burma, Java
1283–1317	Rule of Rama Khamheng at Sukhotai—first notable Thai kingdom
1292	Majapahit state emerges in East Java
End of period	Islam in insular Southeast Asia

PART THREE: TRADITIONAL ASIA

Pre-1300

1122–1282	Buddhist monk Nichiren (Lotus sect) in Japan
1133–1212	Buddhist monk Honen (Jodo sect) in Japan
1167?–1227	Genghis Khan
1173–1262	Buddhist monk Sinran (Jodo Shinshu sect) in Japan
1185–1333	Kamakura shogunate in Japan
1206–1290	Slave Dynasty in Delhi
1221	Retired emperor Toba II revolts against shogunate in Japan
1264–1294	Reign of Kublai Khan
1274, 1281	Mongol invasions of Japan
1275–1292	The Polos in China
1279–1368	Yüan (Mongol) dynasty in China
1290–1320	Khalji sultans in Delhi (Allauddin, r. 1296–1315)
1292–*c.* 1520	Majapahit kingdom on Java (Hayam Wuruk, r. 1350–1389)

1300

1320–1413	Tughluqs in Delhi (Muhammad Tughluq, r. 1325–1351, and Firoz Shah, r. 1351–1388)
1331	Emperor Daigo II revolts against shogunate in Japan
1336–1565	Vijayanagar kingdom in South India
1338–1573	Ashikaga shogunate in Japan
1347–1518	Bahmani kingdom in Deccan
1350–1767	Ayuthia kingdom in Thailand (Trailok, r. 1448–1488)
1353–18th cent.	Lan Xang, founded by Fa Ngum, flourishes in Laos
1368–1644	Ming dynasty in China
1392–1910	Yi dynasty in Korea
1398–1399	Timur pillages Delhi

1400

1403	Malacca ruler converted to Islam—rise of city as commercial power
1403–1424	Reign of Chinese emperor Yung-lo in China
1405–1431	Chinese maritime expeditions into South and Southeast Asia
1414–1451	Sayyid dynasty in Delhi
1426–1788	Second Le dynasty in North Vietnam (Le Thanh Ton, r. 1460–1497)
1431	Thais sack Angkor
1434	Cambodian capital relocates at Phnom Penh
1446	H'angul promulgated in Korea
1451–1526	Lodi dynasty in Delhi

1469–1538	Nanak, founder of Sikhs
1471	Le dynasty absorbs Champa
c. 1472–1538	Ming philosopher Wang Yang-ming in China
1486	Bartholomeu Diaz rounds Cape of Good Hope
1486–1752	Toungoo dynasty in Burma (Bayinnaung, r. 1551–1581)
1498	Vasco da Gama reaches India
1500	
1510	Goa becomes Portuguese colony
1511–1641	Malacca in Portuguese hands
1517	First official Portuguese mission, headed by Tomé Pires, arrives in China
1519	Magellan in Philippines
1526–1530	Reign of Babur in Delhi
1527–1592	Mac rule in North Vietnam
1534–1582	Oda Nobumaga in Japan—reunification
1536–1598	Toyotomi Hideyoshi in Japan
1540–1545	Sher Shah's reign in Delhi
1542	Portuguese arrive in Japan as first Westerners
1542–1616	Tokugawa Ieyasu in Japan
1556–1605	Akbar's reign in India
1557	Portuguese receive Macao as leasehold
1559–1626	Nurchachi, Manchu leader
1571	Spanish found Manila
1571–1821	Manila galleon trade with Mexico
1592–1643	Abahai, Manchu ruler
1592–1770's	Trinh rule in Hanoi; Nguyen rule in Hué
1600	
1600	Battle of Sekigahara in Japan; Dutch arrive in country
1602	Dutch East India Company founded
1603–1868	Tokugawa shogunate in Japan
1605–1627	Jahangir's reign in India
1619	Dutch East India Company centers operations in Batavia on Java
1627–1656	Shah Jahan's reign—Taj Mahal
1627–1680	Sivaji, founder of Maratha state in Deccan
1635	First English arrive in China
1639	British found Fort St. George at Madras
1641–1824	Malacca in Dutch hands
1644–1912	Ch'ing (Manchu) dynasty in China
1658–1707	Aurangzeb's reign in India
1661–1722	Reign of Chinese emperor K'ang-hsi
1664	French East India company chartered
1668	Bombay acquired by English East India Company

1674	French locate at Pondicherry in India
1689	Sino-Russian Treaty of Nerchinsk
1691	English East India Company establishes Fort William at Calcutta
1700	
1724	Hyderabad state founded
1736–1796	Reign of Chinese emperor Ch'ien-Lung
1740	Laos now divided into three parts: Luang Prabang, Vientiane, Champassak
1747–1826	Durani dynasty in Afghanistan
1753–1885	Alaungpaya (d. 1760) dynasty in Burma
1757	Battle of Plassey; British established in Bengal
1758–1760; 1765–67	Robert Clive governor of Bengal
1772–1785	Warren Hastings governor-general in India
1782	Chakri dynasty in Bangkok
1782	British acquire Penang
1786–1793	Lord Cornwallis governor-general of India
1788–1802	Three Nguyen brothers rule Vietnam
1798	Ceylon becomes colony of England; Dutch East India Company dissolved
1798–1805	Lord Wellesley governor-general of India
1800	
1802	Gia Long institutes united Vietnam rule from Hué
1811–1816	Java temporarily occupied by British
1816	Nepal becomes British protectorate
1819	British acquire Singapore through Raffles
1824–1826	First Anglo-British War
1825–1830	Dutch-Java war; Diponegoro
1826	Straits Settlements formed out of Penang, Malacca, and Singapore
1828–1835	Lord Bentinck governor-general of India
1833	U.S. treaty with Siam (first with an Asian country)
1838	First Anglo-Afghan War
1839–1842	First Sino-British conflict, the "Opium War"
1842	Sino-British Treaty of Nanking
1844	Sino-American Treaty of Wanghsia (Cushing Treaty); Sino-French Treaty of Whampoa
1848–1856	Lord Dalhousie governor-general of India
1853, 1854	Perry in Japan; treaty the latter year
1857	Sepoy Mutiny in India
1858	British crown assumes sovereignty in India from Company, now dissolved; Harris treaty in Japan
1868–1912	Emperor Meiji's reign in Japan

PART FOUR: MODERNIZING ASIA

Pre-1850	
1817–1898	Sir Syed Ahmad Khan, Indian Muslim leader
1836–1886	Ramakrishna, Hindu mystic
1837–1919	Itagaki Taisuke, Japanese statesman
1838–1922	Yamagata Aritomo; Okuma Shigenobu—Japanese statesmen
1841	Brunei sultan cedes Sarawak to James Brooke
1841–1909	Ito Hirobumi, Japanese statesman
1850	
1850–1865	Taiping Rebellion in China
1851–1868	Mongkut's reign in Thailand
1852	Second Anglo-Burmese War
1853–1878	Mindon's reign in Thailand
1855	First Americans in Korea
1856	Thai-U.S. treaty; Sino-British & French conflict
1856–1920	Bal Gangadhar Tilak, Hindu nationalist
1857	First major universities opened in India
1858, 1860	Chinese treaties with West and Russia
1858–1927	K'ang Yu-wei, Chinese reformer
1861–1874	T'ung Chih Restoration in China
1861–1896	José Rizal, Filipino nationalist
1861–1941	Rabindranath Tagore, Hindu poet
1862	First French cessions in Indochina
1863–1902	Vivekananda, Hindu mystic
1866–1915	Gopal Krishna Gokhale, Indian political leader
1866–1925	Sun Yat-sen
1867	Thai-French treaty on Cambodia
1868	Burlingame Treaty between U.S. and China
1868–1910	Chulalongkorn's reign in Thailand
1868–1912	The Meiji emperor's reign in Japan
1869	Opening of Suez Canal
1869–1948	Gandhi
1870	Sino-French treaty
1870's–1908	Tzu Hsi in power in China
1873–1938	Muhammad Iqbal, Indian Muslim leader
1874	French-Annamese treaty
1875	
1876–1948	Muhammad Ali Jinnah, founder of Pakistan
1876	Sino-British convention of Chefoo; Japanese-Korean treaty
1877	Satsuma Rebellion in Japan

1878–1880	Second Anglo-Afghan War
1878–1885	Thibaw's reign in Thailand
1879–1904	Raden Adjang Kartini, Indonesian reformer
1881	Sino-Russian Treaty of St. Petersburg
1882	American-Korean treaty
1885	Indian National Congress Party founded; Chinese renounce claims in Annam and Tonkin and in Burma; Third Anglo-Burmese War
1886	Burma becomes province in Indian Empire
1887	Indochinese Union created; Macao changed from leasehold to colony of Portugal
1888	Brunei, Sarawak, and North Borneo become British protectorates
1889	Meiji Constitution promulgated in Japan
1889–1964	Jawaharlal Nehru
1892	India Councils Act—nominated Indians on certain councils
1893	Durand Line demarcated between Afghanistan and India
1894–1895	Sino-Japanese War
1894–1905	Sun Yat-sen's Prosper China Society
1894–1969	Ho Chi Minh
1895	Malaya Federated States formed
1896	French-British divide Siam into spheres of influence; 15-year Sino-Russian treaty of alliance
1898	Spanish-American War; Filipinos declare independence; "One Hundred Days of Reform" in Peking; Britain obtains 99-year lease of New Territories; Russians into Liaotung Peninsula
1899, 1900	Hay Open-Door Notes
1899–1902	Philippine insurrection
1899–1905	Lord Curzon viceroy of India—partition of Bengal
1900	
1900–1901	Boxer Rebellion
1901	U.S. establishes civilian rule in Philippines; Dutch "ethical policy" in Indonesia; Boxer Protocol
1902	U.S. Cooper Act regarding Philippines; Anglo-Japanese Alliance
1904	British-Tibetan treaty
1904–1905	Russo-Japanese War
1905	Taft-Katsura Agreement
1905–1912	Sun Yat-sen's League of Common Alliance
1906	Muslim League founded in Dacca
1907	Philippine Assembly meets
1908	Budi Utomo formed in Indonesia; Root-Takahira Agreement

1909	Morley-Minto Reforms; British receive four Malay states (Unfederated States) from Thailand; provincial and national elections in China
1910	Korea becomes Japanese colony
1909–1925	Wachirawut's reign in Thailand
1911	Chinese Revolution begins; Bengal partition reversed; Indian capital moved from Calcutta to Delhi
1912	Sarekat Islam formed in Indonesia
1912–1926	Emperor Taisho's reign in Japan
1912–	Sun Yat-sen's party, Kuomintang
1915	Japanese 21 Demands—Bryan's nonrecognition doctrine
1916	Hindu-Muslim Lucknow Pact; Jones Act for Philippines
1917	British promise Indian self-governing institutions; Lansing-Ishii Agreement
1918	Dutch promise Indonesian self-rule; Siberian intervention
1918–1932	Party government in Japan
1919	India Act creating bicameral parliament; Amritsar incident in Punjab; Third Anglo-Afghan War; May 4th incident in Peking
1920	First Indian civil disobedience movement under Ghandi; Indonesian Communist Party founded (first in Asia)
1921–1922	Communist parties established in China and Malaya
1922	Washington Conference
1923	Thailand ends unequal treaties; Japanese Communist Party founded
1924	Sun-Joffe (Chinese-Soviet) agreement
	Sino-Russian treaty of recognition; Mongolian People's Republic established; U.S. Immigration Act excludes Asians
1924–1927	First Chinese united front

1925

1925	First All-India Communist Conference; Japanese-Soviet treaty of recognition
1925–1935	Prajadhipok's reign in Thailand
1926	Kingdom replaces emirate in Afghanistan
1926–	Showa emperor (Hirohito) in Japan
1927	Simon Commission; Indonesian Nationalist Party formed; Geneva Naval Conference
1928	Republic of China relocated at Nanking
1929	Indian Dominion Status announced
1930	Congress proclaims Republic Day in India; London

	Naval Conference; Ho Chi Minh organizes Vietnamese Communist Party
1930–1934	Second Indian civil disobedience campaign
1930–1931	First British-Indian Round Table Conference in London
1931	Second Round Table Conference; Ceylon constitution; Philippine Communist Party founded; Chinese Soviet Republic formed
1931–1932	Japanese take over Manchuria; Stimson nonrecognition doctrine
1932	Third British-Indian Round Table Conference; Thai coup led by Pridi and Phibun; Japanese army attempts coup in Tokyo
1933–	Mohammad Zahir Shah on Afghan throne
1934–1935	Chinese Communist Party's Long March
1935	Last India Act—Burma separated from India
1935–1946	Philippine Commonwealth
1935–1947	Mahidol's reign in Thailand
1935–1949	Yenan border government
1936	U.S. recognizes Afghanistan; Sian kidnapping of Chiang Kai-shek; another Japanese army attempted coup in Tokyo; Anti-Comintern Pact
1937	India provincial elections; Brussels Conference on China
1937–1941	Sino-Japanese undeclared war
1938–1941	U.S. economic sanctions against Japan
1940	Tripartite Pact; Hanoi Convention; Muslims demand partition in India
1941	Russo-Japanese neutrality pact
1941–1945	Pacific War
1942	Cripps mission to India
1943	Cairo Conference; Communist Party of Burma founded
1945	Yalta and Potsdam conferences; Democratic Republic of Vietnam and Republic of Indonesia proclaimed

PART FIVE: POSTWAR ASIA

Pre-1945	
1941–1970	Reign of Norodom Sihanouk in Cambodia
1945	Nationalist Chinese treaty with Russia; Kim Il-Sung emerges in power in North Korea
1945–1949	Indonesia revolutionary period
1945–1952	Occupation of Japan
1945–1965	Sukarno in power in Indonesia

1946	Philippine elections (Roxas president) and independence (July 4); New Delhi Asian Relations Conference; constitutions in Ceylon, Thailand, North Vietnam; constituent elections in Cambodia and Laos; North Vietnam elections and agreement with France
1946–1947	Yoshida Shigeru prime minister of Japan
1946–1948	Malayan Union; Roxas president of Philippines
1946–1954	North Vietnamese–French warfare
1947	Partition of India; Pakistan and Union of India created (August 15); Philippine-U.S. military base agreement; Linggadjati Agreement between Indonesians and Dutch; first Dutch "police action"; constitutions in Burma, Cambodia (and elections), Laos, Japan
1948	Independence of Burma (January 4) and Ceylon (February 4); Democratic Peoples Republic of Korea and Republic of Korea created; Bao Dai-French treaty; Renville Agreement between Dutch and Indonesians; second Dutch "police action"; constitution of Republic of China—Chiang Kai-shek president; Manchuria falls to Chinese Communists
1948–1953	Quirino president of Philippines
1948–1954	Yoshida again prime minister of Japan
1948–1957	Federation of Malaya
1948–1958	Phibun prime minister of Thailand, U Nu prime minister of Burma
1949	India-Bhutan treaty; Thai constitution; State of Vietnam proclaimed; conference on Indonesia at New Delhi; Dutch recognize Indonesian independence; Central Peoples Government of the People's Republic of China established on mainland; Chinese Nationalist regime in exile on Taiwan
1949–1952	Land redistribution in Communist China
1950	Indian constitution promulgated; Union of India becomes Republic (January 26); India-Sikkim treaty; Pathet Lao formed; Baguio Conference; Republic of United States of Indonesia becomes unitary Republic of Indonesia; Colombo Plan inaugurated; Soviet-Chinese Communist treaty of alliance
1950–1953	Korean War
1951	Japan Peace Conference; Japan-U.S. security treaty; Nepali kings end Rana rule; Thai constitution; elections in Burma and Cambodia
1951–1952	First Indian elections
1952	Japan regains independence (April 28); Tsedenbal emerges as leader of Mongolia; South Korea elections

1952–1955	Mutual-aid Chinese Communist economic programs
1953	Chinese Communist census
1953–1954	Chinese Communist elections
1953–1956	Suspension of American aid to Burma
1953–1957	Magsaysay president of Philippines; first Chinese Communist five-year plan
1954	Geneva Conferences on Korea and Indochina; SEATO formed; India-Chinese treaty on Tibet; Chiang Kai-shek re-elected president of Nationalist China; Chinese Communist constitution
1954–1956	Hatoyama Ichiro prime minister of Japan
1954–1959	Mao Tse-tung president of Communist China
1955	Bandung Conference; State of Vietnam becomes Republic of Vietnam; Burma-Japanese reparations agreement; elections in Cambodia, Laos, Malaya, Indonesia
1955–1958	Collectivization phase in Chinese Communist economy
1955–1963	Ngo Dinh Diem president of Republic of Vietnam
1956	Indian States Reorganization Act; Japanese-Philippine reparations agreement; Japan-Russian treaty; Chinese Communist Party constitution; elections in South Korea, Ceylon, Burma, South Vietnam (also constitution)
1957	Second Indian elections; Communist–non-Communist rapprochement in Laos; "One Hundred Flowers Bloom" period in Communist China
1957–1960	Kishi Nobusuke prime minister of Japan
1957–1961	Garcia president of Philippines
1957–1963	Independent Federation of Malaya
1957–1965	Guided Democracy in Indonesia
1958	Chinese Communists promote communes, people's militia, "Great Leap Forward"; Japanese-Indonesia reparations agreement; Laos elections
1958–1959	Second elections in Communist China
1958–1960	Ne Win prime minister of Burma
1958–1962	Chinese Communist second five-year plan
1958–1963	Sarit Thanarat prime minister of Thailand
1958–1969	General Ayub Khan in power in Pakistan
1959	India-China border conflict; elections in Pakistan and South Vietnam
1959–1969	Liu Shao-ch'i president of China
1960	Bombay state partitioned; Sino-Burmese boundary treaty; Sino-Mongolian boundary treaty; Japanese-U.S. security treaty revised; Indonesian parliament abrogated—other legislative organs created; National

	Liberation Front formed in South Vietnam; elections in Burma, North Vietnam (and constitution promulgated), Laos, South Korea, Taiwan
1960–1962	U Nu again prime minister of Burma
1960–1964	Ikeda Hayato prime minister of Japan
1961	India annexes Portuguese colonies; Sino-Nepal border agreement; elections in South Vietnam
1961–1965	Macapagal president of Philippines
1962	India-China border conflicts; Nepal constitution; Ne Win reassumes rule in Burma; Geneva Conference on Laotian neutralization—neutralist, Communist, and rightist factions sign coalition in Laos; elections in India, Pakistan, Cambodia
1963	State of Nagaland created in India; Sino-Pakistan border agreement; Sino-Afghan boundary treaty; Thanom Kittikachon becomes prime minister of Thailand; Park Chung Hee assumes presidency of South Korea; Cambodia first accepts military aid from Communist bloc; Malaysia created; elections in South Vietnam and South Korea
1963–1965	Singapore in Malaysia
1963–1966	Indonesia out of United Nations
1963–1970	Suspension of American aid to Cambodia; Tunku Abdul Rahman, prime minister of Malaysia
1964	Regional Co-operation for Development established by Pakistan, Iran, and Turkey; Afghan constitution; Sato Eisaku becomes prime minister of Japan; elections in North Vietnam; Gulf of Tonkin incident—U.S. retaliatory attacks; elections in Communist China, which explodes its first nuclear device; Pakistan elections
1964–1966	Lal Bahadur Shastri prime minister of India
1965	India-Pakistan border war—U.S. suspends all aid to both; Maldives granted independence; supplementary Burmese-Japanese reparations agreement; Communist attacks on U.S. installations in South Vietnam elicit escalated American intervention—ground troops arrive; Singapore becomes separate independent republic; Indonesia coup involving Sukarno—Suharto rises to power; elections in Afghanistan, Ceylon, Laos
1965–1969	Marcos president of Philippines (first term)
1965–1970	U.S. diplomatic rupture with Cambodia
1966	Punjab state partitioned; Indira Gandhi becomes prime minister of India; Tashkent Conference between India and Pakistan; ASPAC formed; Asian

	Development Bank headquarters located in Manila; elections in Cambodia, South Vietnam, Taiwan
1966–1969	Great Proletarian Cultural Revolution in Communist China
1967	Elections in India, South Vietnam, South Korea
1968	Mauritius granted independence; Thai constitution; North Vietnam elections; Suharto president of Indonesia; U.S.–North Vietnam peace talks open in Paris
1969	General Yahya Khan in top Pakistan office; elections in Afghanistan, Thailand, West Malaysia; Provisional Revolutionary Government proclaimed in South Vietnam; West Irian votes to join Indonesia; President Marcos of Philippines elected for second full term
1970	Elections in Ceylon, Pakistan, East Malaysia; Cambodia coup—Lon Nol regime replaces Norodom Sihanouk; Sukarno dies
1971	Elections in India and North Vietnam; elections scheduled for South Vietnam and Indonesia; secessionist movement fails in East Pakistan; Communist China welcomes first American delegation (Ping-pong team), journalists, and scientists; President Nixon announces plan to visit Communist China

BIBLIOGRAPHY

Books designated by an asterisk (*) are available in paperback.

ASIA

Reference:

Asian Survey. Berkeley, Calif., 1961 to date. (Successor to *Far Eastern Survey*, N.Y., 1932–1961.)

Association for Asian Studies. *Journal of Asian Studies*. Ann Arbor, Mich., 1956 to date. (Successor to *Far Eastern Quarterly*, 1941–1956.) And annual *Bibliography* issue.

Christian Science Monitor. Boston, daily except Sunday.

Far Eastern Economic Review. Hong Kong, weekly. And *Yearbook*, 1960 to date.

Foreign Affairs. New York, quarterly, 1922 to date.

The New York Times.

Times (London).

United Nations. *Official Records* of various organs, including Economic Commission for Asia and the Far East (ECAFE).

U.S. Congress. *Congressional Record*. And various committee reports and hearings, especially those of the (Senate) Foreign Relations Committee and (House) Foreign Affairs Committee.

U.S. Department of State. *Bulletin*.

U.S. *Papers relating to the Foreign Relations of the United States*. 1861 ff.

Wint, Guy, ed. *Asia: A Handbook*. New York: Praeger, 1966.

Politics and History:

Bingham, Woodbridge, *et al*. *A History of Asia*. 2 vols. Boston: Allyn & Bacon, 1964, 1965.

Buss, Claude A. *Asia in the Modern World*. New York: Macmillan, 1964.

Cameron, Meribeth E., *et al*. *China, Japan and the Powers*. 2nd ed. New York: Ronald Press, 1960.

Clyde, Paul, and Burton Beers. *The Far East*. 5th ed. Englewood Cliffs, N.J.: Prentice-Hall, 1971.

Fairbank, John, and Edwin O. Reischauer. *A History of East Asian Civilizations*. Vol. I, *East Asia: The Great Tradition;* Vol. II (with

Albert Craig), *East Asia: The Modern Transformation.* Boston: Houghton Mifflin, 1960, 1965.

Kahin, George M., ed. *Major Governments of Asia.* 2nd ed. Ithaca, N.Y.: Cornell University Press, 1963.

Lach, Donald F. *Asia in the Making of Europe.* Vol. I, Books 1 & 2: *The Century of Discovery.* Chicago: University of Chicago Press, 1965.

Latourette, Kenneth S. *A Short History of the Far East.* 4th ed. New York: Macmillan, 1964.

Michael, Franz H., and George E. Taylor. *The Far East in the Modern World.* Rev. ed. New York: Holt, Rinehart & Winston, 1964.

Vinacke, Harold M. *A History of the Far East in Modern Times.* 6th ed. New York: Appleton-Century-Crofts, 1959.

Culture and Society:

Binyon, Laurence. *Painting in the Far East.** 3rd ed. New York: Dover, 1959.

Bowers, Faubion. *Theater in the Far East.** New York: Grove Press, 1960.

Grousset, René. *The Civilization of the East.* 4 vols. London: H. Hamilton, 1931–1935.

Lee, Sherman E. *A History of Far Eastern Art.* New York: Harry N. Abrams, 1964.

Suzuki, Daisetz T. *Essays in Zen Buddhism.** New York: Grove Press, 1961. And other works on Buddhism.

Yohannen, John D., ed. *A Treasury of Asian Literature.** New York: John Day, 1956.

Economics:

Cressey, George B. *Asia's Lands and Peoples.* 3rd ed. New York: McGraw-Hill, 1963.

Dobby, Ernest H. G. *Monsoon Asia.* 2nd ed. London: University of London Press, 1963.

Ginsburg, Norton S., ed. *The Pattern of Asia.* Englewood Cliffs, N.J.: Prentice-Hall, 1958.

Myrdal, Gunnar. *Asian Drama, An Inquiry into the Poverty of Nations.** 3 vols. New York: Twentieth Century Fund, 1968.

Asia and the United States:

American Assembly. *The United States and the Far East.** 2nd ed. Englewood Cliffs, N.J.: Prentice-Hall, 1962.

Dennett, Tyler. *Americans in Eastern Asia.* New York: Barnes & Noble, 1963. (Reprint)

Greene, Fred. *U.S. Policy and the Security of Asia.** New York: McGraw-Hill, 1968.

Griswold, A. Whitney. *The Far Eastern Policy of the United States.** New York: Harcourt, Brace, 1938.
Reischauer, Edwin O. *Wanted, An Asian Policy.* New York: Alfred A. Knopf, 1955.
U.S. Congress. House Committee on Foreign Affairs. *United States Policy Toward Asia.* Washington, D.C.: Government Printing Office, 1966.
U.S. Senate. Committee on Foreign Relations. *United States Foreign Policy.* 13 parts (Part 5 relates to Asia). Washington, D.C.: Government Printing Office, 1959.
U.S. Senate Committees on Armed Services and Foreign Relations. *Military Situation in the Far East.* 5 vols. Washington, D.C.: Government Printing Office, 1951.
U.S. Department of State. *American Foreign Policy, Basic Documents, 1950–1955.* 2 vols. Washington, D.C.: Government Printing Office, 1957. And subsequent annual *Current Documents.*

SOUTH ASIA

India:

Basham, A. L. *The Wonder That Was India.** 3rd rev. ed. New York: Taplinger, 1968.
Brown, W. H. Norman. *The United States and India and Pakistan.* Rev. ed. Cambridge, Mass.: Harvard University Press, 1963.
Crane, Robert I. *The History of India.** Washington, D.C.: Service Center for Teachers of History, 1965. A bibliographic essay.
De Bary, William *et al*, eds. *Sources of Indian Tradition.* New York: Columbia University Press, 1958.
Gandhi, Mohandas. *Autobiography: The Story of My Experiments with Truth.** Boston: Beacon Press, 1957.
Mahar, J. Michael. *India: A Critical Bibliography.** Tucson: University of Arizona Press, 1964.
Majumdar, R. C., *et al. An Advanced History of India.* 3rd ed. New York: St. Martin's Press, 1967.
Moreland, W. H., and A. C. Chatterjee. *A Short History of India.* 4th ed. New York: David McKay, 1957.
Nehru, Jawaharlal. *The Discovery of India.** 4th ed. London: Meridian Books, 1956.
Piggott, Stuart. *Prehistoric India to 1000 B.C.** 2nd ed. London: Cassell, 1962.
Smith, Vincent A. *The Oxford History of India.* 3rd ed. New York: Oxford University Press, 1958.
Spear, Percival. *India: A Modern History.* Ann Arbor: University of Michigan Press, 1961.

Pakistan and Border Lands:

Callard, Keith. *Political Forces in Pakistan.* New York: Institute of Pacific Relations, 1959.
Karan, Pradynina N. *Nepal: A Physical and Cultural Geography.* Lexington: University of Kentucky Press, 1960.
Khan, Mohammad Ayub. *Friends, Not Masters: A Political Autobiography.* Oxford: Clarendon Press, 1967.
Maron, Stanley, ed. *Pakistan: Society and Culture.* New Haven, Conn.: Human Relations Area Files, 1957.
Wilbur, Donald N. *Afghanistan, Its People, Its Society, Its Culture.* New Haven, Conn.: Human Relations Area Files, 1962.
Wriggins, William H. *Ceylon: Dilemmas of a New Nation.* Princeton, N.J.: Princeton University Press, 1960.

SOUTHEAST ASIA

General Surveys:

Cady, John F. *Southeast Asia: Its Historical Development.* New York: McGraw-Hill, 1964.
Fifield, Russell H. *The Diplomacy of Southeast Asia, 1945–1958.* New York: Harper & Row, 1958.
———. *Southeast Asia in United States Policy.** New York: Praeger, 1963.
Hall, Daniel G. E. *A History of South-East Asia.* 3rd ed. New York: St. Martin's Press, 1968.
Harrison, Brian. *South-East Asia: A Short History.* 3rd ed. New York: St. Martin's Press, 1966.
Journal of Southeast Asian History. Singapore, 1957 to date.
Kahin, George, ed. *Governments and Politics of Southeast Asia.** 2nd ed. Ithaca, N.Y.: Cornell University Press, 1964.
Purcell, Victor. *The Chinese in Southeast Asia.* 2nd ed. New York: Oxford University Press, 1965.
Shaplen, Robert. *Time Out of Hand: Revolution and Reaction in Southeast Asia.** New York: Harper & Row, 1969.
Tregonning, Kennedy G. *Southeast Asia: A Critical Bibliography.** Tucson: University of Arizona Press, 1969.

Mainland Southeast Asia:

Blanchard, Wendell, ed. *Thailand.* New Haven, Conn.: Human Relations Area Files, 1958.
Buttinger, Joseph. *Vietnam: A Political History.** New York: Praeger, 1968.
Fall, Bernard B. *The Two Vietnams.* 2nd rev. ed. New York: Praeger, 1967.

Hammer, Ellen J. *The Struggle for Indochina, 1940–1955.** Stanford, Calif.: Stanford University Press, 1954.
Lebar, Frank M., and Adrienne Suddard, eds. *Laos.* New York: Taplinger, 1960.
*The Pentagon Papers.** New York: Bantam Books, 1971.
Shaplen, Robert. *The Lost Revolution: The U.S. in Vietnam.** New York: Harper & Row, 1965.
Steinberg, David J. *Cambodia: Its People, Its Society, Its Culture.* Rev. ed. New Haven, Conn.: Human Relations Area Files, 1959.
Tinker, Hugh. *The Union of Burma.* 4th ed. London: Oxford University Press, 1967.
Wilson, David A. *Politics in Thailand.* Ithaca, N.Y.: Cornell University Press, 1962.

Insular Southeast Asia:

Corpus, Onofre. *The Philippines.** Englewood Cliffs, N.J.: Prentice Hall, 1965.
Ginsburg, Norton, *et al. Malaya.* Seattle: University of Washington Press, 1958.
Hanna, Willard. *Bung Karno's Indonesia.* New York: American Universities Field Staff, 1961.
Hayden, Joseph R. *The Philippines: A Study in National Development.* New York: Macmillan, 1945.
Kahin, George. *Nationalism and Revolution in Indonesia.* Ithaca, N.Y.: Cornell University Press, 1952.
Phelan, John L. *The Hispanization of the Philippines.* Madison, Wisc.: University of Wisconsin Press, 1949.
Vlekke, Bernard. *Nusantara.* The Hague: W. van Hoeve, 1959.

CHINA

General Surveys:

Couling, Samuel. *Encyclopedia Sinica.* Shanghai: Kelly and Walsh, 1917.
Creel, Herrlee G. *Chinese Thought from Confucius to Mao-Tse-tung.** New York: New American Library, 1953.
Cressey, George B. *Land of 500 Million.* New York: McGraw-Hill, 1955.
De Bary, William T. *et al.*, eds. *Sources of Chinese Tradition.** New York: Columbia University Press, 1960.
FitzGerald, Charles P. *China: A Short Cultural History.** New York: Praeger, 1954.
Goodrich, L. Carrington. *A Short History of the Chinese People.** 3rd ed. New York: Harper & Row, 1959.
Grousset, René. *Chinese Art and Culture.** New York: Grove Press, Inc., 1959.

———. *The Rise and Splendor of the Chinese Empire.** Berkeley: University of California Press, 1953.

Hu Chang-tu *et al. China: Its People, Its Society, Its Culture.* New Haven, Conn.: Human Relations Area Files, 1960.

Hucker, Charles O. *China: A Critical Bibliography.** Tucson: University of Arizona Press, 1962.

———. *Chinese History.** Washington, D.C.: Service Center for Teachers of History, 1968. A bibliographic essay.

Latourette, Kenneth S. *The Chinese: Their History and Culture.* 4th ed. New York: Macmillan, 1964.

China to 1949:

Boxer, Charles R., ed. *South China in the Sixteenth Century.* London: Hakluyt Society, 1953.

Carter, Thomas F., and L. Carrington Goodrich. *The Invention of Printing in China and Its Spread Westward.* 2nd ed. New York: Ronald Press Co., 1955.

Chiang Kai-shek. *China's Destiny.* New York: Macmillan, 1947.

———. *Soviet Russia in China: A Summing Up at Seventy.* New York: Farrar, Straus & Cudahy, 1957.

Creel, Herrlee G. *The Birth of China.** New York: Frederick Ungar, 1937.

Fairbank, John F. *The United States and China.** Rev. ed. Cambridge, Mass.: Harvard University Press, 1958.

Feis, Herbert, *The China Tangle.** Princeton, N.J.: Princeton University Press, 1953.

Hucker, Charles O. *The Traditional Chinese State in Ming Times, 1368–1644.** Tucson: University of Arizona Press, 1961.

MacNair, Harley F. *Modern Chinese History: Selected Readings.* Shanghai: The Commercial Press, Ltd., 1933.

Morse, Hosea B. *The International Relations of the Chinese Empire.* 3 vols. Taipei: Wen Hsing Shu Tien, 1963. (Reprint)

Reischauer, Edwin O. *Ennin's Travels in T'ang China.* New York: Ronald Press, 1955.

Sun Yat-sen. *San Min Chu I.* Trans. Frank W. Price, Shanghai: China Committee, Institute of Pacific Relations, 1927. The Three Peoples Principles.

Teng Ssu-yu and John K. Fairbank. *China's Response to the West: A Documentary Survey, 1839–1923.* Cambridge, Mass.: Harvard University Press, 1954.

United States. Department of State. *United States Relations with China with Special Reference to the Period 1944–1949.* Washington: Government Printing Office, 1949.

Waley, Arthur. *Three Ways of Thought in Ancient China.** Garden City, New York: Barnes & Noble, 1939.

Watson, Burton. *Early Chinese Literature*. New York: Columbia University Press, 1962.
———. *Ssu-ma Ch'ien: Grand Historian of China*. New York: Columbia University Press, 1958.
Williams, S. Wells. *The Middle Kingdom*. 2 vols. Rev. ed. New York: Charles Scribner's Sons, 1883.
Wright, Mary C. *The Last Stand of Chinese Conservatism: The T'ung-chih Restoration, 1862–1874.** Stanford, Calif.: Stanford University Press, 1957.

Communist China:

Barnett, A. Doak. *Communist China and Asia.** New York: Harper & Row, 1960.
Blum, Robert. *The United States and China in World Affairs.** Ed. by A. Doak Barnett. New York: McGraw-Hill, 1966.
Brandt, Conrad, *et al. A Documentary History of Chinese Communism.** Cambridge, Mass.: Harvard University Press, 1952.
China Quarterly. London, 1960 to date.
Cole, Allan B. *Fifty Years of Chinese Communism*. 2nd ed. Washington D.C.: Service Center for Teachers of History, 1969. A bibliographic essay.
FitzGerald, Charles P. *The Birth of Communist China.** New York: Praeger, 1966.
Halpern, Abraham M., ed. *Policies Toward China: Views from Six Continents.** New York: McGraw-Hill, 1965.
Mao Tse-tung. *Selected Works of Mao Tse-tung*. 4 vols. Peking: Foreign Language Press, 1961–1965.
Schurmann, Herbert F. *Ideology and Organization in Communist China*. Berkeley: University of California Press, 1966.
Schwartz, Benjamin. *Chinese Communism and the Rise of Mao.** Cambridge, Mass.: Harvard University Press, 1951.
U.S. Consulate General, Hong Kong. Communist China press translations of varying titles, including *Survey of China Mainland Press*.
Wu Yuan-li. *The Economy of Communist China: An Introduction.** New York: Praeger, 1965.

RIM LANDS

Japan:

Borton, Hugh. *Japan's Modern Century*. 2nd ed. New York: Ronald Press, 1970.
De Bary, William T., *et al.*, eds. *Sources of Japanese Tradition.** New York: Columbia University Press, 1958.
Feis, Herbert, *Japan Subdued*. Princeton: Princeton University Press, 1961.

———. *Road to Pearl Harbor.** Princeton: Princeton University Press, 1950.

Hall, John W. *Japanese History.** Washington, D.C.: Service Center for Teachers of History, 1966. A bibliographic essay.

———, and Richard K. Beardsley. *Twelve Doors to Japan.* New York: McGraw-Hill, 1965.

Japan Tourist Bureau. *Japan Tourist Library.* Tokyo. Second edition.

Kawai, Kazuo. *Japan's American Interlude.* Chicago: University of Chicago Press, 1960.

Kenne, Donald. *Japanese Literature: An Introduction for Western Readers.** New York: Grove Press, 1955.

Murasaki, Shikibu. *The Tale of Genji.* Trans. Arthur Waley. New York: Modern Library, 1960.

Okuma, Count Shigenobu, ed. *Fifty Years of New Japan.* 2 vols. London: Smith Elder, 1909.

Reischauer, Edwin O. *Japan: The Story of a Nation.** Rev. ed., New York: Alfred A. Knopf, 1970.

———. *The United States and Japan.** 3rd ed. Cambridge, Mass.: Harvard University Press, 1965.

Sansom, Sir George B. *A History of Japan to 1934.** 3 vols. Stanford, Calif.: Stanford University Press, 1958–1963.

———. *Japan: A Short Cultural History.* Rev. ed. New York: D. Appleton-Century-Crofts, 1943.

———. *The Western World and Japan.* New York: Alfred A. Knopf, 1950.

Silberman, Bernard S. *Japan and Korea: A Critical Bibliography.** Tucson: University of Arizona Press, 1962.

Warner, Langdon. *The Enduring Art of Japan.** Cambridge, Mass: Harvard University Press, 1958.

Yanaga, Chitoshi. *Japan since Perry.* New York: McGraw-Hill, 1949.

Korea:

Goodrich, Leland M. *Korea: A Study of U.S. Policy in the United Nations.* New York: Council on Foreign Relations, 1956.

Kim, C. I. Eugene, and Han-kyo. *Korea and the Politics of Imperialism.* Berkeley: University of California Press, 1968.

McCune, Shannon. *Korea: Land of the Broken Calm.* Princeton, N.J.: Van Nostrand, 1966.

Paige, Glenn D. *The Korean People's Democratic Republic.** Stanford, Calif.: Hoover Institution Press, 1966.

Scalapino, Robert A., ed. *North Korea Today.* New York: Praeger, 1963.

Mongolia:

Lattimore, Owen. *Nationalism and Revolution in Mongolia.* New York: Oxford University Press, 1955.

Murphy, George G. *Soviet Mongolia*. Berkeley: University of California Press, 1966.

Taiwan:

Mancall, Mark, ed. *Formosa Today*. New York: Praeger, 1964.

INDEX

72 73 74 12 11 10 9 8 7 6 5 4 3 2 1